AKHENATEN TO THE FOUNDING FATHERS

AKHENATEN TO THE FOUNDING FATHERS

THE MYSTERIES OF THE HOOKED X

By Scott F. Wolter, P.G.

North Star Press of St. Cloud, Inc.
St. Cloud, Minnesota

Acknowledgements

Janet Wolter
David & Kim Brody
Darwin Ohman
Jim Adam
Alan Butler
Margaret Starbird
Bill Mann
Leslie Kalen
Don Rose
Eastern Band of Cherokee
Peter Tomlinson
John Freeburg
Paul Cabana, Brian Meere, and everyone at H2 for their support.
Joe Rose
Michael Carr
Steve & Peter Dimarzo, Jr.
Judi Rudebusch
Zena Halpern
Andy & Maria Awes
Kate Reeve
Rick Lynch
Todd Jovonovich
Jerry Lutgen
Julie Snider
Jack Roberts
Thanks to everyone and anyone I've forgotten.

www.HookedX.com

ISBN 978-0-87839-620-7

Printed in the United States of America

Published by
North Star Press of St. Cloud, Inc.
Saint Cloud, Minnesota

www.NorthStarPress.com

Table of Contents

Introduction

So just what is going on with the academics anyway? Isn't it obvious by now that people prior to Columbus visited the Americas? And have for millennia? Why can't historians, anthropologists, archaeologists, linguists, and other disciplines see the obvious voluminous evidence of this? As maddening as this is, one has to fight the urge simply to dismiss the nay-sayers. We need to look deeper and realize there's more going on here. Is it mere protection of the statis quo? Of traditional beliefs? Is it politically motivated or is there a religious component in play?

In the past, when science couldn't back up what archaeologists found, perhaps it made sense to move with extreme caution. But science has matured. What lay in the realm of speculation before has become fact today as geology and other sciences date artifacts with so much more certainty. Yet some still stubbornly refuse to accept the obvious hard science. My advice to those is to get up to date with science. The world is ready, eager for the truth.

There are a multitude of reasons why academia has essentially blown it and continues to get it wrong when it comes to the truth about the pre-Columbian history of this continent. This has long been the case, but I thought the words of the accomplished author and mystic, Manley P. Hall (1901 to 1990) that he wrote during the turbulent and rapidly changing post-World War II era in 1951 summed up the situation well:

> Modern scholars have accepted, without proper reflection, a fabrication of lies fashioned to deceive and to prevent the recognition of facts detrimental, even dangerous, to the ulterior motives of powerful interests. Time will reveal that the continent now known as America was actually discovered and, to a considerable degree, explored more than a thousand years before

> the beginning of the Christian era. The true story was in the keeping of the Mystery Schools, and passed from them to the Secret Societies of the medieval world. The Esoteric Orders of Europe, Asia, and the Near East were in at least irregular communications with the priesthoods of the more advanced Amerindian nations. Plans for the development of the Western hemisphere were formulated in Alexandria, Mecca, Delhi, and Lhasa long before most European Statesmen were aware of the great Utopian program.[1]

The time has now come to bring these facts to the surface, no matter how startling they might be, no matter how they rock the beliefs of many mainstream scholars. New evidence—new science—is changing everything we've come to understand and believe about our history in North America, about history in general. In this book I plan to reexamine previous research and update old issues with new findings.

Besides the problems of academia and traditional beliefs, what else could be raising the ire of the people who are so opposed to the idea of early cultures coming to North America prior to Columbus? I'm convinced one of the biggest issues is what the truth might mean for the worlds' religions. The evidence presented in this book reveals an old story that has caused major tremors in the Catholic faith most notably in the last decade with books like the *DaVinci Code*, which, though fiction, set off dozens of other books refuting the ideas in that book. The reason it caused such concern is because the story has profound elements of truth. Many believe the followers of Jesus and his true teachings, and his bloodline descendants continued to be persecuted long after his death, and the one refuge where they knew they would be safe was in the secret land across the Atlantic.

The artifacts and sites examined and explored here reveal a hidden chapter of North American history whose time has come to be revealed. They reveal not only the story of the people who came to this continent, but also stories of the people they encountered here. It has long been known that Native Americans have oral stories, myths, and legends about these early visitors. Despite the tragic history Native Americans endured, we will explore the possibility that they still have knowledge of those early contacts to this day.

One of the encouraging things that should give people hope is that, unlike the past when new discoveries and scientific advances occurred but sometimes took decades for that information to make it into the public's consciousness, times are changing. This snail's pace transfer of new information has suddenly been given a rocket boost by the advent of the Internet and the introduction of other scientific endeavors (like the mitochondrial DNA studies) that have sparked new interest in how humans moved around the planet, and, that controversial issue, when. The truth about pre-Columbian contact in the Americas is already spreading virtually instantaneously and will continue to do so.

I also believe that massive cultural changes around the world will happen rapidly, especially with other new technologies—like the Ipods and cell phones—proliferating. These devices are opening up the world in places, such as even the relatively closed cultures in the Middle East.

The world is changing, and the speed of that change is escalating. As we entered a new age of the zodiacal calendar on the symbolic day of December 21, 2012, this represents a time of great change and of great opportunity. I believe the work contained in this book, my previous works, and the work of many others who have struggled to get the truth out are important and must be heard. The true history of our world and of the world's religions is of vital importance. While this is just my take on what likely happened, it probably is very close to the truth.

In any case, with over seven billion people on the planet and counting, now is probably a good time to reflect on change. Most people would probably say we need to change the way we as a species are conducting our overall business on earth or we aren't going to make it. I believe before we can go forward into the future, we have to know where we've been. This book will attempt to tell some of the stories of where we have already been.

Summary of Key to the Secret History of North America

AKHENATEN TO THE FOUNDING FATHERS: THE MYSTERIES OF THE HOOKED X is a continuation of the research presented in my previous books, *The Hooked X: Key to the Secret History of North America*, and the book preceding it, *The Kensington Rune Stone: Compelling New Evidence*. In keeping with the format of the first Hooked X book, I will begin with presenting several tidbits of new information and discoveries relating to the Kensington Rune Stone.

Several benefits have already materialized since the historically hostile and dismissive attitude of many academics and skeptics involved with research into the once highly controversial Kensington Rune Stone. Doubt and skepticism has gradually been replaced by a more open and welcoming environment of open discussions. The evidence of authenticity presented in *The Kensington Rune Stone: Compelling New Evidence* prompted several previously reticent individuals, namely, Helmer Voigt, the Rodney Beecher Harvey Family, and of course the Olof Ohman Family to come forward with important new information, which was presented in *The Hooked X*. Due in large part to the change in the public perception of the artifact's authenticity additional new people have come forward, allowing me to share and interpret this new material in "Chapter 1: New Kensington Rune Stone Evidence."

I also introduced several new artifacts and evidence that provided support to the authenticity of the Kensington Stone, such as the three Spirit Pond Rune Stones, the Narragansett Rune Stone, the Newport Tower, the Westford Sword, the Boat Stone, the Tyngsboro Map Stone, the Oxford Astrolabe, and the Larsson Papers. The continually mounting factual evidence is consistent with theses artifacts also being genuine. Collectively they provide a compelling argument of an extensive medieval presence in North America.

This book then provides an update about several of the artifacts and sites reported on in *The Hooked X* with the general theme that they are finally being taken seriously and, where appropriate, protected or moved to safer locations. The key question investigated in the previous book was what is the origin and meaning of the runic character used for the "a" sound on five runic inscriptions found on this continent, yet never seen in the known runic record anywhere in Europe. My research led to the conclusion the symbol represented the religious ideology of the people who came here. The trail led to the identity of the fourteenth century carver of the Kensington Rune Stone through the language, runes, dialect, and grammar on the Island of Gotland and the only clergy there at that time capable of carving an inscription of such complexity and length: the Cistercians.

The connection to the Cistercians and their military brethren they officially founded, the Knights Templar, opened a new door for research that suddenly provided the necessary elements for a plausible explanation for the late medieval artifacts found in North America. At the beginning of the fourteenth century, the Cistercians were at the height of their success with over 750 abbeys stretching from the Holy Land across Europe and into Scandinavia. Not coincidentally, the Knights Templar were also at the height of their success until that fateful day on October 13, 1307, when the King of France and Pope Innocent V conspired to bring down the military monks who carried the swords. Most historians say the Templars ceased to exist after their putdown, which coincided with the steady decline of the Cistercians. Skeptics of my research have said the Templars couldn't have been involved with the Kensington Stone because the survivors would have been old men or dead by 1362. What they fail to acknowledge is that the Roman Catholic Church might have been able to kill people, but they could not kill the religious ideology of these people, which quietly continued on in secret, or "Sub Rosa."

Upon developing my own theory that the *leadership* of the Cistercian/Knights Templar orders likely embraced vastly different religious beliefs diametrically opposed to the Roman Catholic Church, I soon discovered I wasn't alone in this belief. Other authors, such as Alan Butler, were on a similar track with their own research. Butler and others agree the charismatic leader of the Cistercians, Saint Bernard de Clairvaux, was a mystic with a fascination with the Virgin Mary to the point where it became known in Church circles at the time as "The Great Heresy." The evidence I presented to support this then radical ideology was the incorporation of symbols and images related to this fascination in the amazing Gothic architecture the Cistercians introduced into Europe in the twelfth century. The sacred feminine architecture with its allegorical representation of female genitalia, symbollic of where life comes from, and Dualism was a brilliant secret expression of their true faith with the critical element of reverence for the "Sacred Feminine" that I call "Goddess Veneration."

While Butler and other researchers focused on these monastic orders' activities in Europe from late medieval times through the Enlightenment Age, I focused on operations in North America. The new information I brought to the table involved tangible authentic artifacts that shed light on the activities of these orders on this continent.

The research presented in *The Hooked X* was a summary of my pursuit of evidence at various museums, sites, and religious houses across the United States, Scandinavia, and the British Isles. The voluminous factual evidence I found conclusively shows that the Templars and Cistercians did indeed have a meaningful presence in North America during the late medieval period, but the research also left many unanswered questions.

Were the Templars the first Europeans to make contact with North America? Did they also visit Central and South America during this medieval period? What impact might they have had on Native cultures they surely had contact with? Did other cultures visit North America prior to the Templars? Who were they, and what evidence is there to support earlier contact? Why is it that we know nothing about that history today? Is there "lost" information just coming to light or were there certain entities that did not want the public (possibly the Catholic church hierarchy) to know? Are many academics in relevant disciplines really dragging their heels, or are larger forces at work here? Is there a "big secret" behind this hidden history that could alter the course of history moving into the future? The research I present in this book attempts to answer these questions.

Chapter 1
New Kensington Rune Stone Evidence

Before setting off on our journey to the truth about the history of North America and beyond, I feel it's important to share a few discoveries relating to the Kensington Rune Stone that, at first glance, may seem insignificant. In a forensic investigation factual evidence is important no matter how trivial it may seem. Many times I've discovered vitally important information from what was otherwise considered an inoccuous source such as a family photograph. Something in the background or written on the back can provide important clues. We begin with two never-before-published photographs that provide additional context to the man who discovered the artifact in 1898, his family, and the entire Kensington Rune Stone story.

Two New Ohman Photographs

WHAT'S EXCITING about giving presentations about the Kensington Rune Stone is the people who come forward with new information—an interesting story, a new photograph, or something else previously unknown—like Hans Voigt's letter from Olof Ohman that surfaced in September of 2006.[2] Hans Voigt's letter to Ohman that he brought to the attention of the Minnesota Historical Society added clarity a century later to the pervasive rumor in the community about Ohman carving runes on wood years before he found the rune stone. Gunnar Johnson's claim cast doubt about the authenticity of the inscription and Ohman's character. Helmer's grandfather read about this in the newspaper and wrote to Ohman, recalling an event in 1882 while the two of them were working on Mr. Johnson's house. Hans wrote, "At the time I made on a piece of wood some marks which were, after a fashion, to represent runes, as he says. So it seems to me that it is this incident which has popped up in Mr. Johnson's memory."

Helmer Voigt presented the response from Ohman—previously unknown—which included some of his thoughts about the controversy. It was a rare opportunity to peek into the mind of the central character in one of the greatest historical controversies ever. As expected, his musings were not consistent with that of a forger.

On February 27, 2010, after finishing my lecture to a Sons of Norway group at the American Swedish Institute in Minneapolis, an older woman approached with a broad smile. She introduced herself as Muriel Stock and told me she had been born and raised in Kensington. She then held up a photograph and said, "Do you know who these people are?"

I recognized the man with huge hands and a thick mustache. Muriel then turned the picture over. Written on the back was, "Olof Ohman and wife."

My eyes widened with excitement and my first thought was how much Darwin and the rest of the Ohman family would enjoy seeing the picture. A few days later, Darwin and I were in Muriel's home with my laptop and scanner. Muriel and her daughter, Tari Kellogg, explained that her grandmother's brother, Erick Colmark, had been a photographer in Kensington. Judging from Olof's graying hair in this picture compared to his dark hair in an 1893 photo, Muriel's great uncle probably took the picture sometime between 1910 and 1915. Olof was born in 1854 so he was somewhere in his late fifties to early sixties by this time. Karin was born in 1862, so she was likely in her early fifties.

This previously unknown picture of Olof Ohman, and his wife, Karin, surfaced after I gave a lecture on the Kensington Rune Stone on February 27, 2010. Muriel Stock's great uncle, Erick Colmark, was a photographer in Kensington and probably took the picture some time between 1910 and 1914. (Photo courtesy of Muriel Stock)

Days after our visit while traveling in Detroit, Michigan, I received a text from my wife, Janet, that Tari had found another picture. On March 13, 2010, Janet and I stopped by Tari's home to look at the second picture that included what looked to be seven of Olof and Karin's children. We examined both photos and, surprisingly, concluded that Olof and Karin were definitely in the foreground, but the seven other people were not their children. Muriel said the younger man in the center was her great uncle, Erick Colmark, the photographer who took the first picture. The other people were his five sisters and younger brother Carl.

The burning question was why would Olof and Karin Ohman pose for a picture with children from a different family? We speculated that perhaps Olof's celebrity as the discoverer of the Kensington Rune Stone prompted the Colmark parents to ask for a photograph with their children sometime after 1910. This made sense given that prior to 1910 he wouldn't have had much notoriety given the artifact had been dismissed by scholars and relegated to storage inside the granary on the Ohman farm from 1899 until 1907. In August of 1907, Hjalmar Holand took possession of the stone. After studying it for two years, Holand then offered the artifact for sale to the Minnesota Historical Society for $5,000. This prompted the Museum to assign renowned geologist, Newton H. Winchell, to conduct an investigation into the authenticity of the artifact.

In December of 1910, Winchell concluded, ". . . the said stone is not a modern forgery, and must be accepted as a genuine record of an exploration in Minnesota, at the date stated in the inscription."

Karin and Olof Ohman pose for a photograph with the children of the Colmark family sometime between 1910 and 1914. Left to right: Front: Carl Colmark, Olof Ohman, Karin Ohman; standing in back: Unknown, Unknown, Erick Colmark, Unknown, Unknown, and Unknown. (Photo courtesy of Muriel Stock)

This news was no doubt well received by the Ohman family and others in Kensington. Winchell's confirmation of the authenticity of the Kensington Stone appears to have made the Ohmans celebrities in the community and likely explains the picture taken with another family's children.

A Belated Message from Olof

ON DECEMBER 26, 2009, AN IMPORTANT PIECE of new information about the rune stone came from an unlikely source: Olof Ohman himself. He received plenty of help passing the information along until it eventually reached me.

I stumbled upon a miraculous find in a book I had put away six years earlier without ever opening it. Long-time Kensington Rune Stone researcher, Hjalmar Ruud Holand's, *The Kensington Stone,* was published in 1932. My copy was in poor condition–worn and the binding repaired with adhesive tape. How the book ended up in my hands that day is an interesting story in itself.

In June of 2003, I traveled to Heavener, Oklahoma, to see the Heavener Rune Stone and meet its long-time champion Gloria Farley. At eighty-eight years old, Gloria moved slowly but had a razor-sharp mind to match her determination. Her home was filled with books, pictures, and artifacts from many decades of research pursuing evidence of ancient cultures in America. After a few minutes of small talk Gloria insisted we go see her Rune Stone.[3]

Gloria and I had several phone conversations after the visit. In one call, she asked if I believed the Heavener inscription was real. I said, "Yes, I do, Gloria." A couple of weeks later we received word that Gloria had passed away.

A few months after her death, a package arrived with twenty to thirty books. A geologist named Bart Torbert, was asked by Gloria's family to go through her book collection. Bart sent me all her books dealing with rune stones and Norse history. I saw the Holand book in that collection but never opened it at the time because I already had a copy and had it read it years before.

When I finally opened the book in 2009, six years after receiving it, my eyes focused on the familiar handwriting of two individuals I had come to know very well. The first page had an inscription written by Holand to a longtime Kensington Rune Stone supporter, Constant Larson, an attorney and a prominent citizen of Alexandria, Minnesota. Larson, the first president of the Kensington Rune Stone Foundation that built the museum in Alexandria where the stone is currently housed, was also the man who, in 1927, assembled ten prominent businessmen in the community, including himself, to reimburse Holand $2,500 for expenses incurred during his two decades of researching the artifact to acquire it.

Below Holand's inscription, dated December 2, 1931, was another familiar signature made with the slightly shaky hand of an elderly man. Olof Ohman would have been seventy-seven at that time, but knowing his adversarial relationship with Holand over the then twenty-two-year-old dispute over ownership of the artifact, Larson likely collected Ohman's signature at a later time. I suspect Larson was aware of the rift between the two men having been involved in the 1927 rally at Fahlin's Point to raise money to build the monument at the discovery site. In spite of this, one can understand why Larson would want his book signed by these two giants of the unfolding rune stone saga.

My eye caught something else in the lower left corner of the page. It had been stamped by the Runestone Museum. Since the area code of the phone number in Alexandria had changed in 1996, the "612" meant the book had come into their possession some time prior to that. Somehow, it got away from the museum, eventually finding its way into Gloria's library in Oklahoma, then on to me. My initial excitement quickly changed to curiosity as numerous questions formed in my head.

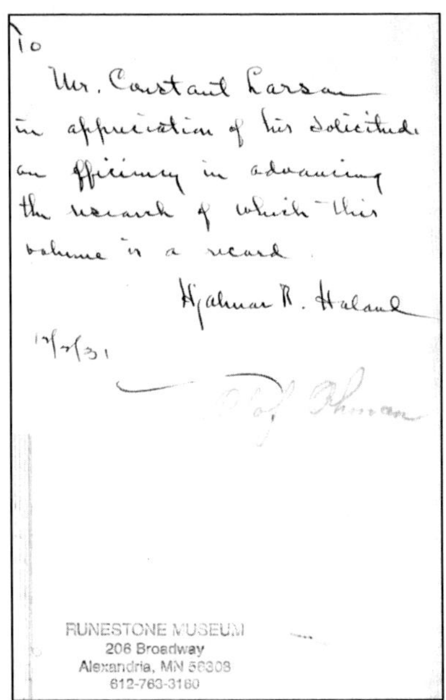

On December 26, 2009, I discovered two familiar signatures in a book entitled, The Kensington Stone, published in 1932 by Hjalmar Ruud Holand. I had received the book three years earlier as a posthumous gift from long-time Heavener Rune Stone researcher Gloria Farley. The inscriptions read: "To Mr. Constant Larson, in appreciation of his solicitude and efficiency in advancing the research of which this volume is a record. Hjalmar R. Holand 12/2/31," and beneath it, "Olof Ohman." (Wolter, 2009)

Opposite the signatures, a small photograph had been glued to the inside cover. The black-and-white image showed five men and a woman sitting on a pile of boulders. I recognized Hjalmar Holand in the middle next to the woman. To his right was a smartly dressed man with a hat who appeared to be Constant Larson.

The picture appears to have been taken at Cormorant Lake, Minnesota, where Holand theorized the medieval Kensington party had "camped near two skerries," as noted in the rune stone in-

Found glued onto the inside cover of the Holand book was a picture of six people sitting on a rock pile. Left to right: Unknown, Constant Larson, Hjalmar Holand, unknown, unknown and unknown.

scription. The "skerries" were thought to be two large glacial boulders with stone holes discovered along the lake shore.

The book was likely an important memento to Mr. Larson of his extensive involvement with the Kensington Rune Stone. Not only did he assembly the group of ten men who brought the artifact to Alexandria for permanent display, but he also wrote a lengthy chapter supporting its authenticity in his book published in 1916 entitled, *History of Douglas and Grant Counties Minnesota: Their People, Industries and Institutions.*

The book was incredible, but the best was yet to come. After turning the next two pages, I found myself staring at a pencil sketch on a piece of lined paper that had also been glued to the page. My eyes recognized the map with the familiar rectangle of the one-hundred-acre Ohman farm. Inside the rectangle was Olof's signature yet again. Below it he wrote, "Where stone was found." To the right of his note was an arrow pointing to a small cross marking the location where he found the Kensington Rune Stone! This map becomes exciting new evidence, validation of the location of the discovery site, pinpointed by the triangulation of the stone holes Janet discovered in 2004.[4]

Samuel Siverts

AS UNEXPECTED AS FINDING THE TREASURES hidden in the Holand book were, a week later I received another surprise. On January 4, 2010, I received a package of documents from a man I had met a couple of years earlier named Ing Siverts. Ing's grandfather was Samuel A. Siverts (1854 to 1941), a cashier at the Kensington bank.

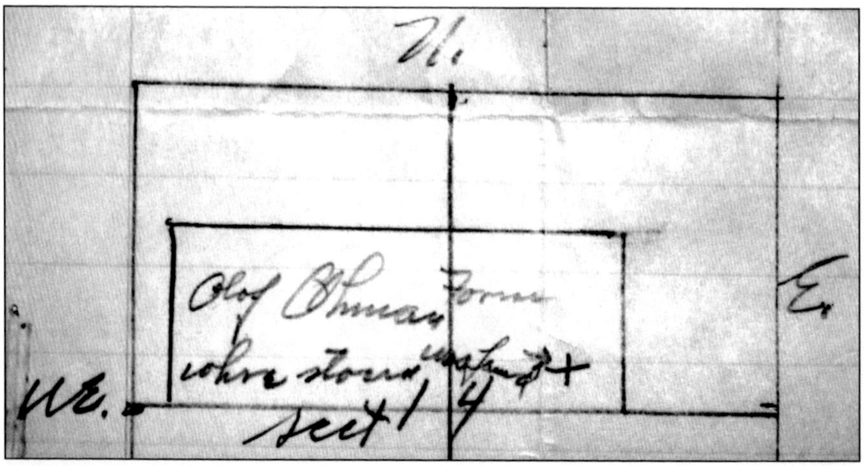

Two pages into the Holand book was a sketch on lined paper that had been glued onto the page. Olof Ohman drew a sketch of his property in "sect[ion] 14" pin-pointing the location where he found the Kensington Rune Stone by writing "Olof Ohman, Forssa; where stone was found." Forssa is the parish in Northern Sweden near the coastal city of Hudiksvall on the Baltic Sea where Olof Ohman immigrated from to the United States.

Siverts had made one of the two copies of the Kensington Rune Stone inscription sent to Professor Olaus Breda at the University of Minnesota in 1899. (Olof Ohman made the other.) Siverts also packed and shipped the artifact to Professor George Curme, at Northwestern University upon his request in February of 1899.

Ing sent me photographs along with letters his grandfather had written. He sent half a dozen photos of Samuel including one with him standing on a dock impeccably dressed holding a northern pike on a stringer.

One of the letters written by Siverts was to Loraine Larson, the daughter of Alexandria attorney and Freemason Constant Larson. Like her father, Loraine Larson was a vocal advocate of the authenticity of the Kensington Rune Stone. A lecture given by her in Duluth in May of 1935 had prompted Sivert's letter, written on the Norwegian Constitution of Syttende Mai (seventeenth of May):

> Miss Loraine Larson, May 17th 1935
> Central High School,
> Duluth, Minn.
>
> Dear Miss Larson,
>
> Your announcement in the *Duluth Herald Review* of your lecture as to the "Kensington Stone" found in 1898, interests me enough to take the liberty to address you regarding the same with a few additional words regarding the stone, about

Samuel Siverts holding a respectable sized northern pike in this circa 1930 photograph. (Courtesy of Ing Siverts, 2010)

which I dare say you know very little if anything. So you will pardon me, if I make some remarks of information as the original facts in this remarkable discovery.

In 1898 I happened to be the first cashier of the Kensington Bank, after having supervised the construction of the bank building, then owned by my old proprietors Mr. Harold Thorson and Mr. Reiter of Alexandria.

Shortly after the bank had opened for business that summer, one day as I happened to be out, there had in the mean time been left with me for investigation as to the inscriptions on the stone, but unfortunately I did not see Mr. Olof Ohman, and indeed I never succeeded to meet him personally, even when I drove to his farm, where I viewed the place, where the stone was originally found, and also the hole and the tree itself had been dug and where the stone had been revealed. Mr. Ohman was never in the bank either to see me, strange to say, but he was a very retired man, as I know of him.

It was me then, who immediately packed up the stone and shipped it to the University of Minnesota, to the then Professor in Norwegian Mr. Breda for a possible translation of the Runics thereon.

But Mr. Breda returned it to me with his skeptical translation and skeptical remarks about runics, which he claimed were fraudulent, and of course I was not a student in the line, so the stone was left in charge of Mr. Olson the jeweler for some time, and as in Morris, Minn., the matter went naturally out of my attention for a long time, and during that time, Mr. Olson had returned the stone to Mr. Ohman, who I understand from Prof. Holand's book, which is before me now and re-read a couple of times, that Mr. Ohman used it for a doorstep before one of his farm houses.

But I am extremely glad over the fact, that it survived again thru Prof. Holand, who spent much time and money to reveal to the European world as well as to this country, that it was genuine, as the original Breda and Scandinavian critics objections have all been overcome, and I presume now, when it is resting in the proper place in Alexandria, Minn., the County seat of Douglas County Minn., I hope it will repose there for good, and not be huckstered away at whatever price might be obtained for it.

The time will come and no doubt has already partially come, when pilgrimages will visit the stone by professional experts, and probably indeed by some of the skeptics from Europe, as all differences of opinion among the learned objections have been revealed to have been all natural differences among the explorers as to their linguistic knowledge of the time the stone was produced and inscribed.

Now if it is not too much to ask of you, I shall be much pleased to know, if I may have a copy of your address at the school in Duluth, where I at one time before living in Kensington did live and run a small bank at Rices Point under the Clarendan Hotel, but which together with all of that part of Michigan Street I understand is all diverted back to a wilderness practically.

I presume there are people at Kensington, who no doubt remember me well, and I would have been present at convention there a few years ago, if I then could have afforded the expenses of the travel. I did offer to come there and give a little talk on the subject of the Stone, but they could not see the way clear to pay my expenses, so it passed off, and now you have already yesterday afternoon given the lecture in the Central High School.

I congratulate you and hope you had a large audience, which the subject was entitled to, so as to give some valuable history facts to the younger generation of this State and Country.

I shall be delighted to receive your reply, if no objection on your part.

Thanking you for attention, I beg to remain an old Kensington resident.

Respectfully Yours,

Siverts's letter introduces a few new interesting facts such as his alluding to the stone being found shortly after the Kensington Bank opened in the summer of 1898. This appears to be consistent with Willie Sarsland's 1949 letter where he wrote that the artifact was unearthed in September. I was surprised to read that Siverts never met Olof Ohman. How the two could miss each other in such a small community is ironic and puzzling.

Mr. Siverts erred about shipping the stone to the University of Minnesota. The record shows that Siverts sent a copy of the inscription to the professor of Scandinavian Languages at the University of Minnesota, Olaus Breda. Siverts actually shipped the stone to the residence of Professor of Germanic languages at Northwestern University, George O. Curme in Chicago, Illinois. Mr. Siverts's lapse in memory can easily be forgiven given his trying to recall details of then thirty-seven-year-old events at the age of eighty-one.[5]

Ing's package had one more surprise. He also sent a copy of a handwritten note Professor Breda had sent his grandfather with his translation and analysis of the Kensington Rune Stone inscription.

"*The inscription is in runic characters, some of the characters are correctly made, some are not.* ᚯ *is written instead of* ᚬ F = å, o } ᚯ use of ᚴ = K
ᚵ ———————— ᚵ = g
ᛔ *is certainly meant for* = p, *while* ᛒ = b
ᚷ ———————— a, *while* X *(early R)* = g
ᛘ ———————— = *v. w. no such Runic char.*

The signs ᛒ, ᛚᛚ, ᛚ, ᛟ, ᛚᛓ, ᛚᛓᛒᛚ, *which indicate numbers, I can make nothing of.*
In English if might be rendered (somewhat freely):—

? Swedes and ? Norwegian on a journey of discovery from Vinland ? West – we camped ? ? one day's journey north from this stone – we fished one day – after we came home

Prof Breda

The inscription is in Runic characters some of the characters are correctly made, some are not. F. i.

ᚼ is written instead of ᚨ = å, o } ᚷ instead of ᚴ - K
ᛉ ——— ᚴ = g }
ᛒ is evidently meant for = p, while B = b
ᚷ ——— = a, while X (copy R) = g
ᛘ ——— = v. w. no such Runic char
ᛟ ——— = ö, o, " " " "

The signs Ᵽ, FF, F,Φ, ᚱE, ᚱFPF, which indicate numbers, I can make nothing of. ᚱ in Runic = 14. Φ in Runic indicates 19. – ᚨ is no Runic char.

I read the inscription ✗:–

Ᵽ (number) göter ak FF (number) norrmen pa apthagelsefarth frå wimlanth of (?) west wi hathe lager F (number) skfar (?) en thags rise nor from thene sten wi war ok fiske en thagh aptir wi kom hem fan Φ (number) man röthe af blod og thoth (?) AVM fraelse af illy (?) Har Φ (number) mans we hawet at se apter wåre skip ᚱE thagh rese from thene öh (?) ahr ᚱFPF (number)

In english it might be rendered (somewhat freely):– ? Swedes and ? norwegians on a journey of discovery from Vinland ? west – we camped ? ? one day's journey north from this stone – we fished one day – after we came home we found ? men red with blood and dead – AVM (?) save from evil (?) – Have ? men at the ocean to look after our ships ? days journey from this island (?) year ? ———

✗ Note that this is a literal transcription and that I am not responsible for bad spelling and language

In January of 1899, then professor of Scandinavian languages at the University of Minnesota, Olaus Breda, sent a translation and his notes of his linguistic analysis of the Kensington Rune Stone inscription. These notes were sent to Samuel Siverts who was the banker in Kensington who had sent a copy of the inscription to Breda. (Courtesy of Ing Siverts, 2010)

we found ? men red with blood and dead – AVM (?) save from evil (?) – Have ? men at the ocean to look after our ships ? days journey from this island (?) year - ? ————————

Note: This is a literal transcription. I am not responsible for bad spelling and language."

The Obelisk at Kensington

ONE OF THE CURIOUS SIDE STORIES in the history of the Kensington Rune Stone was when and how the artifact made its way to Alexandria, Minnesota, in 1927.

Ten businessmen from the Alexandria community each putting up $250, totaling $2,500, paid Hjalmar Holand this sum, and he turned over physical custody of the stone. Many people thought Holand sold the artifact, which he clearly did not. In my 2006 book, *The Kensington Rune Stone: Compelling New Evidence*, I explore the issue of ownership (pages 237-248) that outlines a dispute between Holand and Ohman. The fact that Holand was very clear in stating he was transferring physical custody, not ownership, is very telling.

Ownership however, is not the issue. The mystery of this transaction came to light when an Alexandria resident and local historian contacted me with a very interesting discovery she had made.

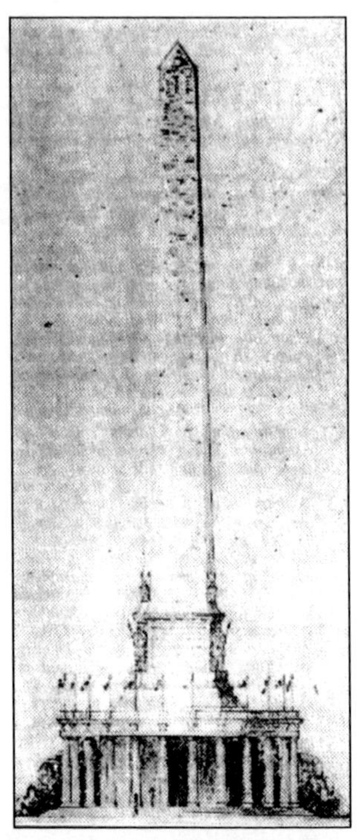

This artist's rendition of the proposed 204-foot tall obelisk at the discovery site appeared in the *Citizen and Alexandria Post News* on July 28, 1927.

These ten men were prominent business leaders in the community of Alexandria, Minnesota, who pooled together and paid Hjalmar Holand $2500 to reimburse him for his twenty years of research expenses on the Kensington Rune Stone. They then brought the artifact to Alexandria and made plans to raise $300,000 to build a 204-foot tall obelisk at the discovery site on the Ohman Farm. Top left to lower right: A.D. Haskell, Carl V. Anderson, C.J. Gunderson, Carl Oscar Franzen, J.A. Wedum, Gordon Duenow, G.A. Kortsch, Constant Larson, Phil Noonan, and Dr. Edwin J. Tanquist.

Julie Snider emailed me with a question, "Did you know that the ten men who brought the Kensington Rune Stone to Alexandria were all Freemasons?" On November 9, 2009, Julie sent me a packet of documents confirming her discovery. Constant Larson and at least five of the ten businessmen he assembled to acquire the artifact in 1927, were Freemasons.

I did not know that and was quite surprised at this revelation. As I thought about the events of 1927, things started to make more sense. These men started an ambitious campaign to preserve, protect and honor the artifact by raising $300,000 to erect a 204-foot-tall obelisk at the discovery site on the Ohman Farm. The rally at Fahlin's Point near Kensington on June 1, 1927, was reportedly attended by 10,000 people and was the kickoff event to raise the money and awareness for what they must have believed was a medieval connection to the Craft of Freemasonry.[6]

At a presentation at a Masonic Lodge in 2011, Mark Campbell, a thirty-third degree Freemason, shared a story after hearing me discuss Julie Snider's discovery about the ten men in Alexandria and the proposed obelisk. Mark said he had recently attended a Masonic meeting in Washington, D.C., and had viewed original plans of the Washington Monument. He said the original dimensions of the monument were intended to be 408 feet tall with a 110-foot diameter, round colonnade. The final height of the Washington Monument is 555-feet due to changes in the design and delays during construction. However, somehow, the ten men in Alexandria must have known about these original dimensions for the obelisk in Washington, almost certainly through Masonic connections, and planned to honor the rune stone with an obelisk of exactly one-half the size.

Julie shared what she had found about each man and asked if I could find anything at the Scottish Rite Temple in Minneapolis. With the help of head librarian, Peter Tomlinson, within a couple of weeks we were able to find the class pictures of two of the men, A.D. Haskell and John Wedum. While working with Julie and Janet, we discussed the obvious question: Why did these men want to erect such an obvious and massive Masonic symbol for what, at that time, everyone was calling a "Viking" artifact?

Perplexed at first, we then wondered: Did they see something on the Rune Stone that resonated with their knowledge as Freemasons? In keeping with the speculative research in *The Hooked X*, it appeared I wasn't the only one thinking the Kensington party of 1362 included ideological followers of the persecuted Knights Templar Order who understood Gnostic tradition and knowledge. But what was it that the ten Freemasons might have seen that told them it wasn't a "Viking" artifact? I was determined to find out.

On September 1, 2010, I got my chance to seek help when I gave a lecture at the Anoka Masonic Lodge where I had given two lectures previously on the Kensington Rune Stone and the Hooked X. John Freeburg invited me to share my latest findings. The last part of my presentation was about the obelisk and the "ten men" from Alexandria.

The room was filled with about seventy-five very attentive people as I listed the possibilities. "Could they have seen the sacred 2:1 ratio (or the 1.62 Golden Ratio) that the stone was split down to by the carver?" "Did they pick up on the number of lines comprising the inscription; three groups of three lines on the face side for a total of nine, and three more lines on the split side for grand total of twelve lines?" I then said, "Symbolically, the twelve lines could represent the twelve apostles in the bible, or as most Freemasons know, they actually represent the twelve primary constellations of the zodiac. These things would likely have resonated, but I think what certainly would have caught the attention of Freemasons versed in the more esoteric aspects were the three Latin letters: AVM."

To Roman Christians, AVM is a common prayer prompt for Ave Virgo Maria, or the Virgin Mary. On the other hand, esoteric Freemason Frank C. Higgins wrote in 1916 about the sacred "Lost Word" of A.U.M. He wrote about a close connection between A.U.M. and the Tetragrammaton, the sacred immutable Hebrew word of the creator seen inside an equilateral triangle. "The symbol of the 'Lost Word' of the Master, says Brother (Albert) Pike, is the A.U.M. of the Persian Magi and the most ancient Brahman, because [behind] the tri-lateral glyph lays the philosophy of the 'Secret Doctrine,' the synthesis of all knowledge."[7]

The word "AUM" represents the three modes of the Creator's existence such as "Knowledge, Power and Perfection" or "Wisdom, Strength and Beauty," called the "triglyph." The triglyph A.U.M. also represents an ancient philosophy of basic truth that includes geometry as the connecting link between matter and spirit. One example is the geometry and mathematics as applied to the great circle known as the earth.

If a circle representing the earth is divided into four equal parts along the four cardinal directions of north, east, south and west, the line connecting east and west is the equator. From there, an equilateral triangle in the northeast quadrant can be made with the vertical axis as its base will have three angles of sixty degrees and its point on the circle will be the exact position of the Great

Pyramid of Giza, in Egypt. A line drawn from the position of the great pyramid to the southern point of the circle, together with the line to the north point and the vertical line connecting them will create a right triangle with corner angles of thirty, sixty, and ninety degrees. This sacred earthy right triangle geometry also applies to the three sacred phases of the sun during its daily trek across the sky and is what the ancients called, "The Wisdom of Solomon."

To keep it simple, Higgins brings in Gematria, where each letter represents a number of the Hebrew language to explain the mathematics, geometry, and symbology of this ancient knowledge of the sun. Sixty is Samech (S), thirty is Lamed (L), forty is Mem (M), and fifty is Nun (N), which forms the skeleton word S-L-M-N. He then fills the "Os" using the eastern religions use of the three mystic "sixes" (6 x 6 x 6 = 216) and by adding the cubes of 3, 4, and 5 (27 + 64 + 125 = 216), the sacred Pythagorean triangle, to complete the true meaning of "SOLOMON", which stands for "SOL," the rising sun, "OM," the midday sun, and "ON," the setting sun.[8]

These three sacred geometrical positions of the sun during its daily trek across the sky that form the 30-60-90 degree angles of the right triangle are called A (90 degrees), U (60 degrees) and M (30 degrees) or A.U.M. To those who understood these complex philosophical and mathematical concepts these three letters was their symbol.

In medieval times, the letters "V" and "U" were interchangeable, and in Latin, there was no difference between the two.[9] This being the case, AVM on the medieval aged Kensington Rune Stone inscription could easily have been intended to have a double meaning. To a Roman Christian, it was acknowledgement to the Blessed Virgin Mary, (Ave Virgo Maria). To the enlightened followers of the Hooked X ideology of the Templar Dualists, it was a symbol of reverence to the "other" Mary (Magdalene), who represented the feminine half of the male/female duality that goes back to the Egyptian Goddess Isis. Once the AVM/A.U.M. was surely recognized by the ten men in Alexandria, Minnesota, the other symbology of the artifact would likely have been recognized once they realized what they were dealing with.

This can be the only logical explanation for why a group of ten men comprised of nearly all Freemasons would have gone to such lengths to mark the discovery spot with one of the ultimate symbols of ancient Freemasonry: an Egyptian obelisk, the ultimate male phallic symbol, which was also used as a giant sundial to track the daily trek of the sun across the sky.

The AVM carved on line eight of the Kensington Rune Stone has been interpreted by scholars to be a Roman Catholic prayer for Ave Virgo Maria. However, it could have had a dual meaning with the other possible meaning being apparent only to those enlightened few with knowledge of the ancient esoteric concept of A.U.M. (Wolter/2010)

One "Degree" North from This Stone

ONE OF THE MOST PUZZLING PHRASES in the Kensington Rune Stone inscription is found on lines three through five that have tentatively been translated as: "We had a camp by two shelters, one day's journey north from this stone. We were fishing (casting or surveying?) one day's (nautical unit or one degree of latitude?) journey from this stone." Could this be what the carver of the Kensington Rune Stone intended? Since I am confident the artifact was created as a land claim, two of the Old Swedish words in this puzzling sentence could indeed mean "surveying" and "one degree of latitude" as a way of documenting its location. The word, surveying, becomes more interesting when considering the amount of surveying necessary to arrange the triangulation of the stone holes at the discovery site that pinpoints its exact location where the Kensington party buried the stone.

When a map of the watershed divides in the upper Midwest is studied, one notices that, not only was the rune stone found on the north-south continental divide, but a surveying party working one degree north of Kensington would also be in the area of the divide. These facts, assuming the word indeed does mean "surveying," puts an emphasis on the apparent importance of watershed headwaters. In a later section, I will present research on another recently discovered inscribed stone found at another interesting headwaters area that could be related to the Templars who carved and buried the Kensington Stone.

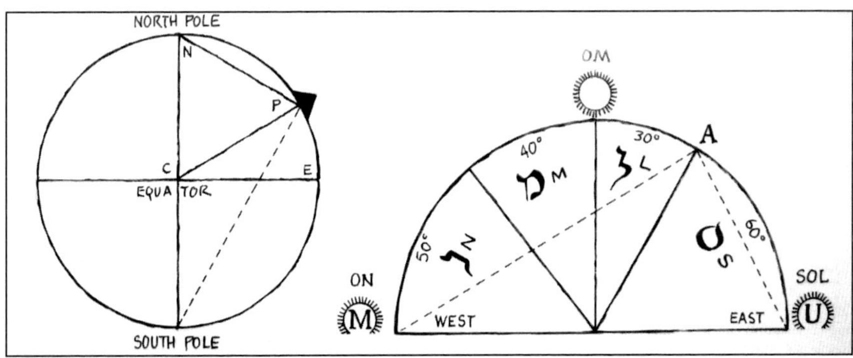

Enlightened ancient Egyptians, Templars, and modern Freemasons understood the mathematics, geometry and symbology of the sacred Pythagorean triangle when allied to the earth (left) and the daily trek of the sun across the sky (right). The three points and angles of the equilateral triangle are represented by "A" (90 degrees), "U" (60 degrees), and "M: (30 degrees) or A.U.M. (Redrawn from Higgins, pp. 24, 26)

What the Carver Didn't Say

NOTABLY ABSENT from the Kensington Rune Stone inscription are a couple of important things. First, lines six, seven, and eight read, "When we came home we found ten men red from blood and death." Many researchers in the past assumed this meant ten men in the Kensington party were ". . . killed by savages."[10] The inscription doesn't say that, and the words could just as easily have meant ten dead Natives. We simply don't know what the carver intended and must be very careful when interpreting what the inscription really means.

1. 8 Götalanders and 22 Northmen upon
2. (this) acquisition journey from
3. Vinland far to the west, we
4. had camp by two shelters (?) one
5. day's journey north from this stone.
6. We were fishing one day. After
7. we came home found 10 man red
8. from blood and death. Ave Maria;
9. Save from evil. 10. [There] are–
10 men by the inland sea to look
11. after our ships— a 14 day's journey.
12. from this peninsula. Year 1362.

The first nine lines of runic text on the Kensington Rune Stone are on the face side and the last three lines are on the split side. (Wolter Courtesy of the Runestone Museum, 2010)

There is another critically important aspect of the inscription that appears to have been overlooked. My recent thesis presented in 2009, of the Kensington Rune Stone being a land claim is supported not only by evidence clearly presented within the inscription, but also by a curious apparently unnoticed omission. Historically, inscribed land claims typically make crystal clear under whose authority the land is being claimed for. Eighteenth century land claims in North America, such as the land claim plaques placed by the French explorer Pierre La Vérendrye, were made in honor and for the French king. Throughout history, land claims were made for kings, lords, nobles, and even in the name of the pope.

The Kensington Rune Stone reads like a land claim, yet there is no obvious mention of who made the claim nor is there any mention of the land being claimed for any king, the pope, or anyone else.

In 1128, the Templars were granted the status of a Sovereign Order. St. Bernard de Clairvaux was their leader as the Templars were officially a Cistercian Order with Hughes de Payens formally installed as the Grand Master.[11] In 1139, the Knights were granted by Pope Innocent II, a St. Bernard protégé, international

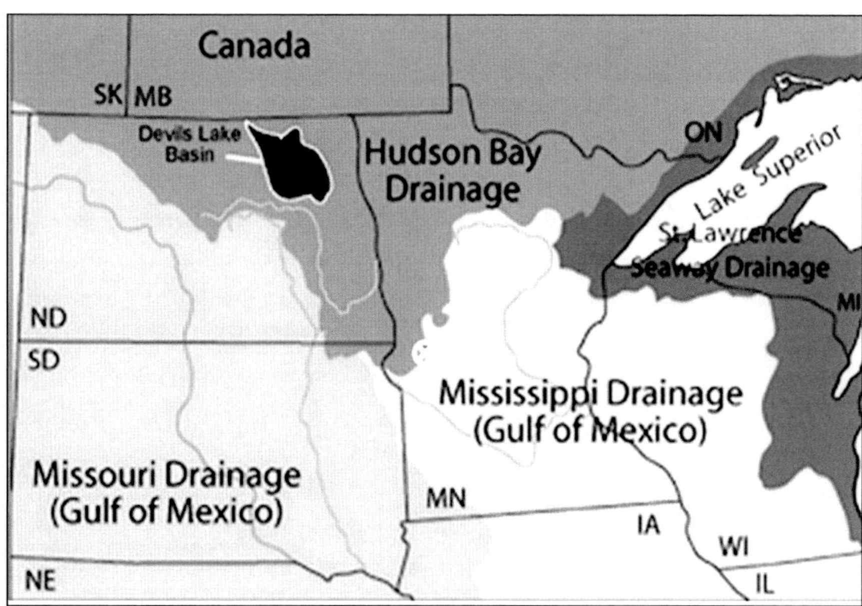

The Kensington Rune Stone was found on the north-south continental divide of North America. A medieval land claim plaque or stone in this case, could give the claimers the right to claim the entire Mississippi-Missouri river watersheds to the Gulf, and the Red-Nelson river watersheds to Hudson Bay, which is almost half of the continent.

independence from obligation to any authority other than himself.[12] This unprecedented status appears to be the key point when considering who was most likely responsible for carving the fourteenth century inscription.

Not only does the lack of any mention of a monarchy or papal authority point to the fugitive Knights Templar and their Cistercian brethren, but there appears to be another piece of evidence within the inscription that points in their direction. Could this renegade outfit that made its way to the heart of the interior of North America have made the claim in their own name? Perhaps the Hooked X symbol emblazoned twenty-two times represents who actually was claiming the land. This all-important symbol that appears to represent the essence of their religious ideology might very well have meant, "We claim this land for our Brethren."

The Dotted R

A SIGNATURE MOMENT in the modern history of the rune stone was triggered by a visit to the Runestone Museum in Alexandria, Minnesota, by Scandinavian runologist, Henrik Williams on September 30, 2010. The professor's actions and words led to a series of events that resulted in my performing yet another examination of the artifact. This time, however, it involved the latest three-dimensional digital microscopic technology. But first, a little background information . . .

In October of 2008, Richard Nielsen, had convinced the Runestone Museum to allow a three-dimensional examination of the artifact using digital technology. For reasons yet to be explained, Nielsen refused to turn over the data he had promised to the museum or to either the professional or academic community for peer review. Ultimately, the museum became frustrated with being unable to secure the large format 3D images they chose not to allow Nielsen into the museum to accompany Williams during his examination of the Kensington inscription.

Upon completion of his hour-and-a-half-long examination, with three museum board members: Jim Adam, Laura McCoy, and Carol Meyer present, Professor Williams made the following pronouncement about the Dotted R on line six: "If the dot is man-made, the Kensington Rune Stone is a genuine medieval artifact."[13] In my 2006 book, *The Kensington Rune Stone: Compelling New Evidence*, Dick Nielsen and I presented evidence that the Dotted R alone proved the Kensington Stone was genuine since it was unknown to modern runic scholars until it was discovered in 1935, and then published for the first time in 1938, yet it is present within the inscription discovered in 1898.

After being highly impressed with the capabilities of the digital microscope during a demonstration in my own laboratory, I contacted the Runestone Museum. They expressed strong interest in pursuing a microscopic examination using this equipment and wanted to take advantage of the new 3D digital microscopic technology that far surpassed any previous work done. The museum also saw an opportunity to provide the appropriate Dotted R data requested by Professor Williams. On February 16, 2011, with Keyence technicians, Michael Vincent and Julia Des Chenes, operating the equipment, the examination took place at the museum.

Before examining the Dotted R, we looked at the characters museum director Julie Blank was curious about. On line eight, Julie thought the second thorn rune in the word "death," the word separator after it, and the Latin "A" in "AVM," showed some differences. After centering the microscopic lens over the middle of the loop on the thorn rune, something unexpected jumped out under high magnification. A circular depression was present in the middle of the plateau of rock that connected to a trench that ended at a circular pit at the bottom of the groove of the loop. (See color section, Figure 1)

It was clear to me that the carver had tried to make a shallow punch mark in the center of the loop. Likely because of weaker, unstable rock associated with a prominent crack running through the bottom part of the loop, the chisel slid down to the lower right and stopped in the pit it made within the outer groove. The carver was trying to make a rare dotted "thorn" rune that, because of the slip of the chisel, had gone unnoticed until now.

The realization of the new discovery was exciting and surprising. If Julie had not asked to look at this rune, I had no plans to go anywhere near it. Already the new technology had paid big dividends.

From there we turned our attention to the Dotted R on line six. As explained in my previous two books, here was the "Magic bullet" that all by itself proved the inscription to be medieval. The first image to appear on the screen was the clearest and most detailed view of the dot I had ever seen. Its uniform shape, depth, and central positioning could only be intentionally man-made. The slightly dull edges and shallowly pitted depression was consistent with the weathering of the original inscription I had documented a decade ago.

Runologists like Henrik Williams, now had the critical data they asked for to make the pronouncement that the world has been waiting for over a century to come from the Scandinavian scholars. (See color section, Figure 2)

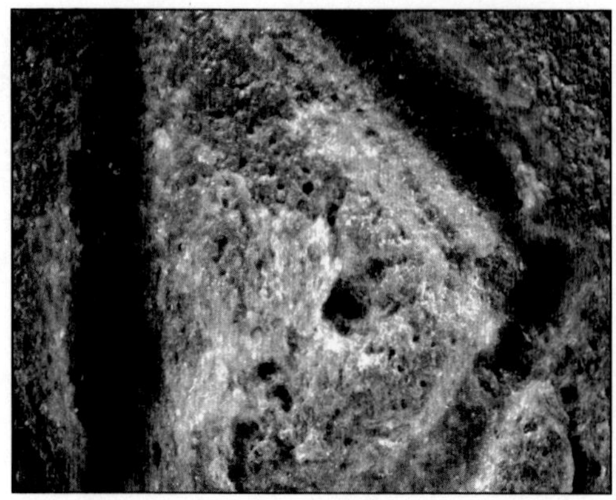

This reflected light image of the area in the upper loop of the first "R"-rune on line six, shows the uniform shape and depth (approximately 400 microns in diameter) of the pit, or "dot," in the upper plateau of rock. Very small-scale pitting (50 microns in diameter or less) can be seen on the glacial surfaces due to weathering of fine-grained feldspar minerals, or plucking out of quartz grains from the surface of the meta-greywacke. (Magnification 30X)

One would think this highly accurate new data would be enthusiastically received by Williams and other academics. However, two months later Williams issued a startling response. He started off by chiding three board members of essentially lying about what he had said and then claimed he was talking about the dotted *thorn* rune on line eight, not the dotted R on line six. Perhaps this was an attempt to wiggle out of the corner he had painted himself into. However, how could he have been referring to the dotted thorn rune when it was unknown to anyone until six months *after* he made his now infamous statement?[14]

Professor Williams's statement went on to talk about geological features within the inscription while disparaging the qualifications of others investigating the stone. Herein lays the problem. Defending the status quo by many academics is what has dogged the investigations from the beginning, and that has now been more than one hundred years.

From my perspective, the mystery of the Kensington Rune Stone was already solved a century ago by the first state geologist of Minnesota, Professor Newton H. Winchell. Winchell, recruited by the Minnesota Historical Society to investigate the authenticity of the artifact in 1909, made exhaustive investigation into the geological, historical, linguistic, and archaeological aspects. This resulted in his emphatic opinion that the Kensington Rune Stone was a genuine medieval artifact. My own professional research, as a geologist, confirms this opinion.

As a licensed geologist in the State of Minnesota, I must conduct myself within certain professional and ethical standards. If I violate those or perform substandard work, complaints can be filed, and I can lose my license to practice my profession. What accountability does academia have? I sometimes worry they answer to no one.[15]

GRAL (Grail)

IN ORDER TO PREEMPTIVELY neutralize criticism, I did some additional testing of the first four runes (not pentadic numbers like the " eight" on line one) that are singled out with punch marks added to specific runes after the inscription was carved that, when put in sequence, spell "GRAL." In medieval Old Swedish, these letters mean "Grail." Whether the carver intended to encode the word Grail within the inscription may never be known with certainty. However, given the weight of related evidence pointing in the direction of a post put-down party connected to the Cistercians and Knights Templar, having Grail on the stone should not be all that surprising.

On August 13, 2012, I went back to the Runestone Museum with the 3D digital microscope and carefully created images to verify that the punches were indeed manmade, and, that they were added *after* the lines were carved. Others had claimed the punch marks were made *prior* to the inscription being carved so the carver would know where to put his lines. In my opinion, this was clearly not the case since guide lines could more easily be made using a piece of limestone as chalk or a piece of charcoal from a campfire.

The results of my analysis were consistent and conclusive. The punch marks clearly were made directly on or immediately adjacent to the lines *after* the four runes were carved. (See color section, Figures 3 & 4)

Pentadic Number Eight (8)

SINCE WE HAD TIME to examine and measure other characters with added punch marks, we also looked at the Pentadic number eight, the very first thing carved on the stone and part of the Dating Code confirming the 1362 date. In *Compelling New Evidence*, Dick Nielsen and I made a joint discovery that illustrated how effective our collaboration was before personalities and money issues took over. The results were as expected—the punch mark is definitely present at the end of the second horizontal bar and extends nearly twice the depth of the groove it was added to. (See color section, Figure 5)

The Wholle Grail

JUST WHEN I THOUGHT there couldn't be anything new on the Kensington Rune Stone I received yet another call. Mark Limburg, a musician living in Minneapolis called me and said, "Scott, I think I've discovered something potentially important that relates to the rune stone." He had been watching *Holy Grail in America* when something struck him.

Mark came by my office on February 23, 2011, with a map of the Merriam Park neighborhood a few blocks south from my office. Mark pointed to an east-west street, Roblyn Avenue, and said, "I was raised in Germany. There's a symbol used for the 'double S' sound that looks like a capitol 'B.' So, if substituted for the 'b,' this street could mean 'Rosslyn,' as in Rosslyn Chapel."

Angling down and meeting Roblyn Avenue was a street named Temple Court. Mark then drew a horizontal rectangle with the all too familiar 2: 1 ratio beginning at Roblyn and Temple. The opposing corner was at the intersection of Howell Street North and Iglehart Avenue, exactly at the location of the Triune Masonic Temple. Only days before, Darwin Ohman, Janet, and I had attended the one hundredth anniversary of the Triune Temple fund-raising dinner for renovations to the building. The celebration was also to commemorate the Triune Lodge being the oldest still operating original Masonic lodge building in the state of Minnesota. During the dinner a Freemason friend, John Freeburg, said the Merriam Park neighborhood area was originally planned to be the site for the Minnesota State Capitol Building located between the two cities.

Mark pointed out another smaller 2:1-sized rectangle in the middle of the larger rectangle that has *four* streets with proper names, Moore, Wilder, Carroll, and Merriam. He then suggested it could be an analogous allegory to

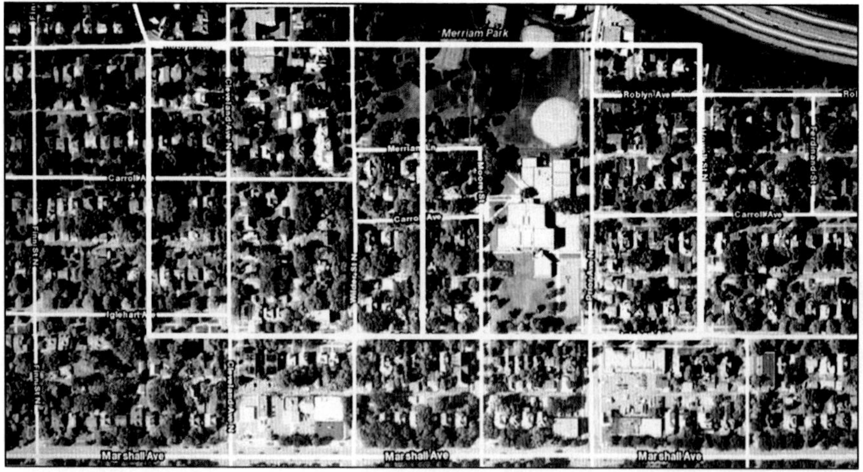

A perfect rectangle with a 2:1 ratio is formed by the streets Temple and Roblyn in the northwest corner and Howell and Iglehart in the southeast corner. Another 2:1 rectangle is formed exactly in the center by Carroll Avenue, Merriam Lane, Moore Street, and Wilder Street North. Could this be analogous to the Hooked X allegory of the female child inside the womb of her mother?

the hook in the "Hooked X" I proposed earlier of a female child inside the womb of her mother?

Another larger 2:1 ratio rectangle is located a block east of the smaller rectangle and both have a small notch in the street in the northeast corner. The large notched rectangle to the east happens to have *eight* streets named after men: Howell, Dewey, Prior, Ferdinand, Carroll, Roblyn (named for two men, Rob and Lyn), and Iglehart. Mark looked at me and said, "Could this be representing the eight Goths on the Kensington Stone?"

Going back to the original rectangle with Temple/Roblyn and Howell/Igelhart at the opposite corners we find *ten* streets running through or around the rectangle named after men, Roblyn (two men), Cleveland, Howell, Iglehart, Prior, Merriam Lane, Moore, Carroll, and Wilder. Ten men are referred to twice in the Kensington inscription. If you then add the smaller rectangle with four men, and the larger rectangle with ten men, they add up to *fourteen* men, yet another important number on the split side of the Kensington Stone. I had already done the math when Mark asked me, "What do the three rectangles add up to?" I then answered, "Four plus eight plus ten equals twenty-two, the same number of 'Northmen' on the first line of the inscription."

At this point that it occurred to me that there might be another confirmation code within the Kensington Rune Stone inscription beyond the Easter Table Dating Code that confirms the 1362 date.[16] Mark's discovery got me thinking about the numbers and the "odd" characters within the inscription. So, I went back and simply tallied all the runes within the inscription and something surprising jumped out. It turns out that the significant numbers within the

Mark Limburg's Merriam Park mystery includes three rectangles with 2:1 ratios with streets named after four, eight, and ten men, that all add up to twenty-two, the same important numbers found on the Kensington Rune Stone.

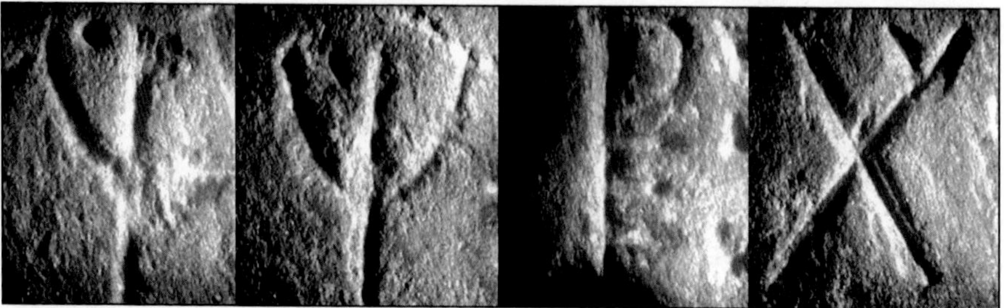

There are eight "g"-runes, ten "w"-runes, fourteen numbers, and twenty-two Hooked X's within the Kensington Rune Stone inscription. These appear to confirm the numbers, 8, 10, 14, and 22 within the inscriptions. (Wolter, 2002)

inscription, 8, 10, 14 and 22, appear to be confirmed by the number of odd characters never seen before in medieval runic inscriptions in Scandinavia. There are eight "g" runes if the backwards "u" rune in "illu" is included which is virtually identical to the first known, backwards "g" on the Kensington Rune Stone. There are also *ten* of the enigmatic "w" runes within the inscription.

Upon tallying the numbers within the inscription, making sure to count the Arabic ten as one symbol, and the two times that "one" is spelled out, there are *fourteen* individual numbers: 8 (Goths), 2, 2 (NorRmen), 2 (Shelters), 1 (day's journey), (We went fishing) 1 (day), 10 (men red with blood and death), 10 (men by the sea), 1, 4, (day's journey), (year) 1, 3, 6, 2. Lastly, there are twenty-two of the all-important Hooked X symbols scattered throughout the inscription.

It can't be a coincidence that the apparent coded symbols represent the never-before-seen runes for "g," "w," and "a," and extremely rare numbers. If ever someone needed convincing that the Kensington Rune Stone is a unique medieval inscription that follows none of the usual standards, here is yet another piece of evidence consistent with the inscription being a message meant to be understood by enlightened ones who knew what the codes were and what they meant.

Like many things in life, unless you become aware of things by observation, reading, or formal education, subtle or hidden details and messages will be missed. In recent years, I have tried to explore and better understand the esoteric side of certain organizations and secret societies. The "initiated" Cistercian/Templars certainly understood coded and encrypted forms of communication as did their ideological descendants, the Rosicrucians.

The Rosicrucian's early seventeenth-century books contained ciphers, cryptogams, codes, acrostics, and anagrams used to perpetuate knowledge that had been in use for thousands of years and used by most secret societies. This appears to be what we have here with these four important numbers (8, 10, 14, and 22) being confirmed by the number of times these three mysterious runic characters, and fourteen individual numbers appear within the inscription.

Mark Limburg's Merriam Park/Triune Temple mystery also includes the mysterious Kensington Stone "w"-rune. The "Grail" prayer my co-author Dick Nielsen and I discovered on the Rune Stone was part of his research.[17] He explained that the "w"-rune that is singled out with a punch on line eleven of the Kensington inscription is in the word that essentially means "water." Mark explained, "If the grail is treasure, the location of where the Holy Grail was buried could have been shown on the Kensington Stone, geographically, by the ten "w"-runes. Maybe the dot within the "w"-rune represents where the Grail was buried within a geographical area that resembles a chalice, made out of water."

At this point Mark pulled out a map of the Twin Cities. He outlined the area where the Mississippi and Minnesota rivers converged. Fort Snelling was built there and it's the place the Dakota called the most sacred in the entire world.[18] I smiled as I saw that the bends of the converging rivers formed a chalice. Mark had highlighted the old north-south Indian trail (now Snelling Avenue) to complete his "w"-rune shape. He then asked, "Didn't you say in one of your lectures that Snelling Avenue is the ninety-three degrees west longitudinal meridian that is exactly ninety degrees west of Rosslyn Chapel in Scotland?"

I nodded and said, "Isn't it also interesting that the forty-five degrees latitude, halfway between the equator and the North Pole, is marked by Roselawn (Rose Line) Avenue? I'm sure it isn't a coincidence that Roselawn and Snelling intersect in the small city of Roseville."

It's highly likely that the Ojibwa understood the geographical significance of this place that to them was sacred. There is an old and very sacred Native burial ground on the east side of the Minnesota River directly across from Fort Snelling. It makes sense that when the Templars came to Minnesota, they may have come up the Mississippi but would have encountered their first major obstacle at St. Anthony Falls; little more than a mile upstream from the closest point on the river to what is now the Merriam Park Neighborhood. At his point, I knew where Mark was going and when he put his dot to complete the geographical "w"-rune of his Grail map right on the Triune Temple.

Running with the idea, I explained to Mark that if there was something to his theory of a Grail treasure being buried by the Templars in the Merriam Park area, the local Twin Cities geology was perfect for them. The surface is covered with a relatively thin veneer of glacial sand and gravel deposits directly on top of the Platteville limestone and Decorah shale that serve as cliff-forming rock that produce the beautiful bluffs along both rivers. Along the Mississippi from Fort Snelling north to St. Anthony Falls, directly below the limestone and shale cap-rock, is the roughly sixty-foot thick St. Peter sandstone. This sandstone is loosely compacted, very well rounded quartz sand and is very easy to tunnel into. In fact, there are hundreds of miles of sewer and storage tunnels under the Twin Cities. During the 1920s and 1930s, Chicago gangsters often took hiatus in houses on the bluffs along the Mississippi River in Minneapolis and St. Paul that had escape tunnels leading to boats on the river.

I was torn between how unlikely this all was, but also how incredible all these seeming coincidences were mounting to a plausible possibility. Mark interjected, "But wait, there's more. Back in the fourteenth and fifteenth centuries in northern England and Scotland, they performed what were called 'Mystery Plays.' One of the main writers and performers of these plays in Rosslyn Chapel was Alexander Scott. In one of his plays, Scott referred to the third person in the Trinity as the 'Wholle Ghost.' This is translated into modern English the Holy Ghost, or Holy Spirit, which was to the Templars and to enlightened Freemasons, the Goddess."

Mark continued, "So, here, we have an interesting medieval spelling, used in the Rosslyn/York area of 'Holy' as 'Wholle.' I was watching your movie, *Holy Grail in America*, and thinking about the street signs in the Merriam Park neighborhood, when something hit me. The Triune Temple is at the corner of the first large rectangle, Howell and Iglehart, which is a perfect anagram for 'The Wholle (Holy) Grail.'"

My head was spinning, but just for good measure, Mark had one more surprise, "Oh, and did I tell you that the address number for the Triune Temple was 1898, the year the Kensington Rune Stone was discovered by Olof Ohman?"

If the early city planners thought the capitol would be here, then maybe they laid out the street system with a clever puzzle related to the Kensington Rune Stone that had been recently discovered. In 1909-1910, the Rune Stone was a hot topic in the local newspapers as articles reporting new findings appeared as Newton Winchell conducted his investigation into the authenticity and ownership of the artifact for the Minnesota Historical Society. Like the ten men (mostly Freemasons) in Alexandria who likely saw the "AVM" and planned to build the 204-foot tall obelisk at the discovery site, the early city planners, who were almost certainly masons as well, probably saw a connection to the "craft" as well.

Exactly what is going on with the street system in Merriam Park is a mystery, but clearly it has something to do with the Kensington Stone and early twentieth century Freemasonry. One doesn't have to be a mason to realize that some members at the highest levels know more about the connection to the Medieval Templar/Cistercian order and modern Freemasonry than they are letting on. This becomes more obvious as the research progresses. From my perspective, if they are unable or unwilling to go public about it, then I guess it becomes my job to do so.

In December of 2010, Mark Limburg published his research in a small book that included many more details than presented here entitled: *The Kensington Rune Stone: More Compelling New Evidence.*[19]

U-Haul Ceremony

AS FRUSTRATING AS THE LAST 115 years have been, the ocean-liner of skepticism is slowly beginning to turn around. On May 28, 2011, the U-Haul Company held an unveiling ceremony of the newest 'super graphic' for the State of Minnesota in Alexandria, Minnesota. Representatives from Alexandria, Douglas County, the Runestone Museum, and the Ohman Family participated in the ceremony on a cool, but sunny day. The incorrect "Viking" connection to the artifact still persists, but the fraud mentality that has persisted for so long is changing. The factual evidence has proven its authenticity; it is simply a marketing campaign now. The U-Haul ceremony that ensures there will be hundreds of billboard of the Kensington Rune Stone traveling around the continent is a big step in the right direction.

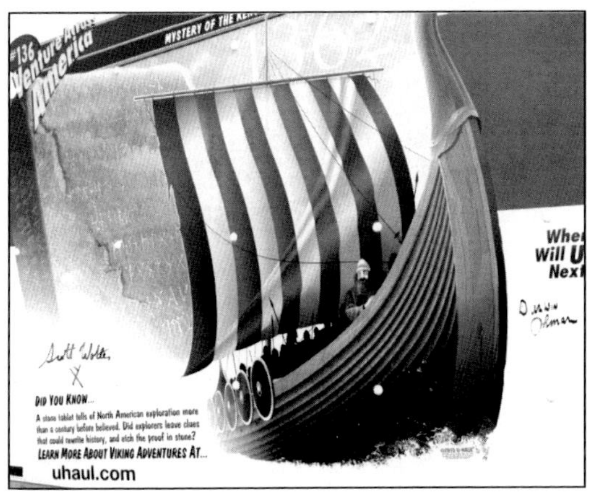

Darwin Ohman and the author both signed the U-Haul truck with the newest 'super graphic' of the Kensington Rune Stone for the State of Minnesota at the unveiling ceremony in Alexandria, Minnesota, on May 28, 2011. (Wolter, 2011)

Chapter 2

Update on Artifacts and Sites

VERY LITTLE STAYS STATIC in the world of exploration and discovery. Before launching into new material, I thought I'd give updates about the artifacts and sites I wrote about in *The Hooked X: Key to the Secret History of North America*. This update also includes recent developments in the effort to preserve a mysterious ship petroglyph we will discuss in this book.

The Westford Knight (Sword)

DAVID BRODY, THE CO-CHAIR of the Westford Knight (Sword) Committee, recently gave Niven Sinclair, the patriarch of the Sinclair Clan in England, an update on the progress on the local effort in Westford to preserve the carving. Niven believes the sword carving is likely connected to his distant ancestor Prince Henry Sinclair, believed to have led an expedition to the North America in 1398, so he certainly has a vested interest in seeing the carving preserved.

Brody reported plans to erect a gazebo-like structure over the carving to protect it from the elements, part of a local Eagle Scout project. They also plan to include a way to redirect surface water and road spray away from the carving.

Unfortunately, a nearby resident objected to the plan. The project is on hold until this is worked out. We wish David and the others the best of luck in their efforts to protect and preserve this important historical artifact.

Upper Peninsula Ship Carving

WHILE I DIDN'T WRITE about the ship carving in the previous book, it was featured in the documentary film, *Holy Grail in America*. During filming I noticed a small chip of the rock had flaked up from the surface in the top right corner of the sail. It had part of a one-eighth-inch-deep carved groove in it. I collected the roughly one-half-inch-thick chip with the hope of conducting weathering studies in my laboratory. Unfortunately, weathering had penetrated the full thickness of the chip of volcanic rock making any definitive relative-age weathering research of the carving impossible.

In August of 2010, I received disturbing news and a photograph. A few yards away from the ship carving are other interesting rock carvings—a human hand, a circle cross symbol, a downward pointing arrow, and a human stick figure with a bird head. Somebody had scratched away the bird head to the point where it was almost completely gone.

I feel partly responsible for the vandalism. It happened soon after the site was featured in our film *Holy Grail in America*. We always make a conscious effort not to mention exact locations of sites for their safety. In the film we said this site was in the Upper Peninsula near Copper Harbor. That seemed a wide enough area. It appears that some one found the site anyway and defaced it.

The local community took action to preserve the rest of the carvings. Ed Lahti (builder of the cover), Mike Lynch (vice-president of CCASC) and Robert Wheeler (president) mounted an effort to preserve the ship carving. On August 21, 2011, they installed a protective cover that should help deter future vandals.

The Westford Boat Stone

On September 20, 2011, I received a phone call from a Kevin Paxon, who had read *The Hooked X*, and had a suggestion as to what the three mysterious characters might be carved below the boat on the Westford Boat Stone. Kevin

This roughly one-foot long carving of a ship is one of several petroglyphs found on rock out-croppings near Copper Harbor on the Upper Peninsula of Michigan. (Wolter, 2009)

Not far from the ship petroglyph are several others carved symbols that include a hand, a circle cross, a human stick figure with a bird head, and a downward pointing arrow. Sometime in 2010, the bird head was vandalized and now is virtually gone. (Wolter, 2009, left; Wolter, 2011, right)

On August 21, 2011, a group comprised Ed Lahti, Mike Lynch, and Robert Wheeler, installed a protective cover to help deter future vandals. (Photo courtesy of Robert Wheeler)

said he looked into the two symbols that could represent Jupiter and the constellation Taurus using an astronomy program and discovered something interesting. The planet Jupiter was in the constellation of Taurus from May of 1395, to June of 1396, and from May of 1407 to June of 1408. He felt the earlier dates could have coincided with the Prince Henry Sinclair voyage thought by many researchers to have taken place around that time.

This historical astronomical method of dating made sense to me and for the first time offered a plausible explanation for these mysterious symbols. Kevin's

Three symbols are carved on the Boat Stone that was found in Westford, Massachusetts. The second could be the astrological symbol for the constellation of Taurus, and the third could be the astronomical symbol for the planet Jupiter. (Wolter, 2007, left; Internet, middle and right)

suggestion did not address the issue of the "1" character, but if this is the correct interpretation then somehow it must figure into the astronomical explanation. Hopefully, Kevin Paxon's suggestion will inspire further investigation.

Narragansett Rune Stone

ON AUGUST 7, 2012, A SHOCKING and unexpected turn of events unfolded involving the Narragansett Rune Stone resulting in a positive outcome that could have been a terrible historical tragedy. The story began when I received an email from a man named Andrew Jollie, who had read my first Hooked X book and wanted to see the Narragansett Rune Stone.

Because of the vandalism of the bird petroglyph that happened in the wake of *Holy Grail in America* film I was now particularly careful about pointing out the location of any in-place artifacts with people I didn't know. I referred Andrew to Rick Lynch, a local resident and long-time researcher who could vet him and direct him to the inscription if he checked out.

I remembered his name when the email came in and didn't think much at first when he said he couldn't locate the boulder near the shore in the bay. He said he had tried three times to find the boulder and was convinced it was gone. Attached was a picture of Andrew standing in the water at the approximate location of the boulder at low tide. I had visited the site four times to study the inscription and knew the area very well. It didn't take me long to realize that Andrew was right—the boulder with the inscription was no longer there!

It didn't take long to come up with a suspect. There was only one person who had the means, the motivation, and the opportunity. Over the course of the next two days, several people worked to compile a body of evidence and a personal profile that fit only one person.

The reason I knew instantly this particular person was the perpetrator was due to the less-than-poor impression he made on Rick Lynch, David Brody, and me when we met him on December 19, 2012. Another resident had invited us to attend the party to solicit support from the residents of the neighborhood to remove the stone from the bay to relocate it to a local museum where it could be protected and studied. As we made our pitch to the neighbors, I saw one person shaking his head. When it was his turn to speak, I was dumbfounded by what he said, "That stone is on my property, so I own it. I can do whatever I want with that stone and could take it out of the water tomorrow if I wanted to."

Right then I knew we were in trouble, but I never dreamed he would be so bold and defiant. I called Paul Roberti, who was stunned when I told him the news, but in the same breath he said he knew who had removed it. A couple of days later Paul told me this man's wife had admitted to their removing the stone, "So people would stop coming on to their property to see the Rune Stone."

On April 16, 2013, I sent an email to Detective Sheila Paquette with the Rhode Island Department of Environmental Management, Division of Law Enforcement-Criminal Investigation Unit, who was working the case. She replied: "Yes. An item matching the description of what we have come to know as the Narragansett Rune Stone, also called the Stone, and the Quidnessett Rock that has been part of an on-going investigation in cooperation with the attorney general and Coastal Resources Management Council for the past eight months was returned today to the custody of the State of Rhode Island."

When I asked for details, she appropriately declined to offer any. It didn't matter. The stone was safe. The only other thing I cared about was where would its final home be. Detective Paquette agreed it should be housed where the public could see it and would be protected from the elements and potential vandalism. This was a happy ending to what could have been a tragic story of the loss of yet another important historical treasure.

The top photo shows the Narragansett Rune Stone boulder in 2011, and its position near the large rocks along the shore. The lower photo shows Andrew Jollie standing in the water on August 6, 2012, where the boulder used to be, confirming it had been stolen. (Richard Lynch/Andrew Jollie)

Newport Tower

IN THE THREE YEARS SINCE I LAST WROTE about the Newport Tower, a number of interesting things have happened, including two newly discovered renditions of the structure in art. The first was a painting that came to light in March of 2009. Rick Lynch explained the discovery in an email: "The Newport Tower painting was discovered hanging on the wall in a back room of Jenks Lodge No. 24 A.F. & A.M. in Pawtucket, Rhode Island, in 2008. Long forgotten and damaged during a break-in at the lodge several years earlier, it hung in obscurity until Brother Russell Kawa brought it to my attention during a fraternal visit to the lodge."

"The date of the painting was 1869. It was painted by George Douglas Brewerton (1820 to 1901), who was not a Mason, yet his father was. Restoration of the painting was going to be costly and the lodge decided to send it to a Newport restorer/gallery for the amount of $15,000. The painting has since been totally restored and is now in the possession of a private collector."

What's interesting about this newly discovered painting is that the Tower is in essentially the same ruined state as it is today with Native Americans campsites nearby and on Goat Island in the Narragansett Bay. The Narragansett Indians have an oral tradition about the builder of the tower. "They were fire-haired men with green eyes who sailed up river in a ship like a gull with a broken wing."

It appears Brewerton believed the tower was pre-Columbian and begs the question of what inspired him to paint the scene he did.

The second artist rendition of the tower was discovered by my wife, Janet, on Halloween night 2011, when she pointed out a picture in a book I'd recently purchased, *The Architectural Heritage of Newport Rhode Island*. The picture turned out to be a detail of a lithograph of Newport from the perspective of Goat Island by John Newell, who reportedly drew the sketch in 1888. Standing to the right of the First Congregational Church, the Newport Tower looks in the same condition as today. What is puzzling about the sketch is the title underneath read: "NEWPORT, R. I. IN 1730."

This romanticized pre-Colonial period painting of the Newport Tower (detail of painting) was discovered at the Jenks Lodge, in Rhode Island, in 2008. It was painted by artist George Douglas Brewerton, in 1869. (Photo courtesy of Richard Lynch)

It's likely Newel romanticized this scene, but why a depiction from 1730? Possibly he was working from older sketches or drawings from that period that are now tucked away or lost. This is sheer speculation of course, but if sketches do or did exist that depict the tower looking essentially the same in 1730 as it does today, this casts more doubt on the Governor Benedict Arnold theory that the "Stone-built Wind-mill" he mentioned in his will dated December 24, 1677, was actually built by Arnold rather than retrofitted for use as a windmill.

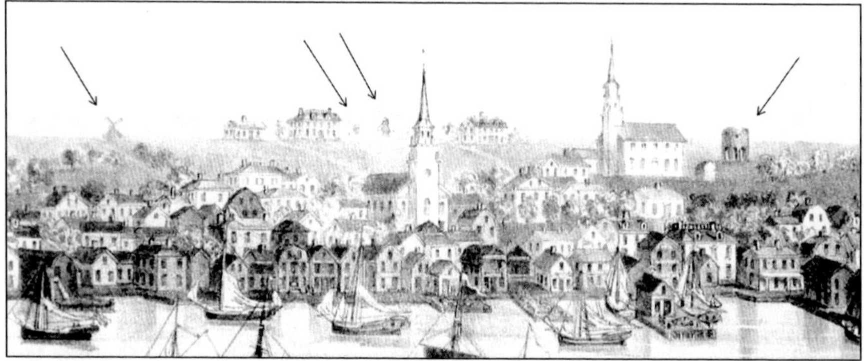

In this close-up view in John Newell's sketch of Newport, Rhode Island, three windmills (arrows from left) and the Newport Tower (arrow from right) can be seen along the horizon. The windmills are shaped with a wider base like the surviving Colonial-aged Jamestown windmil and look nothing like the Newport Tower here sketched in ruins supposedly in 1730.

Nathan Tufts Park in Somerville, Massachusetts, is the site of a stone windmill built by Jean Maillet in 1704. The windmill was constructed only a few decades after the time some believe the Newport Tower in Rhode Island was built, and while it dimensions are similar (approximately thirty feet tall and fifteen feet wide), its design is very different. The Tuft's tower was constructed with a sturdier base of solid stone that tapers with height (left). The Jamestown Windmill, in Rhode Island, built of wood in 1787, is another example of a colonial-age windmill with a wider base that gradually tapers with height (right). (Wolter/2009, 2006)

One other interesting fact from the Newell sketch is that six obvious windmills are depicted in Newell's lithograph, and all six are constructed of wood. They all have different height-to-width dimensions than the tower and taper in diameter with height. This is typical of the structural design of windmills from that period, which does not match the design of the Newport Tower.

Many people are fuzzy on the Benedict Arnold "Windmill Theory" for the Newport Tower, so it seems worthwhile to look at it again. Preeminent tower researcher Philip Ainsworth Means lists the first known reference to the tower as 1675 when ". . . Arnold provides Newport with a windmill to replace the wooden first-in-Newport windmill of Peter Easton, destroyed in late August of this year (1675) by a storm."

The multiple references to ". . . my Stone-built Wind-Mill," and "ye Stone Mill" in 1677 seems reasonable given the tower had indeed been used as windmill. However, the stone structure was already standing and represented the fastest and most convenient way to replace the destroyed windmill and salvage that year's corn harvest.

Arnold immigrated to America leaving Leamington, Warwickshire, England on May 1, 1635, arriving in New England on June 24th. The Chesterton Windmill was built in Warwickshire beginning in 1632 and completed in 1633.[20] Many people claim that Arnold, who was nineteen years old when he left, built the Newport Tower inspired by his memory of the Chesterton Windmill. One obvious problem with this theory is a lack of evidence that Arnold ever saw that windmill or even knew it existed. Another problem is the Chesterton Windmill was built on six columns, and the Newport Tower was built on eight.

The Chesterton Windmill, Warwickshire, England, was originally constructed in 1632, by Sir Edward Peyto, as an observatory and then converted to a windmill. While displaying similar architecture to the Newport Tower, the notable differences are six columns instead of eight, has no fireplace,and the lack of capstone ledges on the columns presumably used to support an ambulatory. (Wolter, 2008)

It's interesting some sources claim Sir Edward Peyto, who was a mathematician and astrologer, originally built the Chesterton Windmill as an observatory. This presents an interesting possible parallel in that the Newport Tower was also originally built as a medieval observatory, albeit in medieval times before being converted to a windmill.

During a few of my technical lectures to professional structural engineers, I've taken informal polls regarding the Newport Tower. I put up an image of the tower without any explanation of what the group was looking at. I asked them if the structure could serve as a windmill. Nearly every time, I hear chuckles as if the idea were ridiculous. When asked specifically why it wouldn't work, they consistently said the laterally forces from wind on the heavy second-story cylinder on the relatively unstable columns would tear the structure apart.

The presence of a first-story wooden ambulatory as evidenced by the capstone ledges at the top of each column, the two- to three-inch indent around the cylinder approximately four feet above the ledges would allow no room for the sails of a windmill to turn. I should remind the reader that, beginning in 2004 when I started to look at the architecture of the structure and who might have built it, the answer came quickly as it had to many other researchers before me: twelfth century Knights Templar round church architecture. In each of the surviving European examples the two-story round church was standing on eight, round heavy stone columns with Romanesque arches between them. These examples, such as the Templar Round Church in Cambridge, England, built in

The white lines represent the structural components made of wood that would be required for a first floor ambulatory that was likely part of the Newport Tower's original construction. On May 30, 2008, a salvage archaeological dig found the remains of two wooden posts both roughly sixteen feet from the northeast and east columns. (Wolter/2007)

1146; all had a first-story ambulatory that encircled the building. Upon looking at the Newport Tower for evidence of a first-story ambulatory, the facts came quickly and convincingly.

The capstone ledges provided structural support for the roof trusses for the first-story ambulatory. Second, roughly four feet above the capstone ledges is a slight indentation in the cylinder to allow for the slanted roof of the ambulatory where it was in contact with the second story. The third critical piece of evidence was discovered May 30, 2008, when Steve Volukas supervised an exploratory "salvage" archaeological dig that unearthed two interesting anomolies when the asphalt walkway was replaced with concrete. At a distance of roughly sixteen feet from both the northeast and east columns, Volukas and his team discovered, "At forty-five centimeters below ground level, a round, red, discolored feature was found within the gray clay layer. The feature measured thirty-eight centimeters by 35 centimeters, although it appeared to continue beyond the south edge of the unit. The center of the feature was 3.8 meters from the base of the east pillar."[21]

These features are likely the remains of wooded posts that provided structural support for the outer wall of the ambulatory. My bet is that any future archaeological dig below the concrete sidewalk will reveal the remains of the other six wooden posts. When all the other factual and anecdotal evidence are combined, the remains of the wooden posts should provide the conclusive evidence of the pre-Columbian origin of this amazing structure.

On September 23, 2011, I placed a call to Scott Wheeler, the trees and grounds supervisor with the City of Newport Department of Public Services, to get an update on the repairs to the Newport Tower the city had recently completed. Scott said the city spent just under fifty thousand dollars and performed an "emergency repair" of an earlier repair of the top two feet of the tower that was made in the early 1900s. The earlier repair was made with a very rigid and strong Portland cement-only based mortar that didn't "give" with expansion and contraction of the structure and was causing rapid deterioration. He also said, "A lot of water was getting into the walls and causing damage below the repaired area," and that "lots of organic material had accumulated at the top and in some areas looked like sod." Scott then said, "Next year there will be a larger conservation analysis to develop a larger restoration and conservation plan where the state of Rhode Island will take the lead."

This news lifted my spirits. I shared my concern during my visit earlier in the spring when the bulge on the top north side that had been visible for a number of years finally collapsed. The material that fell to the ground was relatively minor, but was obviously enough to trigger the emergency repairs.

On December 22, 2007, at 3:00 A.M., or the third morning David Brody and I were at the tower confirming the Venus alignments and the solstice illumination that happened six hours later. We entered the ruin and saw several mortar encrusted stones that had fallen from the inside of the structure. After over eight hundred years, this remarkably constructed and durable structure needs some care. It's great to know those needs are being responsibly met!

A relatively small area at the top above the north window in the Newport Tower that had been bulging for several years finally collapsed and fell to the ground only weeks before this photo was taken by the author on May 16, 2011.

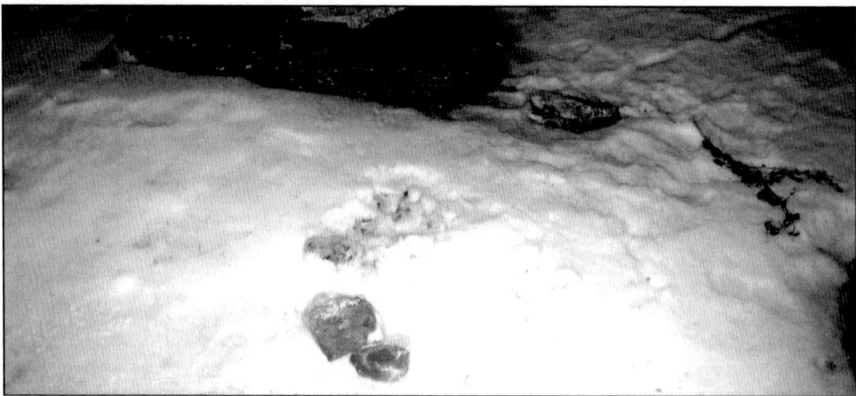

At 3:00 A.M. in the morning on December 22, 2007, when David Brody and I entered the inside of the Newport Tower to conduct research we were greeted with mortar encrusted rocks in the snow that had fallen off the structure during the night. (Wolter, 2007)

The Newport Tower was encased with scaffolding for "emergency repairs" on August 22, 2011, after an area at the top on the north side that had been bulging for years finally collapsed. (Photograph courtesy of Irene Daponte, 2011)

For the fourth year in a row, I traveled to Newport hoping to see the solstice illumination of the egg-shaped keystone on the inside of the tower. I'd been back three times since I first saw it on the solstice in 2007, but each time there was either a blizzard, as in 2008 and 2009, or the clouds didn't part until after the light box had moved off the keystone as in 2010. I planned three days and on the morning of December 19, 2011, the weather was perfect!

David and I arrived at the tower a few minutes before 8:00 A.M., just in time to catch the solar alignment through the south and west windows. This alignment was first discovered by retired Professor William Penhallow, of the University of Rhode Island, who also discovered several solar and lunar

The rising sunlight created a beautiful hexagonal burst in my camera lens as it passed through the both the south and west windows of the Newport Tower on December 19, 2011. This winter solstice solar alignment was intentionally designed into the architecture of the structure by the medieval builders of the structure. (Wolter, 2011)

These pictures were taken on December 19, 2011, as the rectangular box of light moves down and frames out the light tan colored, egg-shaped keystone on the winter solstice. Could this Illumination event have been designed by the builders as not only an allegorical fertilization inside the womb (nave), but also an allegorical orgasm upon stimulation of the clitoris (egg-shaped keystone) of the Goddess? (Wolter/2011)

alignments the builders had incorporated into the architecture. As I photographed the spectacular light show, I noticed a growing number of people walking up to witness the grand finale at 9:00 A.M. Rick Lynch introduced us to the men—mostly Freemasons from his and other lodges.

As the light-box passing through the south window moved out of the west window and then down along the inside wall toward the egg-shaped keystone, an excited crowd of people began to build. At 9:00 A.M. the rectangular shaped box of sunlight framed out the light-tan keystone. As we watched in awe as it lit up like a shimmering beacon, I thought about a comment I'd recently read in a book, *The Story of V*, by Catherine Blackledge. Her discussion of various cultures phrases for female genetalia prompted the thought that the egg shape is also a symbol of the clitoris—another layer to the sacred feminine symbolism of this Knights Templar-built round church.

In my previous Hooked X book (2009), I proposed that the illumination event on the winter solstice was an allegorical fertilization of the Orphic egg by the shaft of light from the sun, considered a male deity in most ancient religions that penetrates the nave of the church, or womb of the Goddess. In light of Catherine Blackledge's research, could the illumination of the egg-shaped keystone also have been designed as an allegorical orgasm?[22]

While some readers might blush about the allegorical clitoris and orgasm in the Newport Tower, its presence should come as no surprise. Two thousand years of repression of open discussion of human sexuality by organized religion has corrupted human thought about a subject that is a beautiful and important part of life. These matters were certainly not lost on ancient cultures, and in the case of the symbolism incorporated into Newport Tower the procreation of human life was also not lost on the Templars.

When thinking about the two keystones in the west, northwest archway of the Newport Tower that form a long-range alignment that extends through the Kensington Rune Stone discovery site, another interesting apparent connection to the Templars appeared. The notched keystone on the exterior of the west, northwest archway appears to contain additional symbolism beyond the Mark Master Mason's keystone shape so symbolically important to early operative stone masons and to modern Freemasons.[23]

Historically, the honor of placing the final keystone in a structure was given to the master Mason who carved the notches in the upper corners of the wedge-shaped block of stone. He also carved the Tau Cross on the stone as the Mason's Mark. I have performed a close examination of the notched keystone on the exterior of the Newport Tower and indeed there certainly is a Tau-shaped mark in the middle of the stone. I have never published this fact previously because the "T"-shaped mark looked more like coincidental cracks in the rock rather than intentional man-made carved lines. However, in light of the research on the Cross of Lorraine symbology presented later in this book, a second look at the notched keystone is required.

A closer look at the "T"-shaped lines on the keystone reveals another, shorter line that crosses the vertical line and is parallel to the

The notched keystone in the west-northwest archway of the Newport Tower has what appears to be the Cross of Lorraine carved between the notches. The lines could also be coincidental cracking in the rock, but this seems unlikely given the symbol is so intimately tied to the Knights Templar, who almost certainly built the structure sometime before 1400 A.D. (Wolter, 2012)

top horizontal line. Amazingly, this makes an undeniable version of the Cross of Lorraine. The question becomes, is it intentionally man-made or the result of the natural fracturing inherent in the stone? Perhaps it is an element of both. A skilled stonemason certainly understands how to work with the natural partings, sedimentary beddings planes, and fractures that are a part of all rocks, and the Templar mason who made this keystone may have subtly enhanced natural fractures.

Whatever the situation was at the time this incredible structure was built, the presence of yet another vitally important symbol to the Knights Templar as the Cross of Lorraine, in a notched keystone that aligns to another medieval Templar artifact, the Kensington Rune Stone, adds to an astonishing and ever-growing list of "coincidences."

Another interesting item came up about the Newport Tower during my December 2011 visit. A man who had attended David's and my lectures at the Bristol Masonic Lodge, in Massachusetts, the previous evening showed up at the tower the next morning along with several other people. Unfortunately, it was overcast, thereby cancelling the lightshow for that day. The smiling tall, dark, and slender man walked up to me carrying something in his hand. He said, "I enjoyed your lecture last night, and I decided to bring you a gift." He then handed a softball sized black rock with weathered white crystals on the surface.

He said the rock was a very rare, highly magnetic rock called cumberlandite, the official state rock of Rhode Island. He then shared a story that triggered a thought in my mind. He explained how he was into far-eastern martial arts and was practicing his art in Touro Park next to the tower very close to where we were standing. "I was aligning my inner energy lines and suddenly felt a very strong magnetic energy coming from the south column," he said. He then walked up to the south column and pointed to a large black rock with the same white weathered crystals on the surface about three feet off the ground.

Not being into martial arts. I don't understand how or if a person can detect such energy fields or magnetism, but I learned long ago there are many things I don't understand and am certainly in no position to judge. In fact, the more I've read about the esoteric side of ancient cultures including the Templars, the more I'm convinced they were able to detect these unseen energy fields. This made me think that the highly magnetic and very rare rock held some significance, likely both spiritual and practical, to the builders for it to be placed in the structure. Why the south column is unclear. Perhaps it had something to do with the four cardinal directions?

Back at the lab in Minnesota, I took a closer look at the rock. We made a thin section so we could identify its composition. It was indeed highly magnetic, comprised of the primary minerals plagioclase (a feldspar), olivine ((Mg, Fe) 2SiO4), magnetite (Fe3O4), and ilmenite (FeTiO3). Because it contained such high iron content, it was mined by the early colonists for farm tools and cannons. Unfortunately, during the Revolutionary War, cannons made with cumberlandite ore cracked due to the brittle nature of the iron.[24] In thin sections, the opaque minerals of magnetite and ilmenite comprised roughly forty percent of the rock.

Another reason occurred to me that would have made this rock attractive to the Templars, the mineral titanium. The high titanium content in ilmenite when combined with iron could be used in the manufacture of very strong and lightweight steel. Some have speculated that one of the things that gave the Templars an advantage in battle was superior armor as a result of their superior knowledge in metal-works they called "alchemy."

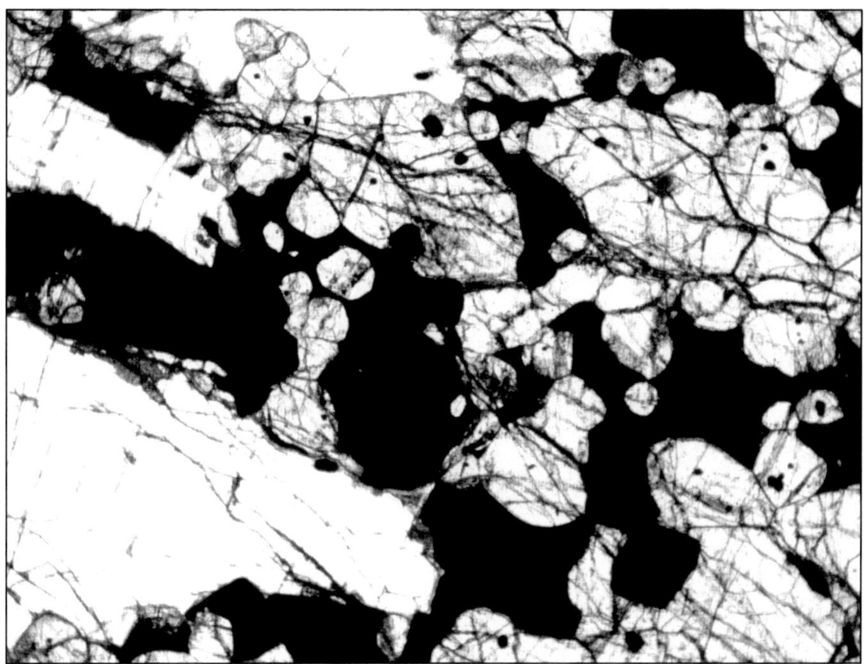

Cumberlandite is highly magnetic and is the state rock of Rhode Island. A large piece of Cumberlandite was added to the south column of the Newport Tower during its original construction. The black opaque minerals in this thin section (magnified forty times under plane polarized light) are magnetite and ilmenite; both contain a high amount of iron and titanium. (Wolter/2011)

To bring further intrigue to the mix with this extremely rare rock type, at the only known site where this material was mined, roughly four square acres near the town of Cumberland, Rhode Island, there is a Cistercian Abbey, called "Our Lady of the Valley." This order of strict observance monks known as Trappist, relocated from Nova Scotia in 1902 when the Abbey Petit Clairvaux, established there in 1892, was destroyed by fire.[25]

The Cistercians, under the leadership of Saint Bernard of Clairvaux, wrote the charter for and officially established the Knights Templar order in 1128. The popular Templar legend about the "Money Pit" at Oak Island, Nova Scotia, where the Templars were rumored to have buried their treasure that some believed included the Ark of the Covenant. A quick Internet search reveals many stories about the numerous unsuccessful attempts to find the treasure on Oak Island that has taken six lives over the last century and a half. I personally believe there was something buried there long ago by the fugitive Templar order, but whatever might have been there was relocated at least three hundred years ago.

A bit of irony, Rick Lynch passed along this fact in an email on January 2, 2012: "As a last bit of curious information, Cumberlandite in metaphysical circles is known as the 'Stone of Virgo.'"

In any case, that a Cistercian Abbey was founded in Nova Scotia and then relocated to Cumberland near the Newport Tower and the Narragansett Rune Stone, and who knows what else that hasn't yet been discovered, seems like more than a coincidence. My Canadian grandfather, Grant Austin, passed along a saying many years ago, "Scotty, if there's empty beers cans lying around, there's been some drinking going on." This fact about the Cistercian Abbey at Cumberland and its curious history seems to be yet one more "empty beer can."

One additional update on the Newport Tower gives me an excuse to share a terrific photograph taken by Rick Lynch. He captured Venus in the western sky in a position consistent with my proposed Venus alignments as the intended use for the two small windows at the top of the tower on the southeast and west sides. In my previous book I theorized that, based on the Templars reverence for the planet, symbolizing the goddess in the heavens, the Newport Tower was used as both calendar and clock because of Venus's precise movements through the skies during its annual, eight-year and forty-year cycles. The cloudy skies didn't allow Brody and me to make Venus observations during the three pre-dawn mornings we spent at the tower in December 2007. We knew she was there, but I wanted to see it with my own eyes. Thanks to Rick, I finally got my chance.

The small white dot in the sky directly above the Newport Tower is the planet Venus in the western sky in January of 2009. The position of Venus in this photo is consistent with the alignments through the two small windows at the top on the southeast and west sides that I proposed to be in the tower in 2008. (Photo courtesy of Richard Lynch)

In December of 2011, Janet and I watched a program on pre-Columbian Mayan civilization called *Chichen Itza*, on H2, History's second cable channel. The narrator began describing a unique stone observatory used exclusively for making astronomical observations of the planet Venus called El Caracol.

This stone observatory structure, which sits atop a large flat-topped stone platform is circular and roughly two stories tall with small rectangular

At the Chichen Itza ruins in Mexico, there is a two-story, round stone observatory called El Caracol that dates back to circa 900 A.D. This tower has a small rectangular window near the top that was used to observe the planet Venus (upper left) and serves as a pre-Columbian analog to the southeast and west windows at the top of the Newport Tower in Rhode Island. (Wolter/2012)

windows for viewing Venus at the top that are eerily reminiscent of the Newport Tower's small windows at the top of the structure. My point in bringing this observatory up is that it serves as a strong pre-Columbian parallel to the Venus alignments I proposed in the Newport Tower in 2008.

Margaret Starbird

ABOUT A MONTH AFTER the documentary film, *Holy Grail in America*, which was based, in part, on the research in my book *The Hooked X: Key to the Secret History of North America* aired on the History Channel, I received an email from an author referred by a fan of her books. The name Margaret Starbird was familiar, and I recalled listening to her lecture on a CD included with her book, *Mary Magdalene, Bride in Exile*, which I had purchased a couple years earlier. I enjoyed the lecture immensely, but I became distracted by other research and hadn't yet read the book when she contacted me.

The subject matter of the documentary clearly resonated with Margaret's own research, and she shared the following information in her email:

> I'm the author of the book that first launched Dan Brown, *The Woman with the Alabaster Jar*, mentioned in *The Da Vinci Code*. On pages 94-97 of my book, published in 1993, I explain the use of the letter "X" as a symbol for light and enlightenment in medieval art and artifact and for the "alternative Christianity" of the Middle Ages—the Church of the Holy Grail. Since the Knights Templar were the alleged guardians of the "Grail Family," there are good reasons to connect them with the "Church of Amor" based on enlightenment. The letter X is found in numerous watermarks of medieval heretics who translated their Bibles into the vernacular and were persecuted by the Roman Church, as were their Templar mentors who refused to join in the "Albigensian Crusade" against the Cathars (1209-1250).
>
> Freemasons today say grace before meals by crossing their arms across their chests and facing east toward the rising sun. The X symbol was the alternative to the upright cross on which Jesus suffered, which was not honored by the alternative Christians who viewed that cross as an instrument of torture. Numerous paintings of Mary Magdalene have the letter "X" worked into the image signaling the alternative faith of the "underground stream" surviving under the nose of the Inquisition—the belief that Jesus was fully human and married, and that his bloodline survived in Western Europe: i.e. the "Grail" bloodline, the "sang real," of whom the Templars were the guardians.

I knew instantly I had found a new friend. Within days after she read *The Hooked X*, and I had finished, *The Woman with the Alabaster Jar*, we talked on the phone. Her passion for the subject matter was infectious, and we laughed about the serendipity of reaching my conclusions about the heretical religious beliefs of the Cistercian/Templar brethren, and their attempt to restore the balance between the masculine and feminine aspects of the Godhead, without prior knowledge of her research. I chuckled to myself more than once about how this wasn't the first time this kind of thing had happened and it likely wouldn't be the last.

What also struck me about Margaret was her impassioned hope of the restoration of the repressed feminine aspects in both the Christian faith and our modern culture. She had many questions after watching the film and reading this book, but also offered several intelligent insights from her background as a biblical scholar.

On October 27, 2009, Margaret provided the biblical reference for the likely religious motive for the illumination event designed into the Newport Tower that is found in the second chapter of the Book of Acts (2:1-18). Starbird wrote, "The incident in Acts is known as the 'birthday' of the Christian Church. An illumination of a keystone in the Newport Tower at 'nine o'-clock in the morning' on the winter solstice would convey a similar and powerful symbolism: the 'birth' of the 'New Illumination,' or 'New Covenant,' in the 'New World.'"

Margaret's informed words echoed my own interpretation pretty closely, even though my knowledge of the bible is limited to say the least. Her discovery of the parallels in the Book of Acts is profound and adds yet another new layer of evidence that goes to the heart of the religious motivation behind the builders of the tower. If in the minds of some pre-Columbian skeptics the medieval origin of the tower is still in doubt, Margaret Starbird's contribution just might be the final nail in the coffin of the Colonial windmill theory as the reason the tower was built.

Chapter 3

The Hooked X

Here is a brief summary of what we have learned about the Hooked X symbol and a table of the nine known examples of the Hooked X symbol, what period they date to, and when they were first publically reported. This book adds three new examples including one with four Hooked X symbols that appear in what is believed to be a mysterious late twelfth-century document. If found to be legitimate, this document would represent *conclusive* evidence of the suspected connection of the Hooked X symbol to the medieval orders of the Cistercians and Knights Templar and to later Masonic organizations that appear to have evolved in some manner from those orders.

Artifact	Time Period	First Reported
Narragansett Rune Stone	Unknown	Circa 1977
Kensington Rune Stone	1362	1898
Spirit Pond Rune Stones (3)	1401-1402	1971
Rosslyn Chapel, Scotland	1446	2009
Christopher Columbus Sigla	1492	2009
Larsson Papers, Sweden (2)	1883-1885	2004
The Cremona Document (4)	1177-1180	2010
Anglo-Saxon Broach	Circa 9th century	2011
Copiale Cipher	Circa 1760	2011

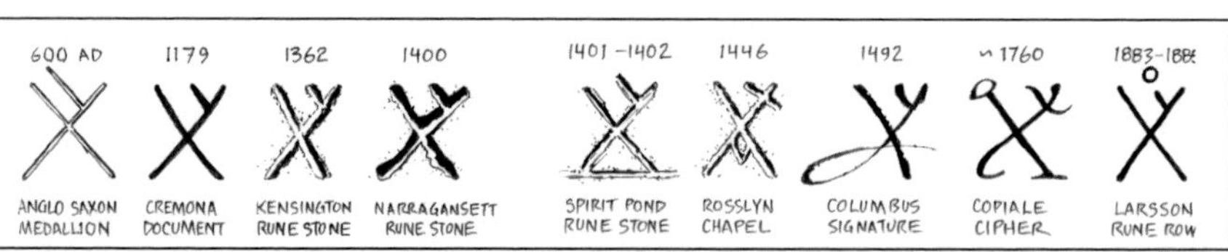

The Hooked X symbol occurs on five North America rune stones, and in Europe, one carved in stone and four more times in documents that, in total, span just over seven hundred years. What all ten examples have in common is an association with the medieval Knights Templar order and their ideological descendants which became occult and esoteric Masonic secret societies. (Sketch by Dan Wiemer)

In my previous book, *The Hooked X*, I provided multiple examples of the Hooked X symbol in Columbus's mysterious sigla he started using after he came back from the Caribbean the first time. Since then, I noticed another Hooked X symbol associated with the famous navigator. On page one of the *Book of Privileges*, a document completed in 1502 that outlined all the favors owed to him by the Spanish crown, is what I am certain is another example of the symbol that reveals his true ideological beliefs.[26] In the left margin of the page is a red circle cross with a crossed rod and sword that makes an unmistakable Hooked X!

Several people have sent me pictures of the page that appears to show another Hooked X highlighted in red ink. It might very well be another example of the mysterious symbol, but it could also be a stylized "X" character. Whether two additional Hooked X examples associated with the famous explorer or only one, there is no doubt in my mind as to where his true allegiance lay.

REMAX Realty?

WHAT SHOULD BE APPARENT in this book is not only a common ideological thread that weaves through time involving several secret organizations, but also common symbols. The Hooked X is one. Later, several examples of modern symbols will be presented that suggest an influence by modern secret organizations like the Freemasons. In many cases, it is difficult to determine whether a Freemason was involved in the use of secret symbols, but invariably it turns out one was.

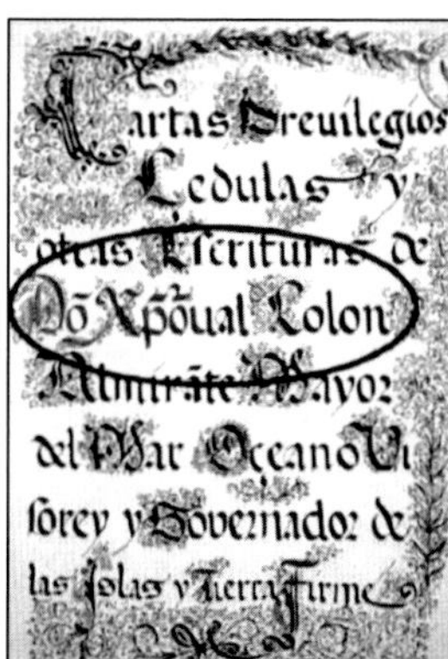

In Christopher Columbus's *Book of Privileges* there are two examples of the Hooked X symbol. One could be argued is a stylized X symbol (left), but the other found on page one of the document, is a crossed rod and sword making the unmistakable symbol (middle). Interestingly, the crossed sword and staff Hooked X symbology is still used to this day as seen in this example of the Masonic Knights Templar Grand Commandery banner in the Grand Lodge of Montana (right). (Internet; Internet; Wolter, 2012)

One example is a sign almost everyone in the United States will recognize as a large real estate company whose logo incorporates the Templar colors of red and white along with a single angled blue stripe. When the logo is flipped upside down, a very prominent and obvious Hooked X is revealed.

The question, of course, is: was this intentional or an interesting coincidence? Readers will have to decide for themselves if there might be an underlying motive. However, it will quickly become apparent in the other examples of modern recognizable logos so common in our society that a common thread of symbols and colors recurs often. Creators of these logos and symbols can easily plead plausible denial, and there's no way to prove their intent. However, in the Remax logo and other examples to be presented, there might be too much smoke not to have something burning somewhere.

While examples of the Hooked X and it's association with highly secretive organizations continue to materialize, we need to be cognizant of other symbols used by followers of the these groups and their alternate ideology relative to the Roman Church. The "X" symbol is certainly one of the symbols that recurs frequently during the research presented in this book. One notable example showed up in the summer of 2011 in the artwork of arguably the most famous artist in the history of the world.

Leonardo DaVinci's New Salvador Mundi

ON JUNE 29, 2011, JUDI RUDEBUSCH forwarded a link to a *New York Times* article announcing that a long lost painting by Leonardo DaVinci had recently surfaced. The painting is of the common *Salvador Mundi* (Savior of the World) image with Christ holding a glass orb in his left hand and his right hand (with the index and middle fingers crossed) upraised in blessing. The painting reportedly once belonged to King Charles I and II, but went missing for over 200 years. It is believed to be worth in the neighborhood of two hundred million dollars.

What immediately struck Judi, and me, the moment we saw it was the obvious "X" in the garment emblazoned across Jesus' chest. DaVinci has long been rumored to be a heretic and is alleged to have been a grand master of the Priory of Sion from 1510-1519.[27] If true, then the prominent "X" in the lost painting is likely a clear symbol to the enlightened ones of both DaVinci's

This long lost Leonardo DaVinci painting of the *Salvador Mundi* came to light in a *New York Times* article on June 29, 2011. In subsequent published articles, two images of the painting were posted that while very similar they are definitely not the same. One thing that is clearly the same is the prominent "X" within the garment on Christ's chest that could be DaVinci's veiled reference to his alternate religious beliefs. (Internet, Internet)

and possibly Jesus' true religious beliefs. The timing of this new painting's discovery is also very curious. With the coming of the New Age, many people with gnostic and esoteric leanings have told me personally that things will be coming forward that hint ever stronger the previously hidden beliefs and agenda that is diametrically opposed to the Roman Church. (See color section, Figures 37 & 38)

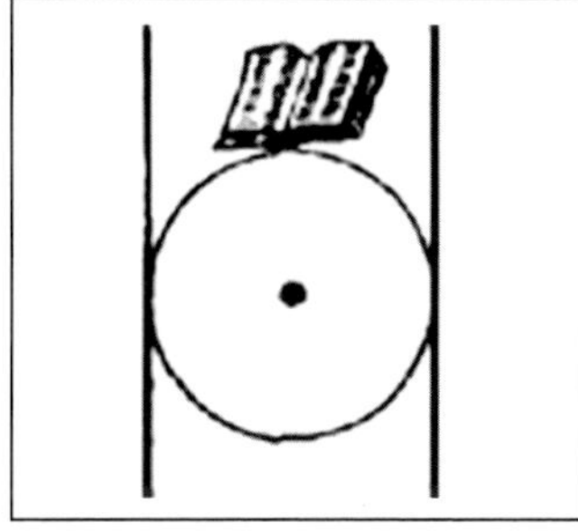

The point within the circle is an ancient symbol that in modern times is called the "circumpunct." One of the many allegorical concepts of the symbol is "The heavens revolving around the earth". The two vertical lines represent the summer (left side) and winter (right side) solstices. In Freemasonry, the vertical lines also symbolize the Patron Saints of John the Baptist and John the Evangelist, whose feast days coincide with the solstices. The bible above the circle teaches Masons to consult the Bible or other sacred texts to achieve balance and direction in their lives.

In Leonardo DaVinci's *The Last Supper*, Margaret Starbird pointed out a gold grail cup above the head of the disciple at the far left (yellow box on left). Upon closer inspection the cup transforms into a geometric pattern that is the right half of the "circumpunct" with two vertical lines (right). In Freemasonry, the right vertical line on the east side of the circle is symbolic of the winter solstice and pagan belief in the resurrection of the sun as the days get longer. This symbol suggests that DaVinci had knowledge that only a members of secret society would be privy to in the sixteenth century.

The many news stories swirling about the DaVinci painting had two accompanying images, one in black and white and the other in color. While the imagery was the same, the images were not. The reason for the differences was not explained, and, like many of DaVinci's paintings, there were many things within the artwork that suggested mysterious messages to those who knew what to look for. Not the least being Jesus' overall androgynous look, reminiscent of the many statue carvings of the "heretic" Pharaoh Akhenaten, at Armana, Egypt. My association of the ancient king of Egypt and "King" Jesus will become apparent later.

The newly discovered painting inspired research into DaVinci and the symbolism in his paintings, which invariably led us to examine his masterpiece in the refectory of the Convent of Santa Maria delle Grazie in Milan, Italy. One thing was pointed out to me by Margaret Starbird. On the far left side of the painting, on a wall directly above the head of Bartholomew, is what looks like a gold Grail cup.[28] When a high resolution image is made of the cup and magnified, it turns out that it is actually a half circle with a vertical line attached to the right (east) side. This symbol is certainly not random and clearly DaVinci had something else in mind besides a cleverly disguised Grail cup when he painted it.

In Freemasonry, the point within a circle is one of the oldest symbols on earth and is called the "circumpunct." Besides being the alchemical symbol for gold it also represents many symbolic and allegorical concepts such as, "man within the universe," "the heavens revolving around the earth," the "open eye," or in Egyptian hieroglyphics as the symbol for the sun. If two vertical lines are attached to the east and west sides of the circle, the symbol represent the summer and winter solstices.[29] The two solstices are also symbolic of the two patron saints of Freemasonry, John the Baptist and John the Evangelist. Their feast days fall on the longest and shortest days of the year and, due to wandering calendars over many centuries, the dates celebrated with pagan feasts for thousands of years now fall on June 24 and December 27.[30]

In DaVinci's *Last Supper*, the Grail cup is actually the right half or winter side of the solstice symbol which is allegorically represented in Freemasonry by John the Evangelist. The Winter solstice has long symbolized resurrection, or "rebirth of the sun" as the days began to get longer. Perhaps DaVinci was subversively foretelling a *literal* resurrection of the sun as opposed to the belief in the resurrection of Jesus after the Crucifixion that was soon to follow this feast. What the symbol also reveals is DaVinci's extensive knowledge of heretical pagan symbolism that would have been consistent with the knowledge base of a grand master of the Priory of Sion.[31] While this evidence certainly doesn't prove he was a grand master, the symbolism found in these and his other paintings are consistent with the long rumored allegation.

Newgrange Venus Temple

ON ONE OF THE TRIPS FOR THE FILMING of the *America Unearthed*™ series, the crew and I traveled to Dublin, Ireland, and then roughly thirty miles north to an area known as the Boyne Valley to the 5,000-year-old megalithic structure known as Newgrange. On November 11, 2012, my friend and Templar historian, Alan Butler, joined us for a most enjoyable day shooting for an episode on mysterious stone structures in North America that incorporated summer and winter solstice illumination events into their construction.

While standing at the entrance of the massive stone and earthen mound reciting our lines and peering into the light box that allows sunlight to enter the chamber lined with large stones to illuminate the floor of the back recess at the extreme end inside at 9:00 A.M. on the winter solstice, I noticed something. The front edge of the lintel stone directly above the light box opening had X's carved into it. After looking closer we realized there were vertical lines between the X's clearly delineating they were not lozenges.

On the front edge of the lintel stone over the light box that allows the light of the sun to enter the chamber at Newgrange there are eight X's carved into the stone. (Wolter, 2012)

The other curious thing about these X's was that the lines were not grooves carved into the stone, but were standing out from the surface roughly one-half inch. This meant whoever carved them went to much more effort to create them by removing the stone around them, than if they had simply carved the lines into the surface.

While Alan and I were standing in amazement, appreciating the effort of the carver, one of the cameramen in our crew, Colin Threinen, asked, "How many X's are there?" I quickly counted them. This time Alan and I were not so amazed. There were eight of them. At the same instant we looked at each other and said, "Venus."

We both knew that in addition to the sun's rays entering the chamber at Newgrange at sunrise on the winter solstice, so too would the light of Venus shortly before. Both our minds began to race as we bandied back and forth the idea that perhaps Newgrange was not only constructed by ancient Irish people over 5,000 years ago to capture the light of the sun, but also as a Temple to the planet Venus! By the end of the day we were both convinced Newgrange was most likely built *primarily* with Venus, the Goddess in the heavens, in mind.

This realization of the undoubted involvement of Venus at Newgrange brought another thought to mind. Only a couple of miles north of Newgrange lay the ruins of Mellifont, the first Cistercian Abbey in Ireland, established in 1146. The next day the crew and I traveled to see the ruins, and the one remaining structure has an unmistakable architecture that matches the mysterious round tower that sits on eight heavy columns at Newport in Rhode Island. Neither Alan nor I found it to be a coincidence that Newgrange was on the

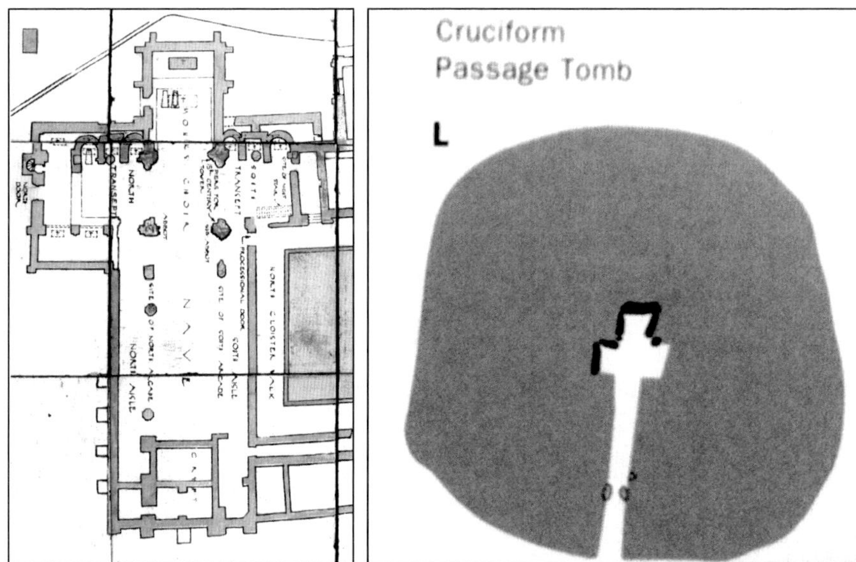

The cruciform shape of many medieval churches including the example here at the Cistercian Abbey at Mellifont in Ireland is strikingly similar to the cruciform shape of the Stone Age chambers such as Newgrange, Knowth, and Dowth in the Boyne River Valley in Ireland. These chambers, situated on the lands or "Grange" of the Cistercians at Mellifont, likely were the inspiration for the cruciform shape of their churches and cathedrals. (Wolter, 2012; Brennan, 1994)

land owned by Cistercians at Mellifont. Historians say the chamber wasn't discovered until 1699.[32] However, Alan and I speculated, on camera, that we were certain the monks had to have been well aware of the massive structure and almost certainly understood its true function centuries earlier.

Martin Brennan's book about Newgrange and other Stone Age sites in the Boyne River Valley, *The Stones of Time*, notes that the sun enters the chamber at Newgrange and illuminates the back recess at the innermost point in the structure just before 9:00 A.M.[33] This fact instantly brought to mind the Newport Tower illumination of the egg-shaped keystone event that happens on the winter solstice at 9:00 A.M.!

Another revelation dawned on me as I read Brennan's book and studied the drawings of the Newgrange chamber ground plan. The area where the beam of sunlight hits at the end of the chamber is divided into three roughly equal-sized spaces. These spaces are called the end, right and left recesses. The shape of the chamber and the three recesses is strikingly similar to the typical footprint of many Christian churches which when viewed from above make a crucifix. In fact, this shape is called a cruciform style.

Large stone basins were found in the right recesses at Newgrange (left) and Knowth (right). Thought by archaeologists to have been used for burials, they likely were used for ritual bathing and almost certainly inspired the practice in monastic orders like the Cistercians. (Courtesy of Ken Williams)

Over ninety of the ninety-nine Cistercian churches on the island of Gotland are small and do not have crossing transepts. However, nearly every one of them has stone-made baptismal fonts that are roughly the same size as stone basins inside the Irish Stone Age megalithic mound structures of Knowth, Newgrange and Dowth. The ornately carved and painted font at Vall Church sits in the middle of the church (left) while the highly weathered sandstone font at Lojsta Church sits where the right transept would be when looking at the altar (right). It seems highly likely the tradition of ritual bathing by the Cistercians was inspired by the Stone Age cultures who built the "re-birth" on the winter solstice earthen mounds that dotted their lands in Ireland. (Wolter, 2004; Wolter, 2004)

Not only did this strike me as the possible inspiration for this common church design, but the stone basin I saw in the right-hand recess at Newgrange resembled baptismal fonts I'd seen in all ninety-nine churches on the Island of Gotland several years earlier. Most archaeologists and researchers believe these stone basins were where the bones of individuals were placed during a ritual for the dead. To me it seemed just as likely the basins were used for ritual bathing. Further, along with the design of the innermost recesses of the chambers, the stone basins were likely the inspiration for the Cistercians who built many of their churches and cathedrals using this cruciform design and lavatoriums in their monasteries with stone fonts or elaborate stone fountains for ritual bathing.

At this point, the now boiling cauldron of coincidences was rapidly coming together. In my previous Hooked X book, I concluded the Newport Tower was originally built by the Knights Templar sometime between 1200 and 1400 A.D. This monastic military order was originally founded by the Cistercians in 1128. Certainly at least one or two Cistercian monks would have traveled to the New World on the Templar voyage that resulted in the construction of the Newport Tower. The highly educated monks would have been responsible for ensuring the illumination of the egg-shaped keystone occurred at exactly 9:00 A.M. on the winter solstice. It was a critical element of the ideological beliefs as well as their functioning observatory.

The question now becomes, could the ancient Monotheistic Dualism ideology I have insisted the Cistercians and their Templar brethren embraced have evolved from the beliefs of the megalithic Stone Age people who built structures like Newgrange and later Stonehenge? It seems all the more likely as well as their reverence for the astronomical movement of the stars, planets, moon, and the sun.

At the ruined Cistercian Abbey of Mellifont the partially intact lavabo remains where the monks practiced daily ritual bathing of their head, hands and feet, before and after meals. Originally constructed in 1142, the first Cistercian Abbey in Ireland had extensive lands called "granges," which included the Stone Age megalith of Newgrange. It seems a near certainty there is a connection between the solar illuminations at Newgrange and the Newport Tower that both occur at 9:00 A.M. on the winter solstice. (Wolter, 2012)

The Copiale Cipher

On October 27, 2011, I received the same email link from two different friends of a short *YouTube* video about Kevin Knight, a University of Southern California researcher who had recently cracked the code of a 105-page enciphered book that dated back to the 1760s. After watching the video, I clicked onto the article about the story, which had a link to an on-line copy of the original manuscript. Fellow researcher and friend, Judi Rudebusch, one of those who sent me the link, asked me to look closely at the X-like character on the thumbnail sized image of the example page. When I pulled up the high resolution version of the example page from the manuscript something immediately jumped out at me, a Hooked X!

Instantly, I flashed back to the hooked characters in the Larsson Papers found in Sweden in 2004 that dated back to 1883 and 1884. Could they be connected somehow? Before the day was out, I'd found out that the book was from the East Berlin Academy in Germany, and could be dated back to circa 1760. The manuscript deciphered by Knight and his Swedish co-researchers from the University of Uppsala, Beata Megyesi and Christiane Shaefer, records the rituals and apparent political leanings of a secret society in Germany. Within the text are eight, still un-deciphered larger characters which include the stylized Hooked X Knight and his colleagues called "Big X."

After studying the dozens of examples of the character in the manuscript, some interesting details became apparent. First, like the Hooked X carved on the pillar at Rosslyn Chapel the "hook" extends both above and below the upper right arm. Another curious feature of the Copiale Cipher Hooked X is the circle at the top of the upper left arm. The circle is an obvious code reminiscent of the punch marks at the ends of the carved lines on many characters on the Kensington Rune Stone added by the carver after he carved the inscription. The character also has what appears to be a dot at the top of the upper right arm as well. This could be a simple stylization made by the scribe or it could be yet another code.

Clearly the Hooked/"Big" X symbol in the Copiale manuscript is being used as a reference to another contemporary secret society. This is consistent with my own interpretation of how the Hooked X was used on the five North American rune stones, both for the "a" sound within the text of the inscription and as an important symbol of their religious and political ideology, essentially saying who they were. Some have argued that my land claim thesis for the Kensington Rune

The Copiale Cipher contains seven oversized symbols within the coded manuscript including what appears to be a stylized "Hooked X" the scribe called "Big X" (left). The symbol is being used to reference an apparent rival Masonic order and contains a number of interesting modifications that are likely codes of some kind. The bar of the "X" crosses over both sides of the upper right arm and is similar to the bar in the "Hooked X" carved into one of the pillars inside Rosslyn Chapel in Scotland (middle). The upper left and right bars have a small circle and dot which appear to have been added by the scribe much like the carver of the Kensington Rune Stone added a punch to the lower right leg to one of the "R" runes (right). (Internet; Wolter, 2008 & 2002)

Stone can't be because the inscription makes no reference of the land being claimed in the name of a king or monarch like many French land claim plaques found in North America. The Knights Templar order couldn't use their former name since they were outlawed. They were still a sovereign entity beholden to no monarch, and by 1362 they certainly didn't answer to the pope. I would further argue that the Hooked X symbol, which occurs twenty-two times within the inscription, proclaims clearly who was claiming the land and/or marking a boundary.

The fact that the Hooked X in the Copiale manuscript is larger in size than the majority of the characters may indicate its importance to the secret society. Another interesting possible connection of the German Copiale manuscript and the Kensington inscription is the presence of umlauts, or double dots above numerous characters. These were thought to be a Germanic influence on the Kensington inscription observed by many runic scholars. In our book, *The Kensington Rune Stone: Compelling New Evidence*, my co-author and I speculated that the carver of the inscription was likely a Cistercian monk who may have been educated on the Swedish island of Gotland. The Germanic influence on Gotland in the fourteenth century is well documented as the Gutish law on the island was not only written in Swedish, but German as well. The double dotted umlauts above several of the "a" and "o" runes were likely a result of that medieval Germanic linguistic influence.

In January of 2012, I had a number of discussions about the "Big X" in the Copiale Cipher with John Freeburg, the lodge education officer of the Anoka Masonic Lodge in Minnesota. His assessment of the document is that it is clearly an explanation of masonic rituals and the translation put forth, "Needs work." When I asked his opinion of the Big X he said, "The eighteenth-century Masonic order that wrote this document was likely a Protestant-leaning group who were referencing a rival Catholic-leaning Masonic group with its leadership likely being within the European royal houses."

Joe Rose, another friend and Freemason, has taken an in-depth look at the Copiale Cipher manuscript. He believes the document is a ritual of one of the "high" degrees in France and Germany during the mid-1700s. Joe explained that a "high" degree is one that emphasizes scientific enlightenment that comes after the third degree or master Mason degree. Joe also believes the Big X symbol in the Copiale Cipher refers to what he called "regular" Freemasons that do not progress beyond the third degree.[34]

The importance of the Copiale manuscript and the Hooked X/Big X symbol within it cannot be understated. My thesis that the highly secretive *leadership* of the medieval Knights Templar/Cistercian orders evolved into equally secretive occult and esoteric masonic secret societies during the Age of Enlightenment such as the Rosicrucians, is bolstered by this new discovery. I am also convinced this leadership was comprised dominantly of individuals who were direct descendants of Jesus and Mary Magdalene.

The Copiale Cipher also brings into the discussion once again the discovery of the Larsson Papers in Sweden, in 2004. These papers include two sheets of paper from a recently donated collection to Daum (Institute for Dialectology, Onomastics and Folklore research in Umeå) that contained Swedish writing interspersed between two rune rows, a Masonic box code alphabet, and the same Pentadic numbers used in Arabic placement as on the Kensington Rune Stone. Dated December 1883, and April 16, 1885, the two sheets originated from Edward Larsson (1886 to 1950), who was a tailor by profession. The infamous Hooked X rune is found on both sheets along with several other hooked characters.

The initial reaction to the Larsson Papers of skeptical scholars was to seize the opportunity to reignite the Kensington Rune Stone hoax theory by claiming an immigrant could have brought the Larsson alphabets to America and then used them to carve the inscription. Of course, my geological weathering studies and the Dotted R make this claim impossible. Until they come to terms with what the artifact is, a Knights Templar land claim document with multiple aspects to the inscription, they have no chance of understanding it.

The fact is the Copiale Cipher, which is unquestionably a Masonic document that contains the Big X/Hooked X symbol used to represent a unique Masonic order, provides supporting evidence that the Larsson Papers, which also contains the Hooked X symbol, are indeed connected to a unique Masonic organization most likely in Sweden. The other interesting thing about the Copiale Cipher (originating in Germany), the Larsson Papers and the Kensington Rune Stone (Sweden) are they are all associated with countries in the Baltic Region.

More research needs to be done on both the Copiale Cipher and the Larsson Papers to put them into proper perspective. However, the unquestioned association of these documents with highly secretive Masonic organizations in the period after the demise of the Knights Templar order (officially in 1314) provides factual evidence of a connection between the two groups. This connection has long been speculated by many researchers, and these recently discovered documents provide two critical new pieces of evidence that now make that speculation a near certainty.

Each of the ten known *medieval* examples of the Hooked X symbol appear to be associated in one aspect or another with a Cistercian/Knights Templar/Knights of Christ group involved in clandestine operations in North America. Perhaps the "hook" itself was meant to be pointing to the left on purpose as if saying, "We are taking our people, our royal bloodline, and our ideology to the west." In all ten examples, carved into stone or metal, or written onto parchment or paper, the Hooked X was a highly secret and important coded symbol emblematic of a religious and political ideology that was both figuratively and literally at war with the Roman Catholic Church. The primary reason is they wanted to permanently suppress Jesus' bloodline descendants whose very existence threatened the foundation of the Church: the divinity of Jesus. In essence, the Hooked X *is* the symbol of Jesus' bloodline families.

Chapter 4
New Discoveries

On January 12, 2008, I gave a presentation on the Kensington Rune Stone at the Chanhassen Library in Chanhassen, a small western suburb of Minneapolis, Minnesota. Maria Awes, an investigative producer with WCCO-TV in Minneapolis, who had interviewed me in the past about my work on the Kensington Rune Stone and other projects, told me her husband, Andy, would be there to hear my lecture. Afterwards, Andy introduced himself. Andy had enthusiasm and energy and laid out his vision for making a documentary about the rune stone. Janet and I both knew we had found the right person to work with to make the film we always wanted.

Maria was an excellent researcher and writer with a real talent to succinctly summarize a story from a decade of experience working as an investigative reporter. Her talents proved invaluable in writing the script, planning the travel arrangements, and arranging the experts and questions to be asked for the dozens of interviews we conducted.

Andy maximized every minute, mile, and dollar invested. What he accomplished with his three-man crew was comparable to what other production companies typically did only with much larger crews. The best part was we all got along well personally and nearly always agreed on how to tell the story. Bo Hakala's mild demeanor accentuated his immense talent as a videographer. It was fun watching him and Andy craft the interviews and shoot the video that made the film so visually beautiful.

Within a couple of weeks, we had assembled a group of investors with a signed agreement in place. For the next six months our four-man crew of video photographer Bo Hakala, sound, lighting, and "anything else we needed done" guy, Ben Krueger, director, Andy Awes, and me traveled to Europe (twice), Canada, and locales in the United States, retracing my research of the past eight years.

The Premier

ONCE THE FILMING IN EUROPE WAS DONE, Andy pieced together a trailer that he kept secret until he surprised me by unveiling it during our East Coast trip filming of more artifacts and sites. It was an incredible four minutes I couldn't imagine being done any better to sell this project. In January of 2009, they entered the *Secret History of North America* trailer into a contest for best emerging producers at the annual National Association of Television Production Executives Conference and won first place.

Andy and Maria were ecstatic when they called with the news and said every cable network there wanted to talk with them about the project. Within a month we had struck a deal with the History Channel to produce a two-hour documentary. Because History now owned the film, they decided to change the name of the film to *Holy Grail in America*. I wasn't happy about it. Comparison with Dan Brown's *DaVinci Code* came from this, but we knew our story wasn't fiction, and it was really good. Eventually, I realized more people would likely tune in to watch it with the new title. I knew the content was more important.

The film premiered on September 20, 2009, at the Riverview Theatre in South Minneapolis. Everyone who had participating in financing, making the film, or who had been involved in the research was there. Janet and I were humbled to have our work showcased in such a powerful and classy way. It was truly a memorable and historic night. Historic also was having this research begin to reach a worldwide audience. This generated new leads to more sites and artifacts, many relegated to historical obscurity by ego, incompetence, negligence, and apparently in some instances, an intentional effort to conceal. Some of the most interesting and important of these new discoveries are presented here.

Stone Holes

IN THE THREE YEARS SINCE the release of the first Hooked X book several new stone holes have been discovered and recorded. The total number of known stone holes in the Upper Midwest of North America has now surpassed 100. As awareness of these curious man-made artifacts increases, surely more will be found. Currently, South Dakota researcher Judi Rudebusch has taken the lead in compiling a stone holes database. For those who think they may have discovered a stone hole, I'd like to encourage them to contact either Judi or me. We encourage people to send photos and a GPS location if possible.

Because there is no documented modern explanation for the roughly one-inch diameter by anywhere from one to nine inches deep, rounded triangular shaped holes, we continue to postulate the man-made holes are likely of pre-Columbian origin. Their likely purpose was for use as trail markers, marking land boundaries, and for surveying. As presented in my previous book, at least half a dozen stone holes at the Ohman Farm triangulate to pinpoint the location where the Kensington Rune Stone was discovered. This serves as evidence for the intended purpose of the stone holes which likely included other functions.

In 1806, when Lewis and Clark embarked on their historic adventure across the newly purchased land from France known as the Louisiana Purchase, they received the following instruction from Thomas Jefferson, "Beginning at the mouth of the Missouri, you will take observations of latitude and longitude, at all remarkable points on the river, and especially at the mouths of rivers, at rapids, at islands, and other places and objects distinguished by such natural marks and characters, of a durable kind, as that they may with certainty be recognized hereafter."

This interesting quote makes one wonder if one of those "remarkable points" of "a durable kind" could have been stone holes left by earlier Templar visitors. Admittedly, this is sheer speculation. However, the reader will soon see it seems likely the third president of the United States received secret information about pre-Columbian Templar visits to North America. The association of the numerous stone holes at the Ohman Farm with the Templar relic known as the Kensington Rune Stone, and the existence of well over one hundred known stone holes of a similar type across the continent makes the knowledge of these artifacts by certain founding fathers a distinct possibility.

On December 26, 2011, Janet and I visited the Darrell Quaas farm in Dassel, Minnesota, to examine this stone hole. The roughly one-ton glacial boulder has an approximately one-inch-wide by four-inch-deep hole with a rounded triangular shape typical of the stone holes found all over the Upper Midwest over to the East Coast of North America. As more people become aware of them, many more are sure to be found both in North American and likely other continents as well. (Wolter, 2011)

The Du Luth Stone

AFTER *HOLY GRAIL IN AMERICA* AIRED on the History Channel on September 20, 2009, I received a flood of emails, letters, and phone calls. Aside from a couple people with apocalyptic predictions for daring to write about such sensitive Christian subject matter, the vast majority of comments were very supportive, and several offered exciting new leads. One of those leads came from a man I'd known for years who, like me, was an avid collector of Lake Superior agates.

Daryl Johnson called and said he'd heard a lecture by a woman who talked about the history of Pine County, Minnesota. During her slide program she showed a picture of a glacial boulder with a familiar name and date carved on the surface. The date was "1679" and the name was "Du Luth."

Daryl didn't know the boulder's location, but I found someone in the community who did. John Ecklund, whose grandfather settled in the community in the 1910s, was very helpful. He said, "There aren't many people left who know the location of the boulder, but I do and would be happy to show it to you." We made plans to see the stone on October 16, 2009, and I invited one other person to join me who could offer additional geological insights. It had been several years since we were in the field together, but I knew my former advisor, mentor, and friend, Professor emeritus Charles L. Matsch, would enjoy seeing this artifact.

John and his son, Eric, led us a couple of hundred yards into the woods on a cool and sunny mid-October day to a large boulder of the familiar sandstone from the Hinckley Formation. We could see the inscription from several yards away, but were struck by the advanced weathering of the carved characters upon closer inspection. I took several pictures with my camera and

In Pine County, Minnesota, a roughly 1,000-pound, sandstone glacial boulder contains an inscription of the date "1679" and the name "Du Luth." The inscription appears to be genuine and would be consistent with the known exploration of land west of the Lake Superior by French explorer, Daniel Greysolon Sieur Du Luth, from 1678 to 1682. (Wolter, 2009)

portable microscope. The carved lines exhibited rounded edges with exposed sand grains in the grooves that were identical to the surfaces on the rest of the boulder. One point Charlie and I agreed on was that the carving wasn't recent, and very likely was made three-hundred thirty years ago.

Two curious features of the carving were the presence of two punch marks that seemed out of place. One was to the upper left of the number "1" and the other was to the lower right of the first "U." Neither punch mark seemed to belong, but they were clearly man-made. Therefore, they were put there for a reason. It would be only a couple of weeks before I would learn of a compelling possibility for the punch marks.

The mysterious punch marks on the Du Luth Stone prompted me to think about punch marks I had seen on other inscriptions. After going back and re-examining the five rune stones with the Hooked X, they all had similar punch marks in curious places. Even though my co-author and I had accounted for most of the punch marks, or dots, I found during my microscopic examination of the Kensington Rune Stone, we didn't have an interpretation for all of them.[35] One word separator, in the middle of line five, stood out because of double punches that made four holes instead of two.

Dot Codes

THE DOUBLE-PUNCHED WORD separator on line five of the Kensington Stone is reminiscent of word separators on the Spirit Pond Map Stone's map side that could also be some kind of code meant to be read by one of the carver's own.

The Narragansett Rune Stone appears to have two, previously unnoticed punch marks at the beginning of the inscription, in much the same position as the Du Luth Stone, and at the end. While a single punch word separator at the end of the second line is possible, it could be the carver's intention to acknowledge God, to possibly bless or protect the message. Another possibility: the punch marks at the beginning and end of the inscription are some kind of watermarks confirming the legitimacy of the message. We will see another example of marks at the beginning and end of another message carved in stone later in the book.

Margaret Starbird was the first to call my attention to what the punch marks could be.[36] Starbird cited Herbert Silberer's book, *Hidden Symbolism of Alchemy and the Occult Arts*, where he explained, "The center of the sun [God] is to be seen in the symbol (a circle with dot in the center)." Apparently, the dot, or punch, without the circle is also an acknowledgement of the presence of God.[37] This would work well for an inscription carved in stone, since carving a circle would be time consuming and difficult.

The practice of acknowledging the Creator with punch marks and dots appears to have been passed on from the medieval period into the Renaissance era through secret societies with Templar connections. Explorer Christopher Columbus incorporated several dots within his mysterious sigla. In the three examples pictured on page 106 of *The Hooked X, Key to the Secret History of North America*, the pattern of dots is different in each Columbus sigla, suggesting either a code or possibly multiple references to God. If indeed these punch marks and dots are acknowledgements by the carvers to the presence of God, these previously overlooked marks represent a whole new aspect of compelling evidence consistent with the medieval origin of these artifacts.

Another interesting example of dot codes I have come across were carved onto a mysterious eighteenth-century powder-horn belonging to Jeff Jones of Pennsylvania. Jeff inherited the powder-horn from a family lineage he claims descended from George Washington. This claim was somewhat problematic in that some researchers claimed that Washington was sterile and, therefore, could not have any direct descendants. However, like many popular myths in our culture, conclusive evidence has not yet been presented.

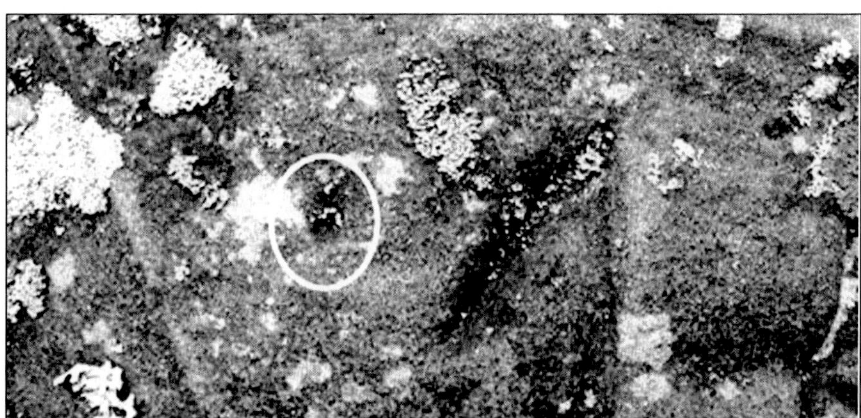

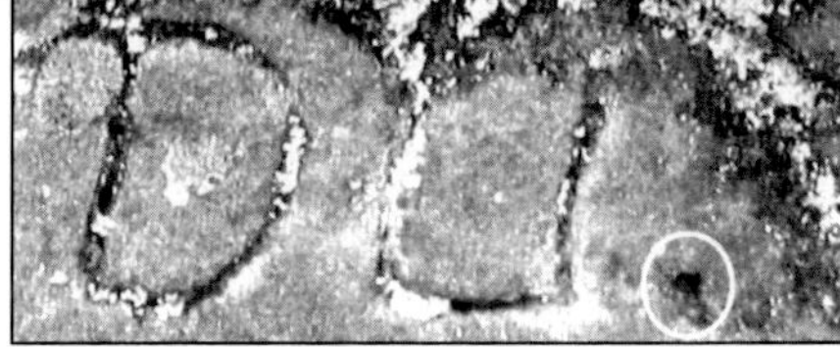

On October 16, 2009, Professor Emeritus Charlie Matsch and I noticed two round, man-made punch marks were present to the upper left of the number "1" (above), and to the lower right of the upper "U" of the "Du Luth" boulder (at right). (Wolter, 2009)

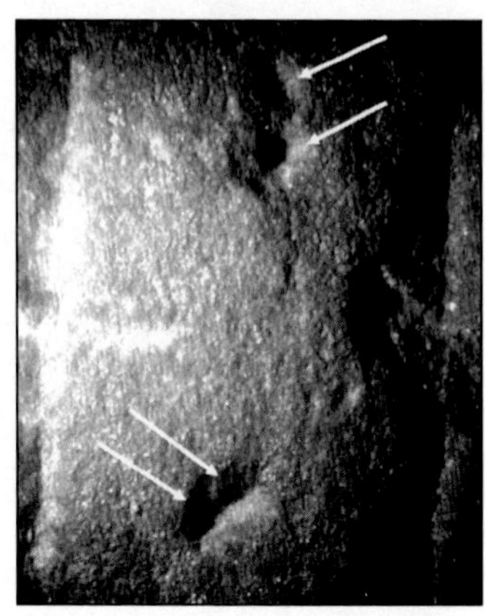

On line five of the Kensington Rune Stone one of the word separators has been double punched, creating four holes instead of two. These added punches could have been an acknowledgement of the presence of God by the Cistercian monk who carved the inscription. Word separators in the five North American runic inscriptions with the Hooked X have two vertically aligned punch marks. (Wolter, 2002)

In 2010, Mr. Jones submitted a DNA sample that did, in fact, produce results consistent with other distant members of the Washington family. No final conclusion yet, but his collection of early American artifacts is quite impressive, and it includes the powder horn. Jeff explained the clearly visible dots on his horn, along with what he called carver's "knockouts" were made to identify specific letters meant to be either dropped or added to create anagrams and secret messages.

A "knockout" is where the carver dug out a shallow pit within a part of a letter that was then blackened out. Three of these knockouts are clearly visible within parts of three letters on Jeff's horn. He believes he has deciphered the

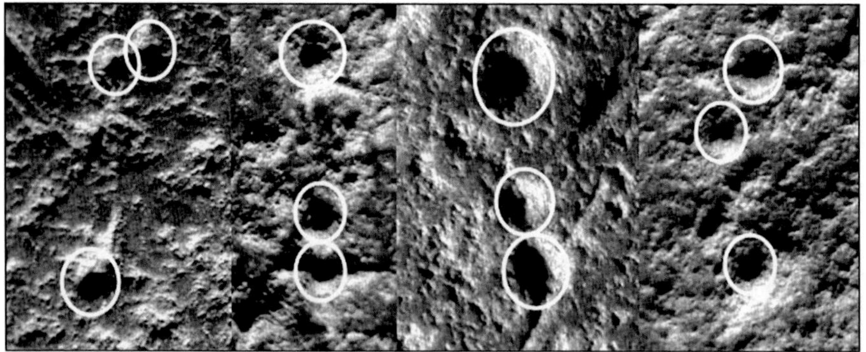

On the Spirit Pond Map Stone (map side) four of the five word separators have three punch marks in what appears to be a random pattern. (Wolter, 2006)

Single punch marks are present at the beginning and the end of the Narragansett Rune Stone inscription, which is comprised of a total of nine runes. (Wolter, 2008)

secret messages his ancestor encoded into the horn that reveals the true identity of his ancestor and his incredible story that has thus far escaped recorded history.

Jeff says the horn was originally made at the time of the Revolutionary War, but wasn't carved until 1839. The message was reportedly carved by his great-great-great-great-great grandfather Chris Jones, and was apparently meant to reveal his multiple alias names that he changed out of necessity during times of intrigue in early American history. Because this ancestor is allegedly George Washington's illegitimate son, he was first named Isaac Newton Martin, after the famous English mathematician and astronomer.

When Martin was an eighteen-year-old Minuteman in 1775, he was captured by the British and eventually ended up on the famous ship *Bounty* when the mutiny led by Fletcher Christian occurred in 1789. Isaac Martin was supposedly killed on Pitcairn Island in 1793, but Jones claims Martin and Christian faked their deaths and reportedly made their way New Orleans by 1808, after changing their names to Jean Lafitte (Fletcher Christian) and Marcus Lafitte (Isaac Martin).[38] Marcus eventually changed his name again to Chris Jones in 1810 after returning from France. If true, it would be one of the most amazing stories in American History.

This late eighteenth-century powder horn contains dots and carved out and then darkened portions of letters called "knockouts," that were made by the carver to create anagrams and secret messages. Jeff Jones, the owner of this powder horn says the dots and knockouts were made by his distant relative to create secret anagram messages. Interestingly, the capital "A" in Aug(ust) has a "v"-shaped crossbar thus producing the encoded symbol "AVM." (Wolter, 2011)

The messages on this horn, however, are not what are important in this discussion. What is important are the dots and other symbols placed within certain texts, whether carved in stone, bone, ivory, or written on paper or parchment. This is an ancient practice used by members of secret societies or groups that likely included our founding fathers. In this case, we might have an artifact directly connected to the family of George Washington, who is, arguably, the most historically well-known member of the Freemasons in the United States.

While punch marks carved into stone or dots drawn on paper during medieval times through the Renaissance could have been acknowledgment of the Creator, it's just as likely they served another purpose–a code. Perhaps both.

We documented several facts that day in the field with Charlie, and later that week with the help of Gilles Durocher, a family friend in Quebec, Canada. Gilles, recently retired after thirty-three years working for the Canadian archives, said Du Luth retired and eventually died in Montreal, in 1710. Gilles was able to find original documents written in Du Luth's own hand that helped answer questions about this interesting early explorer. Another reference helped us trace his steps to what would eventually be the port city named after him, ". . . about the 27th of June, 1679, because it is known that on the 2nd of July, 1679, he planted the banner of France, His Majesty's Arms, 'in the great village of the Nadouecioux, called Izaty's, where never had a Frenchman been no more that at the Songaskitons and Houetbatons, distant six leagues from the former, where I also planted the His Majesty's Arms in that same year, 1679.'"

I visited the site again on November 21, 2009, with Dave Mather, an archaeologist with the Minnesota State Historic Preservation Office. On this visit, we were escorted to the site by landowners. While clearly stating his reasons for being skeptical, it was also clear Dave found the inscription to be very interesting. In addition to making visual observations and trying to learn what we could from the landowners, I had brought a metal detector along and scanned the immediate area around the stone. Hopeful as I was that there might be a buried metal plaque, no metal artifacts were detected.

After the site visit, Dave and I examined a large monument of Hinckley Sandstone in a park within the Askov city limits. The monument was reportedly erected in 1927, and I took both macro and microscopic photographs of the man-made surfaces for relative-age weathering studies. We also collected weathering data from two more monuments of Hinckley Sandstone in the Askov cemetery, dated 1927 and 2008.

Dave could easily understand and appreciate what I was trying to do with the weathering studies and was able to get his other questions answered by Gilles Durocher. After discussing every aspect of this artifact we could think of, we agreed there were few, if any, red flags. All that was needed was for me to complete the laboratory work and for both of us to write our reports.

The following is a list of facts consistent with the boulder being a historically important seventeenth century artifact:

1. The boulder is located several miles east of Askov, Minnesota, in a relatively remote wooded area.
2. The long axis of the boulder is aligned almost due east-west.
3. The inscription was carved into a glacial erratic boulder comprised of Hinckley Sandstone with dimensions of approximately fifty-five by forty-two by thirty inches.
4. The inscription carved into the boulder reads, "· 1679: Du . Luth."
5. The average height of the carved numbers in the date is approximately 3¼ inches, and the average height of the letter in the name is approximately two inches. The average depth of the carved characters was approximately one-quarter inch.
6. The inscription was reportedly first discovered by the landowner, who noticed the man-made carvings sometime between 1964 and 1967. He cleaned off the moss with his fingers and a hunting knife.
7. After being destroyed by the Hinckley fire in 1894, the village of Askov, Minnesota, was rebuilt and then officially incorporated in 1906.
8. The inscribed boulder is situated along the north-south continental divide between the Great Lakes/St. Lawrence Seaway and St. Croix/Mississippi drainage basins.
9. According to French-Canadian historian Gilles Durocher, the numbers and block-style letters are consistent with the pre-1860s French style.
10. The spelling of the French explorer's name on the boulder, "Du Luth," is consistent with one of the multiple known ways the explorer's name was spelled.
11. The historical record in Montreal reports that explorer Daniel Greysolon Sieur Du Luth was in the area of Minnesota in 1679.
12. The presence of two punch-style dots proximate to the inscription is consistent with other Renaissance era North American explorers such as Columbus. Seemingly random dots added to historical inscriptions and manuscripts were often an acknowledgement of God or the Creator.
13. The edges of the carved numbers and characters are significantly rounded from weathering for an unknown period of years.
14. The weathering of the man-made grooves with exposed quartz sand grains had essentially the same appearance as the glacial-age surfaces of the boulder.

15. The siliceous vein running through the boulder produced a three-sixteenth-inch-high ridge from approximately 10,000 to 12,000 years of weathering of the adjacent sandstone.
16. The weathering observed on the two monuments made of Hinckley Sandstone, erected in 1927, was significantly less advanced than the Du Luth inscription.

With an ode to geologist Newton H. Winchell and the language he used in concluding the Kensington Rune Stone was a genuine artifact, I concluded that the Du Luth Stone inscription was also genuine with the following: "The preponderance of the geological, historical, and geographical evidence is consistent with the Du Luth boulder having been carved by the Daniel Greysolon Sieur Du Luth exploration party at the date stated in the inscription."

"In Hoc Signo Vinces"

ON DECEMBER 21, 2010, my birthday, I decided to fly out east, hoping to see the illumination in the Newport Tower. I made a quick stop at the Westford Knight before heading west to Pinnacle Mountain in New Preston, Connecticut.

I had never seen the four Hebrew inscriptions at the top of the Mountain first recorded by Ezra Styles, then president of Yale, and this was going to be the day. The public trail was on the north side of the mountain about 1,000 feet above the base. Forty-five minutes later I reached the treeless top. The area was an outcropping of granite with several large boulders scattered about. The view overlooking Lake Waramaug to the west was breathtaking.

For well over an hour, I scanned the granite bedrock and large boulders but couldn't find the Hebrew inscriptions. A cold wind was sapping my resolve when after deciding to make one more sweep of the area, I spotted them.

Within a minute I found all four Hebrew names carved into glacially rounded granite gneiss surface and each had a semi-circle carved over the letters. While it wouldn't be possible for me to say exactly how old these man-made characters were, I did notice that this particular area of the rock had a lot of fine-grained secondary quartz veins which made the rock smoother and more durable than granite gneiss with less quartz. I wondered if the carver knew this area would make the carvings last longer and concluded that he probably did.

Whether these Hebrew names were carved only a few or several centuries ago was impossible to determine on this day. However, that they dated prior to "contact" was still a distinct possibility.

After a vigorous hike down the mountain, I continued on to the Newport Tower. At 7:30 A.M. there was no sign of the sun peeking through the overcast. A dozen or so Freemasons arrived, including Rick Lynch. I was soon giving short lectures about the Masonic keystones, the various solar, lunar and Venus alignments as well as the illumination. Even though I didn't see the light box, I met some interesting people as the group swelled to about thirty by 9:00 A.M.

Gloria Amendola, who showed me several Templar and Cathar sites in France, surprised me by showing up with her friend, Kim Bacik. We all parted for a late breakfast 11:00 A.M. Just as we sat down, the sun popped out.

Our next stop was to meet Irene Daponte, who had contacted me about an inscribed boulder she had found earlier in the year on the shore of Narragansett Bay near downtown Newport. The tide was quickly receding as Irene led our group to the boulder that was mostly submerged in the sand. As the waves slowly receded, Rick Lynch started shoveling away the sand, eventually exposing a clearly visible, but significantly weathered inscription on the south side of the boulder that read, "IN HOC SIGNO VINCES."

After clearing off barnacles and seaweed from the exposed top of the boulder we noticed two other carvings on the top and northeast sides that were difficult to see. Coming back at night and casting low angle light across these carvings would have to wait for another time.

"In Hoc Signo Vinces" is an old Latin phrase meaning, "In this sign you will conquer." The earliest known use of the phrase was by the Roman

On December 21, 2010, after an hour of shoveling during the receding tide we were finally able to reveal the highly weathered Latin inscription that when translated into English reads: "In this sign you will conquer." Barely readable carvings were noticed on the top and opposite side of the boulder. Inscribed boulders like this one and the Narragansett Rune Stone should be removed from the beach and relocated where they can be protected for future study. (Wolter, 2010)

emperor, Constantine I, adopted a similar Greek phrase as a motto just before the Battle of Milvian Bridge against Maxentius, in 312 A.D.[39] The phrase has been used throughout history on the coat of arms by nobles, on the seal of the Jesuits, by schools, fraternities, and by the modern military. The medieval order of Knights Templar also used the phrase as does modern Freemasonry where it appears on the Knight Templar Cross in the York Rite branch.

My second trip to see the stone was five months later on May 16, 2011. Irene Daponte joined me again along with Steve and Peter Dimarzo, two local amateur archaeologists who have found many interesting artifacts and sites around Narragansett Bay. Low tide was very low at around 1:00 P.M. which allowed us to dig out around the boulder in an attempt to determine its size.

As we began digging sand away, a woman appeared at the seawall overlooking the beach and introduced herself. Carol Pardee lived across the street closest to the boulder and said she remembered the inscription from when she was a little girl, sixty-five years earlier. Carol said her deceased grandparents talked about the inscription long before that. This was helpful information that gave us a minimum age for the inscriptions.

We never did reach the outer edges of the stone before hitting the water table, but were able to get a better look at the other inscribed words we couldn't make out in December.

On our second trip to the stone on May 16, 2011, I was able to create darkness under my rain jacket and shine a flashlight across the previously unreadable carvings on the top and opposites sides of the boulder. The carvings appear to be "Ding, Ding" (underlined in white) as in the sound of a bell. (Wolter, 2011)

With a temporary shelter erected it over the stone creating shade. I then put my dark rain jacket over the stone and stuck my head under it and highlighted the characters with a flashlight. Gradually, I was able to make out the words, "Ding, Ding." We were all a little surprised and confused at first, but on my drive back to Hartford, Connecticut, I talked to Ron Reed, who offered some interesting insight.

Ron, an ex-Navy guy, said whenever an officer left or boarded a military ship, a bell was rung. The bell "dings" two times for a lieutenant and four times for the captain. Ron also reminded me that the US Naval Academy was moved from Annapolis, Maryland, to Newport, Rhode Island, for four years in 1861, and the Naval War College was established in Newport in 1884. We discussed the possibility that the inscriptions could have been carved by a zealous naval recruit. The weathering of the carvings by wave action on the beach could certainly be consistent with a hundred or so years.

However, one cannot exclude the possible origin related to the medieval Knights Templar, who we know were in Narragansett Bay centuries before Newport was founded.

Newport Tower Masonic Medal

ONE OF THE FREEMASONS we met at the Newport Tower was the incoming grand master for Rhode Island, Chip Halstrom. Chip joined us to see the "In Hoc" Stone. Before walking down to the beach he showed us a very interesting artifact. Out of his pocket he pulled a Masonic medal that had a bust of George Washington inside an oval with the words, "Washington Com(man)d(r)y K(nights) T(emplar), Newport, R.I." Hanging below the top part of the medal was a beautiful rendition of the Newport Tower. Chip said he bought the medal off Ebay. However, neither Chip nor Rick Lynch, both Knights Templar Freemasons, had any idea where such a Masonic metal had come from.

On December 21, 2011, Chip Halstrom, the 2012 incoming grand master of Rhode Island, showed us a Masonic Knights Templar medal with the Newport Tower jewel hanging below an oval with a profile image of George Washington. (Wolter, 2011)

We all agreed the medal dated back to at least the mid-1900s and found it very interest-

Templar.

"In Hoc Signo Vinces."

Knight of the Red Cross .... A.O. ....
Knight of the Temple .... A.O. ....
Knight of Malta (and United Orders), } .... A.O. ....

In .... Commandery (Preceptory), No. .... of .... under the jurisdiction of the Grand Commandery (Sovereign Great Priory), of .... Knights Templars

.... E.C. (Pres. Prec.).
.... Gen. (Preceptor).
.... C.G. (Constable).

........................, Recorder (Registrar).

When a candidate completes the required degree work and becomes a Masonic Knights Templar they get a receipt. In this example found in the 1910 edition of History of Freemasonry and Concordant Orders, the "In Hoc Signo Vinces" phrase is found.

ing that a modern Masonic Knights Templar order would pick what many people erroneously believe was an old stone "Windmill" for such a medal. It made us all wonder if some older Masonic body knew more about the ancient tower than they were telling.

The Tulsa Bull Carving

YET ANOTHER CALL FROM NICK JOHNSON, who had seen the film and had made an interesting discovery. He said he was hiking along the Arkansas River on the south side of Tulsa, Oklahoma, when he spotted a bull carving on a large slab of rock, a mile or so downriver from the power plant that controlled the flow of water. Nick asked three friends to help him get the several-hundred-pound slab of rock out of the river and into the bed of his truck.

He asked if I was interested in examining his find under the microscope. I asked him how soon he could bring it to the lab in St. Paul. On March 12, 2011, Nick arrived. He showed me the stone in his truck. Even in direct sunlight, I could see the two-foot long bull carving with high curving horns with four wavy vertical lines. In front of the bull's snout was a vertical pole with horizontal lines running its length. Both ends of the pole dropped into large areas where the rock had spalled away roughly an eighth of an inch deeper than the pole.

On March 12, 2011, Nick Johnson arrived at the American Petrographic Services Inc. laboratory with his approximately 500-pound slab of sandstone with an Egyptian style Apis Bull carving he found while collecting arrowheads along the Arkansas River, in Tulsa, Oklahoma, March 9, 2011. (Wolter, 2011)

Directly above the bull's hind quarters were four symbols carved in a line along the top edge of the slab. The first symbol was clearly a circle with horns that looked exactly like the astrological symbol for the constellation Taurus. The next three symbols had partially spalled away and were difficult to discern.

Looking at the bull again, I noticed a line carved between the two front legs that appeared to be a fifth leg or possibly the line was drawn as if to indicate motion of one of the legs. Another curious perfectly straight vertical line extended from two-thirds of the way to the end of the tail straight up to the edge of the rock, an inch to the left of the Jupiter symbol.

After our cursory exam of the carving in the back of Nick's truck we placed the slab onto a table with rollers and brought it up into the lab. We centered the digital microscope over the carved lines on the hind end. When the image came up it was clear the stone was fine-grained sandstone and the walls of the grooves were rounded from weathering. At this point, I set the magnification to 200X and generated a three-dimensional image of one wall of the groove. When the 3D image came up on the computer screen, Nick and I, and everyone in the lab were surprised at what we saw. The individual sedimentary layers had differentially eroded back making the once straight and steep carved wall of the groove significantly wider and terraced like the old weathered steps of an ancient stone temple badly in need of repair.

I asked Nick if I could make a small test groove along the bottom edge of the slab over a foot away, but into the same sedimentary layer the carving was in. Nick said, "Go ahead," and I then carved a fresh line to roughly one-quarter-inch, the same depth as the carved lines of the bull. I then placed the microscope over the test groove and took a 3D image at the same magnification. When the image

Directly above the bull's hind quarters were four symbols carved in a line along the top edge of the slab. The first symbol is a circle with horns and the others are spalled away to the point of being not discernible. (Wolter, 2011)

came up this time, the contrast between the two was dramatic. The walls of the groove were straight, smooth, and steeper with no terracing of the sedimentary layers as would be expected. The interpretation was simple and while it was unknown how long it took for the advanced weathering profile to develop in the bull carving it clearly indicated significant age. (See color section, Figures 6 & 7)

Independence Rune Stone

In January of 2008, I received an email with fuzzy, nighttime pictures of what appeared to be a runic inscription carved into a rock wall with some mysterious characters and diamond-shaped lozenges. It looked interesting, but the little background information I was able to get led me to think it was probably something done in the last one hundred years or so, and I forgot about it.

The Independence runic inscription is carved into a five-foot tall vertical limestone rock face only a few miles from the Missouri River near Independence, Missouri. (Wolter, 2011)

In September 2009, my friend Wayne May, sent me some photographs he had taken during a visit to see the inscription a few days earlier. Wayne's pictures, taken in daylight, had very clear characters. He said the carvings looked old to him and that I should take a look at it. In June 2010, I had the opportunity.

Wayne had a friend, Forrest Leggett, who lived near the site and offered to be our guide. Committee Films was in the midst of making another film for the History Channel about pre-Columbian exploration and sent Phil Joncas to meet Forest and me in Kansas City to film our visit. The terrain was a heavily wooded valley. The stream running through it eventually drained into the Missouri River just a few miles away. Phil and I followed Forrest across a field, railroad tracks, a stream and up the opposite bank back into the woods. Forest pointed out massive blocks of limestone bedrock slowly sliding down toward the stream eroding its banks. Suddenly, Forrest stopped and pointed to a wall of limestone bedrock and said, "There it is."

The inscription had blended into the rock face. Upon a closer look, I was struck by how deep and skillfully the characters had been carved. I was also impressed with my initial review of the inscription's weathered appearance. It certainly wasn't fresh, and I would learn from Forrest that the earliest known reference was reportedly in the 1920s.

Phil, Forest and I spent roughly two hours taking measurements, photographs, and a sample of the rock from about fifteen feet away. I was sure the rock was a limestone, but its weathering properties would depend on what kind of a carbonate rock it was, and I could only make that determination in the lab.

Within days I had a thin section made and reviewed it under the polarized light microscope. The rock was very dense and compact micrite (muddy) limestone with occasional fossil shell fragments. When we cut and polished the sample, it showed a clearly defined lighter-color weathering profile at the surface that was roughly one-eighth of an inch deep. By June of 2011, my new Keyence three-dimensional digital microscope allowed high resolution and high magnification images. A control sample collected from the bedrock the inscription was carved into revealed a surprising and very interesting surface under the new digital microscope.

Part of the surface was covered with patches of light-gray lichen with shallow pits on the surface. Where the lichen had come off, it had left a series of circular pits that looked the dimples on a golf ball. It appears the lichen produced acid that attacked the limestone surface, producing the pits. The pitted surface excited me because it gave me something I might be able to use to compare with the inscription if I could get the new microscope down to Missouri.

On October 8, 2011, David Brody and I met in St. Louis, Missouri, and then met up with the landowner who led us back to the inscription across his property in our rental Jeep. The final leg of the journey required moving logs and driving over washed out gulleys on an old elevated railroad bed that nearly swallowed the Jeep. Once at the site, I pulled out a plastic table and set up the digital microscope. David scouted the rock faces along the ravine for more rumored carvings while I did my examination.

This was my first chance to take the new equipment into the field and it didn't disappoint. The lens zoomed into the grooves and the images that came up onto the screen were bright, clear and detailed. One of the things I was looking for were the golf ball-like dimples on the surface of the carved grooves, but there were none to be found.

David found no other inscriptions. I showed him some of the images of the rock surfaces inside the carved grooves. Dave said, "You're not seeing the lichen pits are you?" I shook my head and said, "I would have expected at least some pitting, and it's making my 'spider sense' tingle."

By around 5:00 P.M. it was time to pack up. We thanked the landowner for his hospitality. Later that night, we talked about what needed to happen next.

"It's up the runologists now." I said to David.

On October 8, 2011, I was able to use the latest three-dimensional digital microscopic technology in the field to examine the Independence Rune Stone in Independence, Missouri. (Wolter, 2011)

He agreed and then asked me the question I knew was coming, "So, if you had to say, how old do you think the inscription is?"

I said, "Well, David, I'd say it's between one hundred to one hundred fifty years tops." As much as I would have loved for that inscription to be pre-Columbian, both the science and my gut, said, "No."

Ironically, within only a couple of months we received the news from the runologists we were waiting for. Only a month after David and I had been there, another group visited the site, which included James Frankii, a German professor at Sam Houston University in Houston, Texas. As part of his doctoral studies, Frankii studied Latin, Old French, Old High German, Old Saxon and Old Norse. He and the group concluded the vertically aligned symbols were the date he believes the inscription was carved: 1888. The remainder of the inscription includes the name of the carver, Cyrus Arthur Slater, and his wife, Hannah, both English immigrants, who arrived in America in 1881.[40]

A number of people were very disappointed when they found out the inscription wasn't pre-Columbian. I too, would have loved for the inscription to have been ancient, but it wasn't. This inscription was a good example of why people have to always be careful when dealing with historical mysteries. In this case, both the hard and soft science investigations reached the proper conclusion.

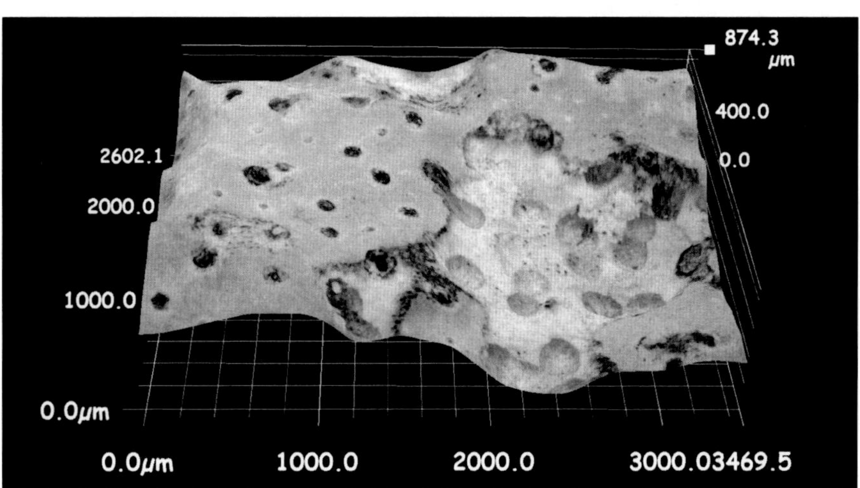

This digital image of the surface of a sample collected from the bedrock outcrop roughly ten feet from the Independence runic inscription. The light gray area is lichen with dark gray spots. Acid from lichen has attacked the surface of the limestone surface leaving circular pits clearly visible in the white area where the lichen has come off. (Wolter, 2011)

Mustang Mountain Runic Inscription

ANOTHER LEAD CAME from Paul Weishaupt, a man who lived near Tucson, Arizona. He forwarded pictures of an inscription he and two friends, Frank Belluardo, Jr., and Jim Cardamone, had found at the entrance to a cave high in the Mustang Mountains. To my surprise, I recognized the characters immediately as Anglo-Saxon runes, but in Arizona? It seems improbable, but I also knew it wasn't a matter of *if* I would see the inscription, but when?–March 19, 2011.

We followed our guides along a desolate road into the Mustang Mountains. It took an hour and a half to reach the saddle between the two peaks. Frank found a couple of pottery shards at an ancient campsite and shared his past experience with archaeologists. Every time he brought up the idea of pre-Columbian exploration, it was roundly dismissed. Frank said eventually he was no longer invited on any more digs. So it goes apparently.

The cave was naturally eroded along a joint fracture extending about forty feet into the mountain. The mouth of the cave was about twenty feet high and, as we entered, I walked across a large flat boulder. Stopping me dead in my tracks were dozens of skillfully carved characters arranged neatly into five rows.

My first impression of the inscription was that it was recently carved. The bottoms of the grooves were white where the dark-gray limestone had been crushed by the chisel. I also noticed the entire face of the boulder was covered with a white calcite coating. The adjacent dark-gray flaked areas exhibited virtually no weathering or buildup of secondary calcite, which covered the limestone boulder's surface the inscription had been cut through. This gave the inscription a freshly made look. But this was not the time to draw any conclusions, so I went to work collecting as much information as I could. After collecting a small sample I chipped off the back side of the stone, I took several photos of the carved characters using my handheld portable microscope.

Paul, Frank, and Jim relayed how they led a group of archaeologists, which included the Arizona state archaeologist, to the site in 2010. They said they were very interested and took many pictures of the Native cave art, but ignored the runic inscription. When they asked the archaeologists for their opinion they replied, "Modern graffiti."

We took pictures of the beautiful Native American wall paintings and carvings inside the cave. Most of the designs were of various patterns, spirals, and one swastika-like sun symbol. All the Native art was covered with black soot from campfires reported set by "illegals" making their way into the country. About halfway into the cave, we found the first word of the runic inscription carved into the east wall, twice. The three- to four-inch-tall runes were bright white from being cut into crystalline calcite lining the wall.

Why these runes were carved two times inside the cave was a mystery, but then we started to think about possible solar alignments. The cave ran almost due north-south into the mountain. The only possibility of sunlight penetrating the cave would be on the winter solstice when the sun would be at its lowest point in the southern sky. Still two days from the spring equinox, we knew we had nine months to think about it.

Before beginning the trek back down the mountain, we scouted around and found two smaller caves. Just inside one of the caves was the rotting corpse of a wild boar. As I moved in to get a closer look, something stirred in the fur. Blending perfectly was a three-foot-long coiled rattlesnake that nervously slunk its way deeper into the cave. As I slowly backed away, I felt empathy for both the ancients and the illegals who risked entering these caves.

The motivation to make the difficult climb and risk the rattlesnakes was likely religious for the Natives who must have considered this cave a sacred site. The bone-white crystalline calcite inside the cave and the chalk-white secondary calcite covering the inscribed boulder might also have inspired the visitors (white monks possibly?) who came before us.

On March 19, 2011, Paul Weishaupt, Frank Belluardo, Jr., and Jim Cardamone, led my family and me on a hike into the Mustang Mountains of southern Arizona, where they found a runic inscription carved into a boulder at the entrance to a small cave. The forty-two-character-long inscription also had a Christian style cross carved a few inches below the last line of runes. (Wolter, 2011)

A week later, we received a call from Michael Carr, who we had met through email correspondence in January of 2011. Michael had contacted me after seeing the film to share his discovery of yet another Hooked X! He forwarded a photo of a small brooch that did indeed have our symbol, along with seven other symbols, scratched into the outer circle.

The Early Saxon, circa sixth-century brooch had a swastika-like design in the center and was unearthed by Hamon Le Strange, a prominent Norfolk baron and master Mason, at a dig in Old Hunstanton, near Norfolk, England, in 1900. Le Strange brought in McKinney Hughes, perhaps the most preeminent excavator at the time, and they discovered a trove of treasure on Le Strange's property. The brooch was found with a skull, but it was away from the main trench where other treasure was found. It was interesting how the Hooked X was standing alone as opposed to being part of a word within a runic inscription.

Knowing Mike had done his graduate work in England and studied Anglo-Saxon runes, I emailed him a picture of the Mustang Mountain inscription for his opinion. His first impression was that the inscription was likely carved to mark a grave, or in this case a tomb. We had thought about the same possibility. We told Michael how the cave had an earthen berm at the entrance that then sloped down moving into the cave. The inscribed boulder was at the bottom of the berm with the inscription facing into the cave. A few feet in the cave, the floor rose up several feet into a small mound. The uneven topography at the mouth of the cave made me wonder if any of the earth had been moved.

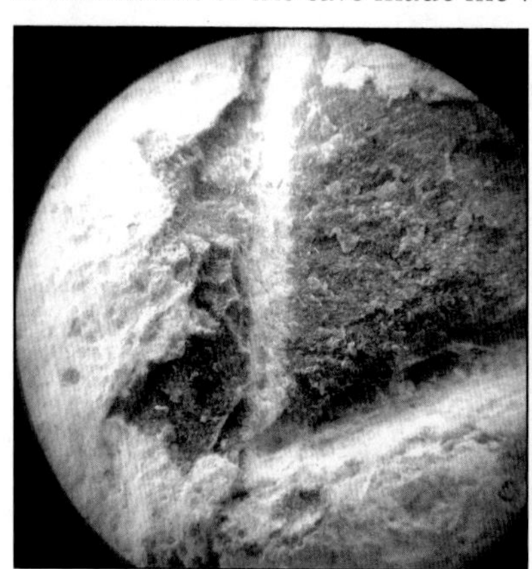

These pictures of the midsection of the second character on the fifth line were taken with a handheld digital microscope at magnification of 3X (left) and 10X (right). The white lines are the grooves created where the chisel stuck the rock, the adjacent gray areas are the flaked limestone, and the surrounding white area is the secondary calcite coating the surface of the boulder. (Wolter, 2012)

The author (dark cap) ponders the runic inscription in front of him carved on a boulder while guides Paul Weishaupt and Frank Belluardo, Jr., and Grant Wolter (bending) look on (left). A group of five spirals were among several Native American carvings and painting found inside the cave (right). (Janet Wolter, 2011; Wolter, 2011)

Michael also mentioned that he found several "exotic" alphabets researching the inscription at monasteries in England. He explained how the monks would craft "secret" alphabets that incorporated standard runic characters together with more obscure symbols. Many of these alphabets were unique to a particular abbey. He then said, "There are some strange combinations in this inscription which actually make it seem more authentic."

We then discussed that most runic scholars in Scandinavia had only studied the corpus of thousands of "public" rune stones scattered throughout the countryside in plain sight. Most of these inscriptions are simple and straight forward, "This stone was raised by Thorvold to honor his brother . . .", or "This stone was carved to commemorate King . . ." They are not used to looking at secret inscriptions with mixed or unusual characters foreign to them. Rune stones like the Kensington, Spirit Pond, Narragansett, and the Mustang Mountain inscriptions are not what they are used to seeing and struggled to decipher them.

This would explain why they reacted so strangely when the Larsson Papers (two sheets of paper dated 1883 and 1884, donated by the family of Edward Larsson, that contained two runic alphabets and include the Hooked X) came forward shortly after our visit to Sweden in October of 2003.[41] They were clearly Masonic in origin and marked the first time the seven mysterious runes on the Kensington Stone had ever been seen. The runic scholars said for over 100 years that the characters didn't exist, yet they did exist secretly within Masonic societies and were likely created much earlier by a scribe monk in a medieval monastery.

Our conversation turned back to the cave and the possibility of it being a tomb. We knew it was time to talk to Paul Wieshaupt. He was quite surprised, but pleased that we had made progress. Before we could suggest it, Paul brought up doing a ground penetrating radar study of the cave. He agreed to look into it, and if he, Frank, and Jim found anything interesting we promised we would help with the next logical step, a dig.

I got another chance to visit the cave on June 1, 2012. We were joined for the filming by Steve Ross, archaeologist with the Arizona State Land Department.

If someone from the twelfth century was buried in the Mustang Mountain cave, we thought they were either in the mound inside the cave or in the berm just outside it. At one point as I sat next to the inscription, I noticed water running down the walls had dissolved the limestone leaving calcite deposits in streams that flowed into a buildup of sand and rock fragments cemented together along the walls about three feet above the present surface next to the inscribed boulder. Suddenly it hit me; the caliche deposits present on both sides of the cave had developed when the ground was at that level. This meant that a large amount of material had been moved from just inside the cave.

Then another thought hit me that prompted me to look at the boulder next to the wall. The previous ground line was higher than the inscribed boulder, meaning it could have been buried *after* it was carved which would explain the lack of weathering.

Earlier, Steve had shared that the site had been recorded to the state archaeologist's office in 1984 and there was no mention in the report about the runic inscription. This meant it was buried and not visible at that time, or the boulder was visible and the inscription was carved after that time. After explaining how caliche deposits develop to the group, everyone understood what the possible implications were.

Mike Carr would eventually provide a translation for us that confirmed this inscription was indeed carved as a memorial. Mike's translation also included a name, Rough Hurech!

The body (in contrast with the soul) fits/lays
Rough Hurech here
He enjoyed (entertainment/joy/merriment) - the secret stolen
Rough Hurech's body - fame and glory
Dust beyond Eden (Eden's Temple)

We made another significant discovery on this visit that confirmed my suspicions of the first trip. The first word of the inscription was carved

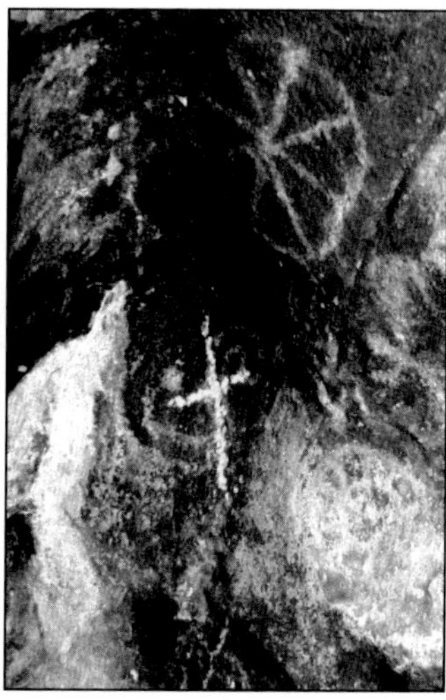

This picture of Janet Wolter, Paul Weishaupt, and Frank Belluardo, Jr., studying the inscription was taken standing atop the small mound of dirt inside the cave (left). A Latin style cross identical to the cross carved below the inscribed boulder was carved over a Native spiral on the upper back wall of the cave (right). (Wolter, 2011; Wolter, 2011)

twice into the east wall roughly halfway into the cave. After pondering why, I speculated that maybe they put it where the sun would hit it on the winter solstice. Photographer, Bo Hakala, said he had an application on his iPhone that might help answer the question. He pulled up the program which when in camera mode, showed a green line marking the horizon, and a curved blue line marking the path of the sun across the southern sky on the winter solstice. Bo then put his camera next to the carved word on the wall and pointed his phone toward the mouth of the cave. Sure enough, the blue line crossed just into an opening at the top of the cave entrance at just before high noon!

After the filming was done we all hiked back down in the shadow of the mountain as the sun fell quickly in the western sky. Paul and Jim returned on December 21 and confirmed at least the first

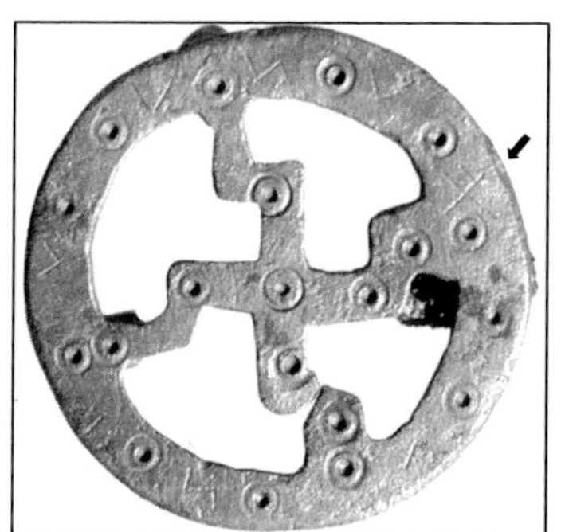

Michael Carr forwarded this picture to me in January, 2011. This Early Saxon (circa sixth century) brooch has a swastika design with eight symbols scratched onto the outer ring including the Hooked X (arrow). The brooch was found with a skull near an excavation in Old Hunstanton, in Norfolk, England, in 1900.

The buildup of material on the limestone cave walls near the entrance was made when water running down leached out calcite from the bedrock. The water evaporated and cemented sand and rock fragments into a hard substance called caliche at the previous ground level. The line of caliche indicated that up to four feet of material had been dug out and used to create the berm just outside the entrance. Could vandals have removed material at the entrance and taken artifacts and remains from a twelfth century burial? (Wolter, 2012)

On November 10, 2011, Bo Hakala places his iPhone against the runic carving on the cave wall using an astronomy application program to check if the sun will illuminate the characters (left). The picture Bo took shows the sun will indeed hit the carved characters at noon for approximately one-half hour on December 21 (right). (Wolter, Hakala, 2011)

word on the cave wall was illuminated by the sun before the clouds moved in just before noon. These confirmed this important discovery, along with the buildup of the berm gave further credibility that this could be a medieval site. If a body was eventually found and it dated to the medieval period, it would be incredibly important and would radically and instantly change history as we know it.

The Millwood Rune Stone

AFTER WATCHING *Holy Grail in America,* Nancy Millwood said she had to get in touch with me. On January 30, 2011, I received an email from my friend, Rick Osmon that a woman in Pensacola, Florida, was trying to contact me. She had a rune stone she had found in North Carolina in 1970. A couple days later Nancy Millwood sent me a half dozen photos of her stone. I immediately recognized the characters as runes, Anglo-Saxon runes. However, several characters had clearly visible single, double and triple dots above them reminiscent of the Scandinavian runes with umlauts like on the Kensington Rune Stone.

Her excitement at finally finding someone who took an interest in her stone was evident. She relayed her forty years of frustration with academics she had contacted who showed little interest in helping her understand what she had found. On February 12, 2011, I met Nancy in Pensacola, Florida.

Nancy revealed her prize. The roughly one-foot by one-foot by an inch-and-a-half-thick slab had the slightly greasy feel of soapstone and was broken across the upper left side. The smaller long piece fit snugly to the larger piece, revealing six lines of text carved deeply into the flat surface that had the undeniable marking of having been cut by human hands. The saw marks on both the front and back sides were very irregular, clearly not consistent with a mechanical saw. The variable thickness of the slab also gave the impression the slab was hand-cut from a larger piece of stone.

The inscription was comprised of forty-five runic characters divided into six lines. Two runes had single dots, eight had double dots above them, and three "M" runes had three dots above each arm.

On February 13, 2011, I met Nancy and Mason Millwood in Pensacola, Florida, to examine the runic inscription she found as an eleven-year old girl in North Carolina in 1970. (Wolter, 2011)

I examined the stone for the next five hours. In addition to taking close-up photographs of the characters, I video-recorded a twenty-minute interview with Nancy where she relayed her entire story. She allowed me to take a small sample of the stone from the back side for testing and loaned me the only photograph she had ever taken of the stone. The faded slide had some water damage, but the inscription was still visible. The slide was dated January 1979 and proved she had the stone since at least that time.

The slide was one of eleven copies, the others had been sent to ten different institutions along with a letter asking for help. Nancy said she never heard back from any of them. As I listened to her story, I could feel her sense of relief that she was close to finally getting some answers. She was like many other everyday people who had found things and simply were curious to know what they were and who made them. Even though I couldn't guarantee her anything, she seemed satisfied that at least I would try.

By June 2013, we had yet to be able to have the inscription translated. I promised her I wouldn't let her be taken advantage of, and until I am confident she and her inscription will not be exploited we will continue to wait.

The Hemlock Chamber

ANOTHER GREAT LEAD from the *Holy Grail in America* film came from a man who lived in Franklin, Pennsylvania. Tom Anderton called and said there was an underground chamber made of cut stone and mortar that he said, "Has a spring flowing in it." Intrigued, I asked Tom for photos. The early springtime images were taken in a wooded area on what appeared to be relatively steep slope in a remote area in the mountains not far from the Allegheny River.

After reviewing his pictures and thinking about the chamber's location near the top of a mountain I wondered if there could be some kind of alignment or illumination event associated with it. I then asked Tom, "What side of the mountain is the chamber on?" After a short pause he said, "It's on the west side." This meant that if there was a solar alignment it would have to be with the setting sun and suggested he be inside the chamber on the summer solstice or within a day or two of it. He said he would and let me know what happened.

By the time June 21st rolled around, I'd forgotten about the chamber and was taken by surprise when the phone rang with an excited voice on the other end. "Scott, you were right. At about 7:30 P.M. Jack Susco and I were standing inside along the wall next to the basin and the sun came in and lit up the whole chamber. It was amazing!"

I knew I had to get out there as soon as I could.

August 30, 2009, Tom and Jack drove Vance Tiede, an archaeologist I thought would find the mysterious chamber interesting, up the mountain road. They walked a logging road that began to parallel the relatively steep mountain slope when Tom said, "I think this is it." He walked a few steps off the trail down to what looked like a pile of stones. Upon looking closer they noticed the stones had been intentionally shaped into blocks and arranged into what turned out to be an air vent. Tom removed a large stone that covered a ten by eight-inch-sized vertical shaft stuffed with rocks about two feet down.

Tom continued down the hill that opened into a small ravine carved by a small spring. The ravine had four large blocks of stone that, upon examining more closely, he noticed had been shaped into roughly five feet long by two-foot-wide by twelve-inch-thick slabs. Just above where the spring flowed out of the ground, Tom began to move several stones that covered the entrance to the chamber. Tom then said, "We keep the entrance covered so animals don't crawl in there. We aren't too worried about people finding it."

Within minutes, Vance and Tom squeezed through the tight entrance that quickly opened up into a roughly twenty-foot-long by six-foot-tall tunnel made of stone walls with neatly placed two-foot wide lintel stones above their heads. They aimed their small flashlights into the darkness ahead, and they heard water trickling. After a few more paces they stepped onto a stone ledge that turned out to be the front edge of a basin with water flowing into it. Shining their beams downward they saw a perfectly cut, four-inch-diameter hole in the front wall where water could flow out of the basin and then seep into the ground.

After squeezing through the entrance, Vance Tiede slides down into the two-foot-wide stone walls of the tunnel leading into the Hemlock Chamber on August 30, 2011.

The two-foot-wide stone walled tunnel entrance leads to a stone basin that spring water flows into and then drains out a four-inch-diameter hole skillfully cut into two blocks allowing water to then seep into the ground.

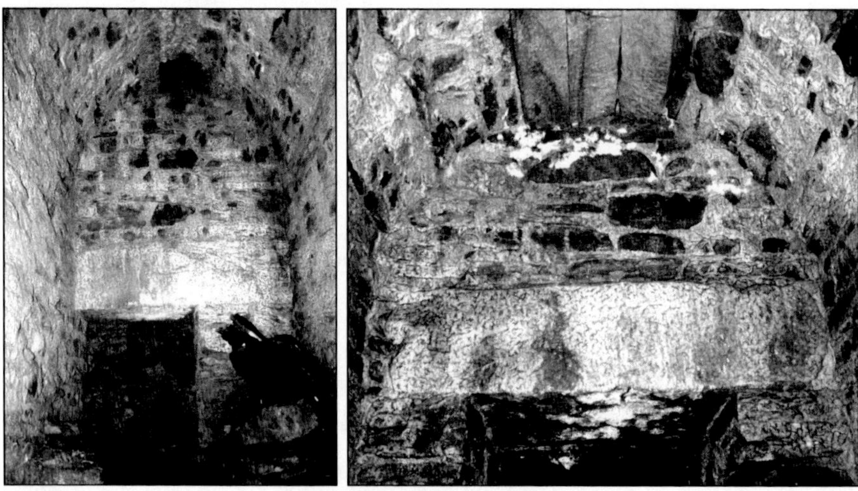

The east end of the spring chamber has a ten-by-eight-inch vent to the surface at the top of the rounded ceiling. The spring flows from a crack in the sandstone bedrock through the two foot wide by three foot tall opening in the lower left side of the back wall (left). Looking back toward the entrance there is a one foot thick lintel stone below a triple keystone securing the ceiling (right).

Above the overflow hole was an eight-inch-wide channel groove on the top front edge to allow water to flow out once the basin filled when the lower hole was plugged. At this point, the chamber widened to four feet. As they stepped up onto the basin, they could see the top of the eight-foot-long chamber was rounded to a maximum of eight and a half feet in height. The barrel vault was secured with a triple keystone that ran the entire length of the ceiling. On the east end of the

Spring water flowing from a crack in the sandstone bedrock along an expertly cut winding groove trickles into a thirty by thirty-inch square cut stone basin inside the Hemlock Chamber. Because of a solar illumination inside the chamber on the summer solstice, the builders likely used it for religious ritual bathing.

The mist-enhanced rays of the setting sun shine along the east stone wall of the entrance to the Hemlock Chamber on June 19, 2011.

ceiling, they noticed the vent opening that led to the pile of stones they had seen at the surface when they arrived. Looking back toward the entrance they noticed the first massive one-foot-thick lintel stone leading back down the tunnel.

The construction of the stone walls in the entrance tunnel was unusual. Sand was used between the stones with a lime mortar then applied on the exterior joints, which kept the sand from falling out. The construction inside the chamber was similar except mortar appeared to also have used to plaster all walls and the ceiling. Much of the plaster had fallen off the inside walls, and it was very dirty. However, the walls were still very white in color, and even tiny flashlights lit up the chamber quite well. The ceiling, dotted with spiders and cave crickets, also had several white calcite stalactites hanging down that were up to a couple of inches long.

Upon learning this, my first thought was maybe the stalactites could be used to date the chamber. However, I'd need to know more about how it was constructed on the exterior or if there was anything used to waterproof it. That would require an archaeological dig that might also yield some organic material such as pieces of wood buried at the time it was backfilled that could be dated.

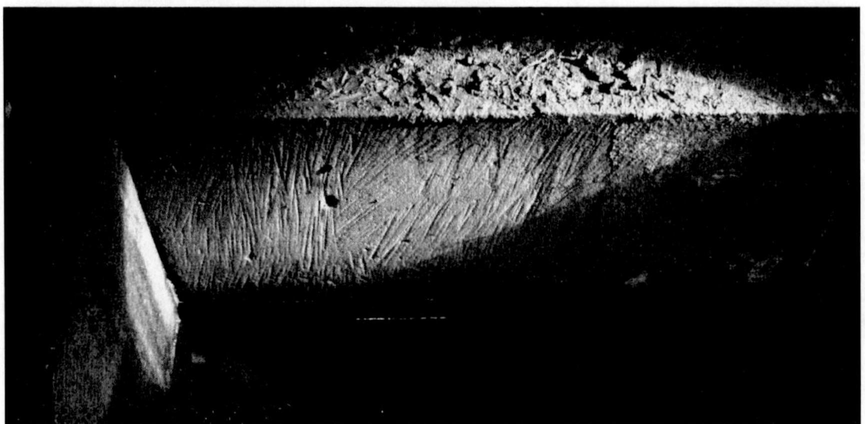

A flashlight highlights the tell-tale scratches along the walls of the stone basin that are consistent with having been done by hand and not modern machinery.

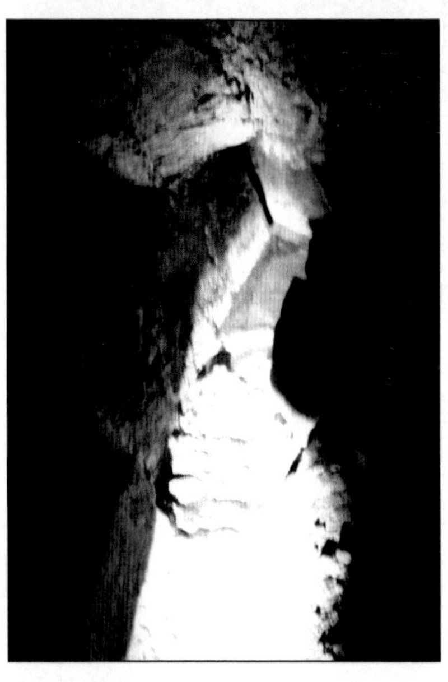

On June 19, 2011, the setting sun cast its light through the misty air inside the mortar and stone underground chamber.

Looking down at the thirty-inch-by-thirty-inch square basin, Vance and Tom listened to the steady trickle of pure, icy cold water and wondered aloud, "What could this structure have been used for?" They kicked around the possibilities they thought people might come up with like a slave tunnel, a bath house, or place for food storage. Upon analysis, none of these made any sense, especially because the location was so remote. The only thing they could come up with that seemed the least bit plausible was that this chamber was used for ritual bathing. The fact that the rays of the setting sun on the summer solstice illuminated the chamber cannot be a coincidence and suggested its likely intended use in a religious ritual.

As exciting as it was to review the chamber photos with Vance in late August, I knew someone had to go back on the summer solstice. On June 19, 2011, David Brody and Tom returned to the chamber, hoping for a clear day. They decided to stay inside and stand along the south wall as the sun set in

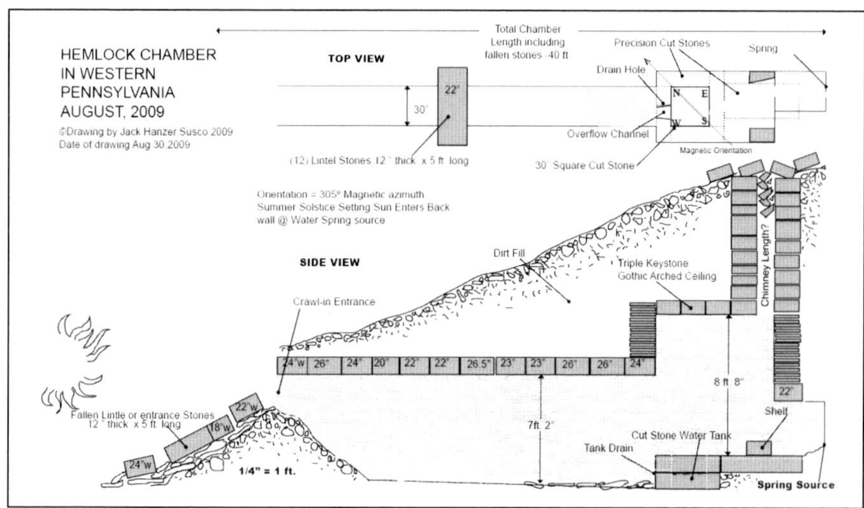

In 2009, Jack Susco made this excellent detailed cross-sectional drawing of the underground Hemlock Chamber near Franklin, Pennsylvania.

the western sky. They had set up a video camera to record the event and took still photos over the course of the forty-five-minute-long show as it unfolded. As the mist-enhanced beam of sunlight worked its way inward along the north stone wall of the entrance, David and Tom were transfixed.

The sun's rays created a beam of light that hit the front wall of the basin and shot through the four-inch diameter hole over the top of the water in the basin. The sunlight reflecting off the ripples on the surface from the trickling water and enhanced by the white plaster walls produced a spectacular light show in the chamber. As amazing as this was the best was yet to come.

As they waited in the dark, David and Tom talked about the high quality construction of the chamber that belied a utilitarian purpose and seemed more intent on, as David suggested, "Pleasing their Gods." He also observed that the large stones showed no evidence of the "plug and feather" method of splitting the largest stones—placing wood pegs or cork (or engineered metal rods that create tensional force in modern times) into drilled holes and then causing them to expand by wetting them. Sometimes ice was intentionally allowed to form in the drilled holes in winter to break the stone. David then cast his flashlight beam at a low angle to the wall of the cistern where he could see the tell-tale scratches that clearly indicated the work was not done with modern machinery and added, "They used good old-fashioned hand tools to skillfully shape the masonry."

As the sun continued to sink in the western sky, the light beam rose above the top of the stone basin and shot back up the winding channel cut into the stone blocks on the chamber floor. David and Tom were speechless as the laser beam-like sunlight illuminated the crack in the sandstone bedrock where the spring water flowed from the earth. It was a spectacular allegorical fertilization of mother earth with the male solar deity in the heavens.

Experiencing the illumination, David and Tom felt that making anything other than an esoteric spiritual or religious interpretation seem ridiculous. The only unanswered questions were who built this incredible structure and when did they do it? My first inclination, upon examining the photos, was to suspect the Knights Templar, who likely were in this area during the late medieval period. Oil was known to the Natives in the region, who set ceremonial fires to the volatile dark liquid that floated on the river and became trapped by fallen trees and debris. The Templars likely would have understood the value and importance of oil that was first discovered in the modern era on this continent at Oil City, Pennsylvania, in the mid-1800s.[42] However, as much as I would like to believe the Templars were responsible for the chamber's construction, I highly doubt they were. In fact, because of the heavy Masonic influence in the area, especially in Franklin, there likely was another more plausible explanation.

The City of Franklin, Pennsylvania, was laid out by Andrew Ellicott, who also laid out the incredible sacred geometry of Washington, D.C. I suspect those responsible for construction of the Hemlock Chamber were a side order of esoteric Freemasons. The fact that the chamber aligns with the summer solstice and not the winter solstice is also significant. Arguably, the most important day of recognition in Freemasonry is John the Baptist's feast day on June 24th, which is when the ancients celebrated the summer solstice by paying homage to the forces of nature including fire, water, and plants.[43] Because of the connection of the summer solstice to Freemasonry, together with the fact that there was a lot of oil money in this area in the past one hundred and fifty years, my guess is that's probably how old the chamber is. At some future time, some archaeological work might be done that could shed more light on the origins of this incredible site.

Meteor Impact Sites

OVER THE PAST FIVE YEARS, Janet and I have noticed a disproportionately high percentage of pre-Columbian artifacts and sites within or near ultramafic volcanic rocks deposits and extra-terrestrial meteor and possible comet impact areas. Examples that jumped out early include the Ohio Serpent Mound, the Southern Illinois area of Little Egypt where the Burrows Cave artifacts were reportedly found and the massive, recently discovered impact site that includes most of the area around Lake Superior where there are tens of thousands of ancient copper mines dating back over six millennia. We speculate that one of the primary reasons ancient visitors from other continents came to North and South America was for precious metals and other economic minerals such as gold, silver, lead, zinc, copper, nickel, titanium, various gemstones including diamonds, and oil.

It's no secret that geologically, precious metals are found in rocks that have been disturbed by tectonic forces. This allows mineral-laden hydrothermal solutions to move and concentrate along fractures in the earth produced by faulting associated with earthquakes, upwelling of molten rock at depth, and extra-terrestrial impacts. Early explorers to North America, and most certainly the medieval Templars, were primarily interested in finding new sources of these highly valuable metals, especially gold. It's no secret in geology that one of the ways to locate these minerals is by looking for areas with high magnetic anomalies.

If our speculation is correct that early explorers possessed ancient knowledge of how to locate areas of high magnetic gravity using an early version of a magnetic compass, and the secrets of sophisticated skills of metalworking called alchemy, it shouldn't come as a surprise to see this association of ancient sites and extra-terrestrial impacts. When large meteorites hit the earth in the distant past, they literally punched holes into the crust of the earth, creating a roughly vertical shaft allowing molten rock and solutions to move along this fractured zone, concentrating precious metals. One analogy of the process is similar to what happens when a rock is thrown through an ice-covered pond or lake and water shoots back up and out of the hole in the ice. A classic example of this association is the Serpent Mound in Adams County in Southern Ohio.

Serpent Mound of Ohio

As ONE OF THE CROWN JEWELS of the ancient mound building cultures, the Serpent Mound has puzzled archaeologists as to its origin since it was first surveyed by Squier and Davis back in 1847. If out-stretched, the total length including the head and egg would be approximately 1,400 feet. The undulating mound averages twenty feet in width and five feet in height. However, at the center of the snake's body, the mound is thirty feet wide at the base and gets slightly smaller toward the tail and the head.[44]

The Serpent Mound was built on the southwestern rim of a roughly five-mile diameter impact crater estimated to be roughly 240 million years old.[45] While the geology of the area is relatively well understood, the identity of the builders of the mound is not.[46] During a visit to the mound on August 11, 2009, with Beverly Moseley, a professional artist and long-time member of the Midwest Epigraphic Society, it was a special treat to receive a tour of the interpretive center that included interesting dioramas Bev had made himself. The interpretive displays were inconclusive about the age of the mound. However, soil depth accumulations and archaeoastronomical calculations of the

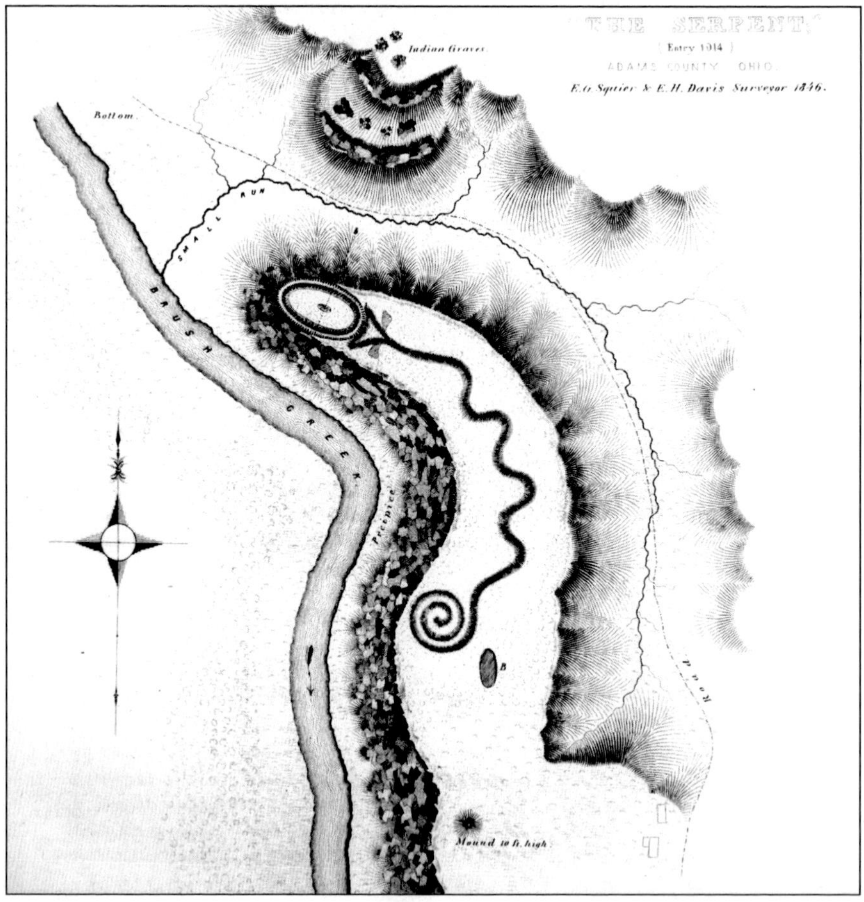

E.G Squier and E.H. Davis produced the first known sketch of the Serpent Mound in Adams County, Ohio, in 1846.

Likely unaware they were replicating where a circle of megalithic stones once stood, a spiritual group of people hold hands inside the berm of earth that makes up the egg in the mouth of the Serpent Mound in Southern Ohio on August 11, 2009. In 1848, Squire and Davis reported, ". . . a small circular elevation of large stones much burned once existed in its center; but they have been thrown down and scattered by some ignorant visitor, under the prevailing impression that gold was hidden beneath them." (Wolter, 2009)

A nine-foot-long, four-foot-wide by roughly twenty-four-inch-thick monolith lies partially buried in the valley below the Serpent Head outcrop in Adams County, Ohio. This stone was likely one of the standing stones that once stood inside the egg of the Serpent Mound and was thrown down the cliff by settlers. (Photo courtesy of *Ancient American Magazine,* Issue #89, photos © Patricia Mason and Jeffrey Wilson, M.S. Professor of Astronomy)

alignment of the mound with the pole star Draconis-*alpha* both date the original construction to over 5,000 years ago.[47]

One other fact that appears consistent with the five millennia date is the reported presence of a circle of standing stones similar to Stonehenge, in Southern England, that once stood inside a perfectly formed oval embankment of earth protruding from the mouth. According to Squier and Davis, "The ground within the oval is slightly elevated, a small circular elevation of large stones much burned once existed in its centre, but they have been thrown down and scattered by some ignorant visitor, under the prevailing impression that gold was hidden beneath them."[48]

In 2009, Wayne May, publisher of *Ancient American Magazine*, hiked below the bluffs where the Serpent Mound resides and found one of the standing stones referred to by Squier and Davis. The stone shows a clear and distinct weathering line marking the above and below

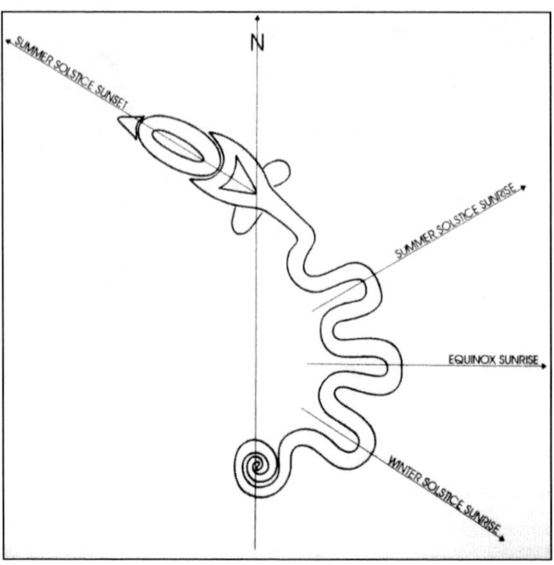

This image shows the solar alignments of the Serpent Mound in Adams County, Ohio. (Redrawn by Dan Wiemer from Hamilton, 2001)

grade ends. It would likely take many decades if not centuries for such a well-developed weathering line to develop.[49]

Hamilton (2001) presented his thesis that the builders of the Serpent Mound incorporated elements of sacred geometry, symbolism, sophisticated mound architecture construction and contains ". . . at least twelve verifiable, geo-astronomical alignments contributed by competent archaeological researchers, independent of one another." The solstice alignments in the bends of the serpent's body impressed me the most. Combined with the other scientifically advanced aspects of this incredible structure it's a strong candidate for its builders having brought this technology to North America from across the Atlantic.

The question is: Why did the ancients build this incredibly sophisticated mound structure on the rim of an impact crater? Since there is no history of mining in the immediate area or economic minerals often associated with meteorite impacts there had to be another reason. The likely reason was the early cultures that lived here must have had the ability to tap into some type of increased energy or magnetic anomaly related to the impact zone. This would not be unprecedented as the earliest temple sites in Europe were built along ancient salt lines, which were later determined to correspond with regular longitudinal lines of increased magnetism. Later we will see these longitudinal lines of increased magnetism in North America correspond to author Bill Mann's "Templar Meridians."

Jacques de Mahieu's Research

In 1981, Jacques de Mahieu (1915-1990), a French scholar and Nazi collaborator wrote *Les Templiers en Amerique* (*The Templars in America*), expounding his theories about the Knights Templar exploration voyages prior to their putdown in 1307. The copy I was able to purchase was in French, so I sought out help from a friend.

John Freeburg asked a French-speaking friend of his to read Mahieu's book and give his interpretation of its contents. On December 15, 2011, John and I met with Jean-Paul Schirle-Keller, who relayed that Mahieu's research seemed credible. One comment that resonated with me was when Jean-Paul explained how Mahieu wrote about how the medieval French people wondered why the Templars were obsessed with the French seaport on the Atlantic Ocean at La Rochelle. It seemed silly at the time to risk sailing so far around the Iberian Peninsula and into the Mediterranean Sea when overland routes across France were a fraction of the distance.

In addition, Mahieu reported that the French also didn't understand how the Templars always seemed to have freshly minted silver currency when all the known silver mines in Europe and Africa had been long-depleted by the Romans. The answer is obvious—they had other secret sources of silver, most likely the American continents. Mahieu presents a compelling body of historical and circumstantial evidence that, in the grand scheme of the murky history of the order, fits together nicely.

At this point, it is appropriate to put professor Mahieu, his Nazi past, and his research into proper perspective. A quick Internet search will find a brief synopsis of the man whose research is labeled multiple times as "racist." Mahieu is an easy target given his Nazi background, but in this discussion his politics are irrelevant and unimportant.

However, given his known association with the Nazis during World War II, it may have provided an opportunity that, at any other time and place in history, could never have been afforded. While the German army was pillaging Europe, the Vatican sought and obtained a tenuous truce of sorts (I'll leave the appropriate historians to explain the nature of that interesting relationship) with the invading Germans that likely afforded certain academics like Mahieu unrestricted access to their archives. Given his detailed and reasoned arguments about the Templars, it seems likely that he obtained secret documents about the activities of the order that other scholars and researchers before or since that time have never seen. Given the contentious nature of the relationship of the Templars and the Roman Catholic Church at the time of their dissolution, whatever secret documents they obtained and the likely important information within them would have been kept off limits to anyone.

Mahieu himself suggests that the strategic port at La Rochelle served as the starting point for secret voyages of the Templars in the twelfth, thirteenth, and fourteenth centuries to ports in Africa, South, Central, and North America, and likely beyond. One of their primary objectives was to locate and mine silver, gold, copper, tin, lead, zinc, titanium, and other minerals. At one point, Jean-Paul said the story about the Templars always having silver made sense to him and shared this story he said probably relates back to their time, "To this day in France when somebody talks about money, they say, 'I need to make some silver, or give me some silver.'"

After the liberation of France in 1944, Mahieu fled to Argentina via the Vatican ratline and studied at the University of Mendoza in Buenos Aries. Mahieu conducted archaeological studies at many pre-Columbian sites in South America, formulating theories about both the Knights Templar and Vikings visiting South and Central America many centuries ago.

In 2002, I was sent a picture of a runic inscription from Sierra del Medina in Tucumán, Argentina, South America. I don't recall who sent it to me or any information about a translation of the inscription. This rune stone has puzzled me and my colleagues ever since. By chance in September of 2011, I was introduced to Alegandro Vega Ossorio, a South American researcher who was very cordial and knew all about the mysterious boulder inscribed with Scandinavian runes. On November 27, 2011, I received the following reply which finally put my mind at ease after nearly a decade of wondering: "Yes of course we saw this inscription, because Jacques de Mahieu found it in Tucuman Province. As you know Xavier de Mahieu works with us and Commission de Exploraciones Arqueologicas is continuing the task of Jacques.

"Yes we have this stone. Also we have several samples of different scripts from pre-Columbian times in Argentina. Following the translation of Jacques Team in 1970, the script means: 'A dos dias la casa (Aldea) de Sven' (English would be something like this 'At two days, Sven House')."

Chapter 5
Archaeopetrography

Sometimes, no matter how much examination and testing is done on an inscription or artifact carved in stone, a definitive conclusion about its age or authenticity cannot be made. However, in the three cases presented in this section, I was able to apply microscopic analysis effectively on three mysterious historical artifacts and collect enough factual data to render a definitive opinion regarding authenticity. If genuine, the historical importance of the artifacts in this section cannot be overstated.

Burrows Cave "Isis" Stone

IN *HOLY GRAIL IN AMERICA*, producers Andy and Maria Awes wanted to include a segment about the Burrows Cave artifacts in spite of my hesitation. I'd always thought the artifacts and the story were interesting, but I wasn't sure if they were appropriate to include. Regardless, they found a clever way to weave them in and left the audience with the appropriate conclusion that Burrows Cave remains an open question. Up to this point, none have been able to document definitively whether any of the artifacts were genuine or not. That is until April of 2010.

Amateur archaeologist, Russell Burrows, then living in Olney, Illinois, reported that he had discovered an opening to a cave system that including thirteen sealed tombs with passageways filled with mostly stone artifacts. From 1982 until 1987, Russell reportedly removed somewhere between 4,000 to 7,000 artifacts from the cave system somewhere in southern Illinois.

In May of 2009, I had a chance to meet Russell. He seemed sincere when talking about the cave. At the time, he was considering ways to open the cave, but like so many times before, there was always an excuse why he couldn't do it.

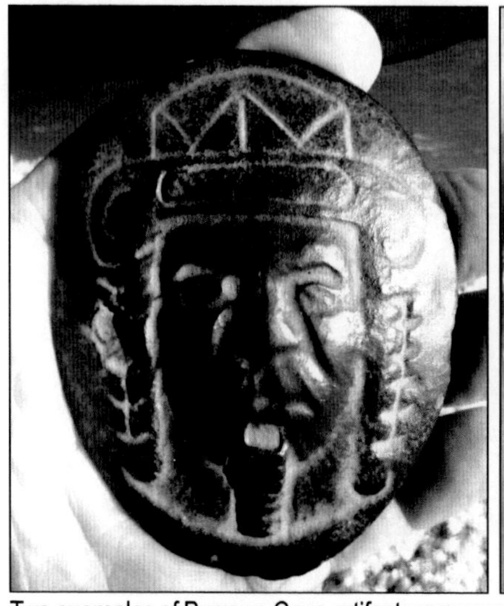

Two examples of Burrows Cave artifacts represent the most common geological types. The "black stones" (left) are calcareous concretions, and the white plates are high white marble (right). (Wolter, 2008)

This photograph of the "Isis" stone was taken by Warren Dexter, in 1987, five years after Russell Burrows reportedly discovered a cave in Southern Illinois filled with thirteen tombs and thousands of stone artifacts. (Courtesy of the New England Antiquities Research Association library at the New Hampshire Technical Institute in Concord, New Hampshire.)

I did not have a lot of confidence in his explanations. When he left, I recall thinking that whatever the truth might be, he was likely going to take it to the grave with him.

In the years I had been involved with the Burrows Cave mystery, I've looked at roughly two thousand artifacts and purchased dozens myself so I could perform invasive testing without having to worry about damaging other collectors' artifacts. Under the microscope, I had seen various levels of wear and apparent weathering. Unfortunately, when asked for my opinion as to the age, my answer was always the same. Without any knowledge of the environment the artifacts were exposed to, I had no weathering data to use as context. In my opinion, the age and authenticity of the artifacts was inconclusive. This was where the controversy remained until amateur researcher, Jay Wakefield, contacted me on April 18, 2010, about a Burrows Cave artifact he called, "The Isis Stone."

Jay said he could see something on the back side of the artifact and sent a few photos for me to examine. It was very hard to see what he was talking about, so I asked if he would be willing to send me the artifact to examine in the lab. A few days later it arrived. The stone itself was a high white marble with dark-gray areas of mold on both sides. Within the grooves of the carved lines on the front side was fine-grained silty sand, which was also present in recessed areas on the edges and back side. When I looked closely at the two areas Jay had pointed out, my eyes instantly recognized part or all of five letters carved in cursive writing. The three characters on the right side were plainly visible and spelled, "t-h-e" as in "mother" or "father" as commonly occurs on a tombstone.

Under the microscope, it was clear the weathering of the English letters was the same as the blank areas on both sides, yet the "Isis" image carved surfaces were not weathered. I also noticed that there were remnants of mortar on the back side with small amounts present within the depression of one of the English letters. Further, the chipped off edges along the back side had broken through some of the remnant mortar meaning the chipping had to have happened *after* the mortar came in contact with the back side and hardened. Thin-section review of the mortar under the polarized light microscope clearly showed the mortar to contain a finely ground, modern Portland cement.

On the back side of the "Isis" stone, the remains of English cursive writing are present in two areas indicated by white boxes. The letters exhibit the same weathering profile as the original flat surface they are carved into. (Wolter, 2010)

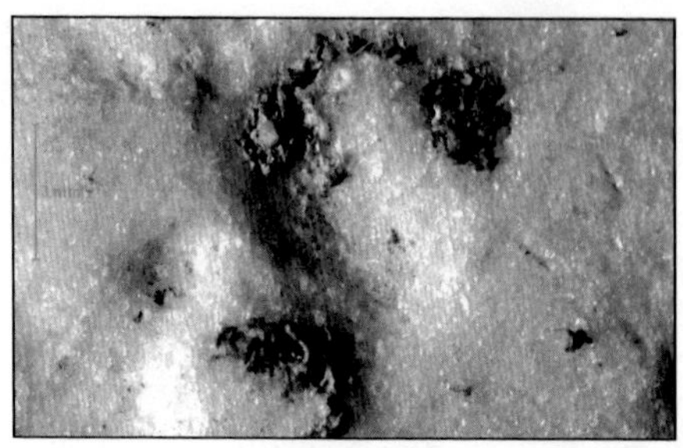

Remnants of modern Portland cement mortar were found within the depressions of the weathered carved cursive letters on the back side of the "Isis" stone. (Wolter, 2010)

A few days later I called Jay and explained my findings. Whoever had made this used an old, weathered, two-inch-thick marble tombstone and carved the kneeling Isis image onto the blank back side. The evidence on the back side laid out a clear and simple sequence of the events that could only have been done by someone intentionally trying to deceive.

At some point after the tombstone had been weathering for many decades to produce the uniform weathering of the surfaces including the carved cursive English text, wet mortar was deposited onto the back side (most likely accidentally since it partially covered a letter). Next, the back side along the edges was chipped away with a chisel in an apparent attempt to, unsuccessfully, remove the remaining tombstone inscription. Lastly, the silty sand was put onto all surfaces to give the appearance of age and disguise the deception.

Jay accepted my findings. After completing my report it was published in issue #89 of *Ancient American Magazine*. Publisher Wayne May deserves a lot of credit for daring to print articles about suspected pre-Columbian artifacts and sites. He receives a lot of undue criticism from mainstream scholars as a result.

The other person I made aware of the test results was Russell Burrows. In fact, he was the first person I called when I reached my conclusions and at first, he accepted them, saying he didn't remember the piece coming from the cave. This statement raised an eyebrow when one considers that researcher

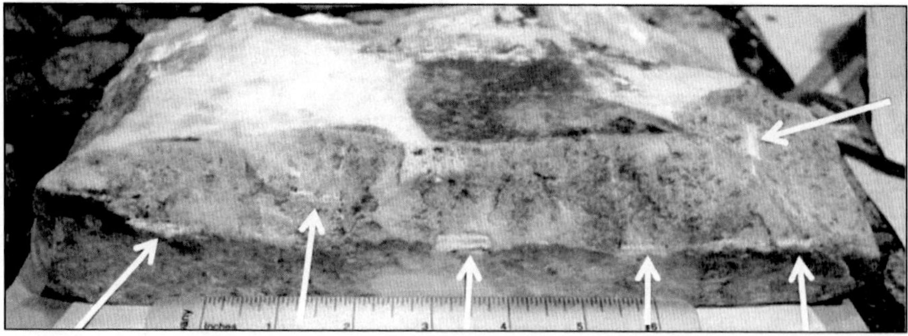

The white arrows indicate ¾-inch-wide chisel impacts where the back side edges were chipped to presumably remove the carved cursive letters. (Wolter, 2010)

The thin dark line marks the contact where the chipped surface (top right) ends. The remnant mortar was cut through, indicating the chipping was done after the modern mortar hardened. (Wolter, 2010)

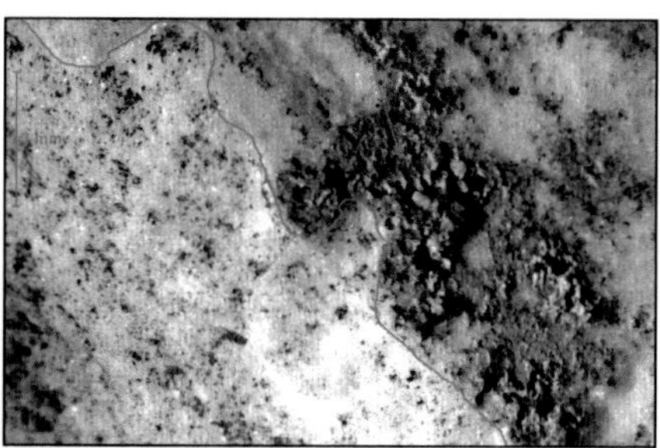

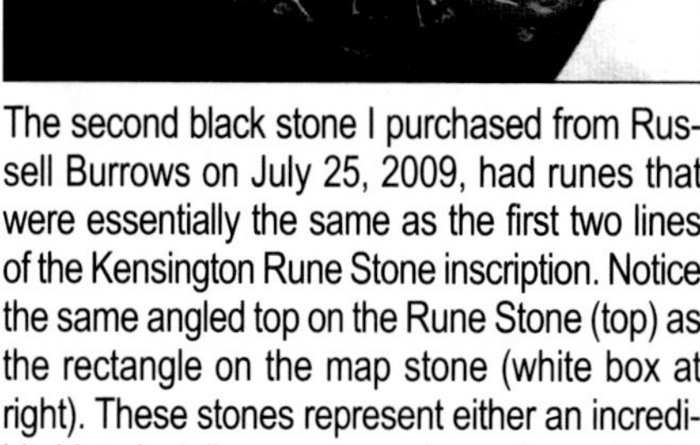

The second black stone I purchased from Russell Burrows on July 25, 2009, had runes that were essentially the same as the first two lines of the Kensington Rune Stone inscription. Notice the same angled top on the Rune Stone (top) as the rectangle on the map stone (white box at right). These stones represent either an incredible historical discovery or a clumsy hoax. In this case, it appears to be the latter. (Wolter, 2009)

One of the black stones Russell Burrows sold to me on July 25, 2009, was a map stone of the Great Lakes with ships, text, and dots representing an apparent sailing route to the west end of Lake Superior that then proceeds west into Minnesota. The dot trail ends near a tall rectangle with an angled top that is eerily reminiscent of the Kensington Rune Stone. (Wolter, 2009)

Warren Dexter photographed the artifact in 1987, in a 1992 book Russell co-authored with Professor Jim Scherz, is the same white marble "Isis" artifact.[50]

To further complicate the Burrows Cave mystery, I found a few more of the suspicious black stones I purchased directly from Russell in July of 2009. Russ told me he had recently been back to Olney, Illinois, and dug up some storage bins where he had stashed artifacts many years ago. He said he had some nice affordable pieces. We struck a deal. Within a week or so, the pieces started to arrive. In one package of a half dozen stones were two that instantly caught my attention. The first was a depiction of the Great Lakes with strange text, boat symbols, and dots that looked as though they were marking a sailing route from Lake Huron across Lake Superior to modern Duluth. From there, six dots heading due west

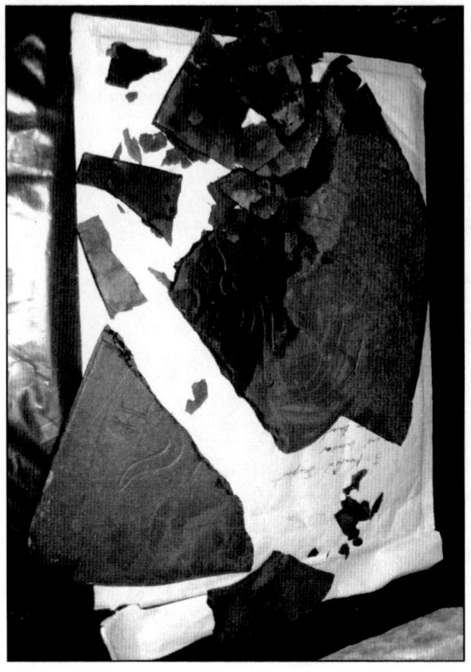

When this Burrows Cave artifact, carved into a highly porous carbonaceous argillite, became saturated when our basement flooded it expanded and broke apart. This piece would never have survived the flooding inside the cave it was reportedly found in that Russell Burrows has repeatedly said has occurred. (Wolter, 2012)

across Minnesota ended at a mysterious, vertically aligned, rectangular box. My first thought was that this area was where the Kensington Rune Stone was found, and that box sure reminded me of it. My skepticism was piqued to say the least, but the next stone I unwrapped had me laughing out loud.

The second stone was a smaller oval-shaped black stone covered on one side with text. Upon taking a closer look I recognized the characters were Scandinavian runes, very familiar runes. In fact, the first four lines were virtually the exact same characters as the first two lines on the Kensington Rune Stone. The remaining text was familiar characters I had seen on many other black stones. When I called Russ and told him what I thought, he said, "Maybe the Templars had been to the cave and the two lines of text were a key?" Of course anything is possible, and as fun as it would have been to have the Templars involved with the cave, I simply could not go there.

I don't believe Russ didn't know what he sent to me and if so, did he really think I would believe these were legitimate? Unlike many of the hundreds of stones I'd seen that appeared to have some weathering, these stones did not appear weathered at all. I dropped the matter with Russ knowing there was no way I would ever get the truth about these stones and put them away.

In spite of the unquestionably fake white-marble artifact and the highly suspect "Kensington" black stones, they don't definitively prove the cave does not exist. There is no question they cast a long, dark shadow over the Burrows Cave mystery. I'm personally convinced the thirty or so white marble artifacts are recycled tombstones intentionally created by someone to deceive and make money. I've wandered through many cemeteries over the years, studying the inscriptions and the various rock types the monuments were made from and have seen thousands carved in high white marble. Marble was a very popular stone for monuments from the mid-1800s to the mid-1900s due largely to being relatively soft (three out of ten on the Moh's hardness scale) which lends itself to beautifully detailed carvings and inscriptions. A very high percentage of the high white marble monuments I measured were two inches thick and exhibited weathering identical to the Isis Stone.

On May 7, 2012, I was able to add another Burrows Cave artifact to the list of probable fakes. This particular artifact has a scene of a Roman soldier in battle with a three-headed dragon that was carved into a very thin and flat, black-colored rock called carbonaceous argillite. The combination of an early spring downpour and a clogged eave downspout caused water to fill up a basement window. Water leaked into the basement and down along the wall the artifact was leaning up against. The leaking water then saturated the bottom half of the roughly twelve-inch-tall artifact. The next morning while cleaning up the mess I found the artifact laying in pieces on the carpet. The highly porous stone absorbed enough water to cause expansion that broke it apart.

While picking up the pieces I thought about the story Russell had told me multiple times about how water had rushed through the cave, washing artifacts out of the tombs and piling them up in the bends of the cave system. I was skeptical of the stories at the time I heard them, but as I picked the pieces of this artifact I knew that story was bogus.

I'm also convinced that some of the black stones are modern fakes as well. However, the fact remains that there are at least 4,000 to 5,000 black stones, many with evidence of weathering that leave many unanswered questions. Who carved them? If it is a hoax, how many people were involved? Who could have had the vast historical knowledge depicted on the stones? Russell certainly didn't do all the artifacts (if he did any of them at all), so who did? The reality is the Burrows Cave mystery is still an open question.

The only person who can answer these questions is Russell. As of 2013, Russell was seventy-seven years old and seemed content to take the secret of the cave with him to the grave. If he doesn't come clean soon, either way, history will no doubt judge him to be a pariah and his cave a fraud. Personally, I don't see him revealing the cave before he dies, and until the cave is found and can shed some context on the weathering environment, we simply cannot pass that judgment. I'm unable and unwilling to pursue any further research on these artifacts. One thing I can say is that the money I spent on Burrows Cave artifacts were a worthwhile investment. I learned much about the controversy and take pride in knowing that I was able to definitively prove at least one, and likely a total of four of the Burrows Cave artifacts are modern fakes.

The Bat Creek Stone

I MET PHIL AND LESLIE KALEN after they contacted the archaeology department at Cambridge University in the UK. A professor of archaeology had apparently heard one of my lectures on the Kensington Rune Stone, and passed along my email address. The Kalens then sent images of the runes they found in a cave on their property in Morristown, Tennessee. After reviewing their photographs, I instantly got excited. The carvings were definitely runes. The only way to figure out what the story was to go to Knoxville.

On August 23, 2008, I met Leslie and Phil in Tennessee. Leslie explained the story of their cave. Shortly after purchasing the house four years ago, neighbors shared old stories about how there were caves under their home. At first, they laughed the stories off as rumors, but eventually curiosity got the best of them. They rented a backhoe, and Phil dug until he discovered the cave.

At their place, I could see mounds of dirt piled around a large depression only a few tens of yards in front of the house. The entrance to the cave was smack in the middle. Phil led me down a short ladder inside the cave. After descending several feet down we walked through a maze of limestone formations carved out by percolating groundwater over millions of years. It was a typical karst type of cave system very common in Tennessee.

The first inscription was the name W.T. Hopkins carved into the limestone wall about a hundred feet from the entrance. Phil led me up a ladder through a pass into another large chamber that went back about another hundred feet. The walls inside this chamber were black with soot, likely from campfires made by people we speculated could have been hiding out in the cave system. There were dozens of dated inscriptions going back as far as 1850. The runes were also carved into the walls of this chamber. As I laid eyes on them I was disappointed.

In addition to the runes, I found four different swastikas and "Hitler" carved into the walls. One of the swastikas was right next to the runes that were also modern and appeared to have been made by the same hand. Even though the inscriptions turned out to be modern, I really enjoyed crawling around in the "Kalen Cave System."

After crawling out of the caves, I sat down with Leslie and Phil and gave my opinion about the carvings. Although disappointed, they clearly understood what they had. Leslie then shared her conversations with the archaeologists who had visited the cave a few weeks prior to my visit and recalled an interesting comment made by one of them after they had reviewed the cave carvings. Jan Smit, head of archaeology at the University of Tennessee, had told Leslie, "If you'd like to see a fake, come to UT and see the Bat Creek Stone."

I knew about the artifact and asked them if they knew what it was. They didn't. Knowing Leslie was Cherokee I thought she'd be interested to know about this inscribed stone discovered in one her tribe's burial mounds in 1889.

The Bat Creek Stone was discovered by Mr. John W. Emmert in an undisturbed grave mound, number three of three mounds found together along the Little Tennessee River near the mouth of Bat Creek on February 15, 1889. Emmert was working on behalf of the Smithsonian Institution's Bureau of Ethnology's Mound Survey Project and reported to his immediate supervisor, Cyrus Thomas, who originally identified the inscription as Paleo-Cherokee. The Bat Creek artifacts sat in the archives in obscurity until 1964, when the inscription

In August of 2008, Phil and Leslie Kalen followed up on rumors and rented a backhoe and discovered the previously sealed entrance to a cave filled with late nineteenth- and twentieth-century inscriptions in the front yard of their Morristown home. (Wolter, 2008)

was noticed by Chicago patent attorney, Henriette Mertz. The artifact had been published up-side down by the Smithsonian Institution, when Mertz turned it around, she believed the characters to be Phoenician.[51]

In 1971, the inscription was found to be a Roman era Paleo-Hebrew Judean text by Dr. Cyrus Gordon (1908 to 2001), who was an American scholar of Near Eastern cultures and ancient languages. In his 1971 book, *Before Columbus: Links Between the Old World and Ancient America*, Gordon wrote, ". . . a Hebrew inscription of Roman date (probably around A.D. 135) was scientifically excavated in Tennessee and published by Cyrus Thomas in the *Twelfth Annual Report of the Bureau of Ethnology to the Secretary of the Smithsonian Institution 1890-1891.* Thomas, without understanding the nature of the writing, published the text upside down on page 394 and quite erroneously surmised it to be in the Cherokee script."[52]

Gordon went on to write, "Though the priority of the discovery goes to Dr. Henriette Mertz, it was Dr. Joseph B. Mahan Jr' s (director of Education and Research at the Columbus, Georgia, Museum of Arts and Crafts), independent rediscovery that led to the results." ". . . that if the Bat Creek Stone is turned right side up, the script is plainly Canaanite."[53]

Gordon translated the text as, "Year 1: Comet (=Messiah) of the Jews. This confirms the Jewish nature of the inscription obviously implied by the very name YHWD. The letter-forms may be dated about A.D. 100 with enough leeway to cover refugees from Judea fleeing from the Romans during the First (A.D. 66-70) or Second (A.D. 132-135) rebellions."[54]

Other artifacts found with the inscribed stone encased in what is thought to be a bundle of birch bark was lost at the time of Emmert's excavation. The bundle was found under the skull of the only body of nine aligned with its head to the south. The other eight bodies were aligned with their heads to the north.

Other artifacts found with the inscribed stone included bone and wood tools, red ochre stones, likely used for face paint, and two brass bracelets.

I explained to Leslie and Phil that upon learning of Gordon's Hebrew translation, the Smithsonian quickly jumped in claiming the inscription was a fake, and, many decades after his death, placed the blame on Emmert as being the forger. Leslie especially was bothered by not only the seemingly baseless fraud claim about the inscription, but was even more put-off by the way Emmert had been thrown under the bus by the Smithsonian. Leslie then explained that her father, Donald Rose, was a senior elder with the Eastern Band of Cherokee Indian and that she would ask him about the stone and what he might know.

It turned out Don was unaware of the Bat Creek Stone as was the tribe. During one of our conversations with members of the tribe another elder, Bob Blankenship, said, "That's another thing they didn't tell us about." They all agreed they wanted to pursue testing the stone and passed a resolution at the Tribal Council to submit a formal request to the Smithsonian to allow me to perform a geological examination of the artifact.

A few weeks prior to the Cherokee's request, History Channel also put a request in to the Smithsonian to have me perform a similar examination in spite of my insistence they wait and let the Cherokee make the request. Committee Films was in the midst of making another documentary entitled, *Who Really Discovered America,* and planned to include the Bat Creek Stone controversy.

As expected, in January of 2010, the Smithsonian refused the History request to examine the artifact, citing the fact it was a sacred funerary object

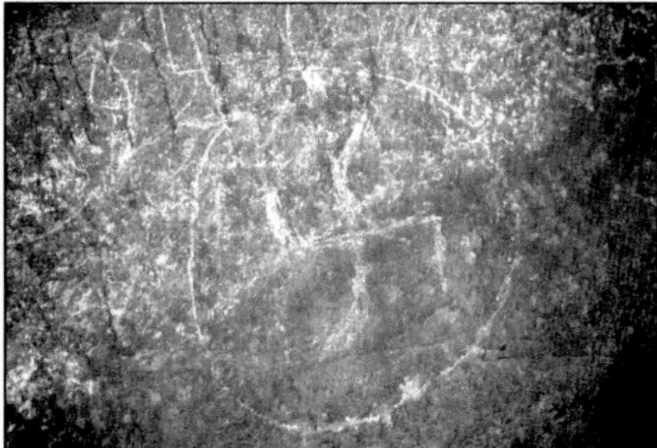

The inscriptions carved in the Kalen Cave dated from 1850, James McClaren, (left) to swastikas dated to 1947 (right). (Wolter, 2008)

The first known photograph of the inscribed stone appeared in the 1890-1891 *Annual Report of the Bureau of Ethnology* on page 394. The inscription is shown up-side down for Hebrew, and the two vertical scratches now on the stone, are not present in the lower right hand corner.

and they were entrusted with the artifact, ". . . on behalf of the Cherokee." This turned out to work to the Cherokee's benefit, for what could the Smithsonian say now other than to approve their request?

This marked the first victory toward learning the truth about this artifact. I then made plans to travel to the McClung Museum at the University of Tennessee, in Knoxville, to examine the artifact they had on indefinite loan from the Smithsonian Institution. I planned to bring my microscopic equipment along to examine the artifact for half a day and then spent the afternoon on the university's scanning electron microscope (SEM) to confirm the chemical make-up of the stone. On May 26, 2010, I received a call from the archaeology department that the SEM was not working properly and that I didn't need to come. Sensing something suspicious, I told the person, "That's no problem. I'll just spend the whole day examining the artifact under my microscope and will come again in a few weeks to do the SEM work."

On May 28, 2010, I arrived at the McClung Museum at 9:00 A.M. where I met up with three women who were serving as witnesses for the Cherokee, Barbara Duncan, Ph.D., who served as the Education director at the Museum of the Cherokee Indian on the Reservation, Sharon Littlejohn, who served as witness for Chief Michael Hicks, and Leslie Kalen Rose, serving as witness for her father and tribal elder Donald Rose.

The people present representing the university and the Smithsonian were Jefferson Chapman Ph.D., senior archaeologist at UT, another archaeologist, and a university registrar. After the artifact had been officially handed over to me by Dr. Mason, I set up my equipment for the examination. While setting up I noticed that people in the room had distinctly split themselves up in a predictable fashion, the three archaeologists on one side of the room and the three women

Inside mound #3 of the Bat Creek complex John Emmert found nine bodies. Seven were aligned shoulder to shoulder in the northern half of the mound with their heads to the north. Two more were discovered in the south-west part of the mound, one with its head to the north, the other with its head to the south. The Bat Creek Stone and other artifacts were found inside a birch bark bundle under the skull of the only body with its head pointing south. (Bureau of Ethnology, Twelfth Annual Report, Figure 272)

representing the Cherokee on the other. Whether intentional or not, I couldn't help but chuckle at the awkwardness of the situation.

At this point, I said to Jeff Chapman, "Hey, Jeff, come over here and sit down. We're going to do this together." To Jeff's credit, he came right over and sat down next to me and took serious interest. We started with the back side of the artifact that had been clearly labeled and numbered by Emmert. The first observation of note was a prominent scratch near one end of stone that was noticeably deeper on the end closest to the center and then trailed off the edge. This groove

The back side of the Bat Creek Stone has the original Smithsonian (Institution) identification names and numbers. Virtually all of the approximately 1-2 mm thick iron oxide-rich weathering rind has peeled off exposing the light brown-colored, un-weathered iron-cemented clayey siltstone. Only a few remnants survive along the top and bottom edges along with a small arrowhead-shaped portion on the lower right side. The scratch made by Emmert with the metal prod at the time of the excavation is on the far right. (Wolter, 2010)

This inscribed stone was found under the skull of one of nine bodies inside a burial mound at the mouth of Bat Creek where it flows into the Little Tennessee River by the Smithsonian's John Emmert, on February 15, 1889. (Wolter, 2010)

was consistent with the gouge made by Emmert, who wrote, "I punched it on the rough side with my steel rod in probing before I came to the skeletons."[55]

Jeff agreed with my interpretation of the prod scratch and seemed to enjoy the microscopic examination. When we turned the stone over to the inscription side, the surface was completely different. The dark-brown of the iron-oxide-rich weathering rind was nearly intact, and just as Emmert noted when he first described the inscribed side of the artifact, the surface was indeed polished.

The clear and distinct inscribed characters jumped off the surface of the stone. Eight characters were clearly visible and arranged in a line with only part of the final character on the far left edge present where the stone had apparently been broken. A ninth character was present that looked like a capital "T" with two horizontal bars, and a dot on the right side of the vertical line. We also noticed two additional characters in the upper left area above the nine previously noted. I spent several minutes examining and photographing each of the nine characters that all exhibited broad, rounded grooves with rounded edges. The once sharper edges and likely "V"-shaped grooves had been rounded from polishing and extensive weathering in the wet mound.

We then turned our attention to the two parallel scratches that were noticeably thinner than the other nine characters. I zoomed into the grooves with the microscope and immediately noticed something was different. The bottom of the grooves was filled with silty clay with a fracture pattern reminiscent of finger grooves made in wet beach sand. Suddenly it hit me "I get it now."

Jeff had been watching closely. He got it too.

These two grooves still had the silty clay in the grooves made when someone scratched the surface of the stone with a sharp instrument. The critical thing is these grooves were not present in the first photographs taken of the stone some time before 1891, or in Emmert's sketch made in February of 1889. This was in sharp contrast to the original nine characters that had none of the silty clay deposits due to extensive weathering that had removed it eons ago. What was eerily ironic was the clay-filled scratches had been made by someone when the artifact was in the custody of the Smithsonian Institution and turned out to be the key evidence to my determining authenticity. At this point I turned to the three women and said, "Well, ladies, it looks like you have a genuine artifact."

They all smiled and seemed genuinely happy. After finishing my work and thanking Jeff and his colleagues, I told them I'd be back in a few weeks to complete the SEM work.

My second flight to Knoxville would be easier since I didn't have to bring the microscope. The morning I was to leave, the same person at UT called and said, "The SEM is acting up again so you don't need to come."

Without hesitating I said, "I'm coming." Sure enough, when I arrived in the SEM lab in the Science and Technology building the next morning, we were told the machine was working fine.

David Joy, head of the Science and Technology Department, asked me about the artifact. I quickly told the Bat Creek story. After a few minutes he said, "Possible first-century Hebrew? Well, this is important."

I agreed. Then we went to work verifying the chemical make-up of the stone and took numerous high magnification photographs. The trips to the University of Tennessee were a success and set the stage for the next step, which was now in the hands of the Eastern Band of Cherokee—asking the Smithsonian for the jawbones so DNA testing could be performed.[56]

Once again Don and Bob needed to appear before the tribal council and asked me to join them and present my geological findings. On October 27, 2010. Leslie and I drove to the reservation. I first presented my geological findings. Bob and Don followed with statements of support for my work and for requesting the bones. Later the council voted in favor of the request, and a letter was sent to the Smithsonian. None of us really believed the Smithsonian would turn over the remains, and after three months of delays and excuses our suspicions were confirmed; they said they couldn't find the bones.

After our exciting day on the reservation, Leslie and I set off for the site where the Bat Creek inscription was discovered. The area was mostly wooded with tall hills and only a few homes scattered amongst the countryside. We hiked along a trail leading to the reservoir that had flooded the Little Tennessee River decades ago.

As we approached the water's edge near the spot on the topographic map marking the approximate location of the mound now underwater, the open tall forest suddenly turned into lush green leafy vines of the foreign vining plant species called Kudzu. The terrain was completely barren of trees, choked off by the invasive plant creating an eerie landscape. We saw no bedrock outcrops except right at the water's edge. The rock was a very soft, silty clay-stone with areas on the surface covered with a reddish-brown iron oxide crust.

On the hike back to the car we found one small outcropping of the same bedrock that allowed me to collect a sample. Leslie asked me if this could have been the source rock for whoever carved the Bat Creek Stone. While it was impossible to know with certainty, I told her in my opinion the rock could very well have come from nearby.

The Bat Creek Stone saga continued to unfold in July of 2011, when Don Rose again went before the Tribal Council to ask their support for a resolution to draft a letter demanding the Smithsonian return the stone, and all the artifacts found with it, to the Eastern Band of Cherokee Indian. The tribe had had enough and wanted the artifacts returned where they would be permanently displayed in their museum on the reservation.[57]

At this same time, a two-person camera crew stopped at the McClung Museum to shoot the artifact still being displayed as a fake and upside down!

At the University of Tennessee, archaeologist Dr. Gerald Schroedl, who believed the stone was a fake, was interviewed. He claimed that anyone who believed the stone was authentic was racist, essentially saying Native Americans were incapable of building such complex mound structures and only visitors from other continents could have built them. At one point in the interview, Schroedl also believed the excavation conducted by Emmert was questionable. "He could have this thing (Bat Creek Stone) in his pocket for all I know, and when he calls up Cyrus Thomas he says, 'Oh, yeah, we found this in the mound.'" He added, "With regard to the bracelets that were supposedly found, again the issue is context. Were they really found in the mound? Who knows?"

After presenting the results of my Bat Creek Stone examination to the Tribal Council of the Eastern Band of Cherokee Indians on October 27, 2010, I posed for a photograph with senior tribal elders Bob Blankenship and Don Rose, who hugs his daughter Leslie Kalen. Blankenship and Rose sponsored my presentation and then made a formal request for the tribe to support asking the Smithsonian Instituiton to return the human remains found with the stone for DNA testing.

When asked his opinion would be if the conveniently missing human remains from the Bat Creek mound were located and tested for DNA and found to be of first-century European descent, his response was, "Well, I would then assume that Emmert had found 2,000-year-old Middle Eastern bones and planted them," as if Emmert knew that in 100 years DNA technology would become standard practice.

Whether Schroedl realized it or not, that statement called into question every archaeological dig the Smithsonian Institution had ever done. Academics cannot pick and choose after the fact which archaeological digs they consider to be legitimate depending upon what artifacts are found. This besmirched the reputation of John Emmert decades after his death apparently for the sake of maintaining the academic historical status quo of no pre-Columbian contact by Europeans in North America.

The next day when Don Rose and Chief Michael Hicks were also interviewed and asked about this, they both said, "We just want to know the truth about our history."

On August 4, 2011, the Eastern Band of Cherokee allowed the proceedings in the tribal council to be filmed and the positive vote for the demand letter to the Smithsonian was unanimous. Before the letter was even signed by Chief Michael Hicks, news of the letter trickled back to the Smithsonian who then stated they would not stand in the way.

In the meantime, Leslie Kalen, personally offended by how Emmert was accused of forgery and had his reputation trampled, decided to take action. She

On October 28, 2011, Leslie Kalen and I hiked through the eerie terrain created by the vining invasive species kudzu that had choked off the native forests along the water's edge near the now drowned site where the Bat Creek Stone was discovered in 1889. (Wolter, 2011)

The other artifacts found with the Bat Creek Stone in 1889 were photographed in 1970 and appeared in the January, 1971 issue of *Argosy* magazine. This is also the earliest known image that shows the two vertical scratches in the upper left area that are not present in the first known photo published in 1890. (Wolter, 2011)

researched Emmert's background and located several direct descendants who knew nothing about his discovery of the Bat Creek Stone or the accusations made against Emmert. With the help of her friend James Dodson, Leslie learned that John W. Emmert was a Southern Confederate who fought and was wounded twice during the Civil War. He was also a highly respected constable and a Freemason with the Shelby Lodge #162. There was a strict vetting process one must go through to become both a member of law enforcement and a Mason.

Leslie's research and connection with Emmert's descendants led to a ceremony in Bristol, North Carolina, where she personally financed the placement of a new granite obelisk tombstone for Emmert on November 19, 2011.

Leslie Kalen (far left in black hoop dress) and James Dodson (second from left) pose with the John W. Emmert Family at the dedication ceremony in Bristol, Virginia/Tennessee, on November 19, 2011. (Wolter, 2011)

Tucson Lead Artifacts

After having been involved with pre-Columbian research in North America for over a decade, I thought I had seen it all. I am almost embarrassed to admit that I had never heard of the Tucson Lead Artifacts prior to November of 2011. I was introduced to a new set of mysterious artifacts that the academicians had written off decades ago. By chance, Maria Awes with Committee Films was searching the Internet for interesting artifacts and sites they could film me examining as part of preparation for a pitch for what would become the television series *America Unearthed,*™ with me as the host. We were already planning to film the recently discovered runic inscription in the Mustang Mountains south of Tucson, when Maria found the lead artifacts right in Tucson proper at the Arizona Historical Society.

On November 10, 2011, I had the opportunity to review a cache of thirty-two lead artifacts found buried five to six feet deep in caliche-encased alluvial gravel outside of Tucson, Arizona. The lead artifacts, found in the 1920s, include eight crosses (six are two-piece crosses riveted together), seven ceremonial swords, fifteen spears, spear heads and shafts, one clay plaque, and one lead fan-shaped baton.

We were at the Historical Society primarily to film, but I got some time with the artifacts. Prior to that, I discussed the artifacts with Don Burgess, a journalist who wrote a lengthy article in the spring 2009 issue of *Journal of the Southwest*. I had read Don's article and other background material about the artifacts prior to our meeting. It was like "déjà vu all over again" as Yogi Berra so eloquently put it. Don had concluded the artifacts were fakes and like so many others determined to prove their case, his arguments were riddled with issues.

An introductory article, *Invented and Manufactured History*, by Raymond H. Thompson, director emeritus, Arizona State Museum and editorial advisor for the journal, leading into Don's paper, clearly was designed to bias the reader. Then in the article, Don didn't score many points with me when he interjected with his take on the Kensington Rune Stone. He intimated there was new research writing, ". . . some believers in the 'first famous rune stone' claimed they had new proof, but the doubters concluded it was another hoax."

As much as I wanted to, I didn't bring the Kensington Stone up during our discussion on camera. What I did bring up were issues I had with his "reasons for rejecting the artifacts as authentic."[58]

The geological features I observed during my initial review of the lead artifacts in November of 2011 were interesting enough for a closer look. Katherine Reeve, the department head of the library and archives, was extremely gracious, and when I asked to come back with the digital microscope to examine a few select pieces, she went out of her way to accommodate my request.

On January 31, 2012, I showed up at the museum where Kate was waiting for me. She led me into her office where the six artifacts I had requested to look at were waiting. I set up the digital microscope and went to work. After collecting images and data of the artifacts, I made a copy of a 352-page report written by Thomas W. Bent in 1964 entitled *The Tucson Artifacts: A narrative report of the discovery, the unearthing, and the failure of the subsequent investigations to solve this mystery*. Bent's report had never been published and while many of the facts listed are the same, it presents a completely different perspective on the artifacts than Don Burgess's article.

In Bent's Chapter 13, "Publicity Promotes Controversy," he reproduces an article published by the *Arizona Daily Star* in December of 1925, entitled, "Leaden Relicts May Mean New Chapter of History: Roman Jews in 'Terra Calalus,' America, From 775 A.D. to 900; Announcement of the Discovery of Leaden Artifacts Bearing Inscriptions in Latin and Hebrew" by Clifton J. Sarle, Ph.D., and Mrs. Laura Coleman Ostrander.

This article does a great job of describing the facts and context surrounding the discovery, the subsequent excavations, the inscriptions, and the controversy at the time. I have purposefully omitted the sections of this announcement that dealt with the speculative aspects of the inscriptions, such as who might have been responsible for carving them, and present here what I believe is the relevant factual information.

> Leaden artifacts of great antiquity have been unearthed near Tucson, Arizona, during the past year. All of the objects bear significant drawings, a number of them inscriptions in Latin and two in both Hebrew and Latin. Many dates also are given. The story revealed opens a new chapter in the pre-Columbian history of America. It is a record of colonization in America by Europeans, in 775 A.D., and a brief chronicle of their life here, covering a period of 125 years.
>
> To many, on first consideration, the claim that the Atlantic was crossed and America colonized by Mediterranean people 717 years before the coming of Columbus will seem preposterous. But to others, however startling as this discovery may seem, it will appear quite in line with the volume of evidence gleaned in recent years in various fields of investigation, which points convincingly to Old and New World maritime intercommunication back even into centuries B.C.

Cross Found Near Tucson

A chance find by Mr. Charles E. Manier of a pair of large leaden crosses protruding from a gravel stratum near the base of a low-lying bluff which flanks the westerly side of the floodplain of the Santa Cruz River for several miles below Tucson, was the beginning of this most important discovery. The Silverbell highway follows approximately the boundary line between this bluff and the floodplain, and one traveling this road passes a number of old lime kilns, long abandoned, which were built into the face of the bluff.

On September 13, 1924, Mr. Manier, accompanied by his father, who was visiting him from California, was returning along this road from an auto ride, when, at the suggestion of the latter, they stopped to examine one of these kilns. This kiln, like the others, was constructed by digging a large well-like pit in the edge of a bluff, which was then lined with adobe blocks and faced with brick. A trench was then excavated leading inward to the base of the kiln where through an orifice the lime, when burnt, was removed. Rain-wash of the many seasons had exposed the ends of these crosses on one side of the cut and led to Mr. Manier's fortunate discovery.

Inscriptions Discovered

When discovered, these crosses were fastened together in such a manner as to appear as one, and it was only while washing the dirt from them after carrying them to his home in Tucson, and a neighbor had called his attention to an apparent line of division running around the side of the cross, that they were separated. It was then found that they had been fastened together by leaden pegs. The opposed faces were smoothly finished and coated with a wax-like substance, the removal of which revealed carved inscriptions in Latin, drawings and dates.

On January 31, 2012, I had an opportunity to examine five of the Tucson lead artifacts with my digital microscope which included #1A (cross), #13 (ceremonial fan), #18 (serpent entwined circle cross), #20 (crescent cross) and #12 (sword with lizard effigy). (Wolter, 2012)

The dates and facts, set forth by translation, aroused Mr. Manier's keenest interest, and he determined to excavate in hopes of finding other material that might add to these astonishing statements and prove or disprove the antiquity indicated by the dates. A few weeks later he joined forces with Mr. Thomas W. Bent (1896 to 1972) and the work was begun. Later, these gentlemen invited C.J. Searle, until recently and for eight years professor of geology at the University of Arizona, Tucson, to advise them as the best method of conducting the excavation and to make a study of the field relations of their find, including, if possible, a stratigraphic correlation with the prehistoric aboriginal culture of the region, to which he had given some study. Shortly thereafter, at Dr. Searle's suggestion, Mrs. Laura Coleman Ostrander, a teacher of history in the Tucson public schools was invited to collaborate with him in the preparation of both popular and technical articles on their discovery. This article, therefore, should be regarded merely as an announcement.

Excavation Carried Forward

Excavation thenceforward was conducted in such a manner as to maintain at all times, as nearly as possible a vertical face from top to bottom in the soil and to a depth a little below the level at which it had been determined the objects occur. In this way objects encountered as excavation progressed would be free from falling earth and most likely to be immediately sighted, lessening the chance of injury by the workman. This method also provided for the examination of many of the objects while still imbedded in the soil, and the study of the uninterrupted full five or six feet of overlying soil, the taking of measurements, photographing and the calling of competent and authenticated witnesses as to the conditions under which the objects were found.

Intermittently, as funds have been available, the excavation has been carried on. Today the excavation is roughly triangular in outline. The base of the triangle, 80 feet long, begins at the side of the highway and its apex extends the same distance back into the gravel bluff, well past the lime kiln. An old land surface gradually rising towards the back of the excavation, and on which these objects were strewn as they fell from the hands of man over one thousand years ago, has been uncovered. The

This view looking north of the excavation site along Silverbell Road shows the lime kiln in the left center and was taken on April 5, 1925. (Photo courtesy of the Arizona Historical Society)

finds include several other crosses, a paddle-shaped object (ceremonial) and a number of heavy two-edged swords and short hand spears. A number of the weapons are heavily scarred and few are broken as though done in combat, and the general disposition of these finds portrays the confusion of a pitch battle. How much additional material will be found as exploration uncovers more of this old land surface cannot be told. Perhaps we may find the ashes of their fires or the place where they smelted the ore for the lead of their crosses.

Imbedded in Caliche

The surface on which these finds were made was buried from three and a half to six feet in depth, increasing gradually as excavation penetrated the bluff. The objects themselves are generally found firmly imbedded in a lime-cemented gravel, often so resistant that objects have to be removed with a pick. The material overlying in general is coarse, angular and poorly assorted and showing very indistinct stratification. Many water-worn limestone boulders, often too large for a man to lift,

Charles E. Manier holds one of the swords found at the excavation site he discovered on September 13, 1924. (Courtesy of the Arizona Historical Society)

Latin inscriptions and three profiles are carved onto the smooth inner surface of artifact #1A. (Wolter, 2011)

lie in a plane just above the relics. This seems a well-defined feature, which may be traced for some distance, showing in the sides of the dry flaring washes, which deeply dissect a plain bounded at its lower edge by the bluff, through which the floodwaters from the flanks of the Tucson Mountains are discharged to the channel of the Santa Cruz. At the top of the section is a well-defined darker stratum often fifteen inches or more thick, a true soil, in which scant vegetation of the dry slopes finds root. Immediately below the soil and formed by evaporation of lime-charged groundwater, is a thick zone solidly cemented by deposition of lime and of white color, known locally by the Mexican name 'Caliche,' by geologists as desert limestone. In fact, cementation of the subsoil is the rule and has greatly retarded the work of excavation.

Unbroken Ground

The depth at which these objects are buried, the firm cementation of the gravel stratum in which they occur, the unbroken and undisturbed condition of the caliche shell and overlying soil, form a seal which nature has placed upon these artifacts, not to be counterfeited, and has remained unbroken through the centuries which the dates incised upon these cruciform tablets by the old scribe, who signed himself 'O. L.,' indicate. The covering of these objects was brought about by rain and stream action bearing material from higher to lower ground under the impelling force of gravity. Subsequent to the burial of these objects, torrential rains have done much to modify these slopes and have carved them into many minor reliefs.

Dr. C.J. Searle, Ph.D., holding the spear between John S. Bent (left) and his brother Thomas W. Bent, was a former professor of geology, who advised them on proper methodology for conducting their field excavations. (Photo courtesy of the Arizona Historical Society)

An episode in the history of the region, possibly later, perhaps antecedent and surviving for several centuries after the passing of these Roman Jews, was the coming of a race of people who left the litter of broken pottery near the watering hole. Certainly at this particular locality the aborigines came much later. Fragments of their pottery have been found upon the recent surface scattered in the last formed stratum, the soil even covering the top of the bluff. The underlying strata, the lowest of which concerns us as bearing the artifacts may in their arrangement and order of formation be compared to the layers of a cake. The bottom layer is laid down first and the top last and the frosting (or soil) added last of all. This pottery is in the main of the type designated by archaeologists, from the paints used in the ornamentation, 'red-on-gray,' and there is also some of a later type found here, designated 'black-on-white." *These potteries will be recognized by all archaeologists as pre-Columbian and lying as they do at a stratigraphically high horizon, and overlapping this site, is another proof of the greater antiquity of the leaden artifacts.*

Could Not Be Forged

The great antiquity of these leaden objects, as shown by the dates, and the unique combination of details, the outgrowth of the peculiar conditions obtaining in the western Old World during the early Middle Ages, in the aboriginal setting of America, could not well be forged or duplicated, and the field relations, which have been carefully studied, confirm the genuineness of the record carried by these artifacts as beyond the shadow taken to the excavation and shadow of a doubt. Furthermore, competent witnesses have been taken to the excavation and shown, many of them numbered among the scientific faculty of the University of Arizona, and they have uniformly expressed themselves as convinced of the genuineness of Mr. Manier's discovery.

Upon reading Bent's report, I was struck by his commitment to detail in the documentation and the care that went into the excavations of the first twenty-seven artifacts. Credit for this belongs to C.J. Sarle, Ph.D., who advised Bent and Manier on the proper methodology for documenting finds as their excavations progressed. The data collected is better than some professional reports I've read. I was also astounded at how Don Burgess and other skeptics could be so flippant in their conclusions that the artifacts were fraudulent when the provenance of their discovery was so well documented with consistent and clear facts.

The following is a chronological listing of the thirty-two artifacts collected and includes the date discovered, who found it, the type of artifact, and the depth from the surface where it was found:

ARTICLE	DATE DISCOVERED	DISCOVERER	TYPE	DEPTH
#1	September 13, 1924	Charles Manier	Cross	65"
#2	September 14, 1924	Professor Rupper	Caliche Tablet	67"
#3	November 28, 1924	Thomas Bent	Cross	65"
#4	November 30, 1924	Charles Manier	Cross	58"
#5	December 5, 1924	Manier & Bent	Cross	58"
#6	January 24, 1925	Mexican Worker	Cross	66"
#7	January 24, 1925	Mexican Worker	Cross	66"
#8	February 13, 1925	Charles Manier	Sword	64"
#9	March 4, 1925	Group	Hollow Spear	54"
#10	March 27, 1925	Group	Solid Spear	59"
#11	March 28, 1925	Dr. A.E. Douglas	Sword	60"
#12	April 4, 1925	Manier & Bent	Sword	62"
#13	April 4, 1925	Manier & Bent	Fan	62"
#14	May 26, 1925	Charles Manier	Spear Head	58"
#15	May 26, 1925	Charles Manier	Broken Sword	42"
#16/23	July 10, 1925	Charles Manier	Broken Sword	Unknown*
#17	August 27, 1925	Antonio Corella	Broken Sword Tip	72"
#18	August 29, 1925	Antonio Corella	Serpent Cross	72"
#19/21	August 30, 1925	Mexican Worker	Spear/Shaft	72"
#20	September 1, 1925	Mexican Worker	Crescent Cross	72"
#21/19	September 2, 1925	L.A. Borquez	Spear/Shaft	72"
#22	September 2, 1925	Mexican Worker	Spear Head	72"
#23/16	September 18, 1925	Mexican Worker	Broken Spear	63"
#24	November 6, 1925	Placido Ochoa	Broken Sword	78"
#25/28	November 6, 1925	Ricardo Balancuela	Broken Spear	72"
#26	November 7, 1925	Mexican Worker	Sword	72"
#27	November 13, 1925	John Bent	Broken Spear Point	72"
#28/25	February 11, 1928	U of Arizona	Broken Spear	54"
#29	February 9, 1928	U of Arizona	Broken Spear Shaft	54"
#30	February 11, 1928	Dr. Gurdon Butler	Broken Spear Shaft	54"**
#31	March 3, 1928	Charles B. Conrad	Broken Spear	Unknown
#32	March 15, 1928	John S. Bent	Broken Handle	65"

* Found in debris when thrown on pile unnoticed by workers

** This artifact was the third piece of the broken spear that fits together with artifacts 25 & 28.

It became clear reading the background information and specifically, Thomas Bent's thorough report that, like so many other pre-Columbian mysteries in North America, aspects of the human element played the dominant role in the evaluation of the Tucson artifacts as opposed to hard science. The skeptics asserted themselves within days of Manier's initial discovery—the two halves of the cross he brought to the Arizona State Museum at the University of Arizona, where the date was translated to circa 800 A.D. by Frank Fowler of the Classics department.

On September 21, 1924, the discovery was first reported by the *Arizona Daily Star* where Fowler reportedly claimed the inscriptions were "poor and disjointed and that it was improbable that the tablets could be more than nine hundred years old." Upon reading this statement I felt that déjà vu again. Like the Kensington Rune Stone, early experts were quick to dismiss an artifact that likely had them baffled. Time and again, when faced with something that challenged their current knowledge base and the status quo, history demonstrated that scholars feel compelled to render an opinion whether they have factual support or not.

Even the University of Arizona, who independently worked the Silverbell Road site under the direction of Byron E. Cummings, former dean and professor of archaeology, from mid-January to March 9, 1928, would be a huge let-down for Bent and Manier.[59] After finding five artifacts during their time at the site, it took Cummings two years to submit the promised report and he never turned over any field notes or photographs to Bent and Manier.

This is eerily reminiscent of the promise made to the Runestone Museum by the Swedish investigation team when I traveled to Stockholm and left the Kensington Rune Stone for four months. One of the conditions for allowing them to investigate the artifact

Artifact #10 left a perfect mold in the caliche that encased it fifty-nine inches below the surface when it was excavated on March 27, 1925. (Photo courtesy of the Arizona Historical Society)

This close-up shows artifact #12 and #13 in situ prior to extraction on April 5, 1925. (Photo courtesy of the Arizona Historical Society)

was that, upon completion of their research, they would issue a final report. That report never materialized.

One story I have never shared during my early involvement with the Kensington Rune Stone, happened when I returned to Sweden to ensure the stone's safe return to Minnesota. After spending three months at the Historical Museum in Stockholm, it was brought north to the Hälsinglands Museum in Hudiksvall, Sweden, for a special one month exhibition. On the last day of my stay, the leader of the scientific investigation team, Runo Löfvendahl, came to Hudiksvall where he and I spent seven hours alone looking at the artifact.

During that time, we discussed the geological aspects of the stone, and he agreed with what I had documented in my report. Upon completing our examination, we went down to the lobby of the museum and wrote down our findings on a sheet of paper. After listing the geological points we'd agreed to, I drew a line at the bottom, signed my name, and then slid the paper over to Runo and said, "Sign it." With tears welling in his eyes, he looked at me and said, "I can't."

As frustrating as it has been dealing with academics both in Sweden and the United States, it must have been very difficult for a seemingly honest person like Runo to have to sneak away from his colleagues to feel comfortable conducting intelligent research. This experience convinced me there were larger negative forces at work in Scandinavia other than just problems of the human condition.

In another interesting parallel with the Kensington Rune Stone, the University of Arizona entered into an agreement with the Bent and Manier to purchase the artifacts upon satisfactory completion of their excavations at the discovery site for $16,000. In 1909-1910, the Minnesota Historical Society also reached a tentative agreement with then custodian of the artifact, Hjalmar Holand, to purchase the Kensington Rune Stone for $5,000 after an investigation conducted by Professor Newton H. Winchell. In both cases, the investigations were conducted, but, due in part to the negative opinions of people with limited knowledge of the facts, neither purchase was consummated.[60]

Thomas Bent's frustration with the academic community in general and the University of Arizona's involvement in the excavations is evident throughout his report and it's hard not to sympathize with him. Writing with the benefit of his intimate personal involvement, a comprehensive knowledge of the facts, and forty years of reflection, Bent comes across as credible with a sound and reasonable reflection of all aspects of the mysterious history of the artifacts. Bent laments at the unfounded negative opinions of "experts," most of who never personally saw the artifacts or the discovery site. He refutes criticism with relevant facts that contradict the unfounded claims with up to six-foot deep, undisturbed, caliche-encrusted alluvial deposits covering the artifacts as the factual rock of Gibraltar in this case.

In spite of the disappointing results of the University of Arizona digs lead by Byron Cummings, Bent was an ardent defender of the genuineness of the artifacts who responded to criticism from scholars in the East with the following quote that appeared in *The New York Times* on December 13, 1925: "Such an attitude is to be expected; the archaeologists in New York naturally want the last word in establishing the validity of the finds. I can safely say that any one of the men who have viewed the scene of the excavations will say again, as they have already, that the finds are genuine."

Regardless of these opinions there were a number of compelling geological facts I was able to document that are consistent with lengthy burial.

Geological Examination

The five artifacts I selected for closer examination were #1A, #12, #13, #18, and #20. These artifacts exhibited interesting secondary deposits of calcite and other minerals that filled in or covered parts or all of the carved lines in the lead. The back side of artifact #1A had a very rough surface with white secondary calcite deposits (caliche) within depressions in the metal intermittently scattered over the entire surface. Under magnification, sand grains of various sizes were present cemented onto the cross after burial. Several recessed areas on the back side also had fibrous green malachite, and deep-blue azurite, both copper carbonate minerals that form from the weathering of copper ores. The source copper was likely present as an impurity within the lead deposits originally smelted to make the artifacts, which then weathered out over time within the sand and gravel deposits the cross was discovered in. (See color section, Figures 8 & 9)

I wanted to take a closer look at the calcite deposits within the grooves of the carved lines on the surface of the other four artifacts (#12, #13, #18, and #20). Most grooves were filled with calcite deposits essentially the same as hard water scale deposits on leaky pipes. Under the proper conditions these deposits don't necessarily take a long time to form. However, in this case the artifacts had to first become buried within the sand and gravel before the process started. This process likely took at least many decades and most likely many centuries.

A group of people being shown the location of a find by a man crouching at the base of the caliche cemented wall of the excavation in February of 1928. (Photo courtesy of the Arizona Historical Society)

University of Arizona President, Byron Cummings, who was also a professor of archaeology, points to one of the artifacts still in place prior to extraction during excavations supervised by the University of Arizona, in February of 1928. (Photo courtesy of the Arizona Historical Society)

Two days after the second examination on February 2, 2012, I drove out to Silverbell Road to examine the lone surviving lime kiln and the discovery site where the artifacts were found. The lime kiln was situated roughly fifty feet off the road. As I walked around the kiln, I noticed layers of crushed limestone gravel and lime accumulated along the perimeter of the deteriorating brick chamber. The rust-red adobe bricks comprising the roughly eight-foot diameter circular chamber

On February 10, 2004, Runo Löfvendahl and the author (standing) examined the Kensington Rune Stone for seven hours at Halsinglands Museum in Hudisvall, Sweden. (Wolter, 2004)

where limestone was put into the kiln to be fired was crumbling, leaving a trail of debris on the slope leading into the old trench. I could imagine how Charles Manier had walked up the trench to the bottom of the lime kiln and found the first lead cross sticking out of the eroding cliché cemented sand and gravel bank.

I then drove northwest along Silverbell Road roughly one-quarter mile to the actual discovery site directly across the road from Christopher Columbus Park. David and I chuckled at the irony of the name of the park and its proximity to the artifacts' discovery site. We had also been told the area where the excavations took place in the 1920s had been bulldozed flat with a roughly fifteen-foot high sand and gravel bank for us to examine.

Studying a map of the area, I noticed the Santa Cruz River was only a hundred yards from where the artifacts were discovered. It makes sense this site would have been near a significant waterway.

At the exposed sand and gravel bank, I climbed to the top. The alluvial deposits were essentially the same as the hundreds of gravel pits in Minnesota, Iowa, Wisconsin, and Michigan where I've searched for Lake Superior agates over the past thirty years. We have some caliche cemented deposits but we have a lot less limestone and other carbonate rocks in our gravels than here. The dominant rock type comprising these gravels was limestone, which was the source of the secondary calcite cement.

The sequence of sand and gravel layers from the surface to the six-foot level was essentially the same as described by Thomas Bent and geologists who visited the excavation. The upper four feet was moderately cemented sand and gravel with pockets of loser material. The next roughly twelve-inch-thick layer below contained well-defined cross-bedded sand and gravel layers deposited during a heavy storm run-off event in the distant past. I was later asked about cross-bedding by my son, Grant. "If you have a foot of material deposited in one storm wouldn't it only take a half a dozen events to build up six feet of sand and gravel deposits?"

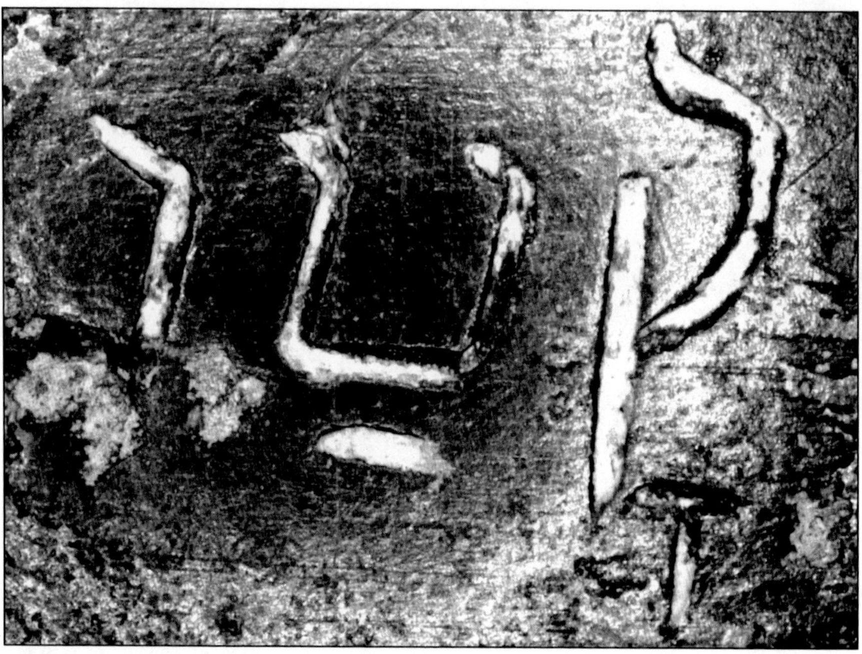

The grooves within the Hebrew characters on artifact #20 are partially filled with secondary calcite deposits (20X). (Wolter, 2012)

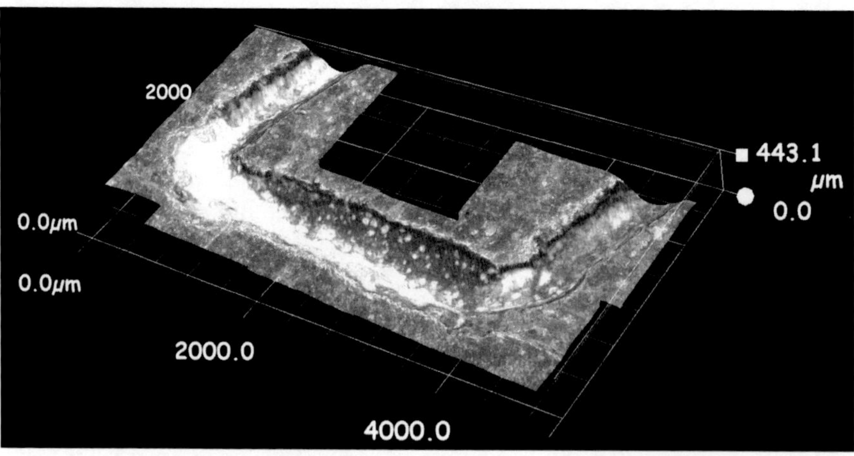

A closer view of the lower portion of the Hebrew "Tet" on artifact #20 shows minor amounts of white secondary calcite in the otherwise clean lead grooves (200X). (Wolter, 2012)

I answered, "No, it'd take a lot longer than that. The reason is after a stream deposits a foot of new gravel in one area, it'll move over and flow into an adjacent low spot until it fills up to the same level. A stream might take dozens of storm events to build up to the same level as the first cross-bedded layer before it flows over it again, depositing new material. That's why it's reasonable to have taken roughly twelve hundred years for the six feet of material to have been laid down over the artifacts."

After having twice reviewed the lead artifacts, the discovery site, and the lone remaining lime kiln along Silverbell Road, and after reading Thomas Bent's detailed report, I can respond to points, made at the time, of why the artifacts were fraudulent when the geological evidence alone made it clear they were indeed ancient:

1. Planting could be duplicated.
   There is no known evidence of planting other than the assertion made years after the fact that a reported hole behind one of the spears was made when "the forger" pushed the spear into the caliche and then slid it out slightly. This hearsay is not supported with photos taken at the time when the University of Arizona was in control of the dig. Further, carbonate cemented sediment like caliche would not allow such a hole to be made if a hard shaft were inserted into it. Hard caliche would resist penetration and poorly

A different area on artifact #20 shows grooves that are near to completely full of white secondary calcite that has also accumulated on the surface of the lead partially covering some of the grooves. (Wolter, 2012)

developed caliche would collapse, creating a large void, not a hole matching the exact shape of the spear shaft.

2. A cutting edge cannot be made of lead, and there is no known archaeological or historical evidence that weapons were ever made of lead.
3. The weapons show signs of having been modified with tools such as a rasp or pliers and a hammer.
4. One of the crosses and other artifacts weighs sixty-four pounds and is too heavy to have been carried through an arduous military campaign.
   All three of these assertions are based upon the incorrect premise that artifacts were used in battle. Nobody in their right military mind, today or in the past, would make a sword intended for battle out of lead. They are more than likely ceremonial objects making conclusions 2, 3, and 4 irrelevant.
5. The crosses and other artifacts were made of lead with composition similar to that of common pot metal.
   Here again, since they are likely ceremonial objects the lead composition of the artifacts is irrelevant. However, assays of the lead in the 1920s concluded that it was of a composition consistent with ore deposits within a few miles of the discovery site.
6. There is no evidence of burials or a battle in the area.
   Since they are not weapons intended for battle this conclusion is irrelevant.
7. In one instance a hole had been created in the vertical wall of the trench for the insertion of a lead shaft.

On February 2, 2012, I visited the lone remaining lime kiln along Silverbell Road in southwestern Tucson, Arizona. These lime kilns were constructed in the early 1880s to make lime for plaster and mortar for the construction of buildings. It was along the weathered trench leading the bottom of one of these kilns that Charles Manier found the first lead cross on September 13, 1924. (Wolter, 2011)

This is hearsay evidence and not consistent with the physical behavior of caliche sediments.

8. The inscriptions say nothing of any real meaning.

   The inscriptions include memorials to the dead among many other things. I find it hard to believe that anyone at the time really thought that memorials to the deceased were meaningless. Further, the fact the artifacts are genuine makes everything carved into them of extreme historical value.

9. Most of the inscriptions are identical to material in three common contemporary Latin grammars.

   My son, Grant Wolter, took it as a challenge to translate some of the Latin inscriptions using Internet translation programs. The messages he deciphered were not "meaningless," and in fact fascinating. He said several of the words could not be found in any of the translation programs. It turns out researchers in the past were also unable to find several words in the inscriptions.

10. The artifact site is part of a Pleistocene deposit, and anything under the surface would have to be at least 10,000 years old.

    The Pleistocene deposit geologists looked at was not the site where the artifacts were found. Natural caliche deposits can develop within decades under the right conditions and by association with the dated artifacts; it appears

At an exposed bank at the discovery site of the Tucson lead artifacts on February 2, 2012, the author points out the roughly one-foot thick layer of cross-bedded sand and gravel deposited during one heavy storm runoff event in the distant past. The lighter colored, massive layer below the cross-bedded layer is much harder due to the heavy buildup of secondary caliche. It was within this roughly six-foot deep caliche layer that the lead artifacts were excavated from. (Wolter, 2012)

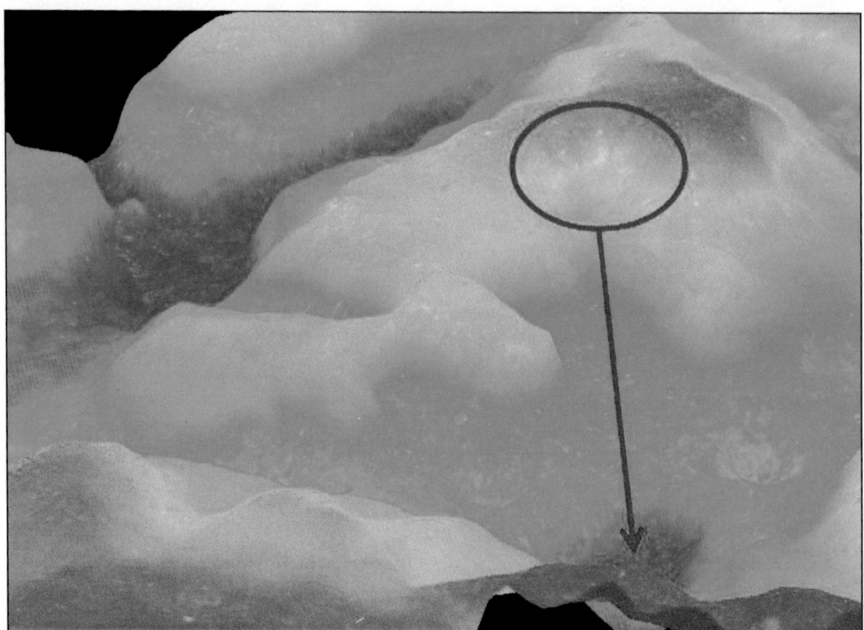

Figure 1. This head-on view shows where the carver's point-chisel struck the center of the plateau of rock in the "thorn" rune in the word "death" on line eight of the Kensingston Rune Stone, and then cut a channel downward when the chisel slipped. The chisel stopped after running into the previously carved groove comprising the loop of the character, creating a deeper hole. (25X) (Wolter, 2011)

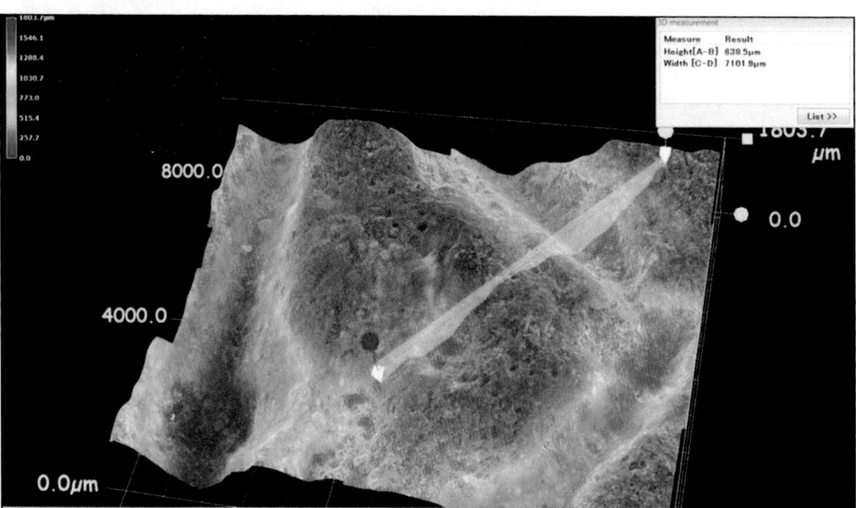

Figure 2. The 3D imaging capabilities of the Keyence microscope includes the ability to create cross-sectional profiles where desired. In this image across the upper part of the Dotted R shows the maximum depths and cross-sectional profile of both the pit and a carved line. (Wolter, 2011)

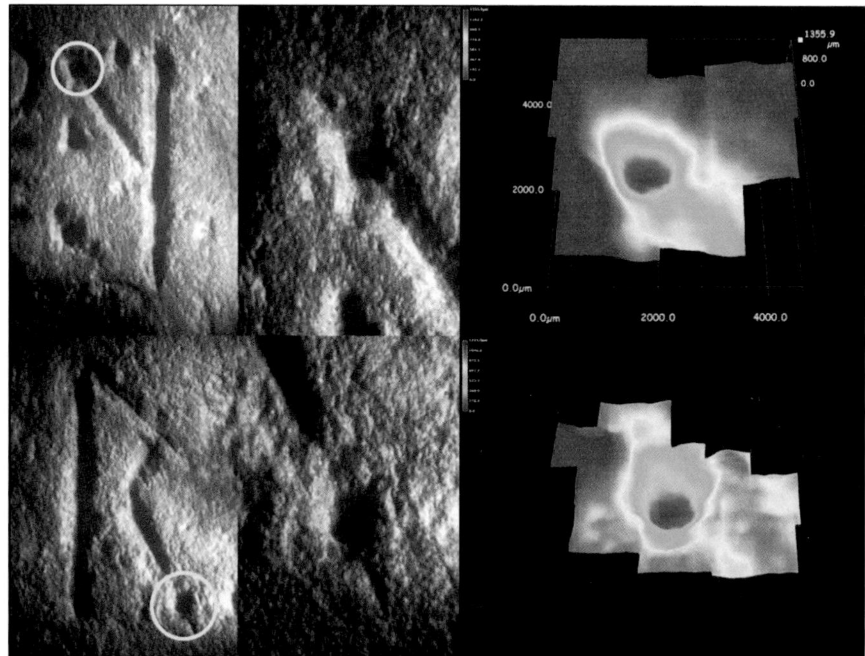

Figure 3 (composite).

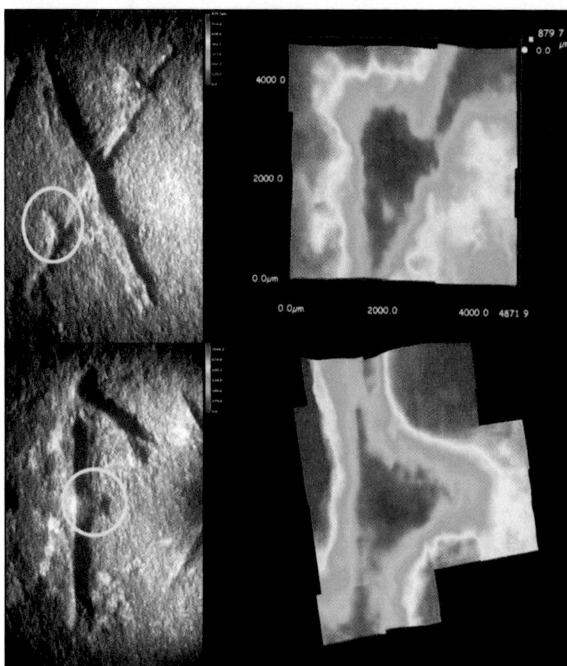

Figure 4 (composite).

The first four runic characters on the Kensington Rune Stone that were modified by the carver after the inscription was carved were the letters "g", "r", "a", and "l". These modifications added both directly onto and adjacent to specific carved lines were definitively confirmed to be manmade and therefore intentional by using 3D digital microscopy in September of 2012. The rainbow colors applied to the digital images on the right represent the yellow circled areas on pictures of these runes on the left taken by the author in 2002. These colors correlate to depth with red being the highest elevation documented and blue being the lowest. (Wolter 2002 [top]; Wolter, 2012 [bottom])

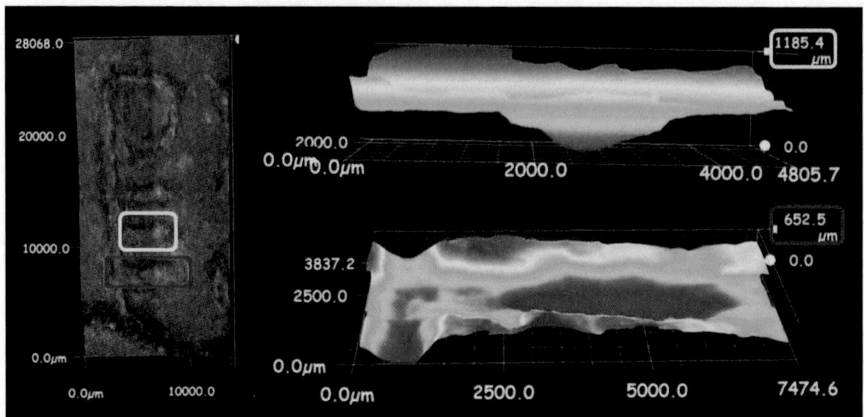

Figure 5 (composite). The punch mark made at the end of the second horizontal bar in the Pentadic number eight in the Kensington Rune Stone inscription was positively confirmed to be man-made using digital 3D microscopic technology in September of 2012. The cone shaped depression of the punch mark (top right) is nearly twice as deep (1185 microns) as the average maximum depth of the lines carved in the character (approximately 650 microns) and was clearly added after the inscription was carved (bottom right). (Wolter, 2012)

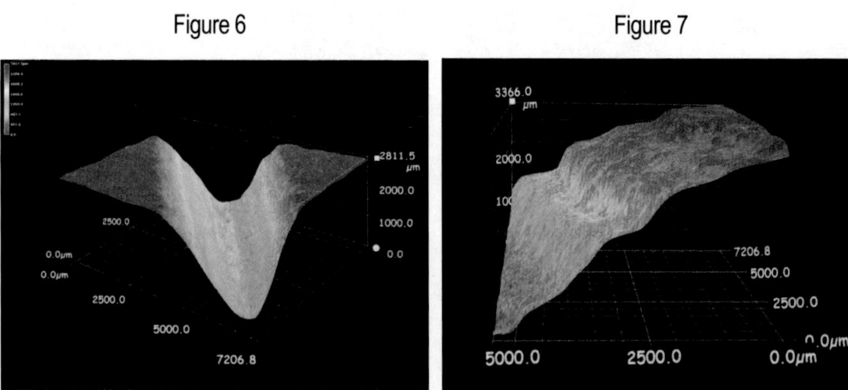

Figure 6

Figure 7

The new digital microscope visually illustrated a classic "v"-shape in the test groove carved into the same layer as the bull carving (Figure 6). This was in contrast to the broader, terraced profile along sedimentary layers of the carved grooves of the bull that was consistent with an advanced weathering profile and significant age (Figure 7). (Wolter, 2011)

Figure 8.

Figure 9.

A closer view of the malachite and azurite on the backside of Artifact #1A (top) shows its fibrous nature indicating it formed by the weathering of copper ore likely present within the lead over an extended period of time (like many centuries) while buried within the caliche-encrusted sand and gravel deposits. (Wolter, 2012)

Figure 10. As Enrico Altmann and I walked around the altar of Eglise Notre Dame Church, France, at exactly 9:00 a.m. on March 30, 2010, we noticed statues of Mary and child on a pedestal wrapped in red and gold robes and flanked by candleholders with red and white candles. On either side of the statues and candles were twin stone columns wrapped in red cloth and awash in vertical columns of sunlight passing though the upper level windows of the church. (Wolter, 2010)

Figure 11. In one of the stain-glass windows at Eglise Notre Dame Church, France, two of the banners held by men opposite Mary and Child have names clearly suggesting an Egyptian origin. On the left is "Osias," an apparent reference to the male God Osiris, and to the right is Amon R, an ode to the rising sun of the New Religion of Egypt that revered the rising verses the setting sun (Amen Ra) first introduced by the "heretic" pharaoh Akenaton? (Wolter, 2010)

Figure 12. On January 6, 2012, Bill Mann shared his Knights Templar Preceptor jewel with eight-pointed white cross with gold Maple leaves of Canada and the red-colored Cross of Lorraine in the center. On the red and white colored neck ribbon is a pin with a shield with black and white colors of the Cistercians, the ideological brethren of the Templars, and symbolic of the religious concept of "Dualism." Across the shield is the name of his Templar Preceptory (Commandary in the United States), Godfrey De Bouillon No 3. The red ribbon with gold trim held his 32 degree Scottish Rite Templar jewel. What Mann said was even more important to him was his Mide' win Shaman's bundle with cedar, sage, sweet-grass, tobacco, and the secret hidden "5th Element" of the medicine cloth which reflects the red of the Templars.(Wolter, 2012)

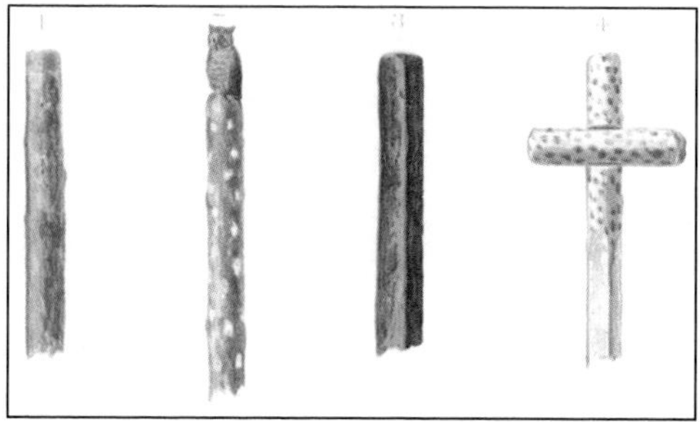

Figure 13. The four sacred posts of the Mide'wigan for the four degrees are placed in the ground and are four feet high and six to eight inches in diameter. The posts are round and painted the following colors: red with a green strip around the top (first degree), red with white spots with a stuffed owl on top (second degree), cut square verses round and painted black (third degree), and an equilateral cross. (Bureau of Ethnology, Seventh Annual Report, Plate XV)

Figure 14. There are several specific methods of face painting of the Mide' Shaman during the four degrees. The four colors used are various combinations of red, white, green, and black. In the third degree within the Mille Lacs Society, in Minnesota, circa 1830, the Mide' paint red and white spots on their faces. In this portrait, the Mide' Shaman wears a red-and-white striped scarf reminiscent of the stripes of the America flag. (Bureau of Ethnology, Seventh Annual Report, Plate VI)

Figure 15. The Cross of Lorraine originated from the True Cross with the scroll affixed near the top by the Romans who mockingly inscribed "Jesus of Nazareth, King of the Jews." This particular painting is a thirteenth century depiction found at Saint Catherine's Monastery at Mount Sinai.

Figure 16. A tilted Cross of Lorraine adorns the pillbox shaped "White Hat" worn in the Lodge by a 33rd-degree Freemason. This cross is the patron symbol of the Knights Templar that was bestowed upon them by King Baldwin II after they captured Jerusalem from the Saracens in 1099. The angle of the tilted cross is 22.5 degrees; the same angle of declination of the planet Venus at its maximum height in the sky as a morning and evening "star." (Internet)

Figure 17.

Figure 18.

Both Nabisco Corporation and the American Lung Association incorporate the Cross of Lorraine into their logos. The American Lung Association chose the symbol to represent their "crusade" against lung disease, but could there also be some kind of an association with the first century bloodline families? (Internet/Internet)

Figure 19. A red Cross of Lorraine (on a white background) tilted forty-five degrees from vertical is found in the logo of one of the biggest energy companies in the world; Exxon Energy. One interpretation of the red and white colored logo could be that the Cross of Lorraine symbolized the bloodline families that were brought across the Atlantic Ocean, symbolized by the blue band at the bottom, to the New Jerusalem to the west which is the direction the Cross of Lorraine is pointing. (Internet)

Figure 20. This painting of the Mandan Chief, Mato-Tope (Four Bears), was painted by Karl Bodmer, in 1833, and shows the sacred colors of both the Israelites and the Mandan of blue, red and yellow. (Wolter, 2012)

Figure 21.

Figure 22.

These two examples of the Washington Family crest incorporate red and white horizontal stripes and both red and white five-pointed stars. The crest with white stars was found on the Jenyn's Roll that dates to circa 1390. The crest with red stars appears in stained glass at Selby Abbey in Yorkshire and dates to the fifteenth century. Notice the "X's" conveniently located around the crest in the stained glass. (Internet/Internet)

Figure 23. On the evening of June 30, 2009, Donald Ruh showed us the artifacts I had watched him find in a videorecording he made inside a small cave on the side of a mountain in the Panther Mountain Impact Area. (Wolter, 2009)

Figure 24. The rounded chest of this ten-inch long ceramic jaguar vessel gives the impression of rounded ends when they are actually square. This style (to say nothing about the red color on a white background) is strikingly similar to the Knights Templar cross used by the order in the thirteenth century. The ceramic vessel was reportedly unearthed from a tomb in western Panama, in 2011, and based on the style of the cross was likely made between seven to eight hundred years ago. (Wolter, 2011)

Figure 25. The stained glass window at Hodnet Church, in Shropshire, England, depicts the authors of the four Gospels, Mathew, Mark, Luke and John. The far right figure that allegedly represents St. John (or Luke?) appears to be a woman. The three other figures are bearded and have their left foot forward. The thinly-disguised female figure does not have a beard, is wearing a woman's gown, appears to have breasts, has her right foot forward, and is holding a gold chalice. If it wasn't obvious the figure is Mary Magdalene the red and greens color of her clothes and the ribbons in front of each saint create a male peak symbol (left two), and a female "V" symbol provides conclusive evidence. (Courtesy of Graham Phillips)

Figure 26.

Figure 27.

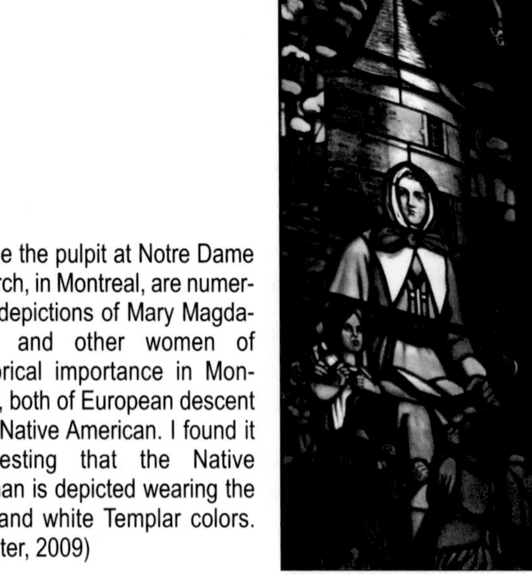

Inside the pulpit at Notre Dame Church, in Montreal, are numerous depictions of Mary Magdalene and other women of historical importance in Montreal, both of European descent and Native American. I found it interesting that the Native woman is depicted wearing the red and white Templar colors. (Wolter, 2009)

Inside Notre Dame Church in Montreal was a painting of a golden haired woman wearing orange, green-and-blue vestments holding three Canadian maple leaves with an Egyptian lily atop the crown on her head. In her lap is what looks like a baby girl with short curly red hair. The painting appears to depict Mary Magdalene with a daughter (Sarah?) and a crown over her head symbolic of royalty (Figure 28). In one of the Stations of the Cross paintings in the church was the Magdalene with the same golden hair wearing green and orange (Figure 29). Notice also the left hand of the child is making the secret "M" sign as an acknowledgement of the 13th apostle whose lap she is sitting on. (Wolter, 2009)

Figures 30, 31, & 32. While researching his genealogy in Scotland in September of 2012, Steve St. Clair discovered his family was granted land by their blood relatives the deMorville Family in 1170. The deMorville Family crest is a Lion Rampant on a blue shield wearing a gold crown. Steve was unaware the lion symbolizes the Royal family of King Jesus who was part of the Hebrew tribe of Judah. On the Nova Scotia flag is compelling symbolism that appears to suggest the designers knew about the legend of Prince Henry Sinclair, a prominent Knights Templar symbolized by the red and white colors of the lion inside a shield. The lion's tail is in the shape of a scimitar, an Arabic sword, likely representing the medieval Templars respect for the Arabs and their proficiency with numbers, mathematics and geometry. The large blue-colored "X" symbolizes the azure blue color of royalty of the heretics in the eyes of the Roman Catholic Church who embraced Monotheistic Dualism originally begun by Jesus' distant ancestor Pharaoh Akhenaten. The upright Lion Rampant is also the official emblem of Jerusalem whose primary colors are blue, yellow and white. (Courtesy of Steve St. Clair, 2012; Wolter, 2012; Internet)

Figure 33.

Figure 34.

The official flag of Nova Scotia includes the yellow shield completing the four color symbology of blue (water), white (purity), yellow (the sun), and red of the Templars and the bloodline of Jesus and Mary Magdaline some of them carried in their veins. The Canadian Flag contains additional interesting symbolism beyond the obvious red and white colors of the Templars who first came to the shores of what is now Canada in the twelfth century. The numerology of twelve points on the Maple Leaf could very likely represent the twelve constellations of the Zodiac. (Wolter, 2012; Internet)

Figure 35.

Figure 36.

Modern stained- glass windows depict John the Baptist baptizing his disciple Jesus with the Holy Spirit, which is actually the sun-God Ra, in the form of the dove which has its rays shining down on both men. In both images, Jesus, has his arms crossed in the classic Osiris pose of the heretics who embraced the Hooked X ideology of Monotheistic Dualism. (Wolter, 2011)

Figure 37.

Figure 38.

David Tenier's mid-seventeenth century painting of the monks' St. Paul and St. Anthony contains symbolism that likely reflected his true ideological beliefs which included the contrasting dark and light halves of Dualism. Another of the many symbols in the painting the author sees can be found in the "X" created by the stick in St. Anthony's hand and the one leaning against the block of rock. Could the upper left vertical edge of the rock above the stick be intentional to create the Hooked X? (Internet)

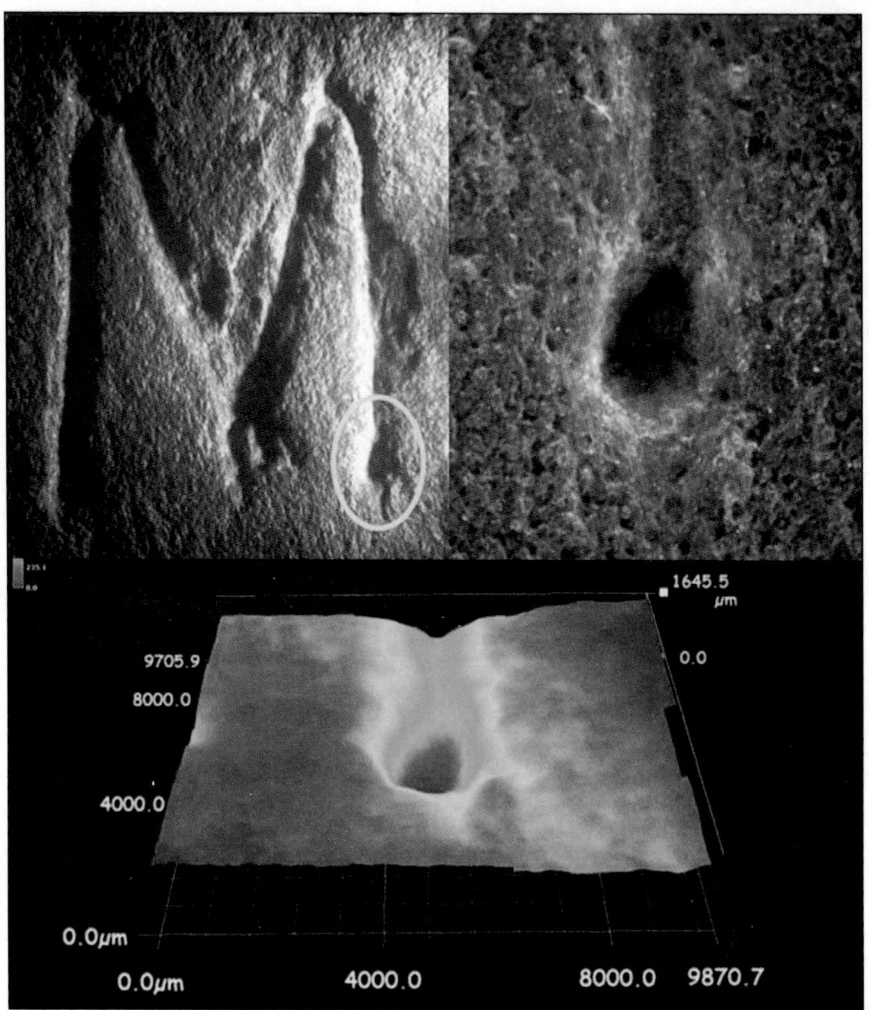

Figure 39 (composite). There is an intentional punch mark that was added to the bottom end of the far right leg of the Latin M on line eight by the carver of the Kensington Rune Stone inscription who was almost certainly a fourteenth century Cistercian Monk or Templar Knight. The punch mark was likely added as an acknowledgment to who they believed was the thirteenth apostle: Mary Magdalene. The rainbow-colored 3D digital image clearly shows the man-made depression. (Wolter, 2002, 2013)

Figure 40. Curiously, in the stained glass window in a Catholic Church in Kansas City, Missouri, is a ship with the stylized M, symbolic of Mary Magdalene, is sailing west following the five-pointed star of Venus as an evening star. Could the ship with the Cross of Lorraine on the mast sailing west be an acknowledgment of the story of her escape to southern France? (Wolter, 2011)

Figure 41.
Helena Roerich as painted by her husband Nicolas Roerich in 1937. The small metal box on the left is believed to contain a meteorite which to people involved in mysticism is considered a sacred object from the heavens. Three other symbolic objects in the painting include the book on the table and the yellow and red roses.

the site with up to six feet of caliche cemented alluvial material is actually 1,200 years old.

Nay sayers also trotted out the old argument about the lack of accepted contemporary pre-Columbian evidence anywhere in the vicinity. Putting the new runic inscription south of Tucson aside, this argument is another red herring. As I've said many times, a lack of evidence proves nothing. Simply being out of context for the currently known history of North America is not a viable argument to support the claim the artifacts are forgeries or fake. In fact, the geological evidence is consistent with lengthy burial and, therefore, supports the artifacts' authenticity, which requires a yet another new chapter of North America history be written.

There is one symbol that occurs twice on artifact #20 that instantly jumped out at me. Near the pointed ends of the crescent in the upper half of the cross is what looked like a dead ringer for the compass and square symbol, the most common symbol of Freemasonry. In this case, it cannot be related to modern Freemasonry being found on an eighth or ninth century artifact. Therefore, there must another explanation for it. Some research produced a plausible and highly likely explanation.

The compass and square symbols resemble magic squares that date back thousands of years and were used for their mystical and magical properties in China, India, and the Middle East.[61] While magic squares can be many sizes and incorporate many numbers and mathematical arrangements, the simplest example is comprised of three rows and three columns with a total of nine squares. Inside each box are the numbers 1 through 9 arranged in such way

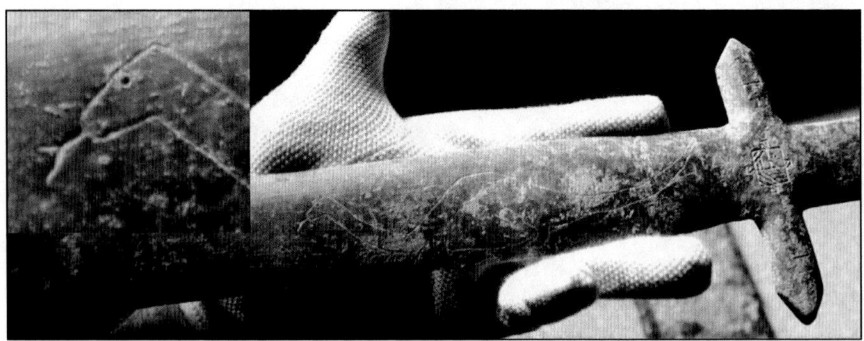

Artifact #12 is a 17½" long sword with what looks like a dinosaur carved into the blade. The dinosaur argument has been one of the skeptic's main arguments against authenticity. However, the creature has a forked tongue (inset) which has not been found in the dinosaur fossil record. This image is most likely that of one of many species of lizard found in the Tucson area. (Wolter, 2011)

that if all rows and columns are added up they will equal 15 as will the two diagonals. This sequence is 4, 9, and 2 for the top row, 3, 5, and 7 for the middle row and 8, 1, and 6 for the bottom row.

By using Gematria, the ancient art and science of substituting numbers for alphabetic letters (usually Hebrew or Greek), words or messages can be encoded. Freemason William Burkle believes that by connecting the numbers 8, 9, and 6 for the compass symbol and 3, 1, and 7 for the square symbol within the Hebrew magic square, when decoded, it likely stands for the equivalent of the Tetragrammaton, or the immutable word of the Creator.

It's highly likely the symbol has a sacred ancient Kabalistic meaning for the compass and square-like symbols on this particular artifact since it is associated with Hebrew words and early Jewish religious symbols.

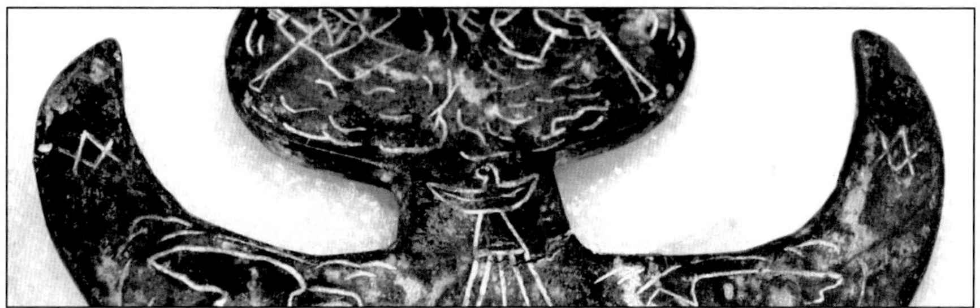

Near the points of the crescent on artifact #20 was two carved symbols that looked exactly like the compass and square of Freemasonry. (Wolter, 2011)

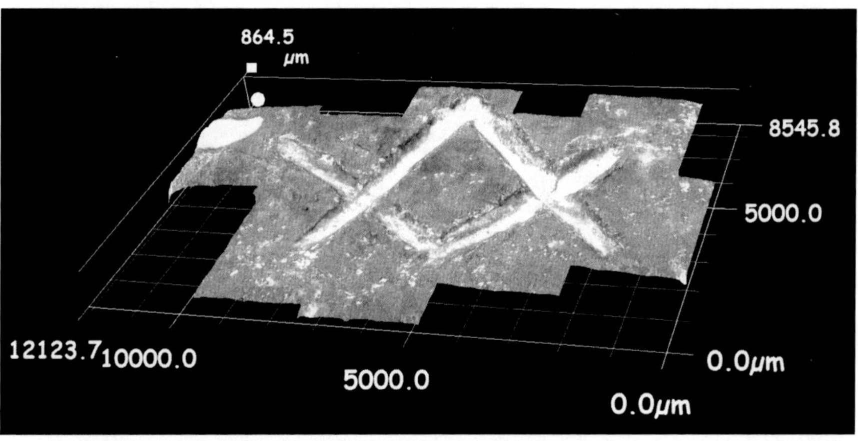

A close-up view of the compass and square symbol on the left side of the crescent on artifact #20 shows the grooves partially filled with white secondary calcite deposited over the centuries when it was buried under nearly six feet of sand and gravel near Tucson, Arizona. (Wolter, 2012)

There is another pre-Columbian example in the New World of the compass and square that indicates highly sophisticated cultures in Columbia, Panama, and Costa Rica that had an amazing grasp of the ancient arts and sciences. In October of 2010, I was introduced to the some amazing pre-Columbian gold statuary by Greg Cavalli. The metallic artifacts were crafted in exquisite detail out of an alloy comprised of copper, zinc, and gold called tumbaga. One of the largest artifacts in his collection contained something that had me scratching my head. The thirty-inch tall, five-and-a-half pound tumbaga statue of a female holding an infant in her arms was wearing only an apron covering her front and back pelvic regions. Incredibly, the design etched onto the apron was a dead ringer for the compass and square symbol of Freemasonry.[62]

Another interesting side note to the lead artifacts relates to a 2001 book by Crichton Miller where he recounts his rediscovering the ancient surveying and navigational device he calls the "working cross." Miller successfully applied for a United Kingdom patent on the device, which bolsters his claim. Artifact #18 is a Christian style cross with an

This Masonic-like apron worn by this thirty-inch-tall female tumbaga statue from the Tairona region of Columbia has a design reminiscent of an inverted compass and square. (Tom Shearer, 2012)

entwined serpent that has both Latin and Hebrew inscriptions. The artifact also has football-shaped flared fins inscribed in Latin roughly one-third of the way up the long cross. At roughly two-thirds of the length there is horizontal bar reminiscent of the Christian cross with a circle joining the four cardinal points of the crossing bars creating a common symbol called the "Circle Cross," which is essentially the same as Miller's working cross.

Miller discusses the Tucson lead artifacts, and the tone of his writing is in support of their authenticity. What surprised me was he made no mention of the circle cross/working cross on artifact #18. He convincingly argued that ancient sailors up through to the Knights Templar used his device, but knowledge of the working cross used to build among other edifices, the Pyramids of Giza, was lost when Roman Christianity rose to prominence. Miller believes that much of the knowledge of the ancients was lost to humanity when the library at Alexandria, Egypt, was burned by the Catholic Church in the third century A.D.

Artifact #18 of the Tucson lead artifacts has a circle cross with a lead serpent entwined around it. This artifact appears to support Crichton Miller's rediscovery of the "Working Cross" that he convincingly argues would have been required knowledge for ancient cultures to successfully navigate the oceans. (Wolter, 2011 & 2005)

The lost Jewish colony of the eighth and ninth centuries who found their way to what is now Tucson apparently did have this knowledge and artifact #18 supports that supposition. If Miller's research is correct, having the working cross would have been a requirement to successfully navigating across the Atlantic Ocean to North America.

Given the well-established provenance of the discovery and extraction of the artifacts together with the complete lack of evidence of planting or other nefarious activity these artifacts, and the numerous centuries estimate for the caliche and copper carbonates to form on the artifacts, they must be accepted as genuine historical artifacts.

Chapter 6

France

On December 2, 2009, I received a call from Rene Barnett, who asked to interview me on her radio show about our research on the Templars. After the interview she convinced me I just had to visit France. To further entice me, she sent a DVD of a documentary film, *Bloodline,* she had made with her former business partner, Bruce Burgess. The film was the story about their investigation into the bloodline of Jesus and his wife, Mary Magdalene, and Rene and Bruce's meeting with Ben Hammott, from London. They talked about the discovery of a cave in the mountains of southern France reportedly near the small mountaintop village of Rennes-le-Château, made famous by the book, *Holy Blood, Holy Grail.*

The film was believable not only from the people featured in the film, which included a member of the so-called Priory of Sion, a secret society that protects both the living and deceased members of the sacred bloodline of the Royal Family. The film's focus was on retracing Ben's steps during his search for the hidden tomb allegedly found by the priest, Abbé François Bérenger Saunière, (1852 to 1917) who discovered parchments inside a hollow pillar in the altar of his church at Rennes Le Château, in 1891.

Ben and fellow researcher Sandy Hamblett, followed clues they found inside the Church of Mary Magdalene eventually discovering four bottles with coded messages, three inscribed stones, and a chest containing artifacts with yet another coded message. This incredible treasure hunt culminated in Ben's discovering a small hole inside a cave in the mountains near Rennes that served as a ventilation shaft for a tomb. Ben was able to lower a boroscope camera down the ventilation shaft into the tomb and filmed its contents.

On the front of the altar in the Church of Mary Magdalene at Rennes-le-Château in Southern France, a kneeling Mary Magdalene has her fingers entwined in the same manner as the fingers on the body inside the tomb Ben Hammott reportedly discovered prior to 2007. (Wolter, 2010)

If the legend that abounds in this region of Southern France is true, then what Ben had discovered was very likely the final resting place of Mary Magdalene. Ben was eventually able to cut away part of the shroud covering the body on the marble slab and reveal a mummified body whose face looked distinctly feminine. What I found most interesting is the fingers were entwined in the same manner as the statue of Mary Magdaline inside Saunière's Church.

While watching the film, Janet and I were torn between utter fascination with the filmmaker's investigation, Ben's incredible discoveries, and the possible implications these discoveries could have. At the same time, we had a hard time believing what we were seeing. After watching the film, I called Rene and asked questions, most that could only be answered by Ben. Rene said, "I'm taking a week-long trip to France and meeting up with Ben and Sandy in March. Why don't you join us?" Since I had always planned to visit France someday, this seemed like the perfect opportunity to go.

On March 28, 2010, I arrived in Paris and took the train to my hotel in the heart of the city directly across the river from Notre Dame Cathedral. As I walked the perimeter of the cathedral I saw dozens of examples of the sacred feminine architecture so beautifully crafted in this structure.

Perhaps the most impressive artifact I saw in the Louvre was a granite sarcophagus covered with scenes and hieroglyphics with incredible detail. How did the Egyptians make something that incredible so long ago? The only effective way to cut and polish granite is with diamonds, and they likely had access to the diamond mines in the southern part of the continent. Even with diamonds, the technology to produce such stunning artwork required ancient knowledge not known today. We forget how technologically advanced the Egyptian culture was and one only needs to spend time in this museum to fully appreciate it. I thought, *If this advanced culture could create these amazing things, they could probably build a boat capable of sailing across the Atlantic.*

The twin towers (left) on the west side of the magnificently lit Notre Dame Cathedral after dark on March 28, 2010. The towers symbolize the sacred feminine architecture incorporated into the Gothic Cathedrals of Europe of the upright knees of a woman with her allegorical birth canal exposed in the birthing position. (Wolter, 2010)

The massive six-foot tall granite sarcophagus (below) with incredible detailed carvings on all sides was one of the most impressive Egyptian artifacts I saw in the Louvre. The artisan who crafted the carvings likely had diamond tools to have been able to so skillfully carve rock as hard as granite. (Wolter, 2010)

My last stop was Saint Sulpice Church. My goal here was to get inside and confirm that the same "AVM" symbolism was here that we saw prominently displayed in the Notre Dame Basilica and the Grand Seminary in Montreal, Canada, during my trip to Montreal in October of 2009.

Montreal, first named Ville-Marie, was founded in 1642 by a group of highly devoted mystics who sailed from La Rochelle, France, and were supported by rich members of the secret Compagnie du Saint-Sacrement. Later, they received donations from the Sulpician priest Alexander Le Rageois de

Bretonvilliers.[63] On this island, the new independent colony of seventeenth-century mystics, "New Jerusalem,"[64] the parish was dedicated to Mary (Magdalene?) and in 1672, the church of Notre Dame was built on the island.

Within the Notre Dame Basilica I found many examples of Templar style crosses, various stylized AVMs, and two Tetragrammatons (four Hebrew letters that correspond to YHWH, transliterated IAUE or Yahweh) with not four, but three Hebrew letters within the Delta, "Hey" "Waw" "Hey" which in Latin spells "Eve," that seemed to be an ode of reverence to the "other" Mary. The close ties of the new colony to the Sulpicians in Paris seemed like more than a coincidence. Daniel Graysolon Du Luth, the first French explorer to travel west of Lake Superior (and carve his name on a sandstone boulder in 1679), started in Montreal and lived right next to the Notre Dame Basilica on Notre Dame and St. Sulpice Streets. Could he have known about the region through membership in a secret society that had knowledge of the Templar party that made it to Kensington? Then, also, the AVM (A.U.M.) on the Kensington Rune Stone has ancient Masonic ties to esoteric knowledge that only the most initiated were privy to. To one group of people, AVM is a symbol of reverence to the Virgin Mary. To others, such as enlightened Templars and Sulpicians it is an allegiance to Mary Magdalene. Inside the Church at St. Sulpice in Paris, I found the same stylized AVM on the marble frontispiece in the Lady's Chapel.

What also stuck out inside St. Sulpice Church is the gnomon (the part of a sundial that casts the shadow) used to record the summer and winter solstices and the equinoxes throughout the year. The winter solstice is marked by a beam of sunlight passing through a small round hole in a stained-glass window on the south wall that hits a mark near the top of a roughly thirty-five-foot obelisk. This documenting of the annual movements of the sun is consistent with the pagan beliefs of many esoteric secret societies that are rumored to be affiliated with the Sulpicians both in France and Montreal.

The same stylized AVM is found at St. Sulpice Church in Paris, France, (left) and at the Notre Dame Basilica (middle) and the Grand Seminary (right) in Montreal, Canada. (Wolter, 2010)

I met up with Rene Barnett, Ben Hammott, Sandy Hamblett, and a friend from Germany, Enrico Altmann in Chartres. The spires of Chartres Cathedral towered over the landscape. The massive size of the cathedral became evident when we arrived for a tour. What struck me most besides its size were the detailed carvings of the various biblical scenes.

On the outer side of the wall encircling the apse were various one-half life-sized biblical scenes carved in limestone. In one scene that I've never seen depicted before was the circumcision of the eight-day-old baby Jesus. This of course confirms his Jewish heritage and very likely his Egyptian heritage as well.

I don't recall ever seeing an image of baby Jesus being circumcised, and the Black Madonna and child here was more vivid than the ones I saw on Gotland. The dark skin on Mary (Isis) and baby Jesus (Horus) allegedly portrays the truth about Mary Magdalene and her Egyptian heritage that is in darkness, or in hiding. To me, this makes a lot more sense than the myth of Mother Mary holding baby Jesus who she supposedly conceived without ever having sex.

We left Chartres for the South of France. I asked both Ben and Sandy about their discoveries at Rennes-le-Château. They shared every minute detail and answered all my questions. Ben said, "Being a geologist, do you think you might be able to help me find another way into the tomb?"

I said, "I don't know, but we can sure give it a try." My thinking was that we might be able to determine the sedimentary bedding trends in the mountain made of limestone and possibly find where the people (Templars?) who carved out the tomb originally got in. It seemed like a long shot but why not give it a try?

Over the next day and a half we meandered toward "Rennes," stopping at interesting churches along way. We stopped in the town of Poitiers to wander through three very old churches including tenth century Byzantine Church of Eglise Notre-

The gnomon inside St. Sulpice Church in Paris, marks the summer solstice with a small beam of sunlight passing through a round hole in a stained-glass window onto the marble square in the foreground. The winter solstice is marked near the top of the obelisk. (Wolter, 2010)

Inside massive Chartres Cathedral is a rare limestone carving of the circumcision of Jesus and a Black Madonna of Isis (Mary Magdalene?) and her son Horus. (Wolter, 2010)

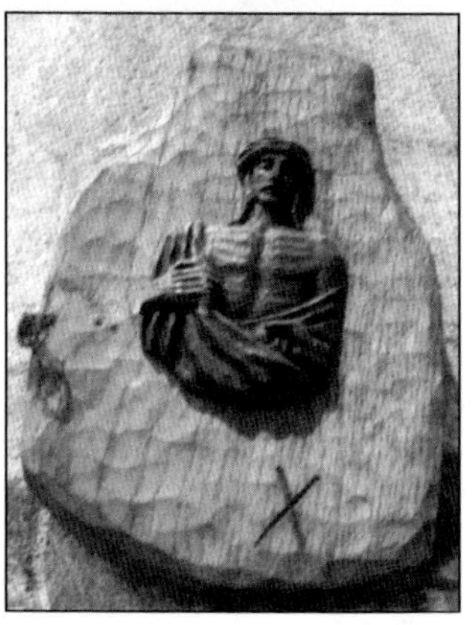

Before leaving Eglise Notre-Dame Church Enrico and I noticed a wooded plaque on a stone column with a depiction of Jesus with an "X" symbol. The "X" can be read as a clever monogram incorporating the letters L V X, (the V and U being interchangeable) or the word "Lux" or "Light," which means knowledge. (Wolter, 2010)

Dame de Poitiers. Enrico and I entered the church at a little before 9:00 A.M. and noticed a priest making his way toward the altar.

Enrico and I then looked behind the altar and noticed what held the congregation's attention. Perched atop an ornate pedestal and wrapped in a bright red cloak adorned with five-pointed stars wearing a crown on her head and holding a fig branch in her left hand and a rod with two large keys in her right was Mary. Seated in her lap was a male child holding up two fingers on his right hand and also wearing a gold colored robe and a crown. On either side of the pedestal, were gold candle-holders with twelve candles each, six red and six white. Behind the Royal Mary and child statues were two large stone columns that were both wrapped in red cloth.

It took a minute to take in the unfolding ceremony Enrico and I had happened upon. When I looked again at that cloth-draped red columns, I noticed sunlight shining through the upper-level windows on the southeast side of the church cast tall rectangles of light onto the red columns. We then looked at the other stone columns surrounding the altar. They too were awash in sunlight in a spectacular illumination event. The priest raised the smoking censer as an offering

On March 30, Ben Hammott, Rene Barnett, Sandy Hamblett, Enrico Altmann, and I walked through the beautiful tenth-century Byzantine Church of Eglise Notre-Dame de Poitiers. The morning sunlight illuminated the stunning beauty of the church's Romanesque architecture. (Wolter, 2010)

to the crowned statues, and then set it in front of the altar. We watched the ceremony as the illuminated columns and the billowing frankincense created a surreal moment we would never forget. (See color section, Figure 10)

I could not help but think of the illumination of the egg-shaped keystone we discovered in the Newport Tower two years earlier that happens at the same 9:00 A.M. time is more than just coincidence. Here we were in a church in the heart of the Southern France witnessing another illumination event where for the better part of two thousand years the Cult of Mary Magdalene has embraced the same "Hooked X" Monotheistic Dualism beliefs as the Cistercian/Templar orders who built the Newport Tower in America.

The ceremony we witnessed, was dedicated to a local story, *The Legend of the Miracle of the Keys*.[65] I think there's more going on. The illumination of the six columns with Mary and child cloaked in red with white five-pointed stars and two candle-holders each with twelve red and white candles sitting front and center of the ceremony reeks of something else. The red and white colors of the Templars, and Upper and Lower Egypt suggest something more ancient. *Lost Keys* seems like a cover for an older story about another Mary and child being kept alive.

In one of the stained-glass window of the Eglise Notre-Dame Church was a scene with Mary/Isis holding baby Jesus/Horus at the top with thirteen male subjects holding white banners. Two names that appear on banners on either side of the mother and child inside a Vesica Piscis are "Osias" and "Amon." These appear to be veiled references to the Egyptian heritage of the Royal Family. Jesus as the male God Osiris, and Amon Ra, the monotheistic sun-God venerated by Akhenaten, who changed the religion of Egypt from worshipping the setting sun, Amen Ra, to the rising sun in the east.[66] (See color section, Figure 11)

Before leaving the church Enrico and I passed by a large stone column with a relatively innocuous wood plaque hanging a few feet above our heads. On the plaque was an image of Jesus. What caught my eye was an "X" carved into the plaque that seemed out of place. On the other hand, when thinking back to Margaret Starbird's comments about how the "X" was the symbol of the heretics whose religious beliefs diametrically opposed the Roman Church. Here again, in this region of France the "X" fits in perfectly.

To the mystics who frequent this area, the "X" is read as a clever monogram incorporating the letters L V X, (the V and U being interchangeable) or the word "Lux" or "Light."[67] In this context the word "Light" is synonymous with knowledge. In a religious context in this case, it is likely the hidden knowledge of the true story of Jesus and Mary Magdalene.

We continued south toward Rennes-le-Château. Along the way we stopped and admired huge bronze statues of Mary/Isis and baby Jesus/Horus on hilltops and ancient castles such as at La Donjon du Faucon Noir.

We stopped in the city of Albi where we visited Sainte-Cécile, the largest brick cathedral in the world (construction began in 1281 and was completed in 1380). It was imposing and had a spooky feeling to it, more like a prison that a house of worship. Inside the church, on the walls on either side of the altar were dreary painted images of people enduring horrific suffering. This was no doubt a powerful motivator or threat to the people that failure to follow church doctrine would result in eternal suffering in Hell.

Near here the Albigensian Crusade began in 1208, after the assassination of Church representative, Pierre de Castelnau, ordered by the Holy See to eradicate the Cathars, who refused to convert to Roman Christianity. They believed in reincarnation and rejected the Old Testament, Sacraments, the Host and the Cross. They were also dualists who believed in the concept of opposites (Good and Evil) through which balance would be achieved in their world.[68] They were the ideological descendants of the same dualists who began in pre-Christian Egypt. The crusade officially ended in 1244 with the final siege at Montségur Castle.

April 1, 2010, we pulled into the village of Couiza, near Rennes-le-Château, which is very small village with connecting buildings crowding the narrow roads. Its now famous tiny church was where Ben and Sandy found Saunière's hidden clues that led to their discoveries.

Sandy had discovered most of the inscribed stones and bottle messages, but Ben found the tomb and thus had the burden of deciding what to

As frankincense rose from the censer placed in front of the altar by the priest six stone columns were illuminated with sunlight passing through the upper level windows of Eglise Notre-Dame de Poitiers Church. This coordinated light show on the spring equinox was certainly no coincidence and represents an ancient pagan festival. (Wolter, 2010)

do about it. Clearly, it weighed on him. I believe initially he really wanted my help in trying to find the original entrance to the tomb. When the day came to climb up the mountain and actually do it, there were too many people around and decided he wasn't ready.

Instead, we made the climb up the mountain near Rennes-le-Bains, where Ben led us to the ruins of a Knights Templar lookout fortress of Château Blanche Fort. The craggy limestone bluff was the perfect strategic location with a beautiful panoramic view of the valleys surrounding it. Little was left of the fort except the stone foundations of two structures. Ben had been to this site many times and explained what he thought they had once looked like. The building he thought had once been a small church had foundation walls built into the bedrock that were still up to six feet high.

I noted the now familiar 2:1 dimensions of the foundation with two-and-a-half thick walls and an inner dimension of roughly eight by sixteen feet. Exactly in the middle of the east-west aligned foundation was a roughly thirty-inch diameter water-filled cistern cut into the limestone bedrock. Even the warrior monks manning their posts at this remote site in the mountains apparently faithfully kept to their religious vows of ritual bathing.

The last morning at Rennes, another friend, Gloria Amendola, along with Sandy Hamblett, offered to drive me to Toulouse to catch my flight home. Still we had nearly a full day to visit a few out-of-the-way Templar sites. We visited a small Templar Commandery Church at Champagne Sur Aude, where a couple of things jumped out at me. First, the most prominent depiction of Mary/Isis was a statue in the Lady Chapel of her clad in gold with golden hair wearing a crown. Gold is the color of Egypt in esoteric circles and this depiction in the Templar Church again harkened to her likely Egyptian heritage. Below the statue on a white marble frontispiece was the same stylized "AVM" I had seen at St. Sulpice in Paris and in Montreal. It seemed the cult of Mary Magdalene had tentacles reaching far and wide. The second thing that caught me by surprise was a statue with two figures in a scene I had seen depicted many times—a monk taking Jesus down from the Cross. Upon walking over for a closer look I was surprised to see that Jesus' eyes were open. He had his arm around the priest, and he was very much alive!

Our final stop before Toulouse was where the Albigensian Crusade ended at Montségur Castle, in 1244. The ruins of the castle were visible from several miles away, sitting atop a mountain of rock that looked like a football standing on end. After winding through the mountains, we pulled over at the base and stared up at the large stone ruins. Gloria told the story of how the overwhelming contingent of knights, sent by the Church in Rome, surrounded the castle and starved out the heretics. Upon their surrender, they were marched down into the meadow before us and burned at the stake.

Gloria added, "The legend says that, as the fires were lit, the prisoners began to sing. Many of the Holy See's knights were profoundly moved by the Cathar's resolve in the face of death and switched sides. They too were promptly burned." Sandy then added, "Did you know that the only order of knights that didn't participate in the Albigensian Crusade were the Knights Templar?"

The tiny mountaintop village of Rennes-le-Château as it looked from the south on April 2, 2010. (Wolter, 2010)

We talked about the persecution of the Cathars and discussed their alternate Christian beliefs which incorporated Dualism, a belief in reincarnation, how they generally regarded men and women as equals, and had no doctrinal objection to contraception, all no-no's with the Catholic Church.[69] These alternate "Good Christian" beliefs and other religious ideological differences surely played a role in the Church's decision to eradicate them. However, we also agreed the strongest motivation for the Albigensian Crusade was the Church's attempt to wipe out what they believed were the bloodline descendants of Jesus and Mary Magdalene.

Since that trip, Ben's continued refusal to bring anyone to the cave, including the French government, raised a red flag. The situation at Rennes-le-Château was strikingly similar to Russell Burrows and his alleged cave in Southern Illinois. While a final conclusion about the existence of Russell's cave and all the artifacts there cannot be reached due to a lack of evidence, our discovery of at least one absolute fake and likely three additional ones has cast a dark shadow over the Burrow's Cave mystery.

Unlike Burrows Cave, however, the mystery surrounding Ben Hammott's tomb has finally been resolved.[70] On March 19, 2012, I received an email from a friend and fellow researcher that Ben was about to issue a confession that his tomb and all the artifacts found by him and Sandy Hamblett were an elaborate hoax perpetrated solely by him. Two days later, Rene Barnett returned my call and confirmed that indeed the rumor was true, that she had interviewed Ben and asked questions live on her radio show the night before. The following morning I listened to the hour-long interview.

Ben seemed to be remorseful, but it's hard to feel sympathy for anyone who carried on such deceit for roughly a decade. Sandy, Rene, and Gloria understandably felt a deep sense of betrayal and anger toward Ben, who deceived a lot of people for

The ruined foundation with a round water-filled cistern cut into the bedrock is all that remains of a tiny church on the mountaintop Knights Templar lookout of Château Blanche Fort. (Wolter, 2010)

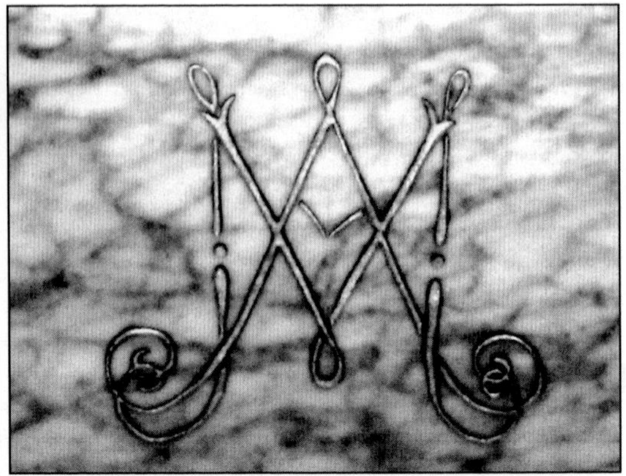

At the Templar Church at Champagne Sur Aude the most prominent depiction of Mary was a statue in the Lady Chapel of her with golden hair, wearing a crown and clad in gold clothing; gold is also the symbolic color of Egyptian royalty. Below the statue on a marble frontispiece was the same stylized AVM as seen in St. Sulpice in Paris and Montreal. (Wolter, 2010)

over a decade. He did achieve a certain level of notoriety and got plenty of attention, but the big payday never materialized. He talked about how he wanted to come clean years earlier, but as he said multiple times during the interview, "I didn't have the guts to do it."

The confession came as a surprise, but not a shock. I was taken by the intrigue of the possibility of a first century tomb related to Jesus' Royal Family at Rennes-le-Château and was excited about being able to help locate the tomb that looked reasonably authentic in Ben's photographs and video.

Ben Hammott's confession serves as a reminder for all researchers investigating controversial subject matter to consider only credible factual evidence and, when it doesn't materialize, one must tread very carefully.

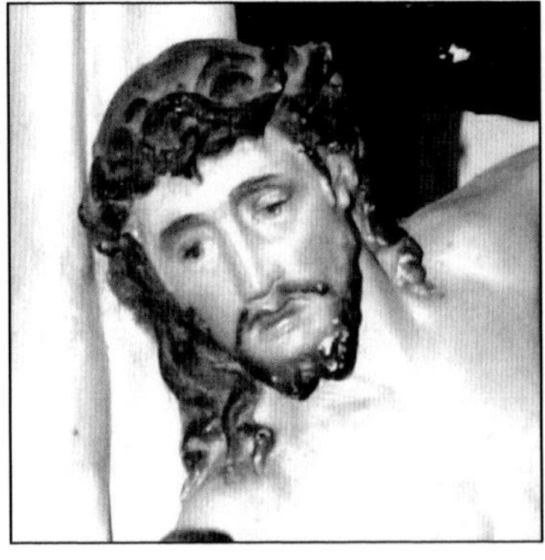

Inside the Templar Church at Champagne Sur Aude, I noticed a ceramic statue of a monk clearly helping Jesus down from the Cross after his Crucifixion. I didn't notice it at first, but Jesus' eyes were open and with his hand around the monk's back he was obviously being depicted as very much alive. (Wolter, 2010)

Chapter 7
Native Americans

There's one area of pre-Columbia research that has been horribly neglected. It seems that people often forget to think about the obvious and miss out on meaningful data. When Europeans came to North America prior to Columbus, they encountered and interacted with the indigenous peoples. Why haven't the scholars taken the Native cultures more seriously as a resource of knowledge? The Smithsonian Institution and other institutions have spent decades digging up their mounds. Surely there is critical evidence there about the visitors from across the oceans. The evidence of contact is so obvious in some cases it cries out. Yet academia has missed the obvious or have suppressed it.

The history of settlement and land acquisition of the United States is complicated. Manifest Destiny was a successful policy from the government's perspective, but was devastating to Native people. Genocide comes to mind, and I think most people of the time understood that. Manifest Destiny also conveniently erased much of the evidence of Pre-Columbian European exploration. Fortunately, that evidence was not completely lost. Surviving Native people still retain a secret knowledge of the early visitors and have expressed to me their prophecies compel them that it is now time to reveal what they know.

Bill Mann's Novel

WILLIAM MANN KNOWS a little something about European contact with Native tribes in the St. Lawrence River area extending from the Atlantic Ocean to the Great Lakes. His unique background and heritage motivated him to research this subject. He is also a non-status Native Algonquin Indian, whose mother, like so many others, found it necessary to hide her true heritage, as her ancestors chose to convert to Catholicism and outwardly became "French" in the early 1800s in order to secure "deed" ownership of the land that they had previously occupied for centuries. Presently, the federal government of Canada has ruled that non-status Indians and Metis should be recognized on the same level of "status" Indians, but it is expected that challenges to this judicial ruling will tie up the federal courts for years to come.

Mann's Masonic resumé includes the following: Member of Oakville Lodge #400, Ancient Free & Accepted Masons of Canada, White Oaks Chapter No. 104, Royal Arch Masons of Canada, Salem Council #9, Royal and Select Master Masons of Ontario, Macassa Bay Lodge No. 9 of Royal Ark Mariners and Sir William York Rite College #57. He's also a thirty-second-degree Scottish Rite Mason, being a member of Murton Lodge of Perfection, Hamilton Sovereign Chapter of Rose Croix, and Moore Sovereign Consistory, Hamilton. Mann is a past preceptor of Godfrey de Bouillon Preceptory #3, Hamilton District No 2, of the United Religious and Military Orders of St. John's of Jerusalem, Palestine, Rhodes and Malta, of the Order of the Temple—Knights Templar of Canada.

These associations are a direct result of the heavy masonic relationships that extend far into his family background. His great-uncle, F.G. Mann was supreme grand master of the Knights Templar in Canada in the 1950s.

Mann has written two books about the Knights Templar in North America prior to Columbus and the secret mapping of the New World.

Being a Freemason, Mann understands the profound impact of the secret societies and members who shaped the early history of the United States and Canada. Most of those figures were Freemasons or members of secret societies with strong ties to affiliated societies in Europe. Most people in the United States are unaware of Thomas Jefferson's likely Masonic affiliation, for example. Any student of American history knows Founding Fathers George Washington, John Adams, Benjamin Franklin, and Andrew Jackson were Freemasons. Most historians make a point to single out the third president as someone *not* a Mason. Jefferson was not a member of a lodge, in this country. However, he was listed as a member through indirect evidence of the Lodge of Nine Sisters (Les Neuf Sceurs) along with Benjamin Franklin, in France. (See color section, Figure 12)

The importance of the Masonic connections between our Founding Fathers and the secret societies of many European countries, most notably France, during the infancy of America cannot be overstated. Not only is the evidence mounting that modern Freemasonry is directly connected to the fugitive medieval

List of Selected Members of the Lodge Les Neuf Sœurs, 1776–1792

B. Foreign Members according to indirect evidence of Masonic documents

	Name	Science or Art	Education	Country where active	Dictionary
75	Campe, J. H.	Social Sc.	P W	Germany	Allg. D.B.
76	Czartoryski, A.C. (Senior)	Social Sc.	W L	Poland	Polski Slov. B.
77	Forster, J. G.	Science	P W L	Eng., Germ., Poland	Allg. D.B.
78	Golitsin, D.	Science	L	Russia	Ency. Slovar
79	*Jefferson, Th.	Social Sc.	W L	France, America	D.A.B.
80	Harpe, F. C. La	Social Sc.	P W L	France, Switz., Russia	D.N.U., Russ, Bio. Slov.
81	Jeffries, J.	Science	—	Eng., America	D.A.B
82	*Paine, Th.	Social Sc.	W L	Eng., Amer., France	D.N.B
83	Pictet, M. A.	Sc. Lit.	P W L	Eng., Switz., France	D.N.U.
84	Raspe, R. E.	Lit., Science	W	Germany, Eng.	D.N.B.
85	*Stanhope, Ch. Earl of	Science	—	England	D.N.B.

296

Nicholas Hans

On page 296 of the book, *Freemasonry on Both Sides of the Atlantic*, Thomas Jefferson (#79) is listed as a member of the Lodge of Nine Sisters through indirect evidence of Masonic documents. On page 295, Benjamin Franklin (#63) is listed as a member through direct evidence of Masonic documents (below).

List of Selected Members of the Lodge Les Neuf Sœurs, 1776–1792

B. Foreign Members according to direct evidence of Masonic documents

	Name	Science or Art	Education	Country where active	Dictionary
56	Bancroft, E.	Sc. Medicine	W	England & America	D.N.B.-D.A.B.
57	Bingley, W.	Theatre	—	France & Holland	Dutch Bio. Dict.
58	Campbell, W.	Science	W	France & England	Amiable
59	Cerutti, J. A.	Social Sci.	W	Italy, France	Ency. Italian
60	Eguia, F.	Medicine	—	Spain	Ency. España
61	Fabroni, G.	Science	P W L	Italy & France	D.B.U., Ital. Ency.
62	*Forster, J. R.	Science	P W	Eng., Russia, Germany	Allg. D.B.-D.N.B.
63	*Franklin, B.	Science Social Sci.	W L	France, England & America	D.N.B.-D.B.U.
64	Izquerdo, E. de R.	Science	P	Spain	Ency. España
65	Jones, J. P.	Navigation	—	America & Russia	D.A.B.
66	Munibe de Pena Florida	Social Sci.	L	Spain	Ency. España
67	Palsa, J.	Music	—	France, Germany	Allg. D.B.
68	Piccini, N.	Music	—	France & Italy	Ency. Italian
69	Pignatelli, F.	Social Sci.	L	Italy, France	Ency. Ital.
70	Santi, G. De	Science	P W	Italy	Ency. Ital.
71	Stroganov A.	Social Sci.	L	Russia	Russ. Bio. Slov.
72	Titius, Cl. H.	Science	P	Germany, Sweden	Allg. D.B.
73	Turschmidt, K.	Music	—	Germany & France	Allg. D.B.
74	Wonsowicz, F.	Nat. Phil.	P	Poland	Amiable

*Member of the American Philosopphical Society; Connection with Education: P—Preofessor; L—Legislator; W—Writer

295

UNESCO of the Eighteenth Century

orders of the Templars, but, because of these international Masonic connections, at least some of our Founding Fathers also knew about the medieval Templar exploration and mapping of North America. It is a pretty safe bet that George Washington, Ben Franklin, and Thomas Jefferson were among that enlightened group.

I first met William in October of 2009, at the Atlantic Conference in Halifax, Nova Scotia. This conference brought scholars and other researchers to discuss early trans-Atlantic contact where I presented my Hooked X research. In December of 2010, Bill asked if I would read a draft of his upcoming new book entitled, *The 13th Pillar*. Having thoroughly enjoyed the historical research presented in his first two books, I was eager to read his latest work. He said, "It's a novel, but I think you're going to like it."

"When did you start writing fiction?" I said.

Bill said, "I think I've written an interesting story and there are other ways to convey information."

After reading what he had sent, I asked him. "Did you write this book as fiction so that, as a Mason, you can say, 'It's fiction?'"

"Yes," he said.

"Can I then assume that, when something's presented as fact, it is indeed fact?"

Again he answered, "Yes."

I smiled and said, "Send me the rest of it."

The story is an Indiana Jones type historical mystery-thriller set both in the present day and the nineteenth century. It involves secret societies, the Templars, and Native Americans, all subjects Bill knows well. It's a good story, but I learned many pearls of wisdom that broadened my understanding of the Native component to the early history of this continent. Some of the secrets revealed in the book represent informed speculation that while not yet universally accepted by academia, are supported by an ever-increasing body of factual evidence. Here are some of these ancient secrets gleaned from Bill's manuscript:

1. A series of ancient longitudinal meridians had been established around the world well before Christ's time, which allowed the ancient mariner—Minoans, Phoenicians, Carthaginians, Greeks, and Romans, to circumnavigate the world.
2. The Knights Templar, among other more physical treasure, rediscovered this knowledge and for the next three hundred years (circa 1150 to 1450) controlled the seas and formed the most advanced maritime fleet in the world at that time.
3. The Templars had established trading routes to the Americas out of La Rochelle on the west coast of France, as early as the twelfth century, thus solidifying their relationships with the Native Americans through strategic intermarriages.
4. The Templars possessed knowledge of many things at this time, including metallurgy, which would have appeared magical to the aboriginals.
5. Native princesses were brought back to France and intermarried with prominent noble families.

6. In 1398 A.D., the hereditary grand master of the Scottish Knights Templar, Prince Henry Sinclair, sailed to what is now Nova Scotia with approximately five hundred knights, some of their families, and a number of Cistercian monks, in order to extend their sanctuary into the New World.
7. New World explorers were agents (and often double and triple agents) for certain ancient secret societies.
8. Prince Henry and his band of knights moved inland after wintering in Nova Scotia and, over the years, established strategic sanctuaries along with permanent relationships within the larger Algonquin Nation, which once stretched from the eastern seaboard to the foothills of the Rocky Mountains.
9. The single mast and crossbeam on the vessels of ancient navigators, including the Templars', allowed sailors to capture the wind and the "crossed sticks" were used to chart the relative distance of constellations or the moon in relation to distance traveled in the boat.
10. Many of the spiritual and physical elements of the Native Mide'win, or the Great Medicine Society, which has been responsible for the continuation of ancient teachings through ceremonies and ritual to the present, can actually be found within modern-day Masonic Templar ritual.
11. The symbol for peace in the Algonquin Nation is a white eagle feather with a thin strip of deer leather, dyed red, wrapped around the stem. Red and white are the colors of the Templars.
12. The Recollets who came to Montreal with Champlain prior to the Jesuits followed earlier Templar maps, which allowed them to traverse North America with the help of their relatives, the Algonquin. These agents remained to re-establish feudal relationships with the Natives.
13. The Sulpicians gained knowledge through their earlier European relationship with the Cistercians who accompanied the Templars to the New World (including Prince Henry and the Kensington Party).
14. The Sulpicians Seminary in Montreal was built on an earlier Templar encampment and observatory. The original cornerstone at Notre Dame de Bon Secours Cathedral displays a number of Templar signs and symbols.

The original cornerstone of the Notre Dame de Bon Secours Church, in Montreal, which was built in 1771 over the ruins of an earlier church. The cornerstone has Templar style crosses with flared ends and several simple AVM designs carved into it. (Wolter, 2011)

15. Artists and royalty hid secrets from the non-initiated through art where secret signs, symbols, and tokens were incorporated into paintings. Hand gestures, poses, the number of included figures, random objects, and the color of clothing meant something totally different when interpreted on a different level.
16. In circa 1642, Champlain, was likely a double agent for both the Knights of Malta (a Catholic order), and Knights Templar working on behalf of the St. Sulpicians, the first missionaries to Montreal.
17. The Jesuits, sent by Cardinal Richelieu, went directly inland past Montreal to the Native villages, hoping to learn the location of the Templar secret. They were only successful in giving the Natives a deadly strain of small pox.
18. In Nicolas Poussin's 1640-1642 painting, *The Shepherd's in Arcadia*, Mary Magdalene with her golden hair and dressed in the gold of Egypt and the blue of Greece, suggest she was indeed pregnant at the time of the Crucifixion and their bloodline was supported throughout the centuries by the Knights Templar.
19. Many elements of the Native Mi'kmaq legend of a man-god who they call "Glooscap" correspond to the circa 1400 time of a Scottish Prince Henry Sinclair, purportedly, brought to North America the Holy Grail, in the form of the Holy Bloodline.
20. The original Knights Templar were members of noble families that could trace their lineage back to either the Norse god-kings or to the House of David and House of Bethany, which became one with the union of Jesus and Mary Magdalene. The northern families were originally pagan and the southern families were Jewish.

After centuries of intermarriage their bloodlines became intertwined and thus were perceived to embrace Catholicism.

21. When these bloodline families secretly gathered in Normandy over nine hundred years ago under the guidance of St. Bernard of Clairvaux, they decided to hide their true faith (the Hooked X ideology) within the Vatican's Roman Catholicism, which controlled most of Europe since the fourth century and the Council of Nicea.
22. The initial Templar refuge established in Acadia (Nova Scotia) was too exposed to the agents of the Church and caused the Knights Templar to move inland, establishing sanctuaries in relation to the ancient meridians. Moving east to west these meridians are located at 56 degrees west longitude (St. Anthony, Newfoundland), 64 (Green Oaks, Nova Scotia), 72 (Montreal), 80 (Toronto), 88 (Oak Park, Chicago), 96, 104, 112 (the final sanctuary).
23. Oak trees were considered signposts to initiated travelers. Red oak meant stop, and the swamp white oak meant keep moving.
24. When Champlain arrived, he gained the Algonquin's favor by helping push back the Iroquois, who were their enemies.
25. French explorer Pierre Gauthier, Sieur de La Vérendrye, whose real name was Pierre Saguirou, was born a full-blooded Algonquin whose parents were killed during hostilities with the Iroquois. His Gauthier godparents had him baptized and raised as a Frenchman.

There are many explosive revelations that jump off the pages of Mann's novel that beg to be explored further. That multiple European cultures have come to North America and both traded and intermarried with the Algonquin Natives should not be a surprise. It should also not be a surprise that, with such a deep blending of cultures, they would also share their religious beliefs, customs, and rituals.

Comparison between Masonic and Mide'win Ceremonies

THE ORIGINS OF THE MIDE'WIN, or "Society of the Mide' or Shamans" is buried in obscurity but was documented as early as 1642 by the Jesuits as being pre-Christian or pagan rituals. The rituals of initiation into the society are strikingly similar to the "Ancient and Accepted Rites" of Scottish Freemasonry, and appear to be highly

PRINCIPAL ALGONQUIAN TRIBES.		
Abnaki.	Menominee.	Ottawa.
Algonquin.	Miami.	Pamlico.
Arapaho.	Micmac.	Pennacook.
Cheyenne.	Mohegan.	Pequot.
Conoy.	Montagnais.	Piankishaw.
Cree.	Montauk.	Pottawotomi.
Delaware.	Munsee.	Powhatan.
Fox.	Nanticoke.	Sac.
Illinois.	Narraganset.	Shawnee.
Kickapoo.	Nauset.	Siksika.
Mahican.	Nipmuc.	Wampanoag.
Massachuset.	Ojibwa.	Wappinger.

This is a list of the thirty-six Native American tribes that comprise the Algonquin Nation. (Bureau of Ethnology, Seventh Annual Report, page 48)

compelling evidence of contact with early explorers who practiced similar rituals. The details of the indoctrination into the Mide'win Society are analogous to the process of becoming a Master Mason (in Templarism, the analog of the fourth degree would be a member of the Order of the Temple).

During a visit to Minnesota in January of 2012, Bill Mann reviewed this section and shared several interesting insights and facts. The following is a comparison of specific aspects of the rituals of both Masonic and Mide' win initiation through the four degrees. I gleaned the details of the Mide' win rituals from the Smithsonian's Seventh Annual Report to the Bureau of Ethnology, for the years 1885 to 1886. When I shared this lengthy document with Bill, he was surprised these sacred rituals had been recorded at all, let alone in such detail.

Not being a Mason myself, to get accurate details of Masonic ritual I used the Internet to find several written sources, and spoke with friends who are Masons. They helped point out the numerous similarities in the rituals between the two groups. The following must be qualified as I am just pointing out similarities based on what is available through the public record, based primarily on what was recorded by a Christian-Jesuit missionary! Because of this knowledge and experience, Bill was quick to point out that the original Masonic degrees of the Blue Lodge were comprised of *four* degrees, not three as it is today.

The four degrees correspond (among other things) to the four Cardinal points (east, west, north, and south), which complete the "square" and reveals a hidden inner fifth element, the eternal spirit within man that aspires to ascend to the sky. In the end, the rituals rely on the same basic principle of turning a boy into a man, or a girl into woman, or both into better, well-rounded people. Their general journey, whether through the Masonic Lodge, the Templar Preceptory, or the Mide'win Mide'wigan, begins by entering the east door and progressing to the west, following the tract of the sun across the sky, and stopping at various stations or posts to acquire knowledge through specific teachings along the way.

The "lodge" itself is constructed according to strict sacred geometrical dimensions and in the same proportion. The two main principles taught to the candidate/initiate are sacred geometry and moral allegory (for Native Americans, its myth and legend). The primary thing the candidate seeks is knowledge or "light."

The equivalents of the four degrees in Freemasonry, Templarism, and the Grand Medicine Society are as follows:

> Freemasonry—1) Entered Apprentice; 2) Learned Apprentice; 3) Master Mason; 4) Select and Master Mason.[71]
>
> Templarism—1) Illustrious Order of the Red Cross; 2) Order of St. Paul (Order of the Mediterranean Pass; 3) Order of St. John (Order of Malta); 4) Order of the Temple.
>
> Mide'win or Grand Medicine Society—1) Birth/Purification (sweat lodge); 2) Life (learning to identify the medicine plants within nature and mixing and applying the medicines); 3) Death; 4) Rebirth (Using the medicines to fast and hibernate like the bear and to gain visions/dreams that are then interpreted by the Elder or Master).

The Mide'win Society is comprised of an indefinite number of Mide' of both sexes, and the rituals for initiation are graded into four separate and distinct degrees. The Mide' shamans kept birch-bark records using detailed incised lines of the number of degrees the owner is entitled. These records are considered sacred and kept private, only brought forward for examination when an accepted candidate has paid his fee, and then only after necessary preparation by fasting and offerings of tobacco.

The following is a comparison of specific aspects of the rituals of both Masonic and Mide'win initiation through the four degrees. The details of the Mide'win rituals came from the Smithsonian's Seventh Annual Report to the Bureau of Ethnology, for the years 1885-1886 as well as other sources.

> **Application for Membership** – A Mide'win candidate's application is reviewed by one of the officiating elders who then calls upon the three assisting Mide' for a conference at his wig'iwam. Tobacco, provided by the candidate,

is distributed and smoked as an offering to the Creator, for his favor in the deliberations. The host then presents the auditors with an account of the candidate's previous life, they determine the presents and gifts intended for the attending members of the society and the fee of gifts to the officiating priests. If all things are favorable, then they select an instructor, or presiding preceptor, who is usually appointed from among these four elders.

A Freemason must petition for membership that must be signed by two Master Masons, at least one from the Lodge he is planning to join. Three members are sent out to interview the candidate who must undergo a background check to ensure they have had no prior felonies and therefore qualified for membership. A vote is then taken by the membership of the Lodge which must be unanimous.

Sponsorship – A candidate to the Mide' can be of either sex and must be confirmed by an officiating elder, who invites three Mide' to visit the candidate to explain the process and confirm them as a reputable member of the tribe with a favorable past. Upon acceptance, tobacco is offered by the candidate who then commences smoking the pipe and after each whiff pays respects to the four cardinal points as well as upward to the Creator, and then downward to Noko'mis, the grandmother of the universe and to those who have already passed.

The candidate must be sponsored by at least two members of the lodge who personally vouch for him.

Payment of Gifts – The candidate is required to provide gifts for the elders who perform the degrees which might include blankets, robes, horses, tobacco, food, and other items. With each degree the amount of gifts increases until four times the number of gifts are required for a candidate to apply for the fourth degree.

A Freemason must pay a fee to progress through the various degrees.

Purification – For four days prior to the initiation ceremony in all four degrees the candidate must be purified in sweat-lodge built to the east of the sacred lodge. The candidate must dwell upon the seriousness and sacred character of the new life they are about to embrace.

The new initiate spends time in the "Chamber of Reflection" before receiving his first degree. He must sit alone at a table with symbols designed to invoke personal reflection upon morality, mortality, and other serious personal matters unique the individual.

Attendees – Many people attend the ceremony to witness the candidate's initiation. These people may include family members, friends, and the Mide' elders, many of whom have traveled great distances to provide support for the initiate as well as participate in the ceremony and associated feasts.

The attendees of a candidate's initiation include those who have already successfully completed that degree. They have traveled afar to provide support for the initiate as well participate in the degree ritual.

Procession – The order of marching to the east entrance is first the candidate, then the preceptor, then the officiating elders, and then immediate family and relatives. Upon entering, all attendees rise and then participate in a march around the inside of the lodge (circumambulation) four times and return to their original positions. The candidate then stands on a blanket before the four Mide' shaman (in the first degree, eight in the second degree).

Masonic degrees involve a similar perambulation of the lodge by the initiate throughout several stations within the degrees. Note: Freemasons I consulted were reticent to divulge further details per their obligations. However, they confirmed the Native's rituals of procession were indeed similar to aspects of Masonic lodge functions.

Ceremony – The initiation ceremony begins with the candidate leading a precession of the Mide' shaman to the east entrance of the Mide'wigan. At the entrance the candidate stops and the shaman and preceptor enter the lodge and march around the enclosure proceeding to their left toward the south and circling four times (eight times in the second degree). The candidate then enters the east door, is addressed by the officiating elder, presents his gifts to the spirits, and then proceeds to march into the enclosure then turning south and then west (following the course of the daily sun) around four times, followed by those in attendance. The ceremony rituals involves singing of sacred songs, smoking tobacco with offerings to the six directions (east, south, west, north, the sky, and the earth), story-telling, speeches, lengthy ceremonial dancing, and feasts.

The representation of the Masonic lodge is the same with the sky (symbolically represented in the Masonic lodge with the stars and other heavenly bodies painted on the ceiling as opposed to the actual sky in the roofless Mide'wigan) and four cardinal points, three of which represent various officers' stations. Relevant speeches are given as the progression of the various degrees unfold. Masonic rituals include music, theatrical performances, transmission of legends, and meals of "fellowship."

"New Life" of the Candidate – The leading elder holds a Mide' sack like a gun and shoots the candidate while preceptor and assistants place their hands on candidate's shoulders and cause his body to tremble. The third time, the elder aims at the kneeling man's breast as if shooting him. After a fourth time, the elder aims and shoots the Mide' sack at the candidates head. He then falls forward to the ground feigning death. Mide' sacks of the elders are then placed onto candidate's back (major body joints in the second and third degrees) and then chant in regular succession to the east, south, west, north, and then to the sky, and touches his body which brings the candidate new life.[72]

Shooting the Mi'gis. (Bureau of Ethnology, Seventh Annual Report, Figure 15)

An important part of the "New Life" ceremony is the mi'gis shell the candidate carries in his mouth. The Mi'gis shell represents the candidate's soul.

In the third degree of the Blue Lodge a similar resurrection sequence occurs where the candidate is "Brought to new life." Note: Here again, the details of this important and sacred ceremony are not to be divulged to non-Mason, or the "Profane." Even though these details can be obtained through an Internet search, out of respect for my Masonic friends they will not be repeated here. However, the points of similarity between the Mide'wiwin and Freemasonic "New Life" ceremonies, where the candidate's "Third Eye" is opened are many.[73]

Presentation of a Mide' Sack – Upon completion of the resurrection ceremony the Chief then presents the new member with a Mide' sack (shaman's pouch). The candidate then offers thanks to the chief and then continues to thank the entire congregation for their presence.

At the appropriate point after the third degree, the candidate is presented with gifts, and upon completion of the degree he receives his Masonic apron. At this point, the Master Mason is now allowed to address the lodge.

Music – Many songs are sung during the four degrees as part of the transference of practical and spiritual information. A Mide' drum and rattles are used in the ceremony.

Masonic lodges have a music book with songs, but rarely do they have the occasion for singing. Music and song has been variously used throughout time within the degrees.

> **Secrets** – The primary secrets imparted to the candidate pertain in large part to being taught the proper use of medicinal plants and remedies for illness. The bulk of the ceremony involves the teaching of moral lessons and offering respect to the Creator and other spirits. The candidate is also taught magic and to become possessed of higher power and increased influence.[74]

The Masonic candidate is progressively brought to the realization of "his own unity with deity," and the resultant responsibilities that entails. These obligations become more extensive as he progresses on his journey through the degrees. Certain progressions do involve aspects of healing and enlightenment (acquisition of ancient knowledge).

> **Secret Words** – Certain phrases are repeatedly sung with varying reverence to impress upon the initiate.

The candidate is required to memorize many secret words and phrases and recite them when called upon during the progression of the various degrees.

> **Guards** – Mide' guards are stationed at the doors of the Mide'wigan (lodge) to prevent intrusion by the uninitiated and theft of the gifts.

"Tyler" is a guard armed with a sword stationed outside the lodge entrance when in session to ward off all "Cowen and eavesdroppers."

> **The Mide'wigan (Grand Medicine Lodge)** – The enclosure in which all four degrees are held is roughly eighty feet long by twenty feet wide with the long axis aligned in an east-west direction, or in the direction where the sun rises in late summer when the ceremonies are performed.

One Mason effectively described the lodge where the Masonic rituals are held with the following: "The Masonic lodge inculcates divine geometry within its structure"

The predominance of the Knights Templar red-and-white colors in the face paint of the Mide' shaman, along with the same colors of the sacred posts, which are analogous to Masonic pillars, cannot simply be a coincidence. These facts together with so many specifics of the Mide' rituals being mirror images to Masonic ritual makes the case for a connection between the two societies a near certainty. Skeptics will have difficulty arguing the rituals of the two groups developed independently on separate continents. Since it is documented by the earliest missionaries and explorers that Mide' rituals were already in practice, there can be only one plausible explanation that validates Bill's thesis. This evidence is consistent with pre-Columbian contact in North America by the Templars with

SCEND VI. PLAYING MURDER.—"JUBELUM" kills him with the Setting Maul and tumbles him into the Canvas.

In the third degree of the Blue Lodge, the candidate is allegorically killed upon being struck with a setting maul later to be "raised' in a resurrection-like ceremony and "given new life." (Cook, page 24, 1909)

Native people that had a profound impact on both cultures.[75] This evidence also supports the theory that the Templars intentionally brought the bloodline of Jesus and Mary Magdalene to North America to protect it from the Church. (See color section, Figures 13 & 14)

Bill insists the Templars not only brought the royal bloodline to America, but made the Natives their Templar brothers and guardians of the sacred bloodline and other Grail secrets. Short of a comprehensive DNA study involving a large number of Native Americans from several tribes, it is difficult to prove this bloodline connection. However, Daniel Graysolon Du Luth does provide an interesting clue. This information comes from the classic volume on the history of Native Americans in Minnesota that ironically, was written by the same man who proclaimed the Kensington Rune Stone genuine in 1910, Professor Newton H. Winchell. On page 524 of *Aborigines of Minnesota,* Winchell wrote the following:

> 1679. The next white man to set foot on Minnesota soil was Duluth, a free, unlicensed fur-trader, who penetrated as far as the "forty Sioux villages" whose central point was Kathio, at the south end of Mille Lacs. Duluth's efforts to establish peace among the Indians of Minnesota were no less than those of Radisson or Chouart. He called the grand council of all the northern nations "at the extremity of Lake Superior" on the fifteenth of September, 1679 and got their good will by means of presents. During the following winter, in order that the peace which they contracted might be lasting, he induced the nations to make reciprocal marriages, and to hold subsidiary meetings in the woods, which he attended. The tribes chiefly concerned were the Assiniboine and the Sioux.[76]

A couple of interesting points come from this citation. First, while the reported intermarriages here are between differing Native tribes, Bill Mann's claim of intermarriages with Europeans seems all the more plausible. The second point is: could it be possible that the meeting place in the woods to discuss and reach agreement on the peace contracts be where the Du Luth Stone was carved? Perhaps the inscribed boulder itself was carved to commemorate the contract and served as a permanent reminder at the divide which was the boundary between tribal lands.

Not only Bill Mann claims Native people in North America intermarried and formed important strategic alliances with the medieval Templars. I have had discussions about pre-Columbian contact with elders from the Cree, Ojibwa, Mi'kmaq, and the Cherokee. To them, it's a given Templars were here in North America. They told me as much during the three-day Atlantic Conference in Halifax, Nova Scotia, in October of 2009. I gave two lectures at the conference on successive days and after my first lecture on the Kensington Rune Stone, I was introduced to Michael Thrasher, an elder with the Cree in Saskatchewan.

Michael and I had a lengthy discussion on the research I presented on the Kensington Rune Stone. He pretty much agreed with everything I speculated on, with the exception of one thing. He said, "Our Templar brothers would never have placed a land claim stone in the ground behind our backs."

When Michael said this I didn't know what to say to him. The inscription clearly reads like a land deed, is double-dated to protect the date with an imbedded code and even says, ". . . acquisition business, or taking up land." When I tried to rationalize the land claim he would have none of it. He was adamant. I couldn't figure out why everything else fit together so well, yet Michael's words stood firmly in the way of my tidy conclusion.

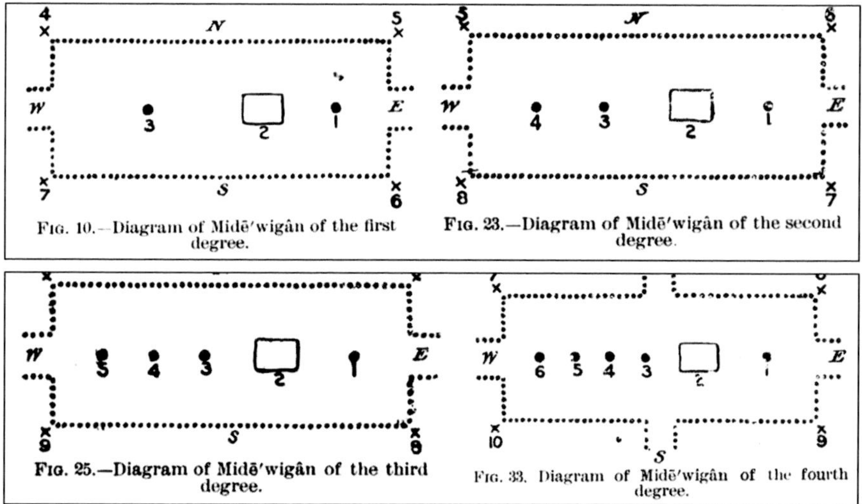

Fig. 10.—Diagram of Midē'wigân of the first degree.

Fig. 23.—Diagram of Midē'wigân of the second degree.

Fig. 25.—Diagram of Midē'wigân of the third degree.

Fig. 33. Diagram of Midē'wigân of the fourth degree.

An increasing number of sacred posts (1, 3, 4, 5, and 6) are added inside the Mide'wigan (lodge) as depicted in these diagrams of the four degrees. During the ceremony, the sacred blanket (#2) is where the initiate dies, and is then allegorically brought back to life by the Mide' shaman. Cedar trees are planted at each of the outer corners of the lodge (4, 5, 6, 7, 8, 9, and 10). In the fourth degree the Mide'wigan has open doorways to the inside on the north and south walls. (Bureau of Ethnology, Seventh Annual Report, Figures 10, 23, 25, and 33)

A general view of the Mide'wigan lodge for the fourth degree. Roughly six paces outside the north and south entrances are small brush structures, called bear nests, for fasting, which are just large enough to admit a body. (Bureau of Ethnology, Seventh Annual Report, Figure 34)

It wasn't until Bill Mann visited in September of 2012 that it dawned on me that Michael was right. Bill and I were driving back from Alexandria after seeing the Kensington Rune Stone at the Runestone Museum. We were discussing the Templar connection and what might have been happening with their Native brethren when the inscription was carved. We were throwing out likely scenarios, when it suddenly hit me. The Templars didn't carve and bury the land claim stone behind the Native's backs—they did it in front of them.

If Bill is right, the Templars indeed warned the Natives that the Christians were coming, and it wasn't going to be good. Then it seems likely they put the land claim document carved in stone in the ground, at this strategic location in 1362, as a preemptive measure, knowing the Europeans would take the land while persecuting the indigenous people as they swept across the continent. The Templars knew first-hand how the Church operated, having had their wealth, property, and very lives taken away only a few decades earlier. Theoretically, the land claim stone would have usurped any future claims to the land, allowing the Templars to protect their "Blood brothers."

Obviously, that scenario didn't play out and is a mystery in itself. Sadly, history played out as the Templars predicted. The Christians did come and what happened to most of the Native tribes of North America can be summed up in one word: genocide. Why the Templars never exercised the land claim can only be speculated. However, as I suggested in my first "Hooked X" book, because the Kensington Rune Stone was carved from a much larger stone and the rest of the slab has never been found, it seems highly likely there is at least another land claim stone out there somewhere.

Bill returned home to Canada, and I placed a call to Michael Thrasher on September 16, 2012. "Michael, do you remember telling me the Templars would never put a land claim stone in the ground behind 'our backs?' I didn't understand what you meant back then, but I do now, and you were right." After explaining my new thinking, Michael agreed the theory made much more sense.

Cross of Lorraine

ANOTHER IMPORTANT ASPECT of all Masonry concerns signs of recognition, which include various handshakes, hand and body gestures, and symbols. One of the symbols rumored to be used as a sign of recognition by the medieval Knights Templar when they came into contact with Natives in North America was the Cross of Lorraine. The Templars were given the Cross of Lorraine as their official emblem and True Cross by King Baldwin II when the Christians captured Jerusalem from the Saracens in 1099.[77] Jerusalem was ruled for a time by the House of Lorraine. This double-barred cross often has a smaller bar on top that represents the scroll inscription of INRI, which the Romans affixed to the True Cross and mockingly stands for "Jesus of Nazareth, King of the Jews."[78] The Lorraine Cross became a sacred but lesser known symbol to the order and still held in esteem by modern-day Masonic Templars. A Cross of Lorraine tilted twenty-two and a half degrees to represent the tilt of the earth, is the symbol of the presiding preceptor of the Knights Templar in Canada, and appears on the "White Hats" of the esteemed thirty-third-degree Scottish Rite Freemasons in the United States.[79] (See color section, Figures 15 & 16)

What I suspect is that the Cross of Lorraine might have been a secret symbol of recognition to allied Native American tribes when they came in contact with Templar parties. To flash the wrong symbol or cross would alert the Natives the visiting party might not be friendly and thus be on their guard. Examples of the Lorraine Cross are found in Indian artwork and adornments. Lorraine Crosses were common trade items with Natives and makes one wonder why that particular style of cross was so popular with them.

To many North American Native tribes, the "rain-cross" was the symbol of the sacred dragonfly they prayed to for rain because the dragonfly appears with the summer rains which allow plants to grow and sustain life. The Pueblo, Navajo, and Hopi Indians of the Southwest United States have used the double-barred cross as a symbol of the dragonfly in rock art, basketry, pottery, textiles, wall paintings, and personal adornments since prehistoric times.

When the Spaniards came in the early sixteenth century the ease of acceptance of their crosses had less to do with acceptance of the foreigner's religion, but the familiarity of the designs in their own culture.[80]

The Bat Creek Stone has a double-barred cross symbol isolated below the single line inscription that strongly resembles a dragonfly. Could this symbol of recognition between indigenous people in North America and early Europeans from the Mediterranean region date back to biblical times? If we assume this premise is true, another interesting question is: could the first-century Europeans connected to whoever created the Bat Creek inscription have taken the double-barred cross from the Natives?

There is more evidence beyond the Bat Creek Stone consistent with this scenario. If we look at one of the main points that have materialized in the writing of this book, that Jesus and Mary Magdalene were not only married, but were royalty with a large amount of tangible assets and a loyal following. The alternate story of Jesus and his followers that has survived two millennia is after they were defeated by the first-century Romans, Mary Magdalene escaped first to Egypt and then eventually disappeared into Southern France where her bloodline descendants carried the secret of that history, hidden from the Church, into the future. When considering the story of Jesus in this context, many of our findings actually do fit together quite well. The one thing abundantly clear is the Cross of Lorraine was very sacred and important to both cultures

To add a little more intrigue and possible evidence to support the Jesus and Mary Magdalene bloodline story, on the fan-shaped baton (Artifact #13) of the Tucson lead artifacts found in 1924, are three Lorraine crosses carved into the lead. Since both Latin and Hebrew occur on the artifacts, the culture that produced them had to have been a unique blend that existed sometime between 775 and 900 A.D. As previously discussed, it turns out such a Jewish princedom apparently did exist at this time in Southern France, which has been the cradle of the legend of the bloodline of Jesus and Mary Magdalene.

The Lorraine crosses on the Tucson baton appear to fill in another interesting historical piece of the puzzle sometime between 200 and 350 years before King Baldwin II bestowed the important symbol upon the Knights Templar in Jerusalem. According to the *Foundation for Medieval Genealogy*, the House of Lorraine can be reliably dated back to the eleventh century, and tentatively dated back through the male line to the eighth century.[81] The timing and location in Southern France for the House of Lorraine fits well for the

Here are two examples of thirty-second-degree Scottish Rite Freemasons wearing jewels with the Cross of Lorraine prominently displayed. The man on the left is Henry G. Thayer, past grand commander of the Knights Templar of Indiana, inspector general from 1887 to 1888; the man on the right is Judge David Sinclair-Bouschor who was a past grand master of the Grand Lodges of Freemasons of Minnesota. (Wolter, 2009)

dates on the Tucson artifacts and may serve as a starting point for researchers possibly to determine who may be connected to a bold pre-Columbian expedition to what is now Southern Arizona.

That many Native American tribes used the Cross of Lorraine as an important and even sacred symbol could potentially lend support to one of Bill Mann's main assertions. If the Lorraine Cross was symbolic of the dynastic families that traced their ancestry back to the royal marriage of Jesus and Mary Magdalene, which includes the leadership of the Knights Templar and the Cistercians, then it would also be a very appropriate symbol for an aboriginal nation that literally carried the royal bloodline in their veins.

On January 10, 2012, a serendipitous moment occurred during Bill's visit when Janet and I took him on a tour of the Twin Cities. Our first stop was at the Washburn water tower in South Minneapolis, tucked into a small neighborhood called Tangletown. The name stems from the curious and random arrangement of the street system that seems to have been inserted into the otherwise usual north-south, east-west layout. At the center of Tangletown, which is the high point in the area, stands an imposing 110-foot tall, eight-sided concrete water tower. Bill's eyes widened, and a smile came to his face as he looked upon the eight concrete Templar knights guarding the water. Near the top, directly above the knights were eight eagles (Phoenixes?) sitting on top of elongated downward pointing triangles (Sacred Feminine).[82]

Janet and I already knew the tower had been designed in 1932 by architect and Freemason Harry Wild Jones. We told Bill we stopped by Jones's old home and talked with the current owners, who knew the history of the previous owner. They said Jones had built a tunnel from his home under the street to his friend and fellow Mason's house. Bill said many Freemasons in the past built tunnels and underground refuges to keep their masonic activities private.

From there we stopped at Fort Snelling where Bill was impressed with the view of the confluence of the Mississippi and Minnesota rivers, a place, "The Dakotahs used to claim superiority over other people, because, their sacred men asserted that the mouth of the Minnesota River was immediately over the center of the earth, and below the center of the heavens."[83] In 1805, Lieutenant Zebulon Pike (1779 to 1813) negotiated a treaty with the Sioux chiefs for the land where Fort Snelling was later built in 1825.[84]

We then drove to the Fort Snelling Chapel constructed of the Platteville Limestone formation, a light-tan stone used to construct many buildings in the Twin Cities. I pointed out the sixty-foot round tower on the south side of the church with Jesus on a cross at the top. Bill looked up, pointed and said, "There's your Cross of Lorraine right there."

After living in this town most of my life and driving by this church thousands of times over the years, I'd never really looked at that cross. Sure enough, not only was the second small cross there, but there was more. The man on the cross was not Jesus, and this person was holding a large sword just like the knights at the water tower. The other interesting thing was the longer lower

This Native American bronze gorget has several X's and a prominently featured Cross of Lorraine symbol at the center. That gorgets are highly revered persona adornments speaks to the importance of this sacred symbol to Native cultures. (Wolter, 2012)

The equilateral Cross of Lorraine (cross bars are spaced equidistant from each end symbolic of Dualism) is seen on the armband of a Yakima man named Inashah, photographed in 1910 (left), and in darker part of the beaded panel (right) worn proudly by a Sioux girl photographed in 1907. This 1 5/8" long pewter Cross of Lorraine was a common trade item with Native Americans in the 1800s (middle). (Photos courtesy of the Library of Congress, Prints & Photographs Division, Edward S. Curtiss Collection, LC-USZ62-110502 and LC-USZ62-119409)

bar of this Lorraine Cross, were actually wings symbolic of the saint this haloed person was supposed to be.

Upon thinking about the wings, it occurred to me that they might also be symbolic of the Native American Thunderbird. In light of our discussions with Bill and his revelations about the early Templar-Native alliance in North America, the dual symbolism seemed to fit beautifully. After all, Pike was a prominent Freemason and perhaps his treaty with the Sioux had more to it than meets the eye.[85] I had recently wondered if that cross was pointing to where the sun rose on the winter solstice. In fact, a few months earlier, I had measured it, and the cross actually pointed almost due south. Following that line south from the chapel tower across the Minnesota River to the east bank lies a very sacred Native burial grounds now called Pilot Knob.[86] To this day that land has not been developed, and I couldn't help but wonder if Pike agreed that land would not be desecrated or developed. Given the inevitability of the white man's advancement upon Indian land, maybe the guarantee of the promised preservation of that sacred land, along with the money, was the best Pike could do.

It turns out that, on the sacred Native land overlooking the confluence of the two mighty rivers, is also a Masonic cemetery called Acacia Park Cemetery (an acacia twig is inserted into the hand of a deceased Mason during his funeral and is symbolic of immortality of the soul[87]). Here again, we see the "bonding of brothers" that apparently continues to this day.

A Cherokee friend, Leslie Kalen, brought up the possibility that the double-barred cross symbol that sits alone below the eight characters on the Bat Creek Stone might be an early version of the Cross of Lorraine. It seemed far-fetched at first, but after seeing the crosses on the Tucson lead baton and seeing a clear connection between the early Hebrews, apparently through the house of Lorraine and the medieval Knights Templar, I began to think that Leslie might be right!

A second look at the Hooked/Big X and one of the smaller characters in the Copiale Cipher clearly shows them to be different depictions of the Cross of Lorraine. The smaller character is an equilateral version with the two parallel bars being equal length spaced equally apart is apparent symbolism of Dualism since no matter which end is up, it looks the same. The Hooked/Big X also has a dot or ball at the top of the upper right bar above the second, smaller curved bar and is reminiscent of the small circle above the large Lorraine Cross on the Tucson Lead Artifact #12, suggesting a possible connection.

To the list of other symbols I've researched with similar Egyptian/Hebrew/Knights Templar/Freemasonry ideological connections through time, it seems the Cross of Lorraine needs to be added. Some examples of these symbols include the obelisk, the Star of David, the planet Venus inspired five-pointed star, egg-shaped and notched keystones, the equilateral triangle, and, of course, the colors red and white, which are symbolic of Upper and Lower Egypt and the Knights Templar.[88] Once these symbols enter people's conscientiousness, they begin to see them all around us in American culture today. Could the people behind these organizations be somehow connected to the first-century royal bloodline families?

I'd found the Lorraine Cross in the logos of the American Cancer Society and Nabisco Foods. I also noticed a familiar sign I'd seen for many years. Now that I had the "eyes to see," it jumped out like a flashing beacon. I was looking at a sign with the logo of one of the biggest energy

The Washburn water tower is 110 feet tall and was designed by architect and Freemason, Harry Wild Jones, and built in 1932. The octagonal tower has eight eagles perched on downward pointing triangles and eight sword-wielding knights symbolically guarding the water in the tower. (Wolter, 2010)

On January 11, 2012, the first rays of the rising sun hit the Lorraine Cross with a saint (who looks a lot like George Washington) holding a sword symbolic of the Templars, at the top of the round tower of the Fort Snelling Chapel at the confluence of the Mississippi and Minnesota rivers. The knight on the cross is pointed directly at the sacred spiritual site and burial ground for the Shakopee Mdewakanton Sioux now called Pilot Knob. (Wolter, 2012)

companies at a local gas station. A big, red Cross of Lorraine on a white background was in the Exxon Energy's logo. Raymond Lowey (1893 to 1986) was born in France, fought for the French army in World War I, and came to the United States in 1919. He was an industrial designer who created the Exxon logo in 1966.[89] (See color section, Figures 17, 18, & 19)

Bill Mann pointed out in September of 2012 that the blue in the logo could represent the Atlantic Ocean the Templars traveled across to the New World. After looking at the logo a little closer, I noticed the Cross of Lorraine was tipping to the left. Could this mean to the west? Could it be possible that the symbolism of the Exxon logo summed up means that the medieval Knights Templar brought the bloodline of Jesus and Mary Magdalene across the Atlantic Ocean to the New World (New Jerusalem) in the west? Whether Raymond Lowey had all of this in mind we'll never know, but it is an intriguing possibility.[90]

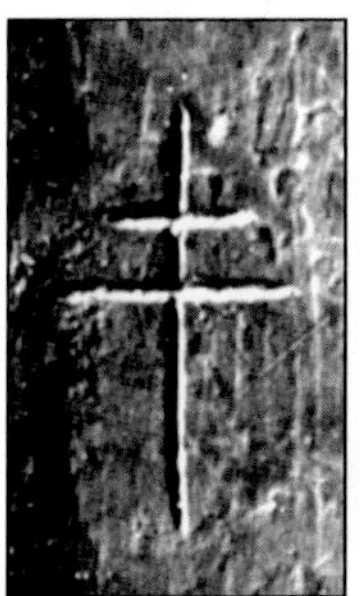

Three Lorraine crosses appear on the Tucson lead fan-shaped baton found in 1924, and date to 765 to 900 a.d. (far left, middle left, and middle right). The second example on the Tucson lead baton shows the Lorraine Cross at the top of a temple in Jerusalem which is consistent with the Templar's reverence for the Lorraine Cross which symbolized the Kingdom of Jerusalem. The mysterious double-barred cross that sits below the inscription on the Bat Creek Stone could be a predecessor of the Cross of Loraine that likely dates back to biblical times (far right). The carved dot next to the Bat Creek "cross" could have been a coded acknowledgment to the Creator by the carver. (Wolter, 2011 & 2010)

The Mandan

THE BAT CREEK STONE INVESTIGATION brought to mind the idea there must be more evidence linking Native American tribes with early visitors to North America beyond the Mide'win secret society. Perhaps the most talked about Native tribe linked with early visitors were the isolated group of "blonde haired, blue eyed" Indians in central North Dakota, the Mandan. The social aspects of the Mandan were complex and highly integrated. They were predominantly an agricultural society with common and private gardens. However, they also participated in summer buffalo hunts, which provided meat and fur critical to their survival.[91]

They also appear to have been dualists reminiscent of the Cathars. According to Catlin, "The Mandan believe in a Great (or Good) Spirit, also of an Evil Spirit, who they say existed long before the Good Spirit, and is far superior in power."[92]

What made the Mandan unique were their ceremonial lodges that were different from other lodges in they had flat fronts and had a greater length than width.[93] Within this medicine-lodge, the Mandan carried out an annual four-day ritual called the *Okipa* ceremony. George Catlin spent two years observing their culture and painting individuals and daily scenes of life within their tribe. Catlin also recorded detailed notes about the *Okipa* ceremony that he witnessed first-hand in 1833-1834, three years before small-pox decimated the Mandan to near extinction.

Catlin was convinced the Mandan were descended from the Hebrews but, according to Henrietta Mertz, was not aware of important details discovered after his time that would have added to his argument. One example is the blue glass bead unique to the Mandan. Mertz writes, "The ancient knowledge of manufacture of the blue glass beads, centered around Egypt and Eastern Mediterranean areas from the seventeenth century B.C., through the fourth century A.D., was a matter unknown to Catlin when he wrote back in 1834."[94]

While reading about the early Egyptian and Hebrew makers of blue glass beads I couldn't help but think about the blue glass medallion with the seven-candled Menorah that Donald Ruh reportedly found in the Sand cave in the Panther Mountain Impact Area of New York.

Mertz goes on to list the following items that parallel both the *Okipa* ceremony and the Exodus story:

1. One head man, or leader, who alone went up to the top of a mountain outside of camp; *Moses to Mount Sinai*, the Lone Man to a mountain to the west of the village.
2. On his descent, he was clothed in white; *Moses in a cloud*, Lone Man with his body painted.
3. Cattle were herded into the village away from the ceremony.
4. Villagers were not permitted near the mountain but remained at a distance, in camp.
5. At the approach of the lone figure toward the village, people trembled and were shaken by fear as if awaiting some dreadful calamity.
6. When the solitary figure arrived at the camp, fear in both cases was dispelled by his reassurance. They no longer were afraid and no combat took place, although both expected it. In both cases the personage received a warm welcome.
7. Immediately upon his arrival at camp, this solitary individual made the rounds of the village, stopping at every house (lodge of the Mandan) and collecting a voluntary contribution.
8. Every person contributed and among the contributions were various types of tools useful in building the sacred edifice.
9. In both accounts, the ritual took place annually, not on a specific day, but rather according to the ripeness of the season.
10. In each case, the lone figure had the means of opening the sacred building used solely on this one occasion during the year.
11. When the building was opened, it was first cleaned and the floor strewn with aromatic and sweet-smelling herbs.
12. Once the building was ready, the young men who were to be anointed entered the prepared room after having gone through a blood purification service.
13. Once in the sacred room and taken their places, the solitary figure who came from the mountain greeted them with a short speech and at that point, introduced a second important personage who was to take over and carry on the sacred rites within the building. In each instance, at the time this second dignitary assumed the leadership, the original person, he who had come down the mountain, stepped aside.
14. The second important character, in each instance, had the sole power, within himself alone, to conduct the rites and retain custody of the sacred vessels and religious paraphernalia pertaining to the ritual. No other individual came near or touched anything.
15. Both stories state that the specifications of the building itself were given to the dignitary who had first gone up the mountain.
16. Within the building, outer screens or doors barred the entryway into the interior, and each entryway was guarded by selected members, priests in one case, sentinels in the other.

17. In the center of the building were four tall poles from which veils, or hangings, of costly and variegated cloth were suspended, shielding the sacred section within.
18. Behind this veil stood the altar, a small structure on which reposed the most sacred object of the Israelites as well as the Mandan.
19. Dimensions of the altar are given in both cases. The Biblical account gave the size as forty-five inches while Catlin estimated forty-eight inches.
20. On this platform rested the most sacred relic of the people, the Israelites and the Mandan.
21. This holy relic was too sacred to be approached by any ordinary man.

About this relic Catlin wrote, ". . . so sacred was that object, and so important its secrets or mysteries, that not I alone, but even the young men, who were passing the ordeal, and all the village, save the conductor of the mysteries, were stopped from approaching it, or knowing what it was. This little mystery-thing, whatever it was, had the appearance from where I sat, of a small tortoise or frog lying on its back, with its head and legs quite extended, and wound and tasseled off with exceedingly delicate *red and blue, and yellow* ribbons or tassels, and other bright colored ornaments and seemed, from the devotions paid to it, to be the very nucleus of their mysteries—the *sanctissimus sanctorum*, from which seemed to emanate all the sanctity of the proceedings, and to which, all seemed to be paying the highest devotional respect."[95]

22. Both the Israelites and Mandan had tiny blue, red and yellow tassels sewed on corners.

Mertz pointed out that, "The Biblical account states that the service cloths for use in the sanctuary shall be woven of violet, purple and scarlet—Josephus gave the colors as: *blue, red and yellow . . .*"

The matching colors of the tassels of the Israelites and the Mandan are the final, convincing piece of evidence that, when combined with other parallel items of the *Okipa* ceremony, and now with the Bat Creek Hebrew inscription very likely over fifteen hundred years old, presents a completely different history of North American that can no longer be ignored. (See color section, Figure 20)

Ironically, Henrietta Mertz (1898 to 1985), would find the Bat Creek artifacts at the Smithsonian Institution only a few years after her *Nephtali* book was published. Her recognition that the characters appeared to be Phoenician and not Cherokee, unwittingly triggered a chain of events that fifty-six years later would culminate in the geological examination by the author that confirmed its authenticity in May of 2010.[96]

Mertz concluded her analysis of the parallels between the Mandan *Okipa* and Exodus ceremonies with the following statements: "Eight thousand miles and two thousand years separated these two records. That the two records run parallel must be conceded. Direct knowledge transmitted from one to the other by some means had to be present. Human history records no equal duplicate parallels. The Mandan, without question, was a direct lineal descendent of the Israelites, AND NO OTHER."[97]

In light of Mertz's concluding statement, the results of my analysis of the distinct parallels between the Mide'win and Knights Templar rituals become important. Here again, the voluminous similarities between them make the possibility of the rituals developing independently of each on separate continents untenable. For the first time to my knowledge, the similarities between these two secret societies have been presented as a confirmation that these two societies definitely had pre-Columbian contact with a deep and profound exchange of culture, which included strategic intermarriage and highly sacred religious ceremonies.

Only three years after Catlin was with the Mandan, the tribe reportedly received blankets from the U.S. military infected with the smallpox virus that essentially wiped out the tribe in 1837.[98] Some researchers have suggested the infection was intentionally spread by the government. I can assure the reader that many informed Native Americans believe it definitely was intentional. While I'm not suggesting a conspiracy, I do find the timing of Catlin's written observations and the demise of the Mandan to be very interesting.

Peace Medals

ANOTHER PIECE OF EVIDENCE strongly suggests a strategic alliance between the Native Americans and Freemasons within the United States government. While history does not suggest that the majority of political interests within our government during this time were sympathetic to Native American interests, there is evidence a small faction within the government were. The pursuit of land through Manifest Destiny became a title wave that overwhelmed both the sympathetic factions and ultimately the Native Americans.

On January 15, 2012, Leslie Kalen sent me a picture of an early clay trade pipe. I noticed the handshake on the pipe looked like it might be a Masonic handshake. Suddenly, I remembered Zachary Taylor's silver presidential peace medal with a similar handshake on the backside. Sure enough, it did have the handshake and what looked like other Masonic symbols. To find out more, I emailed images to a Freemason friend.

He confirmed it was indeed a Masonic handshake and that he saw other things on the back of the medal saying, "The buttons and bars on the cuff of the hand on the left likely represent the three degrees of York Rite Masonry and the downturned pipe could represent a symbolic 'burying of the hatchet' or it's time to end hostilities."

Janet chimed in adding, "Could the veins in the hand possibly represent a river system. I think I see the Mississippi River running horizontal with branches of the Arkansas, Missouri and Ohio rivers converging in what is the center of the continent?"

"Sure!" I responded, "Maybe it was confirmation of a land agreement with the Natives."

Our Freemason friend said. "If you look at the two index fingers, they make a ninety-degree angle. This would be a Masonic symbol indicating this deal was 'on the square' or 'on the level.'"

We agreed there were likely other Masonic symbols on the peace medals, first issued by the administration of George Washington. The British and the Spanish had issued medals to Native chiefs to solidify relations and confirm agreements. When the Americans took over, it was recommended to Washington that medals be produced and exchanged for previously distributed metals by the British. In 1792, the first Washington medals were distributed to chiefs of the Cherokee Nation.[99]

While researching peace medals I found a quote by a Cherokee named Black Fox at a ceremony where the peace medal of a deceased chief was being passed on to new chief on June 28, 1792. "The Dragging Canoe has left the world," he said. "He was consequence in his country. He was a friend both to his own and his white people. But his brother is still in place; and I mention now in public, that I intend presenting him with his deceased brother's medal; for he promises fair to possess sentiments similar to those of his brother, both with regard to the *red and white* [sic]."[100]

This statement by Black Fox cryptically alludes to the "red and white" without giving any context. Skeptics will likely say this statement was a reference to the new Republic of America. However, given the voluminous evidence presented here, it appears this Cherokee Indian was making a coded reference to the Templars that "those in the know," such as enlightened Freemasons and Natives alike would understand. Another curious fact is the colors of the flag of the Wolf Clan of the Cherokee, the largest of the seven clans, are red with white stars.[101]

It is an interesting coincidence that George Washington's early family crests in Durham County, England, dating from the late fourteenth and fifteenth centuries have virtually the same colors and similar design as the Cherokee Wolf Clan. Examples found in England from this period include a Washington family crest in the shape of a shield with red-and-white bands and five-pointed stars found in the Jenyn's Roll of circa 1390, and a shield with red-and-white bands with red five-pointed stars found in stained glass at Selby Abbey, in Yorkshire circa the fifteenth century.[102] The likely connection to the stars and stripes on the flag of the United States is self-evident, but why the similarity to the flag of the Cherokee Wolf Clan is not so clear. (See color section, Figure 21 & 22)

In any case, the salient question about the medals intended solely for the Native chiefs is: Why would Masonic symbolism be on them if Native leaders didn't understand the messages? The obvious answer can only be is they did.

One Ojibwa Native American prophecy keeper said their history was recorded in intervals of 400 years. Shortly before the arrival of Champlain a very important prophecy spread among the Natives: "Their people were to leave the cities and go into the wilderness, because the Christians were coming and it wasn't going to be good. The Templars warned them of the impending arrival, but they already knew about the Spanish incursions to the south and it was only a matter of time before they brought their oppressive religion to the rest of the continent."

I was only a little surprised to hear this, and it made sense. The Templars knew full well what the Church was capable of. By 1600 the Roman Inquisition had begun its rampage across Europe and was ready to extend its tentacles to the North American shores. This would also help explain one mystery historians and archaeologists have puzzled over for two centuries. What became of the mound building cultures, and where did all the people go who lived in the city of Cahokia just east of St. Louis, Missouri? Most of the theories I've heard sound more like guesses. Intentional abandonment sounds very plausible to me.

An Assiniboine elder shared an interesting story about what happened when it became clear that the Christians were going to win the religion war in North America that the Templars had warned his people about. He said that in 1710 it was time for selected Mide'win shamen to load up pack mules with sacred scrolls and bundles containing ancient knowledge and take it into the mountains in the west for safe-keeping. He relayed it was at this

The reverse side of the 1949 Zachary Taylor presidential peace medal features a Masonic handshake along with other symbols designed to send messages to the Native chiefs they were presented to. Another possible symbol within the handshake are veins in the hand representing a river system; possibly the Mississippi River with the Arkansas, Missouri and Ohio Rivers? (Wolter, 2012)

time in Europe that the Masonic United Grand Lodge in England underwent significant changes. For centuries prior, the grand master of the lodge had been a Sinclair. The grand master then became the reigning King of England. This enabled the Church to instill "Christianized" Mide'win rituals into what Natives called "The Three Fires Society."

Senior Cherokee elder Donald Rose related how, when he was a child on the reservation in the 1940s, they were not allowed to speak their Native language in school or learn the "old" ways of Cherokee life. They were essentially brainwashed to erase the Native culture by forcing them to assimilate to the Christian way of life.[103]

Looking back now, it turns out that the policy toward the Native Americans by Christian-led factions within the American and Canadian governments was simple: convert or suffer our wrath. No wonder they hid their secrets.

Evidence of pre-Columbian contact with Native Americans by European and Mediterranean cultures certainly wasn't restricted to what is now North America. Volumous evidence exists of contact in Central and South America as well. In 2010 I had an incredible opportunity to examine dozens of pre-Columbian artifacts from Panama and Columbia, both in the laboratory and in the field.

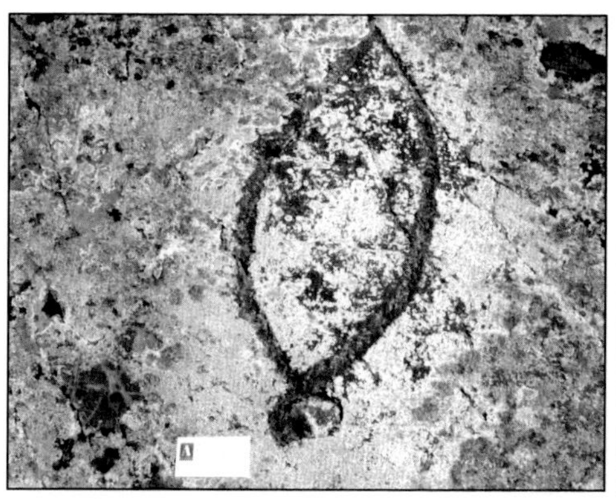

On June 19, 2008, Janet and I spent the day at Jeffers Petroglyphs State Park, in southwestern Minnesota. One of the ancient carvings that instantly caught our eyes was a Vesica Piscis (left), a commonly seen Masonic and Christian symbol. This Goddess symbol of the allegorical birth canal is produced by the intersection of two circles suggesting an advanced knowledge of geometry of the indigenous people likely passed on to them by their Knights Templar brethren. (Wolter, 2008)

Greg Cavalli's Collection

ON SEPTEMBER 1, 2010, I RECEIVED an email from Greg Cavalli, referred to me by Judy Johnson, the secretary and events planner with the Ancient Artifacts Preservation Society. Greg wrote that he heard I might be able to help him with laboratory analysis of his family's pre-Columbian artifact collection. He went on to explain that his great grandfather, Francis Xavier Cavalli, sailed to Panama multiple times beginning in 1863. During mining expeditions into the jungle, and because of his passion for Native history and art, he acquired and reportedly excavated a large collection of artifacts crafted in jade, marble, volcanic rock, carnelian and banded agate, ceramics, and tumbaga, an alloy comprised primarily of copper, zinc, and gold.

Greg sent several documents outlining the history of his family collection, testing of the artifacts he had already contracted and a list of books for me to read. He also sent photographs of his artifacts that looked incredible. He explained he was looking for someone with a scientific background to perform laboratory testing and become acquainted with the material for the ultimate purpose of providing test data for authentication. After several phone conversations, I accepted Greg's invitation to fly out to Los Angeles to meet him.

On October 14, 2010, I met Greg. We drove to Continental Coin & Jewelry Company in Van Nuys, where his collection was stored. Greg showed

On October 15, 2010, Greg Cavalli held an incredible tumbaga (copper and gold alloy) statue reportedly from Panama in his family collection assembled by his great grandfather in the 1860s. (Wolter, 2010)

me dozens of incredible jade and gold tumbaga artifacts, each one larger and more beautiful than the last. My head was spinning as I examined the incredible detail and beauty of each piece.

I told him that my curiosity had been piqued and wanted learn more. I noticed several interesting things on the artifacts and couldn't wait to get some of them under the microscope.

Two months later, Greg visited my lab to discuss moving

On December 11, 2010, I removed a three-quarter inch long bone fragment from one of Greg's tumbaga artifacts called a cacique, for Carbon-14 testing. (Wolter, 2010)

forward with a plan for testing his artifacts. He wanted me to see Panama sites where I could pull some artifacts from the ground myself. If the features on his artifacts were identical to what came out of the ground it would go a long way toward authenticating his collection and any other artifacts I might examine in the future.

On December 11, 2010, Greg showed me one particular tumbaga artifact he said it was an ancient Native chief called a "cacique." He then shook the nine-inch-tall statue. Something inside rattled. Greg then said, "They used to burn the bodies and then put a bone fragment inside a gold statue that was buried in a grave, often with other artifacts." I then told him bone could be dated. He said, "Let's see if we can get it out."

It took about fifteen minutes to get the fragment out through one of the rectangular holes on the backside of the artifact. Once freed, I then slid the brownish-white, three-quarter inch long, slightly curved piece of bone into a plastic sample bag and labeled it.

The test results from Beta Analytical for the bone fragment came back as 1,045 years old, plus or minus fifty years. This fell into the range of between 500 to 1,500 years old as the average age of the cultures that created the voluminous number of artifacts found in what is now Panama ranging into Columbia, South America.

The White Indians of Darien

After sharing my stories about Greg's collection, Leslie Kalen began sending Janet and me books she thought were important. One was "*White Indians of Darien*," by Richard O. Marsh. The book dealth with the White Indians from the mostly unexplored region of eastern Panama in the mid-1920s.

Marsh was sent to Panama by Henry Ford and Roy Firestone to investigate the potential for developing rubber tree plantations for the rapidly expanding automobile industry. While in the dense jungles of Darien, east of the Panama Canal, Marsh encountered three young female Natives with blond hair, light skin, and blues eyes.[104] Intrigued by this, after completing his work, Marsh organized his own scientific expedition the next year to find more white Indians.

The book, a first-person narrative, took many interesting and unexpected turns. Many experienced and qualified scholars were on his expedition, including Smithsonian Institution archaeologist, Professor J.L. Baer, who ultimately died and was buried in Darien. Marsh made a concerted effort to earn the trust of tribal chiefs and Native people they encountered, which eventually paid great dividends. Various tribal leaders shared horror stories with Marsh and his men of how the Panamanian government had taken over their plantations, enslaved the men and raped their women. The Natives hated these people who were encroaching on both their land and culture.

Sympathetic to the Natives and their plight, Marsh helped them organize and mount a revolt that including the indigenous people writing their own Declaration of Independence along with a strategic, but limited violet revolt. Marsh's plan was for the United States to intervene as a peace-keeper while the two sides negotiated a peace treaty. His plan worked beautifully. When the U.S. warship *Cleveland* anchored in the Bay off Cardi near the town of Parvenir, Marsh and several tribal leaders in the revolt were brought aboard the ship.

Marsh met with Dr. South, minister to Panama, who wanted to learn his side of the matter. Seeking to secure a resumption of peace between the Indians and the Panamanians, Dr. South met with Indian chiefs, questioning them about Marsh's involvement in the uprising. They unanimously said he did not take part in the uprising and had only acted as a friend and interpreter.[105]

Marsh made a formal request for political asylum to Commander Wells of the *U.S.S. Cleveland*, which he granted and subsequently was approved by the

This young Navajo boy named Tom Torlino (wearing a Cross of Lorraine among others), from the 1880s, is pictured before being transformed from a "barbarian" savage (left) to a Christianized and "sober industrious citizen."[103]

State Department. Wells presided over military hearings with the tribal chiefs, who absolved Marsh of any involvement in inciting or offering assistance in the revolt. Anderson sided with the Native version of the conflict and much to the heated objection of the Panamanian government, offered political asylum to Marsh.

Eventually, in appreciation for Marsh's assistance and support of the people the chieftains' said to Marsh, "If you want to see White Indians, we'll show you White Indians." Hundreds of White Indians of all ages were brought down from the mountainous jungles of Darien. Marsh learned that White Indians had been born into families of the region for generations and explained their origin:

> Before the coming of the Spaniards there were many white Indians in the region (as the Spaniards noted in their reports). But the White Spaniards treated the Indians so badly that after they were driven out of the country, the Indians turned against those of their own people who also had white skin. They killed many and drove the rest into the mountains and the jungles. They were determined not to have a hated white face in their country.
>
> But white Indian children continued to be born among the brown Indians. The white strain or the white-producing principle was deeply imbedded in the Indian blood. These white babies were not all killed. Fond parents hid them in the mountains and jungles. Finally the Indians passed a law forbidding them to marry. But marriage or not marriage, white babies continued to be born, both to white mothers and brown mothers. The laws of nature were stronger than the laws of man.
>
> This was the situation when I arrived on the San Blas coast. The white type was despised and ostracized. They were forced to live in out of the way places, where no traders or other outsiders could see them. But my arrival, and my conviction that if I could take white Indians to Washington, they would arouse sympathy for the San Blas people, had changed all that.[106]

In 1925, Marsh brought several white teenage males back to the United States with great fanfare, where anthropologists studied the Indians and came up with three possible theories for their existence. The first is they were albinos. This thesis didn't stand up for albinos have white hair, pink eyes, and no pigment in their skin. The Indians had blond hair, brown, green and blue eyes, and pigment in their skin. The second thesis was the Caucasians were the result of an aberrant genetic mutation in the jungle. This theory suffered fatally from a lack of any scientific evidence. The third theory, which was quickly dismissed by scholars at the time, was the white traits were the result of ancient contact with a Norse race.

Only a few weeks before returning the Natives to Panama, Marsh invited three linguists to his residence to study the language of the White Natives.

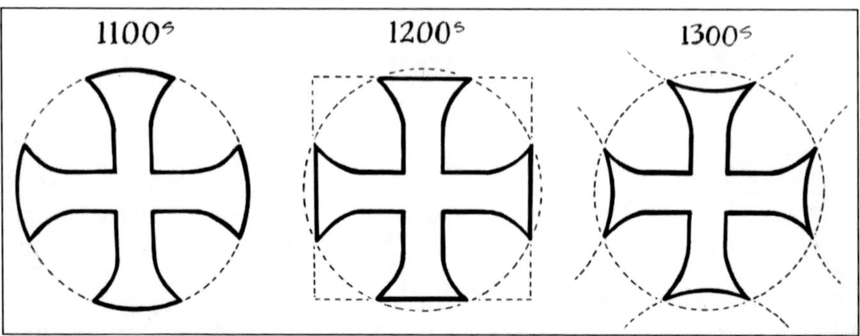

In 2010, Templar researcher Dr. Manual da Silva reported that the style of the Knights Templar four-armed equilateral cross evolved over the roughly two hundred years the order was officially in existence. In the 1100s, the cross fit inside a circle with convex ends to each arm. In the 1200s, the order made the ends straight so as to fit inside a square symbolizing the masonic concept of, "Squaring the circle." By the 1300s, the ends of the arms were concave and it was this detail that can be used to date the various Templar style crosses. (Sketch by Dan Wiemer)

Within days of their departure back to Panama the lead linguist presented their conclusions, "The anthropologists can tell you what they please; Marsh, but some ancient Norse people certainly taught the Tule People their language." They found that the Tule language had a Sanskrit or Aryan structure, not Mongoloid, and they discovered over sixty words identical with early Norse."[107]

Upon reading this I knew there had to be a connection between the various symbols found on the artifacts made by the indigenous people and how they were likely being influenced by other cultures from across the Atlantic and Pacific oceans who came to Panama long before the Inquisition.

Panama

On April 8, 2011, in Atlanta, Georgia, I met Leslie Kalen, to escort her to Panama. Leslie had become quite interested in pre-Columbian research, most notably anything that might shed light on her Cherokee heritage and history. Like me, she found possible Templar connections to many Native American cultures interesting. This definitely included Panama. In Panama, in the city of David, Greg Cavalli greeted us. He showed us his "treasure" room, where Leslie's and my eyes nearly popped out of our heads as we took in the amazing collection. In less than three months he had already assembled a collection of stone carvings, ceramics, and gold tumbaga that would be the envy of any world-class museum.

We quickly started examining each piece. Several artifacts exhibited familiar features and symbols that suggested great sophistication and knowledge and which we had seen in various other cultures from across both the Atlantic and Pacific oceans. On one side of the room Greg had a six-foot tall rack of metal shelves filled with artifacts. Starting at the bottom, I scanned the shelves until I reached the top where my eyes focused on a familiar symbol that initially struck me as unbelievable. After staring at the familiarly shaped cross for several seconds, I wondered, "Could this really be related to them?" Staring at me on the chest of a ten-inch, *white*, ceramic statue of a jaguar was a red square-styled Knights Templar cross used by the order in the thirteenth century.[108] (See color section, Figure 24)

I immediately began to ponder the possibility of Templar contact with Native cultures in Panama during the 1200s. My first thought was, "Why not?" It then occurred to me that we were on the Pacific side of Panama and Greg explained that the artifact had been pulled from the ground only a couple of weeks ago a half-hour's drive away. Did this mean a Templar ship had once anchored on the Pacific side? The idea that contact had occurred on the Caribbean side seemed the most likely. However, it's also possible the jaguar statue had somehow made it's way to the west side via trade at some time in the past.

If this cross was indeed influenced by contact with thirteenth century Templars, then it might explain how and why Christopher Columbus made his way to the Caribbean. He likely was secretly following in the footsteps of his ideological brethren who came here more than 200 years earlier.

Quetzalcoatl

WHILE CONSIDERING THE LIKELY INFLUENCE of the Templars and their Cistercian brethren on the Native cultures of Mesoamerica, the pre-Columbian legend of Quetzalcoatl quickly enters the discussion. According to Manley Hall, Mayan legend describes a band of people who came from the north wearing long black robes who were well received. These people were skilled artisans especially in working metals, and Quetzalcoatl was their leader. He was a white man with a flowing beard who was dressed in a long white robe covered with a design of red crosses. He was identified with the planet Venus, appeared as a great sorcerer and magician who performed miracles. His knowledge was passed on to an order of priests who practiced the arts and sciences, treated the sick, administered sacraments, were diviners and prophets and governed by a master.[109]

This Panamanian pre-Columbian tumbaga gold mask pendant from the Cavalli Collection is 3¾-by-3¾ inches and has a serpent running across the forehead reminiscent of the Egyptian uraeus. A Tumbaga artifact (right) from the Muisca region, Columbia, is a tenth- to sixteenth-century votive figure, its arms crossed over its chest in the classic Osiris pose common in ancient Egypt. (Tom Shearer, 2012; Courtesy of Cleveland Museum of Art)

The Mayan tribal groups believed to have been influenced by Quetzalcoatl had the serpent as its heraldic device.[110, 111] This point immediately brought to mind one of Greg's artifacts that had a symbol that appeared to be directly connected to the ancient pharaohs and priesthood of ancient Egypt. The artifact was a tumbaga mask intended to be worn as a breast pendant with the eyes, nostrils, and mouth cut out from the metal giving the appearance that the mask was speaking. The distinct feature of the mask was the presence of a serpent running across the forehead, reminiscent of the Egyptian uraeus. According to Manley Hall, ". . . the Serpent was often used by the ancients to symbolize wisdom."[112]

The obvious question was, "Could there have been contact with ancient Egyptians that influenced the Panamanians in the distant past?"

The Panama and Columbian artifacts that intrigued me the most were the ones that shed light on the cultural aspects of the people who created them. Many depict common human behavior such as hunting animals, fishing, daily work activities, playing musical instruments, and scenes of sexual activity, giving birth, nurturing the young, and scenes of ancient rituals. One incredible artifact depicts what appears to be a religious ceremony involving eleven people presenting offerings that include fish, a pig, and one individual holding a large monkey. Other individuals depicted include both males and females holding ritual wands, spears, and other artifacts that appear to be playing a role in the ritual. Beneath a cone-roofed shelter with three poles is a lone seated female who seems to be the focus of the ritual. On top of the circular shelter sits a lone parrot-like bird that appears to be presiding over the ceremony. Perhaps this and other rituals depicted in these incredible artifacts are evidentiary remnants of the influence of Quetzalcoatl and his pre-Columbian priesthood.

This apparent religious ceremony depiction of the Native people reportedly from Columbia is eerily reminiscent of a nineteenth-century drawing of the rituals of the Mide'win secret society of the Ojibwa. This particular illustration was received by a fourth-degree Mide' priest of the Mississippi Ojibwa from his father and shows the four degrees presented in profile. What's interesting here are the birds, owls in this case, on top the sacred posts in all four degrees. Could the mysterious Mesoamerican Native ceremony be somehow related to the Mide'win rituals with the sacred owl?

I spotted yet another surprising symbol on the side of the masonic-like apron worn by the female of an incredible male/female pair of tumbaga statues that stood almost three feet in height. A double-headed eagle so common in Freemasonry was on both sides of the vertical sides of the apron.

The artifacts yielded clues of likely influence from other cultures besides the medieval Templars. Tumbaga gold statues commonly were made in male/female pairs that could be interpreted as a representation of Dualism. One pair in particular had the undeniable similarity to the Egyptian god Taweret, who had the

This roughly one-thousand year-old tumbaga artifact with a bird presiding over an apparent religious ceremony of the Native cultures of Columbia, South America, is eerily reminiscent of the rituals of initiation in the Mide'win secret society of the Algonquin Nations in North America. (Wolter, 2012)

head of a hippopotamus, body of a human, feet of a lion, back and tail of a crocodile, and was often depicted carrying an animal. In Egyptian mythology, the hippo, lion, and crocodile were feared animals, but also highly respected.[113] In this case, the male/female pair of statues were carrying a type of lime flask called a Poporo, which is the national symbol of Columbia.

Yet another detail observed in the pre-Columbian metallic statuary is the presence of circumcision of the male genitals. Greg explained to me that unlike most of the human tumbaga statues depicted as anatomically correct nudes,

This copy of a Mide' chart was made by a Mississippi Ojibwa Mide' priest of the fourth degree he received in 1833, an imitation of the one owned by his father. The illustration shows a profile of the four degrees of initiation into the Mide'win Secret Society and includes an owl on top of the sacred post in each degree. (Seventh Annual Report of the Bureau of Ethnology, Plate VIII)

On both sides of the apron on a three-foot tall female tumbaga statue likely from Tairona Region of Columbia, is a double-headed bird (eagle?) that is reminiscent of virtually the same important symbol found in Scottish Rite Freemasonry. (Tom Shearer; Wolter, 2012)

only royalty or the priesthood wore anything resembling clothing. Several of the statues in his collection exhibited exposed male genitals with clear evidence of circumcision. This is consistent with ancient Egyptian and Hebrew religious practice and begs the question of a possible connection. It would be hard to imagine some lesser compelling reason to take a knife and cut the skin off a male's penis.

The many examples of circumcised penises on tumbaga statues reminded me of the circumcision of baby Jesus statue I saw at Chartes Cathedral in France. There was yet another Old World-New World connection in an ever-expanding matrix of pre-Columbian contact data found in the Americas.

Still another aspect of the artifacts reflected a deep understanding of the constellations of the zodiac. Ancient astronomers in cultures around the world including Mesoamerica divided a particular band of twelve star patterns called "houses," encircling the earth each represented by animals. Not surprisingly, this sacred number commonly occurs on the gold artifacts.

Two spectacular examples with this sacred number being featured and likely related to the twelve primary constellations of the zodiac are large gold breastplates. Each breastplate is roughly six inches by six inches in size with a zoomorphic (animal-human combination) figure standing in the middle, surrounded by twelve miniature medallions in one case, and twelve monkeys in the other.

This gold Tumbaga statue holding a lime flask called a Poporo has the diagnostic features of the Egyptian Goddess Taweret. These features include the body of a human, the head of a hippopotamus, paws of a lion and the tail of a crocodile. (Wolter, 2011; Internet)

Another mystery of these Native cultures in Columbia and Panama is where the indigenous people learned these sophisticated skills of working with precious metals. The tumbaga statues are made using the lost wax method of metal-works where the figure is sculpted out of bee's wax with a removable internal core fixed into place with green wood pegs called chaplets, and then the finished art-work is coated with clay.[114] Upon firing, the bee's wax melts away and the clay turns into a hard ceramic mold. A molten alloy of mostly copper, zinc, and anywhere from five- to twenty-five percent gold is then poured into the ceramic mold.

After the mold is broken and removed, the internal core is removed through an opening in the metal. The highly skilled artisan then soldered the detailed adornments to complete the often spectacular pieces of art. The final step converts the entire exterior surface of the statue or pendant to solid gold. This process is an ancient secret of alchemy dating to the Egyptian artisans who used a process of literally turning other metals into gold called "depletion gilding."[115]

Depletion gilding involves immersing the artifacts in a solution of citric acid or urine, which causes the copper, zinc, and silver, if present, to oxidize, forming secondary deposits of copper carbonates that are then polished off, concentrating the gold at the surface. The bulk of the metal in the statues retains the original copper-gold content ratios, but the surface glimmers with the appearance

This thirty-inch statue of a sitting cacique chief exhibits a circumcised penis which reflects upon their apparent religious beliefs which is consistent and possibly connected to the ancient Hebrews and Egyptians. (Tom Shearer, 2012)

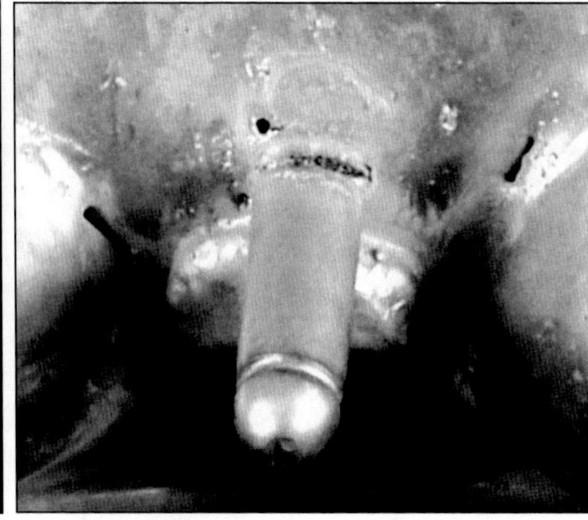

of solid gold. This explains the extensive wear and tiny surfaces scratches I've observed under the microscope during my examination of dozens of these artifacts.

Imagine the Spaniards' confusion when they encountered these people in the seventeenth and eighteenth centuries and thought these magnificent artifacts were solid gold, only to find out upon melting them down they were comprised mostly of copper. Many atrocities were committed against these people by the greedy visitors who mistakenly thought the Natives were trying to fool them.[116]

Where these people acquired this ancient knowledge of such sophisticated metal-works the Natives have been practicing in Columbia, Panama, and Costa Rica for at least 2,000 years is uncertain. However, the evidence preserved in the ceramic, stone, and metallic artifacts along with the legend of Quetzalcoatl suggests pre-Columbian contact most likely with advanced cultures from the Mediterranean region. Quoting Hall:

> In Deganawida, with his Great League, Quetzalcoatl-Kulkulcan and his splendid socialized empires in Mexico and Central America, and Manco Capac, and the communal system which he set up in Peru, we have three clear and definite accounts of initiate-leaders establishing schools of esoteric doctrines in the Western Hemisphere. From a consideration of their attainments and the systems which they inaugurated, we can come to but one conclusion: The Mystery Schools of antiquity were represented in the

These two Mesoamerican gold breastplates, roughly six-by-six inches in size, feature the number twelve in the adornments encircling the human-like figure in the middle. The twelve miniature medallions and monkeys likely represent the twelve constellations of the zodiac. (Tom Shearer, 2012)

> Americas by institutions identical in principle and in purpose with those of Asia and the Mediterranean countries.[117]

My experience with the Greg Cavalli and his incredible collection of Mesoamerican artifacts had a profound impact on me. The symbolism present on the artifacts and the amazing metallurgical skills exhibited was nothing short of incredible. Greg's passion for the artifacts and his desire to understand the cultures that created them was infectious. We spent many hours examining each artifact and discussing the various aspects of who, when, where, and how of their creation.

In January of 2012, Greg was successful in attaining official status for the Cavalli Foundation with the government. Sadly, in 2011, his throat cancer returned, and he lost his battle on February 7, 2012. After his death, his wife, Elizabeth, continued the work of the foundation.

Chapter 8

The "C" Document

In Newport, Rhode Island, at the NEARA Fall Conference Janet and I met up with David Brody and several others. On November 7, 2008, Zena Halpern, longtime NEARA member and friend, asked us to look at something. She showed us a hockey puck-shaped brass object. She said, "Please, do not tell anything about these artifacts." We assured her we would keep things quiet and then turned our attention to the artifacts.[118]

The "seal" as Zena called it, was four inches in diameter by approximately one inch thick and had several strange characters scribed onto one side and a pentagram shaped drawing with more symbols on the other. I was able to push the end of a pin inside a small hole on one side that opened a circular piece on the opposite side. The seal was hollow. Inside was a small pointed piece of metal with the word, "Quetzalquatl" scribbled in cursive writing.

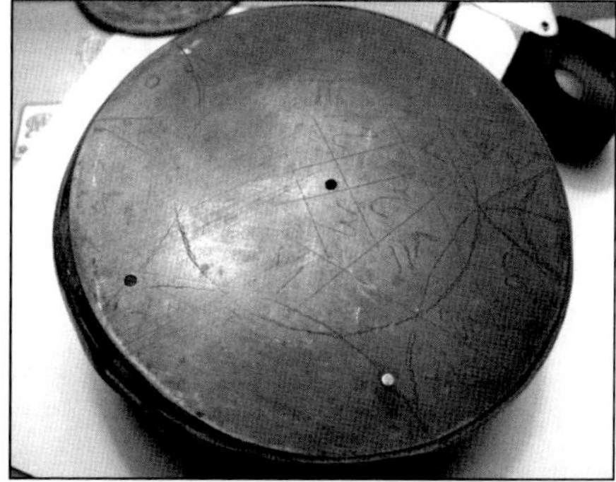

On November 7, 2008, Zena Halpern and Donald Ruh showed David Brody, Janet Wolter and me a four-inch diameter brass seal with inscribed characters and symbols on both sides. The seal was opened by pressing a pin through a small hole in the center of one side (right) which released a thin circular disc on the other. (Wolter, 2008)

Inside the seal was a three-quarter inch long pointed and inscribed piece of brass. (Wolter, 2008)

I asked Zena, "What are these things and where did you get them?"

She said, "I can't tell you where I got them right now, but do you think you can date them?"

I told her that I probably couldn't since I wasn't an expert with metals. She then handed us a couple of pictures of what appeared to be an old piece of paper filled with strange symbols. Zena then said, "The symbols are Theban, an ancient coded alphabet used by the Templars."

David asked, "Zena, what is going on here?"

She said she couldn't go into the details right then, but she and her friend Don Ruh needed help solving a big mystery. When I asked if it had anything to do with the Hooked X Templar research we'd been working on, she said, "Oooh, boy, does it ever!"

We took pictures of everything. Zena and Don appeared to be sitting on something big, but they didn't provide enough background information for us to be of much help. That would eventually change as they slowly revealed more information over the course of the next four years.

The first thing Zena revealed was that the two inscribed stones I had priviously examined in my lab for her had come from this same Neversink Valley area in the Panther Mountain Impact Area in Upper New York and were involved with the story. The so-named, "Living Waters" stone, found in 2004, and "Yod" stone, found by Don in 2001, had six and nine Phoenician letters, respectively, carved into what tuned out to be meta-sedimentary rocks. Because both rocks contained such a high quartz content, neither allowed for conclusive relative-age weathering studies. Quartz is a very chemically stable mineral and, in this case, contributed little in the way of archaeopetrography. At the time she originally sent them, Zena told me nothing about these stones and it was interesting to later learn they were found in the same general area.

The Living Waters stone is a mostly sub-angular to sub-rounded greywacke (geologically similar to the Kensington and Narragansett Rune Stones) comprised of quartz, feldspar, lithic (rock) fragments with a fine-grained matrix of sericite with minor opaque minerals. I cut and polished a small slice off one end of the stone which exhibited a distinct weathering profile roughly half a millimeter deep suggesting significant age. The approximately one and half millimeter-deep carved

The first inscribed stone Zena sent for examination is called the "Living Waters" Stone and arrived at my lab on June 20, 2006. The stone is a greywacke with six inscribed characters (Phoenician?) that exhibit extensive weathering. On the left side is where a small sample was taken for mineral identification. (Wolter, 2006)

grooves had the same weathering appearance as the cut surface which also suggested great age. Without knowing the exact weathering environment where the stone has been it's impossible to pinpoint age. However, the weathering of the inscription clearly indicates it was not carved in the recent past.[119]

Zena then sent a second stone weighing about seven pounds that arrived in March of 2007. This rock had a vulva symbol carved at the center of one of the flat sides of the stone with nine characters partially circling the central symbol. Carved on the opposite side of the stone was a lone, apparently Phoenician character. This stone was meta-sedimentary rock comprised of very fine-grained quartz. There was also a relatively large, very thin piece that had spalled off the top side that had broken through three of the carved characters. This allowed me to examine the cross-sectional profile of the carved grooves that did not show any apparent weathering. Unfortunately, because of the high quartz content this inscription would not lend itself to much fruitful relative-age weathering data.[120]

The Yod Stone was reportedly found by Donald Ruh in 2001, while hiking in the same area near the Neversink River, not far from a large, well-known and apparently ancient carving called the Frost Valley Petroglyph. On July 1, 2009, I was able to examine this impressive spiral petroglyph comprised of a single continuous line carved into a large coarse-grained, greywacke sandstone boulder. Local stories put its known presence back to the early twentieth century, but confirmatory documentation is unavailable.

Some researchers, such as Dr. R.M. de Jonge and Jay Wakefield, believe the Frost Valley petroglyph is an ancient map of northeastern North

A clearly defined, lighter colored weathering profile was observed to a depth of 0.5 mm on the cut and polished surface of the Living Waters Stone. Picture magnified 30 times. (Wolter, 2006)

America with the center of the spiral representing Frost Valley, New York.[121] Whatever Frost Valley Petroglyph's origin, the discovery of two more inscribed stones has deepened the mystery of this area's pre-Columbian history? Could these two new stones be related to the Frost Valley Petroglyph? If so, because of the presence of the apparent Phoenician characters, could these stones be evidence of contact by Mediterranean cultures that date back over 2000 year ago? Assuming this was true, and it certainly could be, why would they have come to this area in the Catskill Mountains?

The other question is what if any association did the brass seal and its parts have that Zena and Don had showed to us? We didn't know it at the time, but it turned out there was a connection.

Zena and Don shared little else about these discoveries until the summer of 2009 when she called me. "Don and I need your help. Would you be willing to hike up a mountain to look for ancient artifacts we think might be hidden in caves?"

Zena Halpern's seven-pound Yod Stone, with its nine characters of Semitic script partially circling a vulva symbol (left). A Hebrew "Yod" symbol is carved on the opposite side (right). (Wolter, 2007)

Instantly intrigued, I said, "Sure, Zena. What specifically would we be looking for?"

She relayed this story: "Remember that brass instrument with the small pointed piece of metal Don and I showed you in Newport last year?"

"Of course" I said.

"And do you remember the two stones I had you look at from Frost Valley?" she asked.

Again I said, "Of course, I do."

Zena paused and said, "Well, there's more to the story, and Don and I think they are all connected."

Zena relayed what sounded like a plot from a James Bond film that began in the summer of 1968. Don Ruh and two friends had recently been discharged from military service during the Vietnam War. Being adventurous, they decided to rent a boat and go scuba diving in the Hudson River. Apparently, while underwater they found two round bulbs that had once been part of decorative posts.

Don gave the decorative bulb he found to his diving buddy. Not long after their day diving in the river, the man's five-year-old son accidently dropped the bulb, which broke open. Inside they found the brass seal. They eventually figured out how to open the seal, thus finding the other objects. The discovery of the seal led Don's friend to purchase a diary that made mention of a medieval document that apparently related to the brass seal.

The contents of the diary led Don's friend to Europe where he was successful in locating and eventually purchasing the original medieval document in Italy. The contents of the document were written in Theban, a coded script reportedly used by the medieval Knights Templar and Cistercian orders. It reportedly took six years for Don's friend to find an expert in Europe who could decode the Theban script that ended up being written by multiple authors in Italian, Latin, and Old French. This led to another round of translations that ultimately revealed an incredible story. This document became known within a tight circle of researchers as the "C" Document.[122]

The Frost Valley Petroglyph was carved into a large coarse-grained greywacke boulder in one continuous line that some researchers believe is an ancient map of northeastern North America with Frost Valley at the center of the spiral. (Wolter, 2007)

There are many details to this story that have been intentionally left out that will be presented in a forthcoming book by Zena Halpern and Donald Ruh entitled *Search for the Cave of Lost Scrolls: One Man's Search for a Secret Codex in a Medieval church and a Historic Discovery in Jerusalem.*

The "C" Document

ZENA HELD TIGHT TO THE CONTENTS of the "C" Document until May of 2010, when she called me and asked, "Would you be willing to sign a non-disclosure agreement? I want to share something with you that's very important."

"Of course I will," I said. After signing the agreement and sending it back to her on June 1, 2010, Zena sent an email that included two attachments.

The first was a picture of a page from the document with several lines of symbols I recognized as Theban, the coded script used by the medieval Templars. When I offered that the paper didn't look like twelfth century velum, Zena agreed and said the pages had been copied and redrawn from an older document. She explained that it took Don's friend six years to get the coded symbols translated, finally finding someone in Spain with knowledge of Theban who could decode the characters. Upon completing the translation, the now-deceased person apparently wrote to the friend, telling him, "Please throw away my telephone numbers and address, I want no one to know that I helped with this document. I live in a Catholic country."

Zena's email included a translation of the subject page with the four gospels, including the name Miriam. This was the first clue this was a potentially history-changing document. The Church has taught Christians the four Gospels included the biblical figure of Luke who according to Church doctrine wrote the third and longest of the canonical Gospels.[123] Obviously, the title page signaled that the "C" Document was at odds with standard Church doctrine and if originally written by a Cistercian/Templar scribe who embraced the heretical (Hooked X) religious ideology, as I believe they did, it would be explosively controversial and explain why it was secretly encoded and kept hidden all these centuries.

The inclusion of Miriam (Mary) brought to mind the research of Graham Phillips whose clever and convincing detective work resulted in the discovery of what he believes is the original alabaster cup legend he says held the blood of Jesus. His research led him to examine a stained-glass window at Hodnet Church, in Shropshire, England. This window prompted him to write the following, "The figure that was supposed to represent St. John appeared to be a woman. The three other figures were bearded but the "John" figure was clean shaven. What's more, it seemed to be wearing a woman's gown and even appeared to have breasts. Could the figure have been a thinly-disguised Mary Magdalene?" It appears that Phillips's research at Hodnet Church might provide support for the "C" Document and vice versa. (See color section, Figure 25)

When I pulled up the second image Zena sent on my computer and I instantly recognized it as a map. The map looked to be a more recent copy of an older map, most likely eighteenth or nineteenth century. It took several seconds, but slowly the lines of a coastline began to look familiar. It was the northeastern seaboard area that included Newfoundland, the St. Lawrence River estuary, Nova Scotia, and Maine. My confusion was due to the island of Nova Scotia being drawn as two parts with the northern half stacked on top of the southern half. Curious, I noticed at the break of both parts was the Star of David.

I looked at the random areas of handwritten text and numerous Roman numbers drawn touching both vertical and horizontal lines that could only represent longitude and latitude. It didn't take long to figure out that indeed these numbers were the correct coordinates for this area of North America, but only if one used Paris as the prime meridian.

After playing on Google Translate, I quickly figured out the text on the map was Old French, which included several interesting words. Only a few was I was able to understand without the on-line translation website. Eventually, I figured

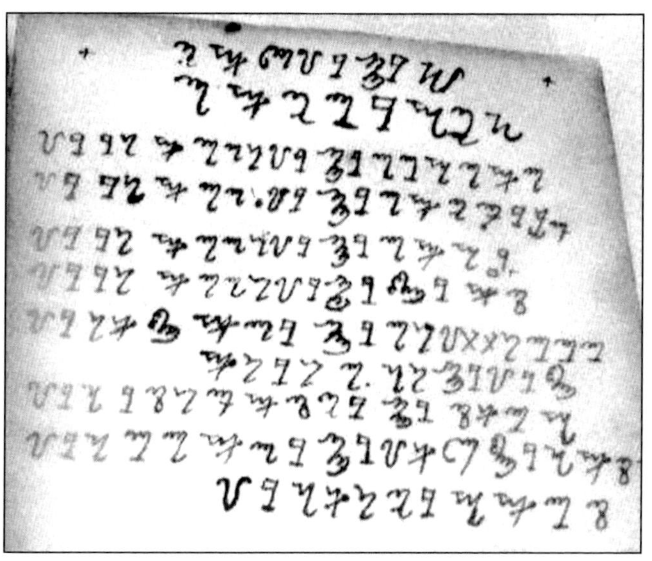

The re-copied title page from the original twelfth century Cremona Document contains eleven lines of the coded Templar script Theban. Notice on the seventh line there appears to be two Hooked X's. Included in the table of subjects are the Gospels of Mathew, Mark, Luke, and *Miriam*. (Photograph courtesy of Don Ruh and Zena Halpern)

out nearly all the words including, "one" (un), "two" (deus), "three" (trois), "four" (quatre), "five" (cinq), "six" (six), "frozen" (froid), "Inuhit" (Inuit), a local Native tribe, "north" (Nord), "west" (ovest), "continuum" (continua), "rose" (Rhodon), which was curiously at forty-five degrees fifteen minutes north latitude, "the monster current" (La courant de monster), "the Goddess" (La Deesse), "the Mother of two" (La Mere de Deus), and "Twenty four of the June" (Le Vingt quatre de juin).[124]

So many things fit beautifully to support mine and other Knight Templar researchers' work it seemed unbelievable. "The Mother of two" was a curious phrase that will no doubt serve to fuel much speculation. What comes to my mind is could this be reference to Jesus and John the Baptist? The other thought was could it be referring to the priestly messiah or the kingly messiah?

"The Goddess" is obvious and in my opinion would be consistent with the Cistercian/Templar reverence of the sacred feminine that has been demonstrated in the architecture of the medieval churches and other structures they financed and built.

"Twenty four of the June" can only be a reference to John the Baptist, one of the patron Saints of the Freemasons and the Knights Templar, along with John the Evangelist. This fact is sure to send chills down the spine of evangelical Christians who will be dazed and confused trying to understand what the truth really is about these two important saints of Christianity.

The biggest surprise didn't appear right away. Sure enough, in the middle of the map below the circle with two horizontal lines was the Roman number forty-five (XLV) and, incredibly, the Roman numeral ten (X) had a hook in the upper right arm! It was the Hooked X, my Hooked X. I was excited. In the top right corner were two more Roman numbers. The number at the top was likely the page number of the document, thirty-seven (XXXVII). Below the apparent page number was what appeared to be the sigla of the person who drew the copy. To the right of that was what likely was the date in Roman numerals of 1179 (MCLXXIX). Here again, the last Roman numeral ten (X) was also hooked.

As I stared at these two examples of what was unmistakably the symbol I'd spent so much time trying to understand and had concluded was linked to the Templars the importance of this document quickly became apparent provided it survived the vetting process.

The line of latitude at forty-five degrees fifteen minutes and longitude of sixty-eight degrees fifty-seven minutes was labeled "Rose" and was likely the optimal place used for making astronomical observations.

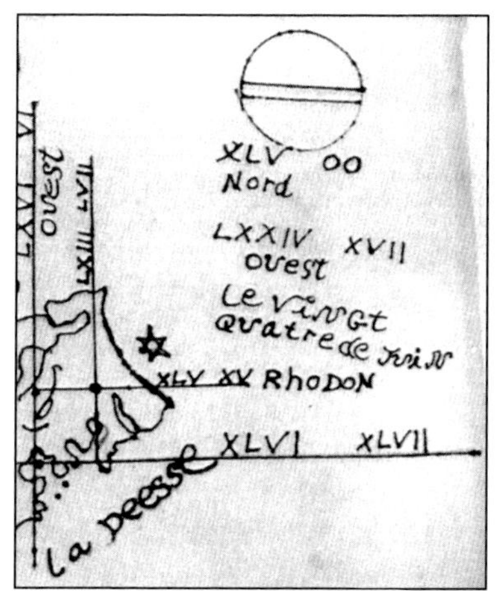

The most intriguing map in the "C" Document includes the southern end of Newfoundland, Nova Scotia broken into two parts and the extreme eastern end of Quebec, and was the first one Zena Halpern sent to me on June 1, 2010. The writing is Old French and the Roman numerals accompany lines of latitude and longitude. This section of the map contains a Roman numeral ten in the form of the Hooked X, in the number XLV (45), under the circle with two horizontal lines. (Courtesy of Don Ruh and Zena Halpern)

My first thought was that this map was too good to be true. This map alone, with the two examples of the Hooked X along with everything else essentially confirmed all my Templar/Cistercian research to date. Unless this map and the "C" Document were proven not to be legitimate, it must now be accepted history that the Templars were making repeated secret trips to North America over three centuries prior to Columbus.

The Hooked X is a symbol representing a religious ideology that was used in multiple ways. In the Larsson Papers, discovered in the Swedish archives in 2003, several runes are "hooked" clearly indicating that the "a"-rune being hooked is not unique. In the "C" Document on the Nova Scotia map, the Roman numeral ten is "hooked" in two places. This shows the symbol was not only used to represent a letter or a sound such as on the Larsson Papers and the Kensington, Spirit Pond, and the Narragansett rune stones, or a coded sigla as in Columbus' signature, or a Mason's mark as found in Rosslyn, but also a Roman number.[125]

Another more practical meaning for the Hooked X is that it is a code for Templar operations in North America since all medieval examples are found either in North America or associated with the Knights Templar. Curiously, all other known examples are linked with secret societies. These facts provide yet another link between the two organizations.

This multiple meaning and usage of the Hooked X is consistent with Templar and Cistercian practice. The "hook" was a code that those "in the know" understood represented the essence of the ideology of the order extant from at least late twelfth through the late nineteenth century. This begs the question: are there more examples of the coded character? The answer is almost certainly yes. However, because these orders both in medieval and later times operated in strict secrecy, the chance of additional secret documents seeing the light of day is remote. If true, it was amazing that Donald Ruh's friend was able to find and purchase the "C" Document. He then reportedly sold the document in 1994 after he had taken his research as far as he could. It is our hope that with the publication of this book and Zena Halpern's work the *original* "C" Document will resurface someday.

Panther Mountain Impact Area

ON JUNE 30, 2009, my son Grant, David Brody, Steve St. Clair, and I planned a hike to the Panther Mountain area. The mountains were very imposing, and the trail leading up was rugged and steep. The weather had been rainy and cool, but the next day was supposed to clear and sunny. This would make for a hot, sweaty climb, but we were all up for it.

Back at the hotel, Don showed us some artifacts he found a few years earlier inside what he called the "Sand Cave." He told us about making the videotape we had watched while he searched and eventually found the small cave only one person could fit into comfortably. In the video, Don narrated as he made his discoveries of the artifacts now laid out on the table. In my opinion, the items appeared to be associated with a solitary religious ritual, and if the Roman coin found amongst the items was an accurate indicator, it dated the artifacts to sometime around the late first century.

Don discovered most of the items buried in sand along a natural rock ledge. Among the items were two small ceramic lamps, two bronze pendants or tokens, one a frowning mask and the other a bust of a female goddess figure. The artifact that intrigued me the most was a medallion made of a bright blue glass with a seven-candled Menorah stamped in the center. The glass was riddled with gas bubbles that didn't seem consistent with modern glass-making techniques. (See color section, Figure 23)

Don also found a ceramic bowl behind a large flat stone that had been placed in a vertical position in the back of the cave. Inside the bowl were several arrowheads. While examining the puzzling group of artifacts, Grant, Steve and I decided we were going to find the cave where they came from the next day.

The next morning, the initial hike up the mountain was steep and slow, but after a half hour or so of climbing we found the first marker Don said we were looking for; a Delta symbol carved into a sandstone rock outcrop. I carefully studied the carved symbol with my hand-lens and took pictures. The grooves appeared to be weathered, and even though I couldn't determine how old they were, I could definitely say they were not recently cut.

Don had a map he said was redrawn from the "C" Document. The lines depicted an asymmetrical square and compass with wavy lines apparently representing the creek roughly a hundred yards away from the Delta symbol.

"The next symbol we're looking for is a Theban 'B.' It should be up there somewhere," Don said, pointing further up the mountain.

I looked at the map, and then asked Don how many times he and his buddy had been on the mountain. He said, "We've been up here collectively about two or three dozen times in the last twenty-five years, but this is the first time with this map." He explained that the sketch had fallen out from behind a framed picture his friend had given to him during a visit in 1996. "A month ago I was digging around in my storage shed behind the house and pulled out this picture. The screws on the back were rusted. When I picked it up, the back side opened, and this sketch and a floppy disc fell out."

This story was sounding more and more like an Indiana Jones movie. It was fun, but at the same time stretched the limit of believability.

Steve asked, "What was on the floppy disc?"

Don said, "It's an amazing story that dates back to the twelfth century. We need to keep looking for the other carvings."

About twenty minutes later we found the next carved character on another outcrop of rock farther up the mountain. This carving was closer to the ground, but was still clear and distinct. The weathering of the grooves of this character was similar to the Delta character and again was obviously not recently made.

After locating the Delta and Theban "B" symbols, then studying the map, it was clear where the third character, a Theban "A," should be. Only one significant rock outcrop was in this area. We scanned the ledges and surfaces for another carving, but we were unable to find it. After discussing the likely possibilities we concluded it must have weathered or spalled off at some point in the past. We also agreed that, according to the map, this had to be the rock outcrop where the symbol once was. Using the points on the "square" portion of the map that represented the carved characters on the rocks we then stretched a tape measure between the "A" rock outcrop and the "B" character farther up the hill.

The two ends of the compass on the map both crossed the lines of the square. After calculating the distance between the outcrops relative to the Theban letters on the map, I placed a red flag in the ground next to the tape

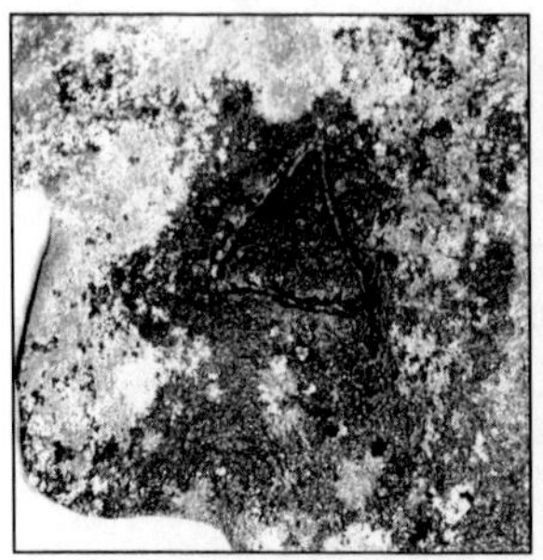

On July 1, 2009, David Brody, Donald Ruh, Steve St. Clair, my son Grant Wolter, and I climbed up the mountain following a map that lead to symbols carved into rock outcrops. We found three of the four symbols pictured above: a Delta, a Theban "B" and an Egyptian style bird. All three symbols had grooves that exhibited weathering and were not recently carved. (Wolter, 2009)

measure. Steve, Grant, and I decided to press on up the mountain to try and find the small cave with the artifacts that Don had found a few years earlier, while David stayed with Don to dig where I'd put the flag in.

The three of us hiked to the elevation and scaled along rock ledges and cliffs trying to find Don's Sand Cave. After three hours of searching with no luck, we hiked back down. Don and David were huddled next to a large boulder. Don said, "After searching for twenty years we finally found the bird carving." Sure enough, an approximately eight-inch-long Egyptian style bird was carved near the bottom into a massive block of sandstone.

On July 1, 2009, Steve St. Clair held a tape measure where the Theban "B" character was carved onto a bedrock outcrop while Grant Wolter held the other end at another outcrop on a very steep part of the mountain. (Wolter, 2009)

Donald Ruh and David Brody pulled this stone inscribed with Roman Numbers and the phrase "IN CAMERA" in Latin letters out of the ground on a mountain in the Panther Mountain Impact Area on July 1, 2009. Two strange carvings were on the backside, one looks like a withered hand and was made using a pecking technique, and the other looks like a Carthaginian Tanit Goddess with its arms raised and was carved using continuous lines. (Wolter, 2009)

Similar to the other carvings, the lines looked weathered and had not been carved in the recent past. While we looked at the bird carving, David said, "That isn't all we found. What do you think of this?" He then handed me an axe head-sized, flat stone.

One of the flat sides of the stone was covered with Roman numbers and Latin letters. Two more carvings of what looked like a five-legged octopus and a figure that to me looked like the ancient Carthaginian Goddess Tanit were on the back side.

On June 30, 2009, Donald Ruh discovered a small stone in a small mound of rocks and dirt near the Neversink River with paleo-Hebrew letters that spell "Yahweh." (Wolter, 2009)

On July 1, 2009, I found a roughly seven-inch long, flat stone in a small pile of dirt and stones with either a bird or notched feather carved on one side. There were two small grooves on the sides in the middle and one end (left) of the stone had been polished to a sharp edge. (Wolter, 2009)

Don said, "We started digging where you put the flag in the ground and pulled out rocks as we went. We found this one about two-feet down," David said. Don then handed me a small white dirt-covered stone and said, "We found this one under the stone with the carvings, but I don't know if it's anything or not."

I rolled the small angular rock in my hands, and then held it up to the sunlight and said, "I think it's probably gypsum. Ancient mariners used optical gypsum to navigate on overcast days to locate the sun. Gypsum polarizes the sun's rays pin-pointing its location"

The Roman numbers on the stone were arranged to indicate the latitude and longitude of 45 degrees, 30 minutes north, and 75 degrees, 53 minutes west. The Latin letters below the numbers clearly spelled, "IN CAMERA."

David said, "'In Camera' is a phrase used in the legal profession for when the judge wants to privately review a document or have a private meeting in his chamber. It means "in tomb," "in chamber," or "in secret." We wondered what this could possibly mean and what location these coordinates might refer to?

We noticed right away the five-legged octopus-thing was made with a series of peck-marks as opposed to grooves like the Tanit carving. This was very interesting as were the lone punch marks in the middle of both carvings.

We decided to visit one more site near the Frost Valley Petroglyph. Don had scouted an area the day before known to be a Native American fertility site next to a small stream flowing off a different ridge of mountains.

On the ride over to the next site, Don showed us a small stone he said he found in the same general area where the Living Waters and Vulva stones were found years earlier. The characters were easy for all of us to recognize—paleo-Hebrew. "Where did you find this?" Steve asked.

Don said, "Across the creek from the fertility stones at the base of a tree. There's a small mound of stones and it was in there."

At that site, Don led us to the pile of stones mixed with dirt and rotted leaves. We decided to check out the rest of the stones and slowly disassembled the pile. We checked the stones for man-made carvings. I picked up a small, flat stone while Grant and Steve were clearing things away. I wiped the dirt off the stone and saw what looked like carved lines. An image appeared that resembled a bird. Looking more closely, I noticed shallow notches on each edge in the middle of the stone. I also found that one end had been sharpened to an edge for some unknown reason. I would eventually call it the Dove Stone, but it was later suggested that the image looked like a notched feather. In the head of the bird or top end of the feather, was a prominent hole or small "dot" reminiscent of the dots in the carvings of the In Camera Stone we'd found earlier in the day.

This stone had me confused. After having time to examine it, I quickly realized I would have difficulty performing any relative-age dating work because it was comprised of very fine-grained silt and clay, minerals that most rocks weather down to. However, like the carved symbols we found on the mountain, the Dove Stone did not appear to have been recently made.

We had found not one, but two carved stones in two different locations. Because we didn't have enough information to understand what we were dealing with, we asked Don to tell us more about the map and the computer disk he had recently found behind the picture.

Don said, "My friend was working in Europe in 1998, and came to visit me with his wife and son when they were here to see a doctor in Connecticut about his Parkinson's disease. He gave me an old picture of Fort Montgomery (New York) figuring it was the last time he would see me, which turned out to be correct. He died two years later in 2000. I hung that picture in my house in Mount Vernon, until I retired in 2007 when I bought a mobile home in upstate New York. I had put the picture in my shed on the property and last month (May of 2009) when Zena was visiting me, I was rummaging around and brought the picture out. The backing had rusty nails that had come loose and while carrying it the map and computer disk fell to the floor."

Don continued, "The next weekend I went to Zena's on Long Island, and we read the printout on the computer disk of the story from the "C" Document that my friend had typed out. You already know what was on the 'compass and square' sketch, and I wanted to get back up on the mountain as soon as possible to see what might be up there. Zena thought you guys could help me and she was right. I thank you," Don said. He then took a deep breath and proceeded to tell us the story in the document and how his friend had spent almost thirty years of his life trying to figure out the document, it's connection to the mountain, and what it all meant.[125]

In August of 2010, I finally read the "C" Document story translated with Don's friend's commentary. It began with a first-hand narrative in *Latin*, written by one of the six Templar Knights about their exploration under the Temple Mount in Jerusalem in the second decade of the twelfth century along with a detailed report of what they found. Much of the speculation of many researchers is essentially confirmed, but there were definitely some surprises. The document then chronicles a late twelfth-century Knights Templar trip to North America with multiple ships with the ultimate destination of the Panther Mountain impact area. The primary goal of the trip was to retrieve ancient scrolls brought to this continent in the first or second century. Incredibly, to get back to the Catskills Mountains, the voyage was led by a woman who knew how to get there. The reason she knew where to go was because she was Native American, and was essentially leading this expedition back to her home.

Chapter 9
Montreal

After the Panther Mountain trip, David, Janet, Grant and I focused on trying to figure out the location of the latitude and longitude on the In Camera stone. When we plotted the coordinates into Google Earth it put us in the woods in southern Quebec south of the St. Lawrence River. This didn't make any sense until we remembered that the current prime meridian, Greenwich, England, was not the prime meridian in the twelfth century. It was Paris, France. Once we corrected the prime meridian to Paris, surprisingly, Google Earth put the coordinates right in the middle of Old Montreal.

Montreal didn't seem to be connected to a twelfth-century Templar voyage to the Catskill Mountains, not until we thought a little more about it. Montreal was the first large city built by the early French colonists in what they called New France. In my first Hooked X book, I wrote about Canadian researcher Francine Bernier's research into the mysterious actions of an early esoteric sect based on the Essene tradition also connected with the order of Sulpicians from France. The original cornerstone of the Notre Dame de Bon Secours Church, in Montreal, built in 1771 has Templar style crosses with flared ends and several simple AVM designs carved into it. Here was a tell-tale connection to the Templars and the Sulpicians, both of whom adopted John the Baptist as their patron saint.[126]

Bon Secours Church built in 1771, was constructed over the ruins of an earlier church established by the early seventeenth-century esoteric Sulpicians. Could this be the location indicated on the In Camera Stone? Could there be something here the Sulpicians wanted to preserve or protect? Perhaps there is something under this sacred ground with a Templar history dating back to the twelfth century, or perhaps even earlier? According to the "C" Document, one of the main goals of the twelfth-century Templar voyage was to re-

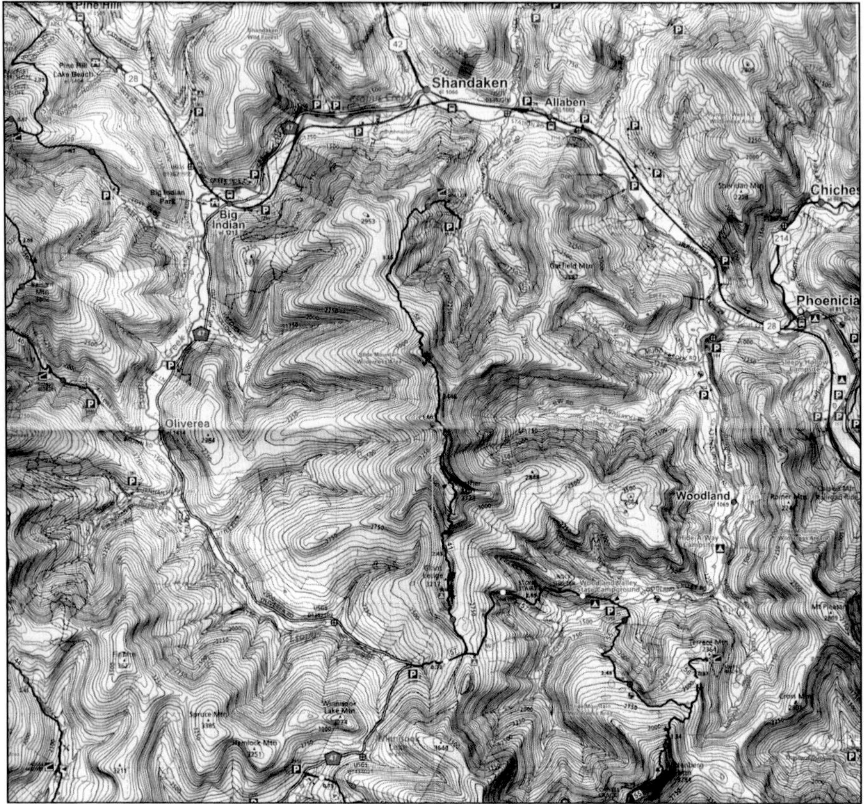

The roughly six-mile diameter Panther Mountain impact crater has rivers that flow in a circular pattern. The unique geomagnetic properties of this area may have been what made this area the attractive and apparently sacred to both the local Natives and their ancient visitors.

trieve ancient first-century scrolls. If so, what could be so important that the information was secretly handed down for hundreds of years until a future returning party could return to secure that location?

On October 21, 2009, David and I headed north from Westford, Massachusetts, toward Montreal. We made our first stop at Mount Monadnock, one of the highest points in Southern New Hampshire. While walking along the glacially rounded granitic bedrock, we found a curious carving, an equilateral triangle with a stone hole closest to the corner in the north direction that had the classic rounded triangular shape. The carved lines looked extensively weathered, but its origin and exact age was unclear. However, any modern hole cut into granite would likely have been made with a mechanical drill producing a round hole; clearly this hole was made with a straight chisel and hammer.

We met up with Canadian researcher Gérard Leduc on the western side of Lake Memphremagog, in Quebec, Canada, just north of Owl's Head Mountain. Owl's Head is where local Freemason's conduct an outdoor summer solstice ritual, I've been told it is an amazing early morning experience. Gérard had offered to show us what he believed was an ancient Templar mill site along a stream a few miles north of Owl's Head mountain.

While hiking along the slate-like rock the stream flowed over and around, it was clear that, in the distant past, somebody tried to build a mill. However, it appeared the construction was abandoned when it was halfway completed.

As the three of us climbed over and around the abandoned ruins, my eyes caught a familiar sight. On the inside surface of the main stone wall running parallel to the stream was a large stone block that had two stone holes. I put my finger into each roughly one-inch diameter hole to feel the familiar rounded triangular shape. If this was a Templar site as Gérard believes, the presence of stone holes exactly like the ones we found at the Ohman Farm in Minnesota, and other suspected Templar sites like Spirit Pond, in Maine was very exciting.

Just beyond the long wall paralleling the stream we found something unusual. Leaning nearly vertical against the bank were half a dozen very large slabs of square-shaped stones. Another pile of slabs lay on the opposite bank that seemed to indicate the construction of this site was not completed and likely abandoned. This evidence brought all kinds of possible scenarios to mind, and I firmly believe some invaluable historical information could be gleaned from a serious archaeological assessment of this fascinating site.

The following morning David and I crossed the Pont Champlain Bridge over the St. Lawrence River into Montreal. We visited the Notre Dame Church. We were especially interested in this church after reading Francine Bernier's book, *The Templar Legacy in Montreal*, and seeing the curious Tri-grammatron inside the pulpit that, when the Hebrew was translated into Latin, spelled, "Eve."

Montreal had been a hotbed of activity in the seventeenth century. The Sulpicians established a seminary here in 1629, Daniel Graysolon Du Luth, who lived across the street from the Notre Dame Church, was one of the earliest French fur traders to explore the Great Lakes region, and of course the medieval coordinates of the In Camera Stone all led us here. On October 22, 2009, we toured the Notre Dame Church.

Just inside the entrance on the east wall we found a large painting of what could only be Mary Magdalene with child. The beautiful woman with

David Brody and I found an equilateral triangle with a stone hole in the north corner at the top of Mount Monadnock, New Hampshire, on October 21, 2009. The rounded triangular shape of the stone hole indicated it was made with a straight chisel and a hammer, and the extensively weathered carved lines of the triangle indicate it was not recently carved. (Wolter, 2009)

long golden hair was wearing orange, green and blue and holding the Canadian maple leaf. That this woman is Mary Magdalene appears to be confirmed in at least two paintings in the church of the fourteen Stations of the Cross. This grieving Magdalene also has golden hair and is wearing green and orange.

The baby in her lap had short curly orange hair and wore a beaded orange necklace. To me, the baby looked like a girl. Could this have been a poorly veiled depiction of Mary Magdalene with her daughter that according to some legends was named Sarah? This begs the question: Why does anyone care about the child of a woman the Roman Catholic Church says was a prostitute?

Curiously, I also noticed the baby was holding up its right arm and was making the same two-fingered gesture that Jesus was making in the *Salvador Mundi* painting by Leonardo DaVinci. The other notable part of this painting was two cherubs holding a crown above Mary's head with a prominent white lily. If this is a picture of Mary Magdalene and her daughter it would be consistent with the

A partially completed stone wall lies parallel to a stream near Lake Memphremagog, in Quebec, Canada, that Canadian researcher Gérard Leduc, believes was constructed by the Knights Templar. (Wolter, 2009)

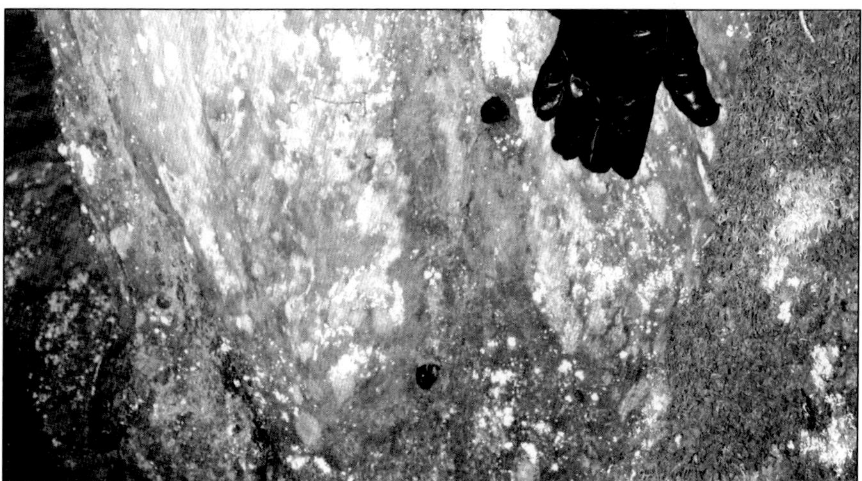

On the inside wall of the abandoned mill we found two rounded triangular stone holes in a large stone slab. (Wolter, 2009)

beliefs of many who believe that Jesus and Mary were not just married with children, but were in fact royalty. (See color section, Figures 26-29)

I had seen a picture of the unusual "Tri-grammaton" in the pulpit. It was stunning. Never before had any of us seen a Tetragrammaton with only

David Brody and Gérard Leduc examine six massive stone slabs that were cut and stacked yet never used at what appears to be an ancient mill site that was abandoned. (Wolter, 2009)

three Hebrew letters, "Hey" "Vuv" "Hey." These letters in Latin spell, E-V-E, Eve, the Mother of All Living. Given the prominent depiction of Mary Magdalene and other women of historical importance in Montreal, both of European descent and Native American, this particular ineffable name of God in Hebrew seemed appropriate.

Inside the pulpit is a rare Tri-grammatron with Hebrew letters that, in Latin, spell, "EVE." (Wolter, 2009)

The "M" Sign

ONE EVENING IN OCTOBER OF 2012, our friend Joe Rose discussed with us a curious element that grew out of his research on the Copiale Cipher. "There's a mysterious hand sign I've noticed in paintings of many famous historical figures that I can't figure out what it means," Joe said. He then held up his hand spreading his pinky and index fingers apart from his ring and middle fingers which were together and asked, "What do you see?"

It looked like an "M." Joe said, "But why are these historical figures dating back to at least the fifteen century depicted with this hand gesture? There's something going on here." A week later, Joe had an answer.

He said, "I think I've got it figured out." He had contacted a fellow Freemason in Europe who put him in contact with another Mason. He had received a box of materials, which included a letter with cryptic verses of poetry. Joe handed it to me. The first thing I noticed was each sentence started with a word that began with an "M."

Joe then asked, "What number is "M" in the alphabet?" Janet and I quickly counted to thirteen. "Right" he said. I then looked back at the letter and counted the number of sentences that began with an "M" word. Also thirteen.

Joe explained that thirteen was a very important number in Freemasonry and to the history of our country. "How many original colonies were there when our country was founded? Have you ever looked closely at the back of a dollar bill? How many rows of stones are there on the pyramid? How many five-pointed stars are above the eagle? How many arrows are clutched in the eagle's claws? How many stripes in the shield over the eagle's body? It goes on and on.

"A skeptic will argue the number is random and simply represents the original thirteen colonies, which it does. However, it means something more. I'm certain it represents the thirteenth apostle who can only be Jesus." Joe said.

Janet said, "How about Mary Magdalene as the thirteenth apostle?"

Joe said, "Of course; how obvious, it has to her."

From there the three of us bantered about how the secret hand sign had to be a subtle acknowledgement that the people who used it were part of a larger cause. That cause was an allegiance to the bloodline families directly descended from the first-century family of Jesus and Mary Magdalene. The reason they honor Mary is because she also symbolizes their reverence to the sacred feminine of the Goddess.

From there, we started researching historical paintings and photographs and found numerous examples of the "M" hand sign being used by people we theorized secretly supported and/or were members of secret societies who opposed the patriarchal oppression of the Roman Catholic Church.[127] To us, the sign was confirmation of the ideology we've always suspected these people embraced. The most obvious example was in the first picture that came up on Google of the famous explorer we all now know was *not* the first to discover America.

I looked again at pictures I'd taken in churches and cathedrals while on my many "churching" expeditions. The first place I looked was at the pictures I'd taken on my two most recent trips to Montreal. The painting of Mary Magdalene

Two of the most famous historical examples of the "M" hand sign are found in the paintings of Christopher Columbus and the Mona Lisa, albeit hers is more subtle. Leonardo DaVinci, who painted the Mona Lisa, is rumored to have been the Grand Master of the Priory of Sion, the historical guardians and members of the bloodlines families of Jesus and Mary Magdalene.(Internet; Internet)

with Sarah inside Notre Dame Church didn't disappoint. The left hand of the child sitting in Mary's lap was flashing the "M" sign as additional confirmation beyond the color of the hair and clothes as to who was really being depicted.

I then found an even more interesting painting inside the Sulpician Seminary we toured that didn't seem at all mysterious when I took it. It was a very common biblical scene just after the Crucifixion with Jesus lying on a bench with Mary Magdalene and two other apparent family members mourning the fallen king. Upon examining this painting again, the woman behind Mary Magdalene suddenly took on significance. I hadn't noticed her right hand on her left shoulder had her middle and ring fingers tucked under a shoulder strap, or her hair, clearly making the secret "M" sign. The woman's left hand also appears to making the "M" sign. Janet noticed the woman seemed to be looking at Magdalene instead of Jesus. Janet also commented that she was certain Mary Magdalene looked pregnant.

Of course, the "M" hand symbolism in this and many other paintings could easily be dismissed by the original artists with plausible denial, and indeed in their time they had to deny anything heretical or risk the wrath of the Roman Catholic Church and the Inquisition. Hiding symbols in plain sight

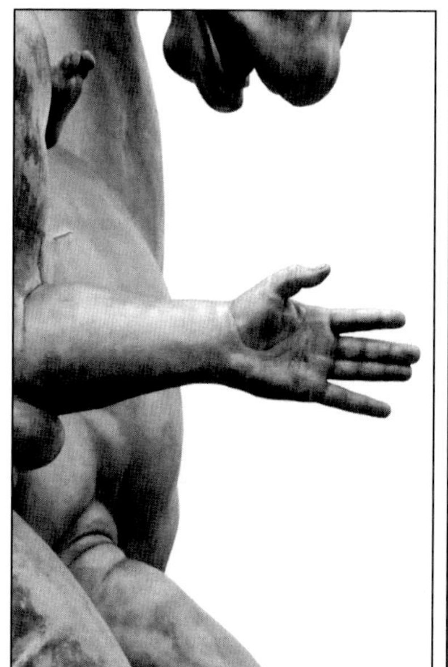

Detail from the statue on the Arlington Memorial Bridge (left). Meade Statue Archangel (right). Both show the "M" sign. (Wolter, 2013)

was one of the strategies of the bloodline "Venus" families and their supporters as a way to preserve the Secret for future generations.

The presence of the "M" sign in modern art and statuary, such as the various examples we found in Washington, D.C., in 2013, indicates the secret of Jesus and Mary Magdalene's marriage with children is still being kept alive to this day.

As always seems to be the case, the "M" sign also appears to go back to the Kensington Rune Stone. For years I assumed the punch mark made at the bottom of the far right leg on the Latin "M" on line eight of the inscription, almost certainly a Cistercian monk or Templar Knight stone mason, was part of a "Grail" prayer. In light of this new discovery, it appears the punched "M" might simply be an acknowledgement by the carver and members of the Kensington party of their reverence of the thirteenth apostle, Mary Magdalene. It might also be a code indicating knowledge she was with child at the time of the Crucifixion.

When thinking about the singling out of the Latin "M" on the Kensington Rune Stone and its likely coded reference to Mary Magdalene, I decided to go back and look at two other mysterious inscribed stones, the Mystery Stone, reportedly found in New Hampshire in 1872, and the Millwood Rune Stone.[128] (See color section, Figure 39)

Two examples of the "M" sign are found on the same statue in Philadelphia called "Religious Freedom." Both a male and female figure make the hand gesture, with the hand up and down in a likely multiple expression of Dualism. Arguably, the most iconic Goddess statue in the United States is also making the "M" sign hand gesture: the Statue of Liberty. (Internet; Internet)

On the bottom line of the Millwood Rune Stone, the third character is a clearly defined Latin "M." Most notable is the two lines at the center cross near the bottom in a similar fashion as the M's scratched into the walls by Templars being held hostage as pleas for protection most likely from Mary Magdalene. Could this be a clue to who may have carved this mysterious inscription? If it was carved by a member of a Templar party, perhaps a Cistercian monk, then the three dots above the arms of the four "M" runes could also be a coded Templar/Cistercian symbol for the Holy Trinity. Perhaps at this point, this is rampant speculation, but knowing the circumstantial evidence suggests the Templars were present in many areas of North America prior to contact, they are as likely a candidate to have created this inscription as any other culture.

In light of my earlier discussion of the assimilation of Native American-Knights Templar cultures that occurred beginning in the twelfth century, the Mystery Stone of New Hampshire looks as though it could be a strong piece of evidence supporting this thesis. As discussed in my first Hooked X book, the M symbol looks very much like the M's carved into the limestone walls at the Templar site of Royston Cave in Hertfordshire, England.

However, there appears to be more going on with the egg-shaped and egg-sized stone reportedly found encased in a "suspicious lump of clay" along the shores of Lake Winnipesaukee in central New Hampshire, in 1972. On four sides of the stone are sets of symbols aligned vertically parallel to the long axis of the stone that appear to have been grouped together intentionally.

The famous sixteenth century Italian painter, Tiziano Vecelli (circa 1489-1576), was apparently a supporter of the "Venus families and almost certainly believed in the bloodline of Jesus and Mary as evidenced by his frequent use of the "M" hand sign by the subjects in his paintings. Examples here include left to right: St. Catherine of Alexandria with her arms also in the Osiris pose, and a bare-breasted Mary Magdalene making the "M" sign over heart. (Internet; Internet)

What I'll call "side one" has a face that appears relatively androgynous and doesn't appear to look either Native or white. To the right of the face is side two that has, from top to bottom, a teepee and a circle (teepee ring or the sacred circle?). Side three, opposite the face side are what appear to be a stylized M that includes a double axe (Goddess) symbol, an "X" with two dots above which are identical to the four double dotted X's on the Kensington Rune Stone, along with a downward pointing crescent (Venus?), and finally a spiral at the bottom. Side four has an ear of corn above what appears to be parts of animals within a circle (ears, a deer leg, and something with three points?).

On the top and the bottom of the stone, which is a very hard, tough, and durable quartzite, are two different octagonal patterns. What isn't apparent in the photos is a hole that runs through the middle the full length of the stone. I also noticed there is also a groove inside the round hole through the stone that exhibits scratches from apparent wear.

In a nutshell, the symbols on the four sides could suggest the following: The face side could represent the Dualism of the intermarriages and as-

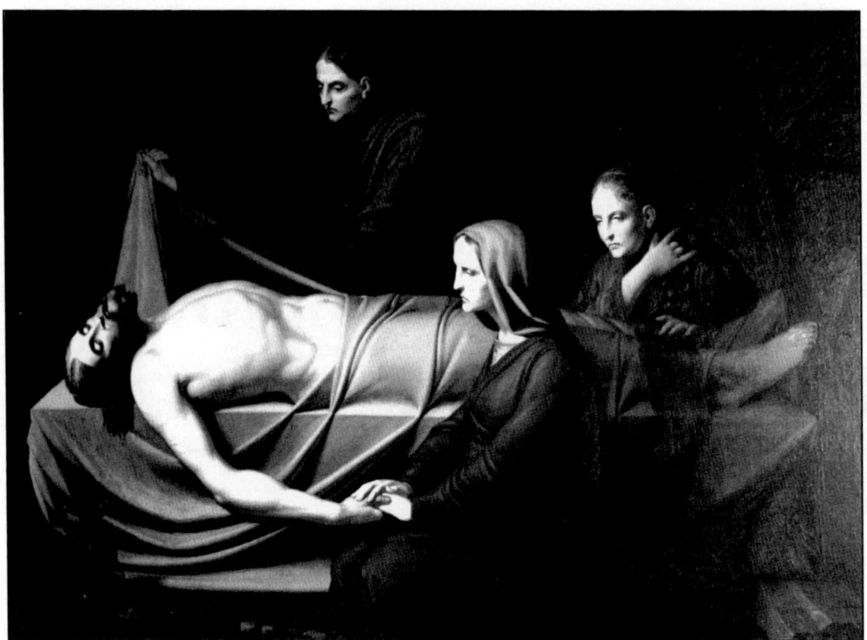

The painting I photographed inside the Sulpician Seminary in Montreal, Canada, of the biblical scene of Jesus lying on a table after the Crucifixion is loaded with symbolism. The woman behind a noticeably pregnant Mary Magdalene has her right hand on her left shoulder with her middle and ring fingers tucked under a shoulder strap making the secret "M" hand sign. She also appears to be staring at Mary Magdalene rather than Jesus apparently confirming the identity of the "Thirteenth Apostle." (Wolter, 2010)

similation of the Templars with the Natives as one people/tribe. Side two appears to be sacred Native symbols. Side three contains sacred Goddess veneration symbols of the Templars, and side four contains the life-giving symbols of food sacred to both cultures. The octagon patterns on the top and bottom are likely symbols that may indicate the "as above, so below" concept of both culture's ideology. The hole through the stone with wear in the groove might suggest it was possibly used at one time as a key. If it indeed is a key, it begs several obvious questions such as, what did it open, where is the thing it opened, and why was this "key" buried on the shores of Lake Winnipesaukee?

The possibilities of what the Mystery Stone may have opened could spur endless speculation. Whatever the vessel was appears to have been very important to both Native Americans and their Templar brethren. Whatever the container was could have come from across the Atlantic and possibly is one of the relics the Templars found under the Temple Mount at the time of the first crusade. If so, the odds are the Templars brought it to North America for safe keeping and it is still here, most likely being guarded by certain Native tribes to this very day.

Nova Scotia

ONE OF THE EXCITING THINGS about research involving signs, symbols, and tokens is once you start to understand what they are you begin to see the world in a different light where symbols are literally all around you. An incredible realization through symbolism came to me while traveling with Steve St. Clair in Nova Scotia. We were filming an episode for the new H2 series I was hosting called *America Unearthed.*™ Steve, a distant relative of Prince Henry Sinclair, was invited to participate due in large part to representing the Sinclair Clan. Many researchers believe Prince Henry Sinclair sailed to Nova Scotia in 1398, with the Templar treasure, whatever that may have been. I think it is likely Prince Henry did bring tangible treasure of some kind, but his most important treasure cargo were family members and others who were the bloodline descendants of Jesus and Mary Magdalene.

Steve shared the findings from his trip to Scotland the previous week where he had investigated his family genealogy, in particular the Herdmanston branch, the earliest St. Clair's in Scotland even before the Rosslyn group. The Herdamanstons had received their land from the DeMorvile Family, who were involved in the killing of the Roman Catholic Archbishop, Thomas Beckett, in 1170, who had been excommunicating certain powerful English families including the St. Clair's. The St. Clair's—direct blood line descendants of the DeMorvile's—gave the St. Clair's land literally two hundred yards from their homestead, Saltoun Castle, which is only eight miles east of Rosslyn Chapel.

Steve pointed out the DeMorvile family financed the building of both Dryburgh Abbey (opened 1150) and Kilwinning Abbey (established circa 1165) which is known to students of Masonic History as Lodge Number 0.

Steve showed me a picture of the deMorville coat of arms—an upright lion with talons drawn and showing its fangs as a symbol of strength. This pose is called a "Lion Rampant," which was facing left inside a shield. Steve reminded me that many of the royal families continued to use the Lion Rampant symbol on their shields in the centuries thereafter. This particular example also had a gold crown on the lion's head, likely symbolic of Jesus actually being a king, and the gold color representing his Egyptian heritage.

I reminded Steve that the lion was also a symbol for Jesus and his family lineage. The lion has often been used as an allegory for Jesus in stories and

The Mystery Stone was reportedly found encased in clay along the shore of Lake Winnipesaukee in New Hampshire in 1872. The symbols carved on fours side of the stone and on the top and bottom ends of the roughly four and a half-inch long egg-shaped stone made of quartzite, could represent the shared ideology during the assimilation of twelfth through fourteenth century Templars into certain East Coast and Great Lakes Tribes. A roughly 3/16-inch-diameter hole runs through the long axis of the stone and contains a groove with scratches suggesting use of the stone as possibly some kind of key. (All photos taken by Wolter, 2007)

movies such as C.S. Lewis's, *Chronicles of Narnia*. The lion in those stories was named Aslan who, like Jesus, was killed and later resurrected. One can be sure that any time there is a symbol or story that relates to Masonic symbolism there will usually be a reference to Jesus and a Freemason behind the scene.

On October 5, 2012, I saw a sign with a Nova Scotia flag. My eyes instantly fixed on the symbol at the center—a red rampant lion inside a shield facing left.

"Steve, look at this," I said. "That's the same lion you showed me yesterday." Sure enough, it was the same red lion on a white background, a point not lost on Steve. He said, "The colors of the Templars." I then pointed out the blue cross of St. Andrew extending to the four corners of the flag. Saint Andrew was the patron saint of the first crusade which I and other researchers, such as Alan Butler, believe were initiated by members of the bloodline families such as Pope Urban II.[129] Besides calling on the Templars to recapture the Holy Land in

Jerusalem for Christendom, their ulterior motive was to secure the perimeter of the city, allowing them to recover relicts under the Temple Mount.

Steve reminded me that the name Nova Scotia means "New Scotland." Looking at the flag symbol again I noticed something unusual about the red lion's tail. Sure enough, it was in the shape of the curved Arab sword, the scimitar. This could only be an acknowledgement of the Templar Knight's respect for the Arab's proficiency with numbers, mathematics, and geometry and that they likely learned a great deal from them during their years controlling the Holy Land. What else could it be? (See color section, Figures 30-34)

Steve and I figured out the rest of the story that to us seemed obvious from the symbolism in the Nova Scotia flag. Whoever designed the flag must have had inside knowledge that the Templars did come to these Canadian shores prior to Columbus, most likely the first time led by Prince Henry Sinclair. They also believed they were the bloodline descendants of first-century royal family of Jesus and Mary Magdalene. The large blue "X" provided further evidence these people did not embrace Roman Christianity, but Monotheistic Dualism faith whose roots extended back to Egypt at the time of Pharaoh Akhenaten's reign.

The Canadian flag's red and white seemed almost too obvious a connection to the Knights Templar, but there seemed to be more going on. The maple leaf symbol has three parts that each has three points. This numerology reminded me of the face side of the Kensington Rune Stone, which was carved by a Cistercian monk traveling with Templar Knights in 1362, has three groups of three lines of runic text for a total of nine. Coincidentally, like the rune stone, which has three more lines of text on the spilt side, the bottom of the maple leaf also has three points, two at the bottom and the stem. The numeric total of twelve in both cases surely cannot be a coincidence and its symbolic meaning will be explained in the final chapter: *Jesus: the Missing Piece.*

The Note

THE "C" DOCUMENT RESEARCH took a surprising, and seemingly ominous turn when I received a call from Zena on April 26, 2011. Her first words were, "Scott, I have a very important question to ask you."

I said, "Go ahead."

"Did you ever do an Internet search on Don's friend?" Zena asked.

I immediately answered, "Yes, but that was at least a year ago."

Zena said, "Oh, my God."

"What are you talking about? Why did you ask me that?' I said.

Zena explained that she had just received a letter from a friend of Don's buddy who now lived in Spain. She said, "Someone put a note inside that letter telling us not to continue pursuing information about him."

At first, I felt a little concern, but as we talked I started to understand the context of the note. I then asked her to send me a copy. A few days later I received the note which instead of being threatening turned out to be extremely helpful.

After talking over the note with Judi Rudebusch, the obvious person referenced from South Dakota, I called Zena and told her the note might be the best thing that ever happened. First, it (assuming it was real) convinced me that Don's buddy did exist, which answered the question that prompted the Internet search in the first place. As the research unfolded, amazing things were materializing that we all began to think too fantastic to be true. So many times I thought this had to be some kind of elaborate hoax. Even though the factual evidence was piling up, we still had serious doubts.

The first thing the three of us did was to search Don's friend's name on the Internet to see if we could find out anything about him. The search came up with no evidence that he ever existed, which created lingering doubts about the overall story. Not only did the note explain the bizarre dead ends we encountered, but the year he reportedly entered the Federal Witness Protection Program was the same year we were told he had died. We all realized that anyone who entered the Witness Protection Program for all intents and purposes essentially was dead.

The other positive thing to come from the note was that Zena now had a fantastic way to entice the readers at the beginning of her book by explaining the reason why she was using an alias for the central figure behind the "C" Document mystery in her book. At that point it all worked out to make lemonade out of what at first seemed to be a big fat lemon.

As this book went to press, more pieces of the story continued to materialize. Don Ruh and his buddy had a number of friends who worked with them as contractors for the U.S. Government. Their business ventures were highly secret, and I can personally understand this since I found out after my own father's death that he also did some clandestine work for the U.S. Government. We all know these secret activities are going on and somebody has to be involved in it.

Apparently, when Don's friend visited Don in the late 1990s while in New York for medical treatments, he left some of the documentation related to his research into the "C" Document with Don. It is unclear how much of the documentation Don knew he was receiving and how much was hidden in places like behind the old photograph. Don has continued to receive additional documentation from the estates of the other men they knew who have recently passed away. His buddy apparently disseminated the documentation amongst his closest friends. Whether they knew what they had is unknown.

At this point, it appears Don is the one who is destined to receive the documentation his friend dispersed amongst his closet friends once he knew his time was limited. This is why he reached out to Zena to help him compile this immensely complicated story into a book.

As the reader has likely already figured out, the redrawn Nova Scotia map with the two Hooked X symbols is what matters most to me. I want to believe that map is legitimate and part of the amazing story of a Knights Templar-led voyage to North America to recover hidden first-century scrolls. Even after all the investigation I've done into the eight known inscribed stones (Living Waters, Vulva, Delta, Theban B, Egyptian Bird, Hebrew, In Camera, and Dove), examination of the brass seal, review of over one-hundred pages of documents and dozens of photographs, I still don't know if this whole story is true or not. Perhaps only parts of it are true. I'm not sure the story will ever be definitive until we find the original "C" Document or something dateable is excavated from the ground.

For now, it remains a fascinating mystery we'll continue to work on until enough factual evidence is collected to decide one way or the other. Until that time, I'm forced to say something I'd rather not. Unfortunately, the current status of all the research leads me to only one conclusion: I simply don't know.

Chapter 10

The Missing Piece: Jesus

Before launching into my thesis about how Jesus and the Royal Family fit into the nearly four-thousand-year-long Hooked X ideological thread, I think it's important to clarify where I'm coming from by starting with what I like to call the "Religion Speech." First and foremost, I want people to know I mean no offense to anyone. What I ask people to do is take whatever faith they might have and set it off to the side for a little while so we can discuss some sensitive issues. From this point on, if readers find the subject matter offensive and they still continue, it's their own fault. The following pragmatic discussion is simply about trying to find the truth, and, in doing so, a variety of possibilities must be discussed. So here we go . . .

In the case of Roman Christianity, I would like to set aside belief in virgin births, and in people physically rising from the dead. Spiritually rising from the dead and ascending to heaven or wherever a spirit might go is another matter. However, until I see the factual evidence to support these claims, I, personally, am not buying it. So, if many of these events could not have happened in the first century, then what did happen? The analysis of evidence presented here represents the most likely explanation of what happened almost two thousand years ago, when viewed purely with science and logic.

For the longest time, I couldn't understand, if the Templars and Cistercians venerated the sacred feminine, or the Goddess, following in the tradition of Akhenaten's Monotheistic Dualism, why did they venerate Jesus if they knew he was just a man and didn't really physically rise from the dead? Upon reading author Ralph Ellis's books, it all came together for me when I began to understand the single most important thing that has dictated the profound changes in the history of religion: the careful tracking of the long-range movements and interaction of the heavenly bodies in the sky by the ancients and specifically, their close tracking of and veneration of the "precession of the equinoxes." It seems appropriate to let Ellis explain this important astronomical phenomenon that serves as the backbone for the history of religion. From his 2009 book, *King Jesus*, Ellis writes:

> The whole business of the constellation of Pisces becoming dominant in A.D. 10, and King Jesus-Justus-Arthur being closely associated with the fish symbolism, is related to the precession of the equinoxes. As we have already seen, the Earth wobbles on its axis like a spinning top, and this wobble makes the rising constellation at the vernal (spring) equinox change over the years. One cycle of the precession takes some 25,800 years, and since there are twelve constellations to pass through during one cycle, then each constellation is dominant for about 2,150 years (depending on its size). This change between constellations every two millennia or so is such an important event that the year-count was zeroed at that time, which is why we count our years from the beginning of the Piscean era (not from the birth of Jesus, as is often assumed).[130]

Ancient cultures around the world tracked these movements of the heavens and compiled detailed knowledge of the constellations of stars, planets, moon, and the sun. Recent archaeological discoveries in the Yucatan Peninsula confirm that astronomical records were kept by the Mayans that spans a 7,000-year-long period.[131] The wisest in these cultures, be it a shaman, medicine man, or high priest, earned their revered status because they were the brightest in their society. One of their most important daily duties was to ensure that the Sun-god Ra (the Aton) rose every day, for without the sun everyone would die.[132]

To ensure the sun would rise, the ancient astronomers made their way to the highest point on a mountain, hill, or to the top of the pyramids and turned their attention to the east. What they saw prior to sunrise was a sky full of stars. On the eastern horizon was one of twelve prominent constellations (the twelve apostles) through which the sun would rise, making it very sacred. Tracking these movements by the ancients has likely gone on for tens of thousands of years, and it has been the change in the ages, or "houses," through the precession of equinoxes that has served as the catalyst to influence the history of religion.

In occult circles, the procession of the equinoxes is responsible for the origin of the "X" symbol used by those at ideological odds with the Roman Catholic Church, those who embraced the teachings of science, which included astronomy. This symbol served as a secret code to those "in the know"

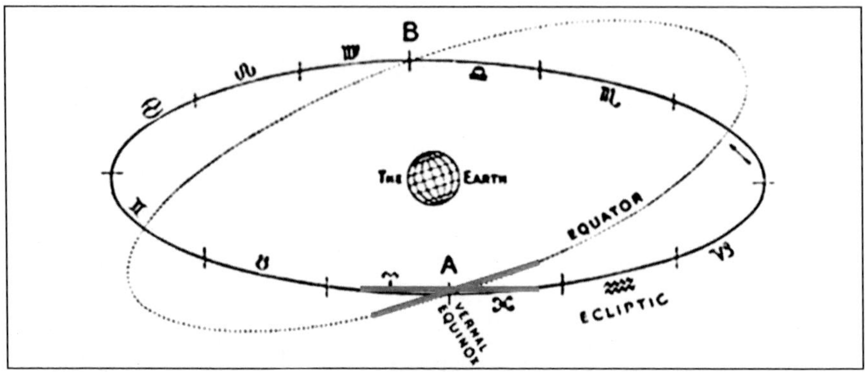

This graphic depicts where the celestial equator intersects the plane of the zodiac during the vernal and autumnal equinoxes. It forms an "X" (at vernal equinox). Quite possibly the X symbol, so often used by the ideological enemies of the Roman Catholic Church, was a secret code for those who understood the astronomical and astrological meanings of the precession of the equinoxes. (Internet)

that they understood the ancient secret knowledge of geometry, mathematics, and astronomy. The secret symbol of the "X" is created where the celestial equator intersects the plane of the zodiac during the annual vernal and autumnal equinoxes in the spring and fall.

"Astronomer priests" also determined that, due to the earth's tilt (22.5 degrees, the same angle of tilt of the Cross of Lorraine on the white hats of the thirty-third-degree Freemasons), it takes approximately 26,000 years for the twelve primary constellations of the zodiac to cycle through their 360 degree procession around the earth through the heavens. The length of time one constellation spends in the eastern sky depends on the size of the constellation, but the average is 2,160 years. Taurus, symbolized by the bull, was a large constellation that lasted nearly 2,700 years. Aries, much smaller, lasted closer to 1,700 years. Exactly how these ancient astronomers determined when it was time to usher in the New Age is unclear. However, we know that the Mayan calendar, or their 26,000 year-long precession of the equinoxes ended on December 21, 2012.

The popular media has made a big deal out of the inaccurate interpretation by doomsayers

A statue of Mary stands on the outside of Notre-Dame Church in Old Montreal with twelve five-pointed stars encircling her head. These stars likely represent the twelve primary constellations of the zodiac that encircle earth and have been tracked by human cultures for hundreds of thousands of years. (Wolter, 2011)

about the end of the Mayan calendar and that it signals the end of the world. This is ridiculous of course for, like most other cycles in life, when one cycle ends, a new cycle begins.

Akhenaten

THE HOOKED X HISTORICAL THREAD I have puzzled over for the past twelve years, I now believe is finally solved. There are certainly many details that need to be filled in, but I believe the evidence demonstrates the thread begins with the "heretic" pharaoh of the eighteenth dynasty of the New Kingdom in Egypt, Amenophis IV, who changed his name to Akhenaten (1358 to 1340 B.C.E.) when he arrived at his new city along the Nile, Amarna. Akhenaten and his queen, Nefertiti, have long been considered by scholars as the ones responsible for changing the long-standing multi-God belief system to a single-God (Aten) form of Dualism we now call, Monotheistic Dualism.

Akhenaten's new religion essentially changed the old religion of veneration of the setting sun to the veneration of the *rising* sun. Simple as it might seem, this change caused great consternation amongst the people. So much so that upon his demise or as many believe, his banishment, the extensive and elaborate carvings of his likeness were defaced and his temples dismantled.

This new religion was prompted by the change in the age as mandated by the astronomer priesthood of which Akhenaten was the high priest. He knew the constellation of Taurus was falling below the horizon in the morning sky, and the constellation of Aries was moving in to replace it. Akhenaten's attempt to unite the followers of both religions is one of the multiple meanings symbolized by the crook and the flail. The flail herds the bulls, or the followers of Taurus, and the crook was used to herd the sheep or the followers of Aries.

Ultimately, Akhenaten's attempt to unite Egypt under the new religion failed. His followers were eventually driven out of Egypt to what is now the Middle East. In his 1933 book, *Moses and Monotheism*, psychologist and author, Sigmund Freud, speculated that the biblical Moses was in fact, pharaoh Akhenaten. This meant that the "Israelites" descended directly from the Egyptian followers of Akhenaten's new religion. This idea is consistent with Ralph Ellis's convincing linguistic argument that Old Hebrew evolved directly from the Egyptian language.

However, recent DNA studies confirm that Akhenaten's mummy was found in the royal tombs at Amarna leading to speculation that the biblical Moses was likely a brother of Akhenaten. In the September 2010, issue of *Na-*

The stone statue of Pharaoh Akhenaten depicts his arms crossed in the "Osiris Pose" over his chest while holding the crook and the flail which are also crossed. In addition to representing the "Hooked X" ideology of Monotheistic Dualism, the crossed crook and flail also symbolized Akhenaten's attempt to combine the Old Religion' of Polytheistic Dualism symbolized by the flail which herds the bulls, or the followers of the constellation of Taurus, with the New Religion symbolized by the crook which herds the sheep, or the followers of the constellation of Aries. Egyptian pharaohs were buried with their arms crossed in the Osirus pose, making an "X" as Ramses is here. (Internet, Internet)

tional Geographic magazine these results were first reported. Under the direction of Egypt's often outspoken Minister of Antiquities Zahi Hawass, they reported, "DNA now confirms the mummy to be a son of Amenhotep III and Queen Tiye–known to be the parents of Akhenaten, the father of King Tut."[133]

Jesus

One of the stories in the Bible Christians seem to agree on is that Jesus was educated in Egypt. Based on the material I've read concerning Jesus, what makes sense to me is that Jesus' education was an initiation in the high priesthood as all Pharaohs-to-be were at that time. Their education was a several years-long process whereby the Egyptian initiates studied the columns of the Temple on which were inscribed the secrets of the seven classic Arts and Sciences.[134]

If true, this education reportedly included seven years studying in India, ". . . sojourned six years amongst the Buddhists, where he found the principal of monotheism still pure," from the time he was twenty years of age until he was twenty-six.[135]

This made perfect sense to me and seemed consistent with his being more than just a simple "carpenter" the Catholic Church wants people to believe. Perhaps the reference to Jesus as a carpenter was simply an allegory for "educator or teacher." According to the research of Robert Feather, Jesus was also educated in the traditions of his unique faith which were contrary to traditional Jewish thinking and practices which included the following:

- Extreme reverence for light and ritual cleanliness/ritual bathing.
- Deep-rooted apocalypticism.
- Expectation of at least two messiahs.
- Continuous references to pre-exilic Egypt.
- Rejection of the Jerusalem Temple and a retrospective devotion to the tabernacle, the place of worship during the time of Moses and the Exodus.
- Dualism.
- Predestination.
- Unique burial practices.[136]
- Adherence to a solar calendar.[137]

As a high priest, Jesus understood that Essene Dualism is where the enlightened ones dwell in the opposite constellation.[138] While humans on earth were venerating the constellation of the zodiac at sunrise as the sun was rising through Pisces (until the winter solstice of 2012 according to the Mayan Calendar) the Creator (the sun) would shine upon the opposite constellation of Virgo. That is until the winter solstice of 2012 when it changed to the house of Leo. Upon reading this it made a lot of sense from the standpoint of trying to understand Dualism, which essentially is the concept of opposites that keep things in balance.

Reading further into Ellis's research, I learned that after completing his education, Jesus was one of these elected high priests of Jerusalem as documented in the Epistle of the Hebrews.[139] I believe it was the rigid and arduous teachings of primarily mathematics, geometry, and astronomy and how to use it that Jesus and his Essene ministry were primarily into. According to the Dead Sea Scrolls, the Essene considered themselves an elite messianic group.[140] No doubt their confidence was due in large part to their breadth of scientific knowledge and more importantly, their application of it. This advanced knowledge was likely used in practical and pragmatic ways that led to strong influence and power. This would explain why so much attention was paid to the Essene and their activities by rival factions such as the Romans, who apparently felt threatened by Jesus and his followers. Ralph Ellis makes the point, ". . . that Jesus and his brethren were part of a rich and influential royal family who were inching ever closer and closer toward taking power in Judea —and perhaps even taking the throne of Rome too, if it fell in their direction."[141]

The Star Prophecy at the time of Jesus that coincided with the change of the age from Aries to Pisces was, "That a king, which means 'messiah' in both Hebrew and Egyptian, would rise in the east to take over the Empire."[142] According to Ellis, the person referred to in the prophecy, along with his mother, appears to be identified by Josephus Flavius, who wrote the commander of the Jewish rebel forces who surrendered to Commander Titus when Jerusalem fell to the Romans was the son of Queen Helena of Adiabene, and his name was King Izus (Jesus).[143]

I am firmly convinced that king was the first Pharaoh of the New Age of Pisces who was baptized by the last Pharaoh of the Age of Aries: John the Baptist. That would explain why John the Baptist is often depicted holding a lamb, or a shepherd's crook, which herds the sheep symbolic of the followers of his teachings. In many of the images of Jesus' baptism, his arms are crossed in the classic Osiris pose, which makes an "X," the infamous symbol of the heretics according to the Roman Church and what I believe is also a symbol of his royal Egyptian heritage.

Some Freemasons I have spoken with who are knowledgeable in the hidden history of Jesus and Mary Magdalene believe John the Baptist was actually Jesus' father. As pharaohs descended from the matriarchal line of Akhenaten, this would make sense since they wanted to keep the bloodline pure and stay within the family line. If true, the John the Baptist/Jesus familial tie would be analogous to Akhenaten and his son, the boy-king Tutankhamen.

In the case of the Knights Templar and the Cistercians, I believe the evidence suggests their *leadership* was a key part of the dynastic royal families with the Templars being the physical guardians of the bloodline, while the Cistercians kept track of the linages to ensure the family line stayed pure. I also believe the Cistercian order was originally founded in the middle eleventh century to establish a monastic order whose primary function was ultimately to protect not only their physical bloodline, but their ancient religious ideology that traced back to Armana, Egypt, at the end of the Age of Taurus (circa 1650 B.C.). If Robert of Molseme, who originally founded the order at Cîteaux, France, in 1098, was not a part of the original plan, St. Bernard of Clairvaux was certainly in on the plan and was the mastermind during his time as the leader of the Cistercians from when he joined in 1113 until his death in 1153.

What scholars have not realized is the bloodline descendants and followers of Jesus and Mary Magdalene implemented the greatest plan of subterfuge in history. In the eleventh century they created incredibly successful monastic orders, the Cistercians and Knights Templar, which aligned with the Catholic Church and used the institution from within to further its own goals. To the Church, the Crusades were a religious mission; to the Cistercians/Knights Templar, it was a military mission with the primary goal of securing the perimeter around Jerusalem so they could retrieve the scrolls, maps, technology, gold, and human remains they knew had been there for a thousand years. For the next two hundred years, they enjoyed unprecedented growth, accumulating great wealth, power, and influence. This success story took a huge hit on October 13, 1307, when the King of France, Philip the Fair, and the Church in Rome conspired to bring down the Knights Templar which not coincidentally led to the decline of the Cistercians thereafter.

The date the Church and the king of France chose could hardly be coincidence. Given the coded reference of the number thirteen to Mary Magdalene by the heretics, they likely picked that date to send a message this bloodline-of-Jesus business would not be tolerated.

In spite of what many believe, the Templars didn't disappear. They went underground. By this time they had established themselves with their allies in the Americas with whom they shared their blood. What's clear is that it was their compatible religious ideologies that led to the bond and to their opposition to the oppressive dogma of the Roman Church. The Cistercians did decline, but they survived and the leadership formed alliances with other religious entities that embraced similar beliefs and long-range goals such as the Sulpicians in Paris. It seems clear that one of the primary goals was to establish a place where they could practice their religion without fear of retribution from the Church. It took three hundred years, but that refuge finally was established in North America in what many then called, "The New Jerusalem." What we now call the United States and Canada.

Our Founding Fathers were well aware of this plan and the genealogy of George Washington suggests that he too was also a part of the bloodline that traces back to the royal family of the first century. I believe this, in part, is why he became the first president of the newly founding republic whose leadership was made of mostly of Freemasons connected to various secret societies that had been in existence since the demise of the Templars. The members of these societies had been ideologically against the Church and European monarchies who sought to limit the personal and religious freedoms of the people they controlled. This has been and continues to be the crux of the conflict that has raged for the past two thousand years.

With the coming of the New Age of Aquarius it appears almost certain this long-standing religious war is about to end. With the advent of the Internet and the instantaneous transfer of information, the historical claims I've made in this book linking the Hooked X families and their ideological thread winding through nearly four thousand years will either be confirmed or refuted. I'm confident they will not only be confirmed, but expanded upon exponentially.

On October 7, 2011, after giving a speech to a group of Masons, a Knights Templar Freemason explained that, when they prayed before the meal prior to my lecture, they all crossed their arms across their chests in the Osiris pose, and he raises his right thumb. I asked why, and he said, "When Masons used to pass each other on the street they would place their right hand below their chest with their thumb raised vertically creating a square. When I pray with my arms crossed, I raise my thumb to make the square of recognition." He then demonstrated by crossing his arms, raising his thumb and said, "I never realized it before, but it makes the Hooked X." (See color section, Figures 35 & 36)

My discussion about Jesus and Mary Magdalene would not be complete if I didn't comment on the recent archaeological discoveries made just outside of Jerusalem that have created a whirlwind of controversy. Readers might recall the Discovery Channel program in 2007 about the incredible discovery of a first-century tomb in East Talpiot, a mile and a half south of the Old City of Jerusalem believed to relate directly to the biblical Jesus, his family, and his closest followers.

There were *two* tombs revealed during the construction of condominiums in March of 1980 and 1981.[144] The first, called the Garden Tomb, was exposed by a blast on March 27, 1980, and revealed the exterior façade over the entrance of an upward chevron above a circle. Inside the roughly square-shaped chamber were a total of six, approximately six-foot-long niches that contained a total of ten ossuaries. Six of the ossuaries were inscribed with the names Jesus, son of Joseph; Mariam called Mara; Joses; Judah son of Jesus; Matthew; and Maria.[145]

The controversy centered on this combination of names that represent either an incredible coincidence or what can only be the family tomb of Jesus and his royal family. Arguments against it being the tomb of *that* Jesus came about because these were common names in the first century. However, when a statistical analysis of the names was run against the roughly six hundred inscribed ossuaries collected from over one thousand tombs that have been opened and studied, this is the only tomb that has this combination of names. This data doesn't prove it is Jesus' tomb, but it seems virtually certain to me that it is.

If we assume this tomb is the final resting place of Jesus and his family, then there are a number of interesting things to consider besides the obvious humanity of the man known as Jesus. The implication of Jesus being human is what created the fervor among Roman Christians who believe both his body

These two late twelfth/early thirteenth century Crusader coins both have an upward triangle with a circle design that is essentially the same as the symbols above the burial chamber to the Talpiot Garden Tomb (top). The first example is found in a coin minted by the Crusaders in the Holy Land between the years 1197-1287 A.D. As possible further confirmation, the back side has small circles in opposing quadrants of the cross and could also be interpreted as the tops of two opposing Talpiot Garden Tomb chevron-circles (middle). The second coin was found by Dr. James Tabor (below right), and is also believed to be a Crusader coin from the same period. Could this be evidence the Templars entered the Jesus Family tomb and incorporated the architecture they saw into the design of the coins? If so, the three circles and dots in a triangle could represent the three skulls found inside the burial chamber that were also arranged in a triangle. Additionally, the vertical columns around the face, presumably of Jesus, may represent the architecture of the antechamber that was intact in the twelfth century, but later destroyed by construction in 1980. (Internet; U. of WI; Internet)

and spirit rose to heaven. It was their well-coordinated protests to Discovery Channel that led to them not replaying the film since its initial release in 2007.

As startling and exciting as finding the tomb of Jesus was, an important revelation in the book for me came on page 100 where Tabor wrote about his research investigating how frequent the name Jesus was during the first century. Of the 600 known ossuaries with names carved onto them, the name Jesus in any form occurs twenty-one times which equals about three and a half percent. However, Tabor argues that of the eighteen instances the name "Jesus" occurs on ossuaries, minus the three in in the Garden tomb, over half a dozen appear to be a reference to Jesus of Nazareth and not the name of the person whose bones are in the box. Of the roughly twelve that remain, they occur as a cluster in close proximity to the Talpiot Garden and Patio tombs and likely represent followers of Jesus.[146]

Without a doubt the biggest bombshell for me was when Tabor wrote that scratched onto the front and lids of at least two of the "Jesus" ossuaries, including the "Jesus son of Joseph" ossuary from the Garden Tomb, are "X" symbols! Skeptics reportedly argued these were mason's marks, but it seems highly unlikely that of the dozens of ossuaries Tabor and his team have examined with similar X's that they were all made by the same first-century stone mason.[147] The only logical conclusion is the "X" is symbolic of something of utmost importance. I maintain it represents the essence of the Egyptian Monotheistic Dualism religion pioneered by Akhenaten that Jesus and his followers later embraced. The "Hooked X" symbol didn't become associated with Jesus and his *true* teachings that harkened back to the secret Egyptian priesthood veneration of the rising sun-God until after his death.

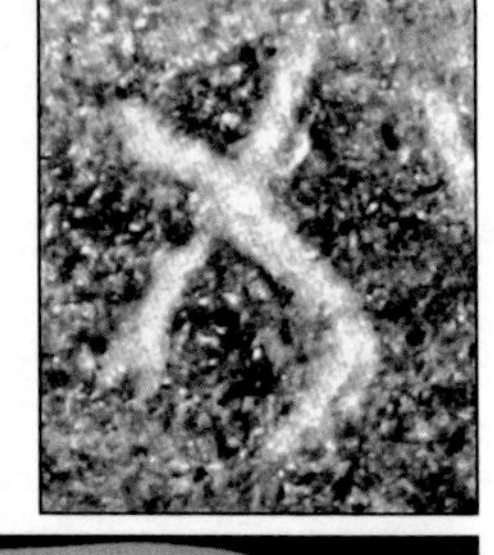

An interesting and potentially important detail of the "X" on the Jesus ossuary is the curious hook on the lower right leg that bends ninety degrees to the lower left. This strange "X" is identical to the first Roman numeral ten caved on the In Camera Stone found in the Catskill Mountains in 2009. The "C" Document indicates that stone, if genuine, could only have been carved by the Templars in the late twelfth century. Could this be evidence that the

This first century ossuary has a large "X" carved beneath the Greek inscription of Caiaphas, the high priest who allegedly turned Jesus over to Pontius Pilate. Like Jesus and his followers, Caiaphas apparently also embraced the same Egyptian Monotheistic Dualism religion pioneered by Akhenaten that was symbolized by the "X." (Internet)

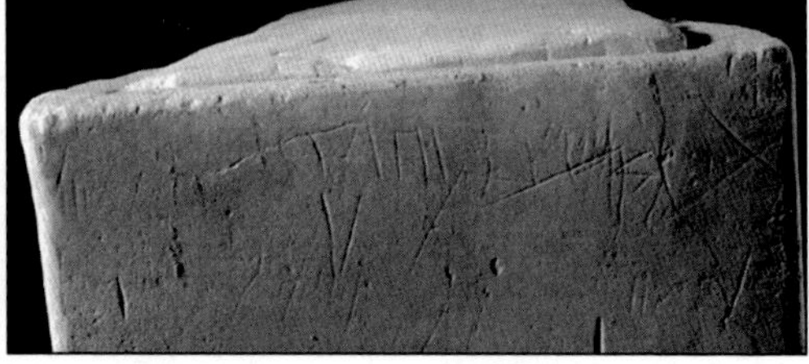

The "Jesus, son of Joseph" ossuary from the Talpiot Garden Tomb in Jerusalem has an "X" symbol on the right side where the inscription begins. The artist drawing below by Jeffrey R. Chadwick shows a curious bend in the lower right leg of the "X," which happens to look very similar to the first Roman numeral ten on the In Camera Stone found in the Catskill Mountains in 2009 (lower right). One could argue a somewhat tenuous connection since the stone was likely carved by someone closely associated with the twelfth-century Templars, devout followers of Jesus and used the Hooked X as a symbol of his religious teachings. (Wolter, 2010; Internet; Internet)

Templars were in the Talpiot Tomb only a few decades earlier and saw the unique "X" carved on the Jesus ossuary? If so, the two "X's" serve as reciprocal supporting evidence.

When thinking about the "X" being used in medieval times to symbolize Jesus and his religious ideology, it necessitated some changes for the Templars who copied the "C" Document Nova Scotia map where "X" is used extensively for the Roman numeral ten. In two instances, the Roman numeral ten is hooked in what can only be a reference to the reverence of Jesus, who came into power when the celestial age changed from Aries to Pisces.

The Hooked X was an unmistakable code used by both the Templars and the subsequent secret societies in Europe who followed in their footsteps.

Janet found something else. On March 10, 2013, she pointed out three small round holes in a right triangle just to the left of the "X" and the Aramaic inscription. This posed more questions. Were these dots manmade? Were they made at the time the inscription was carved? Were they added later, perhaps along with the "X" when somebody entered the tomb? Could the Templars have added the "X" along with the dots when they entered the tomb at the time of the First Crusade? Were these three dots in a triangle left as a calling card on the ossuary just as the three skulls appear to have been left on the floor of the burial chamber? I'm hopeful I'll be able to examine this mysterious ossuary at some point in the future to try and answer these questions.

After I sent the final draft to Simcha, he wrote that he was very impressed with the circa 1200 A.D. Crusader coin that appears to show the chevron-circle Talpiot Garden Tomb architecture on both sides. On March 6, 2013, Simcha's colleague, Dr. James Tabor, posted another coin on his blog with an unmistakable chevron-circle and three dots in an equilateral triangle directly above! The coin has no known minting history, but is believed to date to around that same time as the coin I found, sometime between the 1197 and 1287.

These coins were potentially important pieces of evidence confirming not only that the Talpiot Garden Tomb was, in fact, the family tomb of Jesus and Mary Magdalene, but also that the Templars had entered the tomb shortly after they captured Jerusalem in 1099.

After completing my research into the ossuary "X's" and the Crusader coins, something else crept into my brain. The Hooked X isn't the only secret symbol the Templars quietly introduced to the world. After digesting the research on the tombs found at Talpiot, I started noticing a very basic, yet undeniable architecture that is found all over the world today nearly everywhere. This architecture incorporates the same basic symbology found on the wall outside the burial chamber of the Talpiot Tomb: the upward pointing chevron with the circle below.

Skeptics I'm sure are already rolling their eyes, likely thinking, "Sometimes a peaked roof with a round window simply allows water to run off a building and light to enter a room." This is certainly true, but perhaps there is more to it. It is a fact that after the Templars completed their mission in Jerusalem, in 1118, and returned to Italy and reported to their leader Bernard de Clairvaux, the massive Gothic Cathedrals began to be constructed along with many churches. They were built by the Cistercians and Templar stone masons and/or their money and liberally incorporated the upward pointing chevron with the circle into the architecture. Within these religious houses the circle below the chevron was often used as the Rose window symbolic of their veneration of the sacred feminine. The chevron-circle architecture is also symbolic of the male/female aspect of Dualism with Jesus represented by the chevron and Mary Magdalene by the circle.

If the Templars entered the Garden Tomb of Jesus and his family, it is a certainty they saw these symbols above the entrance to the burial chamber. If so, these symbols would have been of utmost importance and indeed sacred symbols of extreme reverence. After all, these were their distant bloodline ancestors and may have quietly introduced the symbols into the sacred churches and cathedrals they built as a secret acknowledgement they had been inside His tomb.

William A. Turnier designed the Oreo cookie in 1952, twenty-eight years before the Talpiot Garden Tomb was discovered. It is unclear if he was a Freemason, but the symbols are clearly important Masonic and Templar symbols. The design includes twelve Maltese-style Templar crosses, likely symbolic of the twelve primary constellations of the zodiac, surrounding the Cross of Lorraine, which is attached to an oval shape encircling the Oreo name. Opposite the Cross of Lorraine is a stylized AVM. In this case, it must surely be referring to Mary Magdalene.

The "Double Stuf" Oreo with the Cross of Lorraine and Talpiot chevron-circle design was introduced in 1974, six years prior to the Tomb discovery.

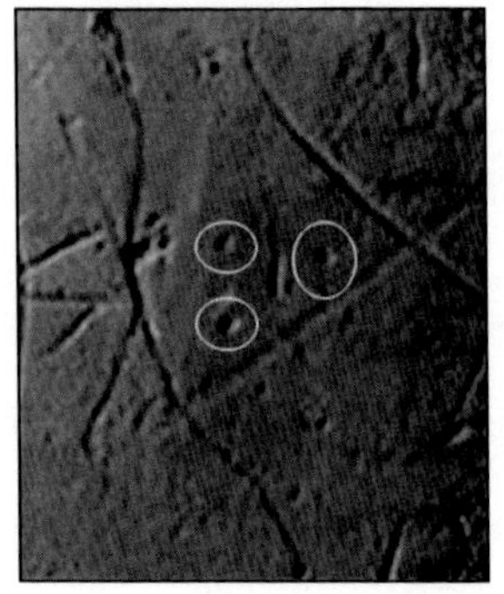

Three mysterious dots in roughly a right triangle are located between the Aramaic "Jesus, son of Joseph" inscription and the unique Hooked X. 3D microscopy should be able to shed light whether these dots are manmade, and if so, when they might have been made. (Internet)

The symbolism in the design of the cookie is the Templar Crosses represent Templar Knights surrounding and protecting the Cross of Lorraine, the bloodline descendants of the Royal Family through time. The chevron-circle is symbolic of the Talpiot Tomb and physical remains of the First Century Royal Family.

Admittedly, this is pretty heavy stuff to put on a popular cookie. However, the symbolism along with the timing when it appeared implies that somebody knew something about the Talpiot tomb prior to its discovery.

I got a very knowledgeable Freemason's take on the design of the cookies. John Freeburg looked carefully at the pictures sent by Channing Mabbett, and was quite impressed. I then asked him, "Assuming these dates for the cookie designs are correct, would it be safe to conclude that somebody knew something about the Tomb before its discovery in 1980?" He looked at me and said, "Oh, yes."

After seeing the upward pointing chevron with the circle carved above the entrance to the Talpiot Garden Tomb of Jesus and his immediate family it dawned on me that symbolic architecture exists all around the world and is primarily found in Christian churches and cathedrals. The Cistercians were primarily responsible for the explosion in the construction of the Gothic cathedrals and churches of Europe beginning in the middle twelfth century. My thesis is they incorporated the chevron and the circle into their religious houses after the Knights Templar entered the tomb and then brought this sacred "Talpiot Tomb" architecture only they were privy to. (Wolter, 2012)

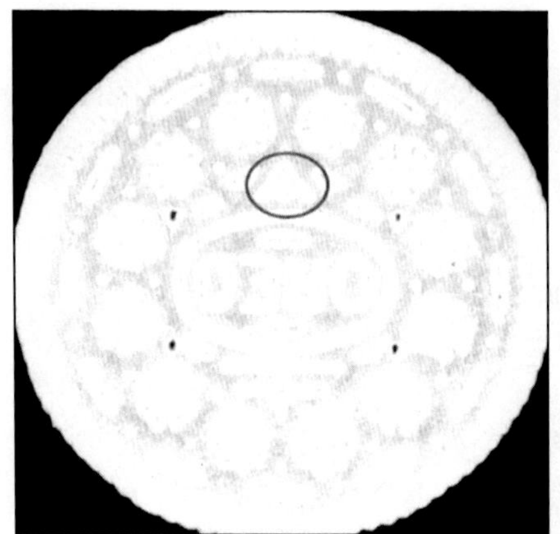

The modern design of the Oreo Cookie was done in 1952 and includes twelve (symbolic of the twelve primary constellations of the zodiac) Maltese style Templar crosses surrounding the Cross of Lorraine attached to an oval shape encircling the Oreo name. Opposite the Cross of Lorraine and circled is a stylized AVM (left with color reversed). The design of the "Double Stuf" Oreo cookie was slightly modified in 1974. The most significant change is the AVM symbol was switched to the chevron-circle symbolism of the Talpiot Tomb (right). (Wolter, 2013)

I can only conclude there must be an obscure Masonic Templar "side" order still in existence today that has known about the tomb for a long time. This knowledge must go back to the Medieval Knights Templar, the only logical candidates to have entered the tomb in the past, most likely at the time of the First Crusade. A day after meeting with John, I met with another knowledgeable Freemason friend who said, "This is not a 'regular' Freemason thing."

The thirteenth-century Crusader coins are likely evidence connecting the Templars to the tomb. Interestingly, the Oreo cookie also looks like a coin. While we're talking about symbolism, isn't it interesting the Oreo has black-and-white colors, which symbolize one aspect of Templar/Cistercian ideology, the concept of Dualism. Examples include the black-and-white-colored Masonic pavement common in Freemasonry, and the Cistercians had their white tunics with black mantles. It's a lot to read into a cookie, but given the facts I suspect it's probably right.

I forwarded the Oreo cookie information to my friend Alan Butler who I thought could give me balanced feedback on this mystery. As usual, he came back with some good stuff. The first thing he offered was a Latin possibility for OREO (OSSUARIUM REGINA ETERNUS OMNIPOTENS). His wife, Kate, who is proficient in Latin, said this was perfectly good Latin for, "Tomb of the Eternal and All Powerful Queen!" Given the AVM, Cross of Lorraine, and Templar Crosses symbolism, this queen could only be referring to Mary Magdalene.

Another interesting possible clue to the tomb appeared when John Freeburg stopped by my office with a series of a dozen antique wooden slides with York Rite Masonic images painted onto glass. He had checked them out from the Minnesota Masonic Historical Society and believed they dated back to the late 1800s. Because of our recent discussions about the likelihood of the Templars having entering the Talpiot Tomb and retaining knowledge to this day, he wondered if one of the slides associated with the York Rite Knights Templar final degrees might have more meaning than he initially thought.

The image was of a Templar knight kneeling with head bowed at the entrance to a tomb with a rectangular shaped doorway carved into bedrock. In his left hand, the knight holds a burning candle, in his right hand a skull. A dressed rectangular slab of rock sits next to the entrance on a larger slab of rock on the ground (antechamber?). On a deeper level, the scene could be interpreted as knowledge of Templar knights paying proper respect prior to entering the tomb of their first-century Royal Family ancestors. Does this image provide additional evidence that somebody knew about the Talpiot Tomb prior to its discovery in 1980?

I also noticed that the dressed slab of rock pushed aside from the entrance on the slide reminded me of another dressed slab of rock with a medieval inscription found in Minnesota. The artist painted the lower left part of the slab of rock in a pattern that is virtually identical to the white triangular calcite area on the Kensington Rune Stone. This almost certainly is a coincidence, but even the approximate shape and dimensions of the two stones is close to the same and had me wondering aloud. John and I agreed the symbolism related to Talpiot and the Rune Stone on the slide was compelling, but far from conclusive. Still, it was also the kind of veiled reference to something deeper that is so very common in the symbolism of Freemasonry and other secret societies.

Perhaps the most important discovery made in the Talpiot Patio Tomb was the ossuary with a carving Tabor and Jacobovici say depicts the Bible story of Jonah and the great fish. This Old Testament story tells how Jonah was swallowed by the great fish (symbolic of the constellation of Pisces?) and after three days was rescued and symbolizes "rebirth" or "resurrection" from the "womb" of the great fish.[148] This Jonah and the fish symbolism of resurrection represent the earliest example that reportedly disappeared by the fourth century.

When they described the head of the human stick figure emerging from the mouth of the fish on the ossuary, ". . . looked like it is wrapped in the style of a mummy."[149] The authors assumed the bandages are seaweed wrapped around

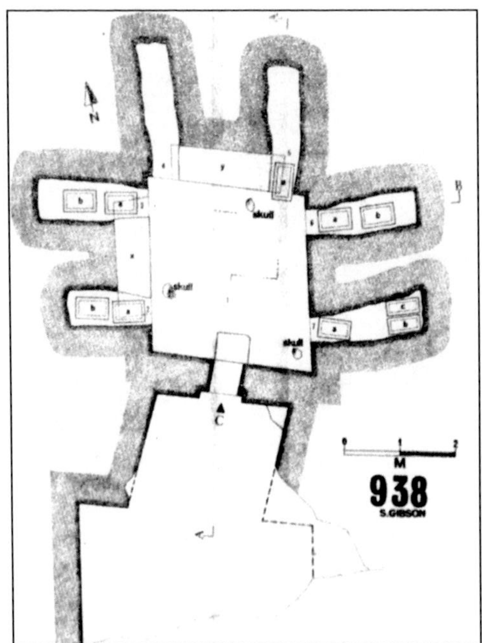

This plan view of the Talpiot Tomb was mapped by Israeli archaeologist Shimon Gibson, in 1980. The antechamber at the bottom was mostly destroyed during construction blasting for condominiums, but the burial chamber remained intact. Inside were two shelves and six niches that contained a total of ten ossuaries. On the floor of the burial chamber three skulls were found placed in an equilateral triangle, likely a tell-tale calling card of the Knights Templar. (Tabor and Jacobovici, Page 29, 2012)

the head, but why couldn't the bandages on the stick figure represent a mummy? While the assumption of seaweed seems to be corroborated by biblical texts, in light of Ralph Ellis's research, the bandages could be another clue to Jesus and his Egyptian heritage.

After reading Tabor and Jacobovici's book, I wanted more details about this incredible tomb and looked at Jacobovici's earlier book co-authored with Charles Pellegrino entitled, *The Jesus Family Tomb*. I was pleasantly surprised to learn new details that shed additional light on the initial discovery of the tomb. Another detail that triggered my speculation was the three skulls excavated from the floor of the main tomb encased in undisturbed red *terra rossa* soil. The Israeli archaeologists mapped the location of the skulls and realized they formed an isosceles triangle with the base oriented toward Jerusalem.[150]

On March 27, 2013, John Freeburg shared a late1800s era wooden slide with an image painted on glass of a kneeling Templar knight holding a burning candle and skull at the entrance of a tomb carved into bedrock. This York Rite Masonic image could suggest knowledge of the Talpiot Tomb by a secret Masonic order prior to its discovery. The dressed rectangular shaped stone on the side has shading that matches the white triangular calcite area on the Kensington Rune Stone possibly suggesting knowledge prior to its discovery as well. (Slide courtesy of the Minnesota Masonic Historical Society)

The St. Louis Arch, symbol of the gateway to the west where Louis & Clark began their exploration up the Missouri River has Masonic symbolism. At its apex, a cross-section of the triangle-shaped structure produces the sacred feminine symbol of the equilateral triangle with the point downward. A similar triangle of skulls was found inside the Talpiot Garden Tomb, containing the remains of Jesus, Mary Magdalene, and others of the first-century royal family. (Wolter, 2011)

The triangular layout of the skulls, which looks more equilateral in shape according to the original sketch made by the archaeologists, reminded me of the three-dot pattern Freemasons often use as important symbolism for multiple purposes. The three-dot triangle also reminded me of the triangle of stone holes at the Ohman Farm that were not part of the stone holes that create the lines that intersect at the location of the Kensington Rune Stone discovery site. Perhaps the three-dot triangle is a sacred symbol within secret organizations that goes back at least two thousand years and includes the triangle of three skulls inside the likely tomb of Jesus and his family.

Whatever the meaning was for the placement of the three skulls inside the Jesus tomb, I agree with Jacobovici's speculation about *who* was responsible for putting them there. In the twelfth century the stone that originally sealed the tomb was removed and then put back in place. But the stone was not replaced properly, which allowed a rare agricultural soil called *terra rossa* to flow into the tomb filling it to a depth of about three feet (one meter) creating a unique geochemical profile on surfaces inside the burial chamber including the ossuaries.[151]

The *terra rossa* soil contained a unique chemical make-up that included titanium and iron and was eventually used through chemical testing to prove that the controversial "James, son of Joseph" ossuary that showed up on the antiquities market around the same time the tenth ossuary from the Jesus tomb went missing could only have come from that same tomb. When added to the five other ossuaries with inscribed names from the Garden Tomb, including "Jesus, son of Joseph" and Mariamene, Mara (Lord), amazingly it could only mean this is with reasonable certainty the tomb of the first-century biblical family of Jesus.

Jacobovici speculates the Templar Knights who entered the tomb in the twelfth century were only interested in the "Jesus" ossuary and responsible for leaving the three skulls arranged in a triangle. I agree it had to be the Templars who entered the tomb nine hundred years ago after capturing Jerusalem and securing the perimeter of the city. The "C" Document is consistent with this premise, which mentions that among other things they found an ossuary that contained the "bones of a man."[152] It makes sense they were looking for the Jesus ossuary almost certainly to collect some (the crossed femurs and skull?) or all of his bones as insurance against future aggression by the Roman Catholic Church.

Another clue it was the Knights Templar who entered the Garden Tomb in Talpiot sits directly above the entrance in the carved architecture of the upward pointing chevron with the circle below it. I would offer two pieces of evidence consistent with the Templars entering the tomb, seeing the chevron and the circle above the entrance to the burial chamber, and then cleverly incorporating that symbolism into their future handiwork.

Reading these books felt like a gale-force of fresh air blown into the subject of biblical history by the use of scientific methodology and sound logical analysis mixed with the proper human sensitivity to such controversial subject matter. Upon closing the second book it felt as though I read what will become known as a classic work in the future. There were a number of points about Jesus made that have been debated before, but for me the truth was definitively put to bed here.

One fact they brought to clarity was that celibacy was not a tenant of first-century pious Jews, in fact their beliefs encouraged them to "Be fruitful, and multiply, and fill the earth."[153] Further, the Roman Christian obsession with virginity did not come from Jesus' time, but grew out of the second- and third-century asceticism. This misconception has led to significant emotional trauma and confusion about sexuality that much of humanity struggles with to this day.

The DNA testing of recovered bone fragments from the Jesus and Mary Magdalene ossuaries proved that the woman inside the Magdalene ossuary was not Jesus' mother or sister. They argue this is consistent with their relationship being almost certainly that of husband and wife.[154] Another critical point was not only were Jesus and Mary Magdalene almost certainly married, but they had at least one child, a boy named Judah, whose bones reside in an ossuary in the Garden Tomb along with his parents and other family members.

Perhaps their most potent argument made from Tabor and Jacobovici was the events that led to the Christian resurrection belief in the revival of the physical corpse after death was simply the misinterpretation of the empty tomb. It was Joseph of Arimathea, who put the body of Jesus in a temporary tomb prior to the Sabbath and later moved it in three days to the family tomb at Talpiot.[155] This explains why his body was gone when followers arrived at the temporary tomb and proves that Jesus was just a man whose bones did not ascend to heaven, but actually lay within an ossuary placed inside the family tomb. Their research also shows the symbology carved on numerous bone boxes is consistent with his followers believing it was the *spirit* of Jesus that ascended to heaven.

Tabor and Jacobovici present what I believe is a conclusive case that they have indeed discovered the tombs of the biblical Jesus, his family, and his followers by using sound archaeological evidence along with scientific testing and analysis to support their arguments. What I respect most about their work is they had the courage to stand behind their conclusions in spite of ferocious opposition of many people driven by religious zealotry rather than scientific method.

I especially like their closing words with respect to their incredible research and what it means which I quote here: "Whatever one's views of Jesus, we should always remember the lessons of the Enlightenment and the very foundation of academic and scientific culture–good history is never the enemy of informed faith. As has ever been the case through the ages it is dogma, ignorance, and bias that should ever remain our common enemy. Our hope is that our decade-long investigation of the Talpiot tombs will serve to dispel those ancient stumbling blocks so that responsible history and informed faith can dwell together in peace."

Mary Magdalene

FOR MUCH OF MY DISCUSSION about the historical aspects of Mary Magdalene and her role in this research I rely on the 2011 publication by Ralph Ellis, *Mary Magdalene: Princess of Provence and the House of Orange.*

Context relative to Ralph's work here is this book benefits from knowledge gained from his nine previous books on the subject of biblical history and the central figure of that time: Jesus. His theories were confidently presented and, for the most part, made a lot of sense to this pragmatist.

Ellis effectively argues that ". . . Mary Magdalene was a powerful and wealthy princess, who was probably the sister-wife of King Jesus in the time-honored Egyptian tradition of a royal sibling betrothal. And being so close to Jesus, she was probably his most intimate and trusted disciple."[156] This would certainly make her an important player at the time and one who would have been revered by followers. However, the true history of the biblical royal family had to be changed, which is exactly what the Church did, creating a largely fictional tome we now call the Bible.

I particularly like Ellis's frank take on this point, "Such deliberate fabrications of biblical verses should alert readers to the obvious fact that the Bible on

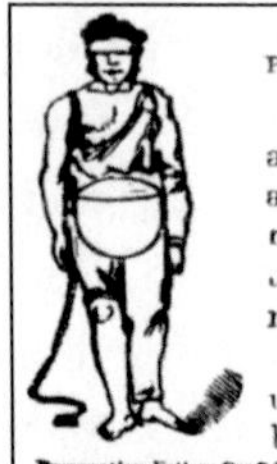

PREPARATION FOR FELLOW CRAFT DEGREE.

Candidate is prepared much the same as in the first degree. The *right* leg, *right* arm, *right* breast, and *right* foot being bare, a slipper on *left* foot and the cable tow twice around his naked right arm near shoulder.

A small white apron with bib turned up and he is "duly and truly prepared" to be made a Fellow Craft.

Preparation Fellow Craft Degree.

Many believe the sect of Jesus was essentially a Masonic organization where the ancient mysteries (the seven classic arts and sciences) were taught to his followers (initiates). Believers argue this legend is secretly preserved to this day within Masonic rituals and art. The stained-glass window in First Presbyterian Catholic Church in Kansas City, Missouri, shows a kneeling pilgrim (candidate prepared for the Fellow Craft degree) kissing the hand of the Church Father (Grand Master of the Lodge) with three pillars in the background which could be symbolic of the three degrees of the Masonic Blue Lodge. (Wolter, 2011; Secret Societies Illustrated, Page 16, 1909)

the family bookshelf should not be taken literally as evidence of what happened in the first century, for we have layer upon layer of deceit in this ancient work. Many of the events it records were deliberately manipulated by Saul, to suit Roman sensitivities and Roman needs, and this was the major revision of the true story that changed Jesus from a Warrior Monarch into a Pauper Carpenter. But each subsequent redaction and translation has overlaid on this unreliable account with yet further alterations to suit the sensitivities of each new era, and the betrothal of a sister-wife was one among many elements that could not be allowed to survive."[157]

So what happened to Mary Magdalene after the Crucifixion? With Jesus exiled in what is now Britain, the most likely result if he survived the Crucifixion as many believe, was that Mary's life would have been in danger. The only thing that made sense was going into exile. Legend has it the pregnant queen first went to Egypt where she gave birth to a daughter many believe was named Sarah. From there, she allegedly escaped in a boat across the Mediterranean Sea to southern France where the "Vine of Mary" legend began. (See color section, Figure 40)

At a Masonic funeral specific arm poses are used to honor a deceased brother. On page 216 of the *Standard Monitor* the following rituals are performed, "The brethren then move in precession round the place of interment, and drop a sprig of evergreen into the grave, after which the Masonic funeral honors are given. The funeral honors are given by extending the hands towards the grave with the palms up. Then cross the arms over the breast, the left above the right,

This ornate life-size sculpture of the entombment of Christ came from the Knights Templar commandery of Reims that was destroyed during the French revolution in 1792. The sculpture was ordered by Francois Jarradin, Commander of the Hospitallers, in 1531. It was later placed in the St. Remi Cathedral in 1803. The sculpture shows a very pregnant and distraught Mary Magdalene with her arms in the air looking at her husband Jesus shortly after being taken down from the cross. Curiously, blood is depicted still flowing from the spear wound on his right side suggesting he was still alive after the Crucifixion. (Photo courtesy of *Christian Tourenne*)

At a Masonic funeral, specific arm poses are used to honor a deceased brother. In the *Standard Monitor,* the following rituals are performed. "The brethren then move in precession round the place of interment, and drop a sprig of evergreen into the grave, after which the Masonic funeral honors are given. The funeral honors are given by extending the hands towards the grave with the palms up. Then cross the arms over the breast, the left above the right, the fingers touching the shoulders. Then raise the hands above the head, looking upward." At Royston Cave in Royston, England, numerous carvings believed made by the Templars in the fourteenth century include one of what appears to be Mary Magdalene with arms raised in the Masonic sign of distress. Curiously, the early sixteenth-century carving of a very pregnant Mary Magdalene at St. Remi has her arms in the same position. What was originally thought to be the Carthaginian Goddess symbol Tanit carved on the In Camera Stone might actually be a depiction of Mary Magdalene. Notice the position of the arms with the left bent ninety degrees in all three examples and the right bent at a lesser angle. The dot in the body/triangle could be symbolic of the long-rumored legend that Mary was pregnant at the time of the Crucifixion. (Internet; Wolter, 2010)

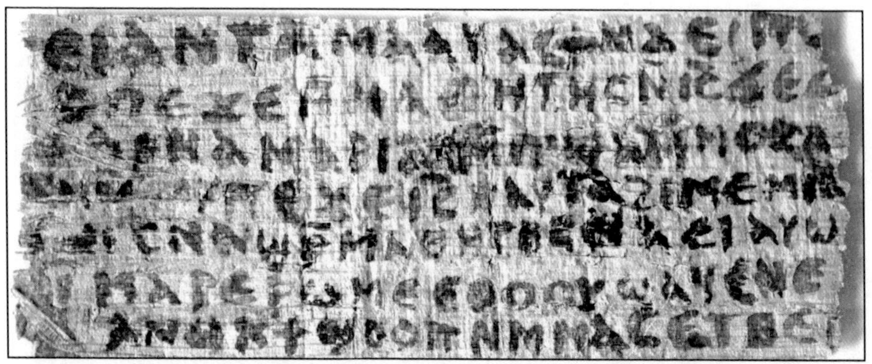

This papyrus fragment was discovered by Professor Karen L. King, of Harvard University who released her findings in 2012. King reported the fourth century Coptic Gospel text includes dialogue between Jesus and his disciples where he says, "Jesus said to them, 'My wife . . . she will be able to be my disciple.'" (Internet)

the fingers touching the shoulders. Then raise the hands above the head, looking upward." Many images of Mary Magdalene depict her in each of these poses suggesting some type of connection to Masonic ritual. The question becomes: why?

And what about the persistent legend that Mary Magdalene was pregnant with a daughter named Sarah at the time of the Crucifixion that I believe is one of the secret messages found in the Hooked X symbol? There is some interesting evidence that supports this, including a stunning life-size sculpture of the entombment of Christ ordered by Francois Jarradin, commander of the Hospitallers, in 1531. It resided at the Knights Templar Commandery of Reims until that building was destroyed during the French Revolution in 1792. The statue now resides at St. Remi Cathedral, where it was moved in 1803.

The sculpture depicts the Royal Family grieving over the body of Jesus with tears flowing from their eyes. A distraught and very pregnant Mary Magdalene has her arms in the air in an interesting position. It's the same position Freemasons use at Masonic funerals and reportedly as a sign of distress to other Masons. The position of Magdalene's arms is very curious and appears to be the same as a carving made by the Knights Templar on the walls of Royston Cave in England. The positioning of the arms has the left arm bent ninety degrees as in a square and the right arm bend at a lesser angle.

While studying these images on May 19, 2013, something prompted me to look at pictures of the In Camera Stone found three years earlier in the Panther Mountain impact area. What we assumed was a carving of the Carthaginian Goddess Tanit, suddenly became something different. I compared the angles of the

One example of believers secretly preserving the alternate story of Jesus and Mary Magdalene might be at the top of the window in the front of First Presbyterian Church in Franklin, Pennsylvania, the stone tracing looks as though two capitol "M's", with a prominently curved female "V" symbol in the middle of each, are on either side of what appears to be a Grail cup. (Wolter, 2010)

arms on the carving with those of the Royston Cave carving and the sculpture at St. Remi. They were the same. Could the Tanit carving on the In Camera Stone actually be a waist-up depiction of Mary Magdalene making the sign of distress?

I immediately forwarded the three images to Zena Halpern and then called her. I asked if she saw the similarity of the arms' positions and she did. We then discussed the dot made in the body on the In Camera Stone, and she said, "A dot on a female body is symbolic of the womb." Again I was struck with a realization. The evidence in the "C" document clearly pointed to the Templars being in the Panther Mountain area in the twelfth century and the most likely candidates to have carved the stone if it indeed dates back to that time. If so, then the carving is not Tanit and can only be symbolic of a pregnant Mary Magdalene with her arms in the air in a sign of distress.

At this point, it is nearly impossible to know for sure what the truth is regarding this persistent legend. However, there is no question whatsoever that many people around the world for many centuries have *believed* the legend of Mary Magdalene to be true.

In September of 2012, another tantalizing piece of evidence surfaced relating to Mary and Jesus being married in the form of a fourth-century papyrus fragment with eight lines of text on the front and six lines on the back written in the Coptic language. The fragment was discovered by Professor Karen L. King, of Harvard University. The Gospel text includes dialogue between Jesus and his disciples where he says, "Jesus said to them, 'My wife . . . she will be able to be my disciple.'"[158] As King stated in her paper, this discovery doesn't prove that Jesus and Mary Magdalene were married, but it moves the idea a major step closer to confirming it.

The implications of the fragment caused heated debate and a predictable reaction from the Vatican, which, of course, claimed the parchment as a fake.[159] What else can they say since it appears this was one fragment they were unable to round up and either destroy or hide away in the bowels of their archives.

On line two of the Kensington Rune Stone inscription there is a "hook" on both the upper right arm and lower left leg of the character. If the "hook" on the upper right arm of the Hooked X character represents the belief that Jesus and Mary Magdalene had a daughter, could the second "hook" on the lower left leg symbolize the belief they also had a son? (Wolter, 2002)

The research in this book unveils evidence that supports the idea that the *belief* in the bloodline of Mary Magdalene and Jesus not only survived and then flourished in Southern France, but eventually made its way to North America during multiple periods in history. The Bat Creek Stone suggests a Hebrew presence in the first/second centuries, the Tucson lead artifacts suggest a Hebrew presence in the eighth/ninth centuries, and the multiple runic inscriptions, Templar/Mide'win rituals and the Newport Tower, suggest a Templar presence from the eleventh through the fourteenth century.

An interesting footnote is the presence of an ossuary that appears to contain the bones of Mary Magdalene in the Talpiot Garden Tomb, suggesting that, at some point after her escape to Southern France, she must have returned to Jerusalem to be buried with her husband and children. Her return to Jerusalem has never been seriously considered to my knowledge and brings up all kinds of interesting possible scenarios. Her wanting to return to be with her husband in death would have been perfectly natural. However, given the volatile political climate with the Romans, it may not have been possible while she was still alive. This brings to mind the likelihood she was brought back by followers after her death, but is there any evidence for this?

Back at the Talpiot tomb, we find that of the six inscribed ossuaries only one is carved in Greek. This ossuary has beautifully decorated carvings befitting

This painting on wood on the ceiling at Rue Bonsecours Church in Montreal, Canada, is a beautiful allegorical depiction of Monotheistic Dualism (Hooked X ideology) and symbolic representation of the Star Prophecy ascribed to the coming new Age of Aquarius. Jesus places the crown onto his wife Mary Magdalene, as she ascends to her equal and rightful place next to her consort. Witnessing the event are twelve angels that represent the twelve primary constellations of the Zodiac and the procession of the equinox who's most recent twenty-six thousand year-long cycle ended on December 21, 2012. (Wolter/2010)

someone highly revered and of significant status. The inscription on this ossuary has been translated as "Mariamene Mara." "Mariamene," a relatively rare form of "Mary," was used by the Jesus' contemporary followers referencing Mary Magdalene. "Mara" is a title of honor equivalent to "Lady," "Lord," or "Master."[160]

Recent DNA test results from the Jesus and Mary Magdalene ossuaries in the Talpiot Garden Tomb shows they likely weren't a brother-sister marriage speculated by Ellis. However, his argument of a royal Egyptian king-queen relationship seems to be reinforced by the title of authority carved into what evidence suggests is the ossuary of the queen and wife of King Jesus: Mary Magdalene.

That this inscription is carved in Greek unlike the rest of the family names in the tomb suggests it was likely carved at a different time. Perhaps she returned in her later years when politics in the region became less dangerous, or her bones were brought back to her final resting place many decades or perhaps even centuries later? It's an intriguing possibility!

So what does all this Talpiot tombs business mean for the Hooked X symbol? One of my first thoughts was of speculation. In my previous book of the Hooked X symbolizing the first-century royal family with the upward-pointing triangle representing Jesus (the father),[161] the downward-pointing triangle as Mary Magdalene (the mother), and the "hook" in the upper right arm that creates a smaller downward-pointing triangle as the long-rumored daughter, Sarah.

While there is no ossuary within the Garden tomb with the name Sarah, there are four other ossuaries without inscriptions as well as skeletons that apparently were never placed within a bone box most likely due to the upheaval caused by the conflict with the Romans. This leaves open the possibility that a daughter could be interred within the tomb. Unfortunately, we might never find out.

There could possibly be a clue to knowledge of the son of Jesus and Mary in the fourteenth century that, while admittedly a long shot, still merits pointing out. On line two of the Kensington Rune Stone is a Hooked X with a second "hook" on the lower left leg of the character. My *Compelling New Evidence* co-author, Dick Nielsen and I speculated the hook singled-out the character used for the letter "a" was part of a "Grail Code." I still believe this to be the case, but the extra hook on that character could also be pointing out the upward-pointing triangle symbolic of another child, a previously unknown son. Given the known Jewish religious traditions of the time, it seems more likely than not that Jesus and Mary Magdalene would have had several children and the ossuary from the Talpiot Garden Tomb with the name, "Judah, son of Jesus" suggests one of those children was a son.[162]

Aquarius

THROUGHOUT THE LAST DECADE I have learned to trust my intuition or "Spider sense" as some people liked to call it. While far from perfect, I have gotten better at knowing when I'm on the right track with my research or simply spinning my wheels. Ralph Ellis, James Tabor, and Simcha Jacobovici's books were an epiphany for me that finally made all the historical pieces of the Hooked X ideology fit together into a logical and cohesive thread.

The Akhenaten-King Jesus-Knights Templar-Modern Freemasonry historical trail, winding through 3,700 years of history, was finally complete to my satisfaction. If I am right about even most of this then the burning question is: what's next? The popular media for the last several years has been all about the impending apocalypse as prophesized with the end of the Mayan calendar on December 21, 2012. Like many other people, I have always scoffed at this myth, knowing the world was not going to end. The "end of the world" predictions by religious zealots have come and gone so many times throughout history that there was no reason to think this prediction would be any different. On the other hand, the new age of Aquarius is very likely to have the opposite effect.

Through my education of the esoteric side of life and religion that is filled with symbolism and allegories, I have learned some pretty interesting things. From prophecy keepers in the Native American tribes of the Ojibwa and the Cherokee, as well as Templar mystics, the arrival of the New Age has a beautiful, and in my opinion, long overdue message of things to come. From what little I know of prophecies, I do know they are very powerful. Say whatever you want, but if the majority of people believe a prophecy to be true, then it is true. The prophecy of the New Age of Aquarius goes something like this: "Women are going to rise up and

In his first public appearance as the first Roman Catholic Pope of the New Age of Aquarius, Pope Francis from Argentina flashed the 'M' hand gesture, not a natural position of the fingers and one that requires intent. Does this mean he's subversively sending the message he is open to the restoration of balance in the world, or is it simply a coincidence? (Associated Press, Gregorio Borgia)

reach their equal and rightful place next to their consort, man, and balance will be restored to the universe."

Some could argue that the process already started decades ago. It is an undeniable fact that woman have made tremendous strides in the last century, most notably in the "New Jerusalem" of the United States of America. Indeed, because of the Internet with its instant access to information and communication, the world is rapidly becoming the international community so many over the last century have predicted. Oppression of women in countries ruled by patriarchal societies is feeling the rumble of the restoration of balance of the sexes that is sure to come.

Let's face it, most reasonable people would probably agree that this dominantly patriarchal world of the last two thousand years hasn't exactly worked out very well. One thing is certain, if we humans as a species are going to make it on this planet, some things have got to change. It seems to me the best way of knowing how to make good decisions at this critical junction in our history, we have to know the truth about where we have already been. And not some sanitized or biased version of history that we have been fed, but the whole truth. I believe that once we know what really happened in the past, only then can we move forward intelligently and with optimism into the future.

Having decided after my father died tragically when I was young man that I would live my life from then on with a "cup is half full" philosophy, I am confident the New Age of Aquarius will inspire that positive change we have all been looking for.

While visiting the Rosicrucian Museum in San Jose, California, a few years ago I was inspired by a painting by the Russian mystic Nicolas Roerich, of his wife and consort Helena Roerich (1879 to 1955), along with her words reportedly uttered in 1933. (See color section, Figure 41)

> The approaching great epoch is associated with the ascendency of woman. As in the best days of humanity, the future epoch will again offer woman her rightful place alongside her eternal fellow traveler and co-worker, man. You must remember that the grandeur of the Cosmos is built by the dual Origin. Is it possible, therefore, to belittle one Element of it?
>
> Helena Roerich Letters 1929-1938

Findings, Interpretations, and Conclusions

New Kensington Rune Stone Evidence Since the First Hooked X Book

1. In a first edition copy of the first book written by Hjalmar Holand on the Kensington Rune Stone a pencil sketch was glued onto one of the pages. The drawing was made by Olof Ohman of his property and pinpoints the location where the rune stone was found. Interpretation: This map confirms where the stone holes intersect as the correct location where the artifact was found by the man who found it.
2. On June 1, 1927, ten businessmen from the Alexandria area, nearly all Freemasons, reimbursed Hjalmar Holand $2,500 and obtained physical custody of the Kensington Rune Stone, held a rally to raise $300,000 to build a 204-foot tall obelisk at the discovery site. Interpretation: The ten Freemasons likely recognized the esoteric Masonic symbolism of the twelve lines of text, the overall 2:1 ratio shape made by the carver, and the Latin letters of AVM.
3. The new Keyence digital microscope generated three-dimensional images of the Dotted R and discovered a previously unknown "thorn" rune on line 8 of the inscription. Interpretation: The new technology confirmed the dot in the Dotted R was man-made and that the carver had difficulty due to friable rock where a joint fracture passed through the loop of the "thorn" rune causing the chisel to carve a linear trench instead of a punch.
4. Darwin Ohman became so frustrated by what he believed was manipulation of the Kensington Rune Stone research by Richard Nielsen and Henrik Williams that he published a chronology of factual events and voiced his profound disappointment with the two researchers. Interpretation: For the author to comment on Mr. Ohman's comments would be inappropriate given my personal involvement in the situation. Mr. Ohman's "Taking a Stand" speaks for itself.

5. The numerous connections of street names, symbolism, and numbers within such a small geographic area near the Triune Masonic Temple in St. Paul, Minnesota, discovered by Mark Limburg are obviously connected to the Kensington Rune Stone. Interpretation: The layout of the streets within such a localized area was likely done by a Freemason around 1909-1910. This was a time when stories of Newton Winchell's investigation were often in the local newspapers and likely inspired the clever street naming and arrangement which occurred around that time.
6. The previously unseen runes of G, W, A, and the fourteen individual numbers occur 8, 10, 22, and 14 times, respectively, within the Kensington Rune Stone inscription. Interpretation: The carver appears to have intentionally used the three unique runes and the numbers to create a confirmation code for the four specific pentadic numbers within the inscription.

Conclusions: Freemasons in the past 115 years have taken a special interest in the Kensington Rune Stone after quietly recognizing various symbolisms and esoteric meaning that has a direct connection to their Masonic rituals and principals. Changes in the overall attitude toward acceptance of the genuineness of the artifact has prompted positive media coverage resulting in more people coming forward with related artifacts and information.

Update on Artifacts and Sites

1. Local citizens have made positive strides to protect and preserve possible pre-Columbian artifacts and sites such as the Westford Sword, the Upper Peninsula of Michigan Ship carving, the Narragansett Rune Stone and the Newport Tower. Interpretation: Positive media attention has prompted action to protect and preserve these artifacts and sites for future research and enjoyment.
2. Two of the three symbols carved on the Westford Boat Stone could be astronomical symbols for the planet Jupiter and the constellation of Taurus the Bull. Interpretation: These symbols could indicate the people who carved the stone used the astronomical methods for navigation and could possibly be used to date the carvings.
3. At Chichen Itza in Mexico, is a two-story round stone observatory called El Caracol. The structure is roughly the same size and has similar dimensions to the Newport Tower and also has tiny rectangular windows near the top used exclusively for making astronomical observations of the planet Venus. Interpretation: The architecture of the

observatory in Mexico with the small square windows serves as a pre-Columbian analog to the Newport Tower which was also used by the builders for making astronomical observations of the planet Venus.

4. Margaret Starbird pointed out a biblical illumination event in the second chapter of the *Book of Acts* (2:1-18), known as the "birthday" of the Christian Church. Interpretation: The illumination in the Newport Tower was incorporated into the architecture for religious reasons consistent with belief in the concept of the allegorical rebirth of the sun as in the early Christian faith.

Conclusions: New evidence will continue to come forward with increased awareness about the ever-increasing number of mysterious artifacts and sites that with careful and thorough investigation will shed new light on the untold history of North America.

Copiale Cipher

1. A mid-eighteenth century encrypted manuscript was decoded by researchers at the University of Southern California and Uppsala University in Stockholm, Sweden, in 2011. The document contained the secret rituals and political leanings of a secret society in Germany. Interpretation: Some researchers believe this is the earliest known record of the ultra-secret organization known as the "Illuminati" that likely still exists today.
2. One of the seven oversized symbols used throughout the document closely resembles the Hooked X and was apparently used to represent a rival Masonic order. Interpretation: The Hooked X symbol used in the Copiale document represents an organization that evolved from the medieval Templar/Cistercian orders that created the numerous Hooked X symbols found in North America, at Rosslyn Chapel, and Columbus's sigla.
3. The Larsson Papers in Sweden include a reference to the "German Style" on the back of one of the sheets. Interpretation: Since both the Copiale Cipher and the Larsson Papers are connected to German Freemasonry and have the Hooked X symbol it seems highly likely there is a connection between them through Masonic secret societies.
4. The Cistercians and Knights Templar used the Hooked X as the symbol of their orders in the twelfth through the fifteenth centuries. Interpretation: The Hooked X was an important symbol used by these orders to identify them.

Conclusions: The Hooked X symbol in the Copiale Cipher provides an apparent link between twelfth- to fifteenth-century Cistercian/Knights Templar orders in the Baltic Region and eighteenth and nineteenth century Masonic orders in the Baltic Region; most notably Germany and Sweden.

Salvador Mundi

1. Rumored to be grand master of the Priory of Sion, Leonardo DaVinci's *Salvador Mundi* painting prominently features an "X" symbol within Jesus' garment. Interpretation: The "X" and other symbology within this and many other DaVinci paintings are veiled messages to those in the know both during his time and into the future.

Conclusions: The "X" has long been a symbol of organizations who embraced both political and religious ideology that is opposed to the dogma of the Roman Catholic Church.

Stone Holes

1. Dozens of stone holes have been discovered in Minnesota and elsewhere within the continental United States. Interpretation: A systematic review of the data collected needs to centralized and researched.

Conclusions: The ever-growing number of stone holes demands proper scientific investigation into their geographic and topography locations, their relative-age using geological weathering methodology, and more research into the likely reasons they were made.

Du Luth Stone

1. The name carved on the boulder is one of the historically correct ways the explorer, Daniel Greysolon Sieur Du Luth, spelled his last name.
2. The block-style letters and the curved style of the numbers carved on the boulder are historically consistent with late seventeenth-century script. Interpretation: The style of script carved onto the boulder is late seventeenth century.
3. The boulder is located at the headwaters of the Great Lakes and Mississippi watersheds, which is consistent with Du Luth's memoirs where he claimed he placed the coat of arms for France in this region.
4. Compared to the weathering of sandstone tombstones, the weathering of the carvings on the Du Luth Stone is consistent with being greater than 300 years old.

5. The two dots carved on the boulder within the proximity of the name could be a coded message. Interpretation: This appears to be a dot code similar to dot codes on other carved inscriptions such as the Kensington, Spirit Pond and Narragansett Rune Stones suggesting a common link with members of secret orders over several centuries.

Conclusions: The cumulative weight of the geological and historical evidence relative to the Du Luth Stone, most notably the relative-age weathering data, is consistent with it being a genuine late eighteenth century inscription made by the explorer Daniel Graysolon Sieur Du Luth.

In Hoc Signo Vinces Stone

1. "In Hoc Signo Vinces" is a Latin phrase used by various military orders going back to the time of Constantine (circa 312 A.D.) in Rome. Interpretation: The phrase was commonly used by military orders throughout history.
2. The words, "Ding" "Ding" are carved on the two different locations on the inland side of the boulder. Interpretation: These two words may have been carved to signify the naval tradition of ringing a bell twice to signal the presence of an officer coming aboard a ship.
3. The inscription is carved into a large greywacke boulder on the shore of Narragansett Bay near the Jamestown Bridge. Interpretation: Greywacke is fine-grained sedimentary rock that lends itself to detailed carvings.
4. The inscription exhibits advanced weathering due primarily to mechanical abrasion from extensive wave action. Interpretation: If continually exposed since being carved the mechanical erosion could have happened relatively quickly.
5. The boulder is located south of the United States Naval Academy in Newport, Rhode Island. Interpretation: The carver could have been a member of the naval academy.

Conclusions: The combination of the relatively rapid rate of erosion from wave action along the beach and the proximity to the military academy is consistent with the inscription most likely having been carved within the past 150 years.

Tulsa Bull Carving

1. The bull carving was reportedly discovered by Nick Johnson on a rock bar in the Arkansas River near Tulsa, Oklahoma, in 2010.

2. No other historical information is known about the carving.
3. The carved grooves of the bull exhibit a differentially eroded and widened profile under magnification. Interpretation: The advanced weathering of the carved lines indicates it was not recently made.

Conclusions: The physical profile of the carved grooves was not recently made. However, until enough historical provenance information can be obtained the age of the carving is unclear and remains an open question.

Independence Rune Stone

1. An English immigrant, Cyrus Arthur Slater, who lived in the area in the late 1800s was a stone mason. His mark is part of the inscription. Interpretation: It appears likely Mr. Slater was involved in creating this inscription.
2. The inscription was carved into a very dense, relatively hard and compact micritic limestone. Interpretation: The inscription was carved into a very durable type of limestone that would tend to withstand weathering relatively well.
3. The weathering of the carved surfaces did not contain any observable micro-pitting of the surface from lichen acid the surrounding rock contained. Interpretation: The lack of lichen acid micro-pitting is consistent with a much shorter length of exposure than surrounding rock the inscription was carved into.

Conclusions: The weathering profile of the Independence Rune Stone inscription is estimated at between 100 to 150 years old as of October of 2011.

Mustang Mountain Rune Stone

1. The five-lined inscription at the mouth of the cave is carved using Anglo-Saxon runes likely from the British Isles.
2. The runic characters were carved into a very dense and compact micritic limestone that exhibits very little apparent weathering. Interpretation: The inscription is either relatively young or is much older and has not undergone much weathering in the relatively dry and protected environment of its location.
3. No secondary carbonate deposits were observed on the carved characters. Interpretation: Little water carrying dissolved carbonate flowed over the characters since the inscription was carved.
4. The average annual rainfall in the area of Arizona where the inscription is located is less than fifteen inches per year. Interpreta-

tion: Water related weathering would be relatively minor and very slow in this area of Arizona.

5. The first five letters of the runic inscription are also carved twice on the east wall of the cave and are illuminated by sunlight only on the winter solstice. Interpretation: The carver intended to have the two carvings illuminated likely as an allegorical resurrection.
6. Sand and rocks are cemented onto the cave walls where water ran down, dissolving calcium carbonate from the limestone that reformed as cement where the ground-line was in the past. Interpretation: A significant amount of the material has been removed from the area at the mouth of the cave near the inscribed boulder, which could have been buried after carving, thus explaining the lack of weathering.
7. The translated runic inscription reads like a memorial or gravestone. Interpretation: The inscription along with the large quantity of material that appears to have been moved suggests there could be a burial here.

Conclusions: Additional geological, archaeological, and runological studies are necessary to reach a more definitive answer for the age of this runic inscription.

Millwood Rune Stone

1. Nancy Millwood discovered the runic inscription in North Carolina, in 1970. Interpretation: Nancy found her rune stone prior to the Spirit Pond (1971) and the Narragansett (circa 1984) Rune Stones were discovered and could not have been impacted by them as some skeptics will no doubt suggest.
2. The inscription appears to be carved using Anglo-Saxon runes and contains several single, double, and triple dotted characters. Interpretation: This inscription is not like the Kensington, Spirit Pond, Narragansett, Heavener, or the Mustang Mountain runic inscriptions and clearly was not copied from them.
3. The inscription is carved into a roughly one-foot by one-foot by one-and-a-half inch-thick hand-cut slab of light-green soapstone. Interpretation: Whoever made this started with a larger piece of stone and cut it into a flat slab prior to carving the inscription.

Conclusions: Additional geological, archaeological, and runological studies are necessary to determine the age of this runic inscription.

Hemlock Chamber

1. The underground structure was made when a trench was quarried into the side of the mountain where a natural spring flowed from the ground. The quarried stone was then used to build the chamber, consisting of skillfully worked quarried fine-grained sandstone. Interpretation: The builders of the chamber were highly skilled stone masons.
2. Only on the summer solstice does the setting sun in the west cast light down the length of the chamber and illuminates the exact opening in the bedrock where water flows out of the ground. Interpretation: The builders intentionally designed the chamber to facilitate the summer solstice illumination event likely for spiritual reasons.
3. A thirty-by-thirty-inch square basin was hand-crafted to fill with spring water channeled by cut stones leading from the opening in the bedrock to the basin. Interpretation: The water-filled basin was likely intended to be used for ritual bathing.
4. At least four large lintel stones equaling a length of at least eight feet at the entrance to the chamber have collapsed due to erosion from the constant flow of spring water. Interpretation: If not recently disturbed by man and the rate of flow from the spring is consistent, the time involved for erosion to produce the amount of collapse is likely more than 150 years.
5. The underground chamber is located near a site once a small remote community along the Allegheny River near Oil City, Pennsylvania. Interpretation: There were people in the area that could have been associated with the chamber in late nineteenth or early twentieth century.

Conclusions: While the primary function of the underground chamber appears to have been for ritual religious or spiritual purposes, additional geological, archaeological, and historical research is necessary to reach a definitely answer to the age of this underground structure.

Burrows Cave Isis Stone

1. The Isis Stone was carved into a two-inch thick, high white marble slab with remnants of six cursive English letters on the back side that exhibit the same weathering profile as the original surfaces of the stone. Interpretation: The cursive letters and the surface they were carved into have been weathering for the same length of time.

2. Remnants of modern Portland cement mortar were present within the weathered cursive characters on the back side. Interpretation: The Isis Stone artifact was made from a modern recycled marble tombstone.
3. A palm-sized black stone artifact Russell Burrows sold me in 2009 contained four rows of runic text that are essentially a perfect match to the first two lines of the Kensington Rune Stone inscription. Interpretation: The only plausible explanation for this artifact is that it was created recently; most likely by Russell Burrows himself.
4. Since 1982 when Russell Burrows reportedly discovered the cave, no other person is known to have ever seen the cave. Interpretation: Russell Burrows is either incredibly selfish or there is no cave filled with artifacts, gold, diamonds, and human remains as he claims.
5. To date, the author has personally reviewed approximately two thousand Burrows Cave artifacts along with photographs of roughly two thousand more. Interpretation: Since Russell Burrows is not capable of manufacturing multiple thousands of artifacts himself, he either has accomplices or at least some of the artifacts came from a legitimate ancient repository.

Conclusions: The weight of evidence to date indicates the cave is most likely a hoax perpetrated by Russell Burrows. Only full disclosure of the cave and its contents by Burrows will restore any credibility to his claims.

The map side of Tucson lead artifact #13 shows an apparent world map with the four sides labeled (clockwise from top) ROMANI, GAVLE, TERRA. CALALUS. T., and BRIIANNIA, along with other religious symbols engraved on the fan-shaped relict created roughly six hundred years after the Bat Creek Stone was carved. (Photo Courtesy of Charles Bent)

Bat Creek Stone

1. The Bat Creek Stone, along with two brass bracelets and bone and wood artifacts were discovered in a bundle under the skull of the only body of nine with its head facing south, inside a Native American grave mound by John W. Emmert on February 15, 1889. Interpretation: Because of the unique burial position and the associated artifacts, there appears to be something unique about this particular individual.
2. In the sketch made by Emmert in 1889, and a photograph of the artifact made in 1891, the two vertical scratches above the inscription are not present that first appear in the January 1971 issue of *Argosy Magazine*. Interpretation: The scratches were added by someone who likely tested the stone while the artifact was in the physical custody of the Smithsonian Institution.
3. The two vertical scratches contain significant deposits of silty-clay within the grooves. Interpretation: Silty-clay develops within grooves when this iron oxide-rich concretion is scratched.
4. The carved grooves of the eight-character inscription are clean and devoid of silty-clay deposits present when the characters were carved due to having completely weathered away. Interpretation: The inscription has experienced extensive weathering consistent with lengthy burial in a wet earthen mound.
5. The two bracelets contained a ratio of copper, zinc, lead, and tin statistically consistent with ancient Mediterranean brass production between 45 B.C. and 200 A.D. Interpretation: The Bat Creek bracelets appear to date to the period of the First Jewish War.
6. The wood artifacts found with the Bat Creek Stone and brass bracelets were carbon dated to 345 A.D. plus or minus 170 years. Interpretation: By association, the Bat Creek inscription is at least 1500 years old.
7. The Smithsonian accused Emmert of forging the Bat Creek inscription without factual basis upon learning it was paleo-Hebrew in 1971 rather than paleo-Cherokee as they previously thought. Interpretation: This action by the Smithsonian gives the impression it was more important for them to preserve the paradigm of no pre-Columbian European contact rather than the honor and integrity of John W. Emmert.

Conclusions: The Bat Creek inscription along with all the other artifacts and remains found in the mound can not be younger than when the bodies of the deceased were buried inside the mound. By association, the C-14 dating of the wood dates the inscription to at least 1,500 years before present, making the Bat Creek inscription a genuine pre-Columbian artifact.

Tucson Lead Artifacts

1. The extraction of nearly all the lead artifacts was performed and witnessed by multiple individuals, including archaeologists and scholars, over the course of six years. No signs of previous burial or "planting" was documented by anyone who participated with the excavations. Interpretation: The veracity of the discovery of the thirty-two artifacts is not in question.
2. Natural deposits of secondary calcite, malachite, and azurite are present on the outer surfaces of all of the artifacts. Interpretation: These deposits took centuries to develop within the caliche cemented alluvial sand and gravel deposits the artifacts were discovered in.
3. The artifacts were discovered beneath forty-eight to seventy-two inches of caliche-cemented sand and gravel deposits. Interpretation The depth of alluvial deposits must have taken approximately 1,200 years to accumulate based on the dates carved on the artifacts found at those levels.

Conclusions: The Tucson lead artifacts must be accepted as genuine pre-Columbian artifacts made by Europeans who traveled to what is now Tucson, Arizona, presumably in the eighth to ninth centuries.

France

1. The same stylized AVM present at St. Sulpice Church in Paris is present throughout Montreal. Interpretation: The Sulpicians who settled in Montreal are directly connected to the Sulpicians in Paris, France.
2. A gnomon that incorporates a thirty-five-foot-tall obelisk and used to record the annual solstices and equinoxes is present inside St. Sulpice Church. Interpretation: The early Church fathers at St. Sulpice appear to have embraced the practice of documenting the annual movements of the sun that is also part of the beliefs of many esoteric secret societies.
3. Inside Chartres Cathedral is a rare limestone carving depicting of the circumcision of Jesus. Interpretation: Circumcision was an ancient Hebrew and Egyptian practice.
4. Statues of the Black Madonna and child are found in numerous churches in France. Interpretation: *Belief* in the story that Jesus and Mary Magdalene were royalty and married still thrives in France.

5. Inside Eglise Notre-Dame Church, five stone columns circling the altar were illuminated by sunlight passing through second-story windows on the Vernal equinox. Interpretation: The illumination event was intentional and serves as a European analog to the illumination of the egg-shaped keystone on the winter solstice in the Newport Tower.
6. "Osias" and "Amon" appear in one of the stained-glass windows inside Eglise Notre-Dame. Interpretation: These names refer to Egypt and the New Religion of Akhenaten that venerated the rising sun.
7. The "X" symbol is prominent throughout Southern France. Interpretation: The "X" is a monogram for the letters L, U, X, meaning "Lux" or "light" which means knowledge.
8. Ben Hammott changed his mind about showing me the location of his tomb with a poor excuse. Interpretation: Either he didn't trust me or there was no cave to show me.
9. On March 19, 2012, Ben Hammott's confessed that the tomb he "discovered" was a hoax perpetrated solely by him. Interpretation: Ben's hoax serves as a reminder always to investigate controversial subject matter carefully and thoroughly.
10. Inside the Templar Church at Champagne Sur Aude is a stylized AVM very similar to the AVMs at St. Sulpice in Paris and Notre Dame Church in Montreal. Interpretation: This appears to represent a connection between the medieval Templars and the seventeenth-century Sulpicians.
11. A statue of the "Virgin" Mary in Champagne Sur Aude had golden hair with a crown and was clad in gold clothing. Interpretation: The person actually depicted was Mary Magdalene.
12. Another statue in Champagne Sur Aude depicted a monk helping a bleeding Jesus down from the Cross. Jesus had his eyes open and his arm around the monk. Interpretation: The scene depicted by the statue implies Jesus survived the Crucifixion.

Conclusions: The symbolism and legends of Southern France preserve the alternate story of the biblical Jesus with royal Egyptian heritage whose wife was Mary Magdalene.

Comparison between Mide'win and Freemasonic Rituals

1. Bill Mann, a high-ranking Canadian Knights Templar Freemason and Ojibwa initiate who has been through the four degrees of the Mide'win Society rituals, reports that that rituals of the two secret so-

cieties are virtually identical. Interpretation: The rituals of these two societies appear to have a common origin.

2. My own comparison of the Mide'win rituals as documented in the 1885-1886 edition of the Bureau of Ethnology Reports to the Smithsonian Institution with Masonic rituals confirms they are nearly identical in most respects. Interpretation: My independent investigation confirms the rituals of the two societies have a common origin.
3. The Bureau of Ethnology documented that the earliest missionaries and explorers reported the Mide' rituals were already in place. Interpretation: The virtually identical Mide' and Templar rituals either developed independently on two different continents at the same time, which is highly unlikely, or there was pre-Columbian contact between the two groups.

Conclusions: The nearly identical four-degree rituals of early French Freemasonry and the Ojibwa Mide'win secret society prior to circa 1600 A.D. could only be so closely related if there was pre-Columbian contact with the Templars.

The Cross of Lorraine

1. The double-barred cross is an ancient sacred symbol in many Native American cultures representing the dragonfly that comes with the summer rains bringing water that allows crops to grow, which sustain life. Interpretation: The sacred symbol was important to many Native Americans prior to European contact.
2. The Cross of Lorraine symbol appears three times on a ceremonial fan labeled artifact #13 of the Tucson lead artifacts. The artifacts appear to have been made by a post Roman-era Jewish colony from what is now France sometime in the eighth or ninth centuries. Interpretation: It appears these people could be connected to the founders of the Knights Templar order who also came from France in the late eleventh century.
3. The double-barred Cross of Lorraine was given to the Knights Templar as their patron symbol by King Baldwin II when the Christians captured Jerusalem from the Saracens in 1099. Interpretation: The Cross of Lorraine is an important symbol to the Knight Templar.
4. The Bat Creek Stone has a double-barred cross standing alone below the eight-character inscription believed to be first century paleo-Hebrew. Interpretation: The symbol could be connected to first- or second-century European visitors and either adopted the symbol from Native Americans or brought it from Europe most likely from an area near or in what is now France.

5. On the front of their white pill-box style hats modern thirty-third-degree Freemasons have a red double-barred Cross of Lorraine tilted 22.5 degrees, representing the tilt of the earth's axis. Interpretation: The Cross of Lorraine is an important symbol, at the very least an ideological link between the medieval Knights Templar to modern Freemasonry.

Conclusions: Like the Mide' win and Templars rituals, the Cross of Lorraine appears to be another important piece of evidence that provides an important pre-Columbian link between Native Americans and the Knights Templar along with their ideological Jewish ancestors from the geographic region in Europe now known as France.

Mandan

1. In 1957, Henrietta Mertz published a book citing twenty-two factual parallels between the four-day Okipa ceremonies of the Mandan as documented by George Catlin in 1833-1834, and the biblical account of the Moses Exodus story by Josephus. Interpretation: The Mandan must have learned the ceremonies from pre-Columbian European cultures coming to North America.

Conclusions: The numerous direct parallels of the Okipa ceremony and the biblical Exodus story are consistent with pre-Columbian European contact with the Native ancestors of the Mandan; or the Mandan are *direct* lineal descendants of those European cultures.

Peace Medals

1. From 1792 to 1889, beginning with George Washington, American presidents authorized the distribution of metallic peace medals as gifts to Native American tribal chiefs. Interpretation: This practice was meant to ingratiate the fledgling government with the indigenous people.
2. Nearly all American presidents were Freemasons during the peace medal era.
3. The peace medals given to Native American chiefs contained various Masonic symbols. Interpretation: The Masonic symbols on the medals were meant to convey secret messages to the Native leaders who must have understood them.

Conclusions: It appears that our early presidents were high-ranking members of secretive Masonic orders who continued communications, in part with peace medals, that had began centuries earlier between Native American chiefs and their medieval Knights Templar brethren.

White Indians of Darien

1. In 1925, Richard O. Marsh brought several white Tule Native teenage males from the Darien Region of Panama to the United States where three linguists studied their language concluding, ". . . some ancient Norse people certainly taught the Tule People their language." Interpretation: Pre-Columbian Norse people had meaningful contact which likely included intermarriages with the Tule people in Panama.

Conclusions: The white Indians of Darien must have had extensive contact with some pre-Columbian groups of Norse people.

Panama and Columbian Gold

1. The Knights Templar used three different styles of equilateral crosses in the twelfth, thirteenth and fourteenth centuries. Interpretation: The style of cross used by the Templars can be used for dating purposes.
2. A human bone extracted by the author from a Tumbaga artifact from the Greg Cavalli collection, in December of 2010, was carbon dated to 1,045 years old, plus or minus fifty years. Interpretation: This date fell within the range of 500 to 1,500 years for the range in known age for most of the Tumbaga artifacts in Panama and Columbia.
3. A white ceramic jaguar from Greg Cavalli's collection has a red equilateral cross painted on its chest consistent with the Templar style of the thirteenth century. Interpretation: The red cross on the white jaguar was likely influenced by Knights Templar who apparently visited Panama in pre-Columbian times.
4. A thirty-inch Columbian tumbaga female statue is wearing a masonic-like apron with a compass and square design. Interpretation: The symbols could represent an understanding of ancient esoteric Masonic knowledge by the indigenous people of Columbia.
5. An ornate Columbian tumbaga artifact of a ritual involving a dozen individuals has a large bird presiding atop a simple covered structure. The scene is reminiscent of the owl that sits atop the sacred post in the four degrees of initiation into the Mide'win Secret Society of the Ojibwa. Interpretation: The tumbaga artifact likely represents similar rituals consistent with a common origin found in both cultures.
6. A thirty-six-inch-tall Columbian tumbaga female statue is wearing a masonic-like apron that displays a double-headed bird looking east and west—virtually identical to the same double-headed eagle symbol

in Scottish Rite Freemasonry. Interpretation: This symbol could represent an understanding of ancient esoteric Masonic knowledge.

7. Another nine-inch-tall Columbian tumbaga statue holding a Poporo has the diagnostic features of the Egyptian Goddess Taweret, which includes the body of the human, the head of a hippopotamus, paws of a lion, and the tail of a crocodile. Hippopotami and lions are not found in Columbia or Panama. Interpretation: There had to have been a profound influence by Mediterranean cultures knowledgeable in Egyptian mythology and religion.
8. The tumbaga statues were manufactured using the lost-wax method and depletion gilding. These sophisticated metalworking skills were known to the ancient Egyptians and kept highly secret within metalworking guilds. Interpretation: Native cultures in Columbia and Panama must have had close cultural ties with whatever groups taught them these closely guarded metalworking secrets.

Conclusions: Numerous examples of secret and sophisticated metalworking skills and symbolism are consistent with pre-Columbian contact between cultures from the Mediterranean and cultures in Central and South America.

The "C" Document

1. The "C" Document is reportedly a twelfth-century Knights Templar document written in a coded cipher that includes maps, the four gospels (including the Gospel of Miriam), and a report of a five-ship Templar voyage to retrieve scrolls brought to North America in the first century. Interpretation: If true, this document appears to shed light on pre-Columbian European contact in North America and the alternate history of Jesus, Mary Magdalene and their followers.
2. Photographs of the document include one of four maps dated to 1179 A.D. alleged to have been redrawn in the eighteenth century and a title page written in Theban characters. These three images include a total of four Hooked X symbols. Two in the title page are used as letters and two on one of the maps are used as Roman numbers. Interpretation: If actually redrawn (likely in the eighteenth century) from original late twelfth-century maps, they represent the earliest known examples of the Hooked X symbol used by medieval Templars.
3. Redrawn twelfth-century maps reportedly chronicle six stops on a Templar voyage from Europe that eventually reached the Catskill Mountains, allegedly to retrieve ancient scrolls hidden there in the first century. According to the "C" Document narrative, knowledge of these scrolls was found by the Templars under the Temple Mount in

the early twelfth century. Interpretation: If true, it would completely rewrite a huge chapter of history of the past two thousand years.

4. Six inscribed stones have been found in the Catskill Mountains over the past decade, including the "Dove Stone" found by the author. Interpretation: These stones have either been planted as part of an extremely elaborate hoax or they further confirm the "C" Document story.
5. The "In Camera Stone," found by David Brody and Don Ruh in 2009, contains several inscribed symbols, including Latin letters and Roman numbers on one side and two different symbols, one carved with continuous lines and the other with pecked dots. Interpretation: The two different techniques used to make the symbols on the back side possibly indicate two different carvers who made the symbols at different times.
6. The Roman numbers are arranged into a pattern consistent with a latitude and longitude. The Latin letters spell "In Camera" which is an old legal term that means either, "In Chamber," "In Tomb," or "In Secret." Interpretation: The inscription appears to indicate an important secret location.
7. Both the first and last Roman number on the "In Camera Stone" have a small bar or hook added to the character. Interpretation: The added bars are likely coded marks certifying the Roman numbers are authentic and correct.
8. The coordinates on the "In Camera Stone" when adjusted to Paris, France, as the prime meridian, pinpoint the location of Old Montreal, in Quebec, Canada. Interpretation: There is something of importance about this location.
9. The note inserted into a letter sent to Zena Halpern explained why Zena, Judi Rudebusch, and the author had such difficulty finding information on the Internet pertaining to Don's friend, the key person who purchased the document in 1971 and then sold it in 1994. Interpretation: The letter explaining that this man went into the Federal Witness Protection Program appeared to answer the question of his existence and why we couldn't find information about him.

Conclusions: The information presented here is just a fraction of the total information related to this document and the artifacts. Although the vetting process of the document and the artifacts is far from complete, the voluminous detailed information known to date appears to be too vast, too complex, and historically consistent to be entirely a modern hoax.

The "M" Sign

1. The "M" sign hand gesture, where the middle and ring fingers are together or crossed and separated from the index and pinky fingers, is an unnatural position requiring intent to create. Interpretation: The hand gesture has important symbolic meaning.
2. The "M" sign has been used in art since at least the early 1600s.
3. "M" is the thirteenth letter in the alphabet. The number thirteen is often found in American symbolism, including the original thirteen colonies, the number of stripes on the American flag, and numerous times on the back of the dollar bill. Interpretation: The number thirteen appears to have the same important symbolic meaning as that "M" sign.
4. King Philip the Fair and Pope Clement the V ordered the arrest of the Knights Templar in France on Friday the 13th, 1307. Interpretation: The selection of that date was intentional and likely designed to send a message to the Templars and their followers that the Roman Church would not tolerate those who did not follow strict Church doctrine.

Conclusions: The "M" sign and the number thirteen are symbols used by supporters with knowledge of the bloodline of Jesus and his wife, Mary Magdalene.

Precession of the Equinoxes

1. The precession of the equinoxes is an approximately 26,000 year cycle that, due to the earth's wobble as it rotates, allows the twelve primary constellations to move through the eastern position in the sky. Ancient astronomers in many cultures around the world have documented the length of time each constellation is in the eastern sky before it disappears below the horizon at approximately 2,160 years. Interpretation: The ability of ancient cultures to track such long-range movements of the stars and other celestial bodies indicates they had a much higher knowledge and intelligence than generally given credit for.
2. The 2,160 year-long average period for each of the twelve primary constellations is called an "age" or "house."
3. In the past approximately 4,000 years, when the constellations of Taurus and Aries descended below the eastern horizon allowing the next constellations to replace them, it has coincided with profound changes in world religions. Interpretation: These last two changes: the Age of Taurus moving to Aries and Aries to Pisces, in accordance with the precession of the equinoxes coincides with significant events in the history of Monotheistic Dualism that I maintain is analogous to the "Hooked X" ideology.
4. Akhenaten tried to change the state religion from Polytheistic Dualism to Monotheistic Dualism at the time of the change in the age

from Taurus to Aries. Interpretation: This historical event marked the beginning of the Hooked X ideology first symbolized by an "X."

5. According to the Mayans and other cultures, the end of the Age of Pisces that gives way to the Age of Aquarius occurred on December 21, 2012. Interpretation: If history is any indication, there will be profound changes in religion that will have world-wide impact.

Conclusions: The precession of the equinoxes has played a pivotal role in the history of the world's religions and the Hooked X ideology.

Akhenaten

1. The eighteenth dynasty pharaoh of the New Kingdom of Egypt, Amenophis IV, changed his name to Akhenaten upon arrival to Amarna. Interpretation: The name change was due to the change in the Age of Taurus to Aries.
2. Akhenaten tried to change Egypt's state religion from Polytheistic Dualism to Monotheistic Dualism. Interpretation: This change was dictated by the change in the ages, apparently mandated according to long-standing Egyptian high priesthood astronomical traditions.
3. The old religion in Egypt venerated the setting sun (Amen) whereas the new religion venerated the rising son (Aten or Aton). Interpretation: Both religions considered the sun to be the single deity or God.
4. Sigmund Freud and many other authors argue that Akhenaten was the biblical Moses and his new religion followers were the "Israelites" who were eventually driven out of Egypt. Interpretation: This is how the Monotheistic Dualism religion (Hooked X ideology) made its way into what are now Israel and the surrounding region.

Conclusions: Akhenaten changed the state religion in Egypt from Polytheistic Dualism to Monotheistic Dualism in accordance with the change of the age from Taurus the Bull, to Aries the Ram. This change in the ages was documented by the Egyptian astronomer priesthood. Akhenaten was the high priest.

Jesus

1. Other than Jesus being educated in Egypt, very little is known of his childhood, youth, and early adulthood. Interpretation: His education likely took several years and involved his initiation in the high priesthood where he learned the seven classic arts and sciences.
2. Jesus' education was apparently consistent with Akhenaten's Monotheistic Dualism and contrary to traditional Jewish thinking. Interpretation: Jesus' Essene sect followed the Egyptian high priest teachings consistent with Akhenaten's new religion.

3. Jesus' Essene priesthood had a deep understanding of mathematics, geometry, and astronomy. Interpretation: This advanced scientific knowledge and the ability to use it in practical and pragmatic ways led to strong influence and power.
4. The Romans felt enough of a threat from Jesus and his Essene sect that they attacked his followers and crucified him. Interpretation: Jesus had to have been a rich and influential person to be perceived as such a serious threat to the Roman leadership.
5. Jesus came into power and prominence as the Age of Aries gave way to the Age of Pisces. Interpretation: Jesus was likely a pharaoh following the Egyptian practice consistent with Akhenaten and his new religion of Monotheistic Dualism.
6. Jesus is often depicted with arms crossed, creating an "X," the classic Osiris pose similar to buried Egyptian pharaohs. Interpretation: This is consistent with his likely Egyptian heritage, the "X" being a symbol of the followers of Monotheistic Dualism religion started by Akhenaten.
7. Medieval Knights Templar were usually buried with their arms crossed over their chest or with their legs crossed. Interpretation: This burial practice likely indicated their acknowledgement of the philosophical and scientific teachings of Jesus, Akhenaten, and Monotheistic Dualism as opposed to the dogma of the Roman Catholic Church.
8. Modern Freemasons cross their chests in the Osiris pose when praying. Interpretation: This prayer practice likely indicates their acknowledgement of the philosophical and scientific teachings of Jesus, Akhenaten, and Monotheistic Dualism as opposed to the dogma of the Roman Catholic Church.
9. The "X" symbol was commonly used by individuals opposed to the Roman Catholic Church. Interpretation: The "X" symbol, which includes the Hooked X in medieval times, was an acknowledgement by followers of the philosophical and scientific teachings of Jesus, Akhenaten, and Monotheistic Dualism as opposed to the dogma of the Roman Catholic Church.
10. The ten ossuaries discovered in the Talpiot Garden Tomb in Israel in 1980 have six names that directly correspond to Jesus and his immediate family. Interpretation: The proximity to Jerusalem and age of the tomb along with the tremendously large mathematically rare odds of this combination of names make it a virtual certainty that tomb contains the remains of the biblical Jesus and his immediate family.
11. An "X" is carved on the ossuary in front of the inscription of "Jesus, son of Joseph." Interpretation: The "X" was symbolic of the acknowledgement of the true teachings of Jesus whose tradition dates back to

the secret Egyptian priesthood and their veneration of the rising sun-God of Monotheistic Dualism.

Conclusions: Jesus was a rich and powerful high priest of the Egyptian tradition of secret philosophical and scientific teachings that coincided with the change in the Age of Aries to Pisces. This important event elevated his power and status to a level that was perceived as a serious threat to the political and military power of the Romans. The Roman attack and suppression of Jesus and his followers ultimately led to the rise of influence and power of the Roman Catholic Church which coincided with forcing the followers of Jesus underground. They have secretly kept the ancient knowledge and the Monotheistic Dualism ideology, which included the Hooked X in medieval times, alive through symbolism, art, and oral stories, for two thousand years.

Talpiot Tomb

1. The architecture of the upward pointing chevron with the circle below on the outside wall above the entrance to the burial chamber would certainly have been seen by anyone who entered the tomb prior to the recent discovery of the tomb in 1980.
2. Terra Rosa soil that seeped into the burial chamber was estimated to have occurred roughly nine hundred years ago when the entrance was not resealed after having been entered by someone. The First Crusade took place in 1098 when Jerusalem was captured from the Muslims by Crusader knights who then controlled the city for the next nearly two hundred years. Interpretation: The Talpiot Garden Tomb was most likely entered by the Knights Templar after the Holy City was captured.
3. The Cistercian/Knights Templar began building the Gothic Cathedrals and churches using the classic upward peak with the circle below often as a Rose Window. Interpretation: The Templars used the Talpiot chevron-circle architecture as a secret acknowledgement to male/female aspect of Dualism and to Jesus with the chevron and Mary Magdalene with the circle.

Conclusion: It appears the Talpiot chevron-circle symbolism has permeated into the architecture of buildings of all types all around the world.

Mary Magdalene

1. Mary Magdalene disappears from the Gospels after the Crucifixion and reappears in the "Vine of Mary" legends that proliferate around the world to this day. Interpretation: Mary Magdalene was likely the wife of Jesus whose life would have been in grave danger after the Jewish revolt which likely triggered her to flee Israel.

2. Many believe Mary Magdalene had children with Jesus and their descendants survive to this day. Interpretation: Belief in such a tradition by so many people around the world for two thousand years likely has a basis in at least some truth.
3. A literal bloodline of Jesus and Mary Magdalene represented a threat that could undermine the central tenet of the Roman Catholic Church: the divinity of Jesus. Interpretation: The Roman Catholic Church believed there were bloodline descendants of the first century royal family and likely spent centuries both in Europe and in North America trying to eradicate them.
4. A recently discovered fourth-century Coptic Gospel parchment fragment contains text where Jesus is speaking to his disciples and says, "My wife . . . She will be able to be my disciple."
5. An ornately adorned ossuary in the Talpiot Garden Tomb has the name Mary Magdalene with a title of honor inscribed in Greek. The other five names in the tomb are inscribed in Aramaic. Interpretation: The Greek inscribed ossuary is likely that of Mary Magdalene and suggests the possibility that she either returned when the politics of the region settled down, or her bones were later brought back by her followers to be buried in the family tomb with her husband.

Conclusions: Mary Magdalene and her husband, Jesus, were rich and powerful royals who both were likely practicing the Egyptian tradition of secret philosophical and scientific teachings of Monotheistic Dualism. Their rise to power due in large part to the change in the Age of Aries to Pisces ignited their followers and prompted the Romans to attack and suppress the revolt. These actions triggered the rise of the patriarchal Roman Christian faith and eventual submergence of Monotheistic Dualism for the past two millennia.

Age of Aquarius

1. The beginning of the Age of Aquarius on December 21, 2012, represents the end of the 26,000 year-long cycle of the precession of the equinoxes. Interpretation: Heralded by many religious groups as the "end of world," in fact, Aquarius represents the end of one very long cycle giving way to the beginning of another.

Conclusions: The coming of the New Age of Aquarius should trigger a time of careful reflection of the accurate historical and religious past of humanity so we can learn from that past to then intelligently move forward into the future.

Notes

1. Hall, Page 186, 1951.
2. Wolter, Page 21, 2009.
3. Wolter/Nielsen, Pages 306-308, 2006.
4. Wolter, Pages 38-44, 2009.
5. Details of the correspondence, newspaper articles and the shipping of the Kensington Stone by Samuel Siverts to George Curme at Northwestern University in Chicago, Illinois, from January thru March of 1899 are reproduced in Wolter/ Nielsen, pages 396-404.
6. For full article about the obelisk and rally at Fahlin's point see Wolter/Nielsen, pages 441-444.
7. Higgins, Page 7, 1916.
8. Higgins, Page 26, 1916.
9. http://medievalwriting.50megs.com/scripts/letters/historyuv.htm.
10. Castle, History of St. Paul and Vicinity, Page 499.
11. Gardner, 2004, Page 238.
12. Gardner, 2004, Page 238.
13. Runestone Museum Memo dated October 1, 2010.
14. Statement by Henrik Williams, Uppsala, Sweden, May 5, 2011.
15. http://www.kensingtonrunestone.us/Take_A_Stand.pdf.
16. See Wolter/Nielsen, Page 59, 2006.
17. Wolter, Page 62, 2006.
18. http://www.fortsnelling.org/index.php?option=com_k2&view=item&layout=item&id=33&Itemid=42.
19. http://www.amazon.com/The-Kensington-Rune-Stone-Compelling/dp/1466406577/ref=sr_1_fkmr1_2?ie=UTF8&qid=1330795067&sr=8-2-fkmr1.
20. Means, Page 114, 1942.
21. Volukas.
22. Blackledge, Page 83, 2009.
23. http://www.sacred-texts.com/mas/dun/dun05.htm.
24. http://en.wikipedia.org/wiki/Cumberlandite.
25. http://www.cumberlandlibrary.org/monasterypage.html.
26. http://www.loc.gov/exhibits/treasures/trt029.html
27. http://en.wikipedia.org/wiki/Priory_of_Sion
28. http://www.margaretstarbird.net/last_supper.html

29. http://symboldictionary.net/?p=2680
30. Hodapp, Page 60, 2010.
31. http://en.wikipedia.org/wiki/Priory_of_Sion.
32. Brennan, Page 18, 1994.
33. Brennan, Page 30, 1994.
34. Joe Rose has written a book about the Cipher entitled: *Freemasonry's Secret Eye: Illuminating the Copiale Cipher*, which includes a translation of the text from an esoteric Masonic perspective. Copies of Rose's work can be obtained at www.jrrbookworks.com.
35. For details about the Dating Code and the Grail Prayer on the Kensington Rune Stone the reader should refer to Wolter/Nielsen, Pages 59-64, 2006, and Wolter, Pages 34-37 & 62-67.
36. Starbird, Page 64, 1993.
37. Silberer, Page 357, 1971.
38. http://en.wikipedia.org/wiki/Mutiny_on_the_Bounty#Crew_list.
39. http://en.wikipedia.org/wiki/In_hoc_signo_vinces.
40. Allen, Page 62, 2012.
41. For more detailed information about the Larsson Papers go to pages 107-112 in my previous book, *The Hooked X: Key to the Secret History of North America* (2009).
42. http://en.wikipedia.org/wiki/History_of_the_petroleum_industry_in_the_United _States.
43. http://www.astrologycom.com/stjohnbaptist.html.
44. Hamilton, Page xxi, 2001.
45. Ancient American, Issue #89, Page 2.
46. http://en.wikipedia.org/wiki/Serpent_Mound_crater
47. Hamilton, Page xxv, 2001.
48. Squire and Davis, Page 97, 1847.
49. Personal Communication with Wayne May in January, 2012.
50. Scherz and Burrows, Page 242, 1982.
51. Mertz, Page 130, 1964.
52. Gordon, Page 179, 1971.
53. Gordon, Page 182, 1971.
54. Gordon, Page 185, 1971.
55. Emmet to Dr. Cyrus Thomas, Page 7, February 25th, 1889.
56. Mary Jo Arnoldi to Barbara Duncan email dated February 14, 2011.
57. Cherokee Council House Resolution/Ordinance No. 794, dated August 4, 2011.
58. Burgess, 2009, Page 93.
59. Bent Report, Chapter XX: Commercialism in the Market Place, 1964.
60. Nielsen/Wolter, Pages 237-248, 2006.
61. http://www.freemasons-freemasonry.com/freemasons_magic_square.html.
62. See pages 199-202 for more on my discoveries with the Tumbaga artifacts of the Cavalli Collection.
63. Bernier, Page 18, 2001.
64. Bernier, Page 26, 2001.
65. http://en.wikipedia.org/wiki/%C3%89glise_Notre-Dame_la_Grande,_Poitiers.
66. http://en.wikipedia.org/wiki/%C3%89glise_Notre-Dame_la_Grande,_Poitiers.
67. Bayley, Page 26, 2006.
68. Bayley, Page 54, 2006.
69. Roux-Perino/Brenon, Page 55, 2006.
70. Ben's real name is Bill Wilkinson; Ben Hammott is an anagram he made up meaning "The Tomb Man."

71. Many Masonic degrees around the world have been "Christianized" to reflect the "Blessed Lord and Savior." Therefore, these degrees reflect the "Birth, Life, Death, and Resurrection of Jesus Christ," but this is certainly not the origin.
72. Hoffman, Page 215, 1885-1886.
73. I spoke with several Freemason's about their interpretation of this aspect of the Third Degree and this explanation is my interpretation of their comments. One thing that was consistent in the meaning of the ceremony in all their comments was the candidate is not brought back to life in the Roman Christian sense as an allegorical Resurrection of Jesus.
74. Hoffman, Page 234, 1885-1886.
75. In personal conversations with Scott Anfinson, the state archaeologist of Minnesota, who doesn't believe the Kensington Rune Stone is genuine and has stated more than once, "I don't find the Kensington Rune Stone to be scientifically interesting." Yet in the same conversation he agreed that, if genuine, it would be the most important historical artifact in Minnesota if not the country. In 2010 and 2011, I invited Scott to attend my many lectures on the Kensington Rune Stone multiple times, but he refused to come. He also stated that even if European explorers had made it to Minnesota, he has seen no evidence they had any lasting influence on Native cultures. This entire section presents convincing evidence that his statement is profoundly incorrect.
76. Duluth's report was made in 1685 to Marquis of Seignelay is printed in Volume I of the report of the Geological and Natural History Survey, page 5.
77. http://en.wikipedia.org/wiki/Knights_Templar.
78. Starbird, Page 96, 1993.
79. http://en.wikipedia.org/wiki/Saint_Catherine's_Monastery,_Mount_Sinai.
80. Bird, Page xvii, 1992.
81. http://en.wikipedia.org/wiki/House_of_Lorraine.
82. http://collections.mnhs.org/MNHistoryMagazine/articles/49/v49i01p019-028.pdf.
83. Neill, Page 1, 1881.
84. http://books.google.com/books?id=E4hxWwCClG0C&pg=PA204&lpg=PA204&dq=treaty+of+st+peters+1805&source=bl&ots=kTfUHVbmfl&sig=WmGJIqQpIS0VusZ_2ohdoKi2SZY&hl=en&sa=X&ei=q1UOT5TVKpSksQKGn83PAw&ved=0CDoQ6AEwBTgK#v=onepage&q=treaty%20of%20st%20peters%201805&f=false.
85. http://books.google.com/books?id=DcCeOEXGyoC&pg=PA342&lpg=PA342&dq=zebulon+pike+freemason&source=bl&ots=tisgY8OEiX&sig=yh8JwpHp3uEEOQnXv1ACb4dUWrs&hl=en&sa=X&ei=2ZVuTL_OOOA2wWd_ZzxAQ&ved=0CC8Q6AEwAg#v=onepage&q=zebulon%20pike%20freemason&f=false.
86. http://www.pilotknobpreservation.org/47849%20Pilot%20Knob%20Guide%20new%20web%20version.pdf.
87. http://www.sacred-texts.com/mas/sof/sof30.htm.
88. Aldred, Page 88, 1988.
89. http://www.loc.gov/exhibits/treasures/trr044.html.
90. On September 18, 2012, I received an email reporting the discovery of a fourth century fragment of papyrus written in Coptic that contains the phrases: "Jesus said to them, 'My wife . . . ,'" and "She will be able to be my disciple." Scholars were quick to point out the fragment was written at least two centuries after Jesus' death and doesn't definitively prove that Jesus was married to Mary Magdalene which is true. However, it sheds a bright new light on the "secret" kept in hiding for almost two thousand years. It is only a matter of time before more definitive documentation surfaces such as a marriage certificate.

91. Bowers, Page 23, 1950.
92. Catlin, Page 156, 1973.
93. Bowers, Page 24, 1950.
94. Mertz, Page 47, 1957.
95. Catlin, Page 162, 1973.
96. Mertz, Page 130, 1964.
97. Mertz, Page 89, 1964.
98. http://en.wikipedia.org/wiki/Mandan.
99. Pucha, Page 6, 1994.
100. Pucha, Page 6, 1994.
101. http://cherokeeregistry.com/index.php?option=com_content&view=article&id=23&Item id=40.
102. http://www.americanheraldry.org/pages/index.php?n=President.Washington.
103. Boorstin, Page 45, 1971.
104. Marsh, Page 55, 1934.
105. Marsh, Page 268, 1934.
106. Marsh, Page 208, 1934.
107. Marsh, Page 220, 1934.
108. da Silva, Page 6, 2011.
109. Hall, Pages 151-153, 1951.
110. Hall, Page 151, 1951.
111. Having visited and examined the incredible Mayan ruins at Chechen Itza in June of 2012, I can attest to the serpent being highly sacred to pre-Columbian Mayans. Nearly every stone temple and structure I saw was adorned with serpents.
112. Hall, Page 156, 1928.
113. http://www.ancientegyptonline.co.uk/taweret.html.
114. Bray, Page 32, 1978.
115. http://www.lehigh.edu/~inarcmet/Peru/analysis/object/01.htm.
116. Bray, Pages 12-14, 1978.
117. Hall, Page 186, 1951.
118. We have since received permission to write about these artifacts.
119. For more detailed information about the petrographic work performed by the author on the "Living Waters" Stone see *The Epigraphic Society of Occasional Papers*, Volume 25.
120. For a more detailed report on both the "Living Waters" and "Vulva" stones by Zena Halpern, see *The Epigraphic Society of Occasional Papers*, Volume 25.
121. De Jonge and Wakefield, Page 12-1, 2002.
122. A comprehensive presentation of the "C" Document research is to be published by Zena Halpern. The author and his wife, Janet, Judi Rudebusch, Steve St. Clair, and David Brody assisted Zena and Don with this research which included three separate trips up the mountain where artifacts and petroglyphs were found.
123. http://en.wikipedia.org/wiki/Gospel_of_Luke.
124. This entry has to be a mistake with the Roman numeral one behind the five when it should be in front. Therefore it must be forty-four degrees (and forty-seven minutes) latitude north.
125. A complete copy of the "C" Document should be forthcoming in Zena Halpern's soon-to-be-published book.
126. Bernier, Page 71, 2001.
127. Readers might enjoy seeing several examples of paintings and photographs of historical figures displaying the "M" hand symbol at: http://www.pseudoreality.org/westside.html
128. Wolter, Pages 155-156, 2009.

129. http://en.wikipedia.org/wiki/Pope_Urban_II.
130. Ellis, Page 435, 2008.
131. http://www.reuters.com/article/2012/05/10/us-science-maya-calendar-idUSBR E8491 D720120510.
132. Ellis, Page 3, 2004.
133. Hawass, Page 48, 2010.
134. Hall, Page 105, 1965.
135. Notovitch, Page 259, 1890.
136. Jewish burials in first century Jerusalem consisted of family members only placing the deceased onto a shelf inside the underground family tomb. They would then anoint the body with perfumes and oils eventually covering it with a sheet which was then left to decompose for roughly a year. The family would then return to collect the bones and place them inside a rectangular shaped stone box made from limestone called an ossuary. The ossuary was large enough to fit the two largest bones of the body, the femurs, crossed inside the bone box with the skull placed on top. Many researchers believe this was the origin of the skull and crossbones flag of pirate ships. This burial practice lasted roughly a century when the Romans crushed the Jewish revolt ending this unique practice.
137. Feather, Page 71, 2005.
138. Hall, Page 156, 2003.
139. Ellis, Page 124, 2008.
140. Feather, Page 55, 2005.
141. Ellis, Page 35, 2011.
142. Ellis, Page 106, 2008.
143. Ellis, Page 45, 2011.
144. Tabor, Page 16, 2012.
145. Tabor, Page 28, 2012.
146. Tabor, Page 102, 2012.
147. Tabor and Jacobovici, Pages 100-101, 2012.
148. Tabor and Jacobovici, Page 79, 2012.
149. Tabor and Jacobovici, Page 84, 2012.
150. Jacobovici and Pellegrino, Page 15, 2007.
151. Jacobovici and Pellegrino, Page 123, 2007.
152. Halpern and Ruh, Page 6, 2012.
153. Tabor and Jacobovici, Page 144, 2012.
154. Tabor and Jacobovici, Page 207, 2012.
155. Tabor and Jacobovici, Page 195, 2012.
156. Ellis, Page 45, 2011.
157. Ellis, Page 115, 2011.
158. http://news.hds.harvard.edu/files/King_JesusSaidToThem_draft_0917.pdf
159. http://www.huffingtonpost.com/2012/09/27/vatican-paper-weighs-on-jesus-wife-scrap-fake_n_1921083.html.
160. Tabor and Jacobovici,P ages 112-113, 2012.
161. On the north wall of the antechamber above the entrance to the Talpiot Garden Tomb an upward-pointing chevron was carved with a circle carved below it. Some scholars speculated the circle was an unfinished wreath symbolic of a Royal Bloodline. The circle in combination with a curious chevron could simply be symbolic of the Family tomb of a Royal male or King.
162. Jacobovici and Pellegrino, Page 18, 2007.

References

Aldred, Cyril, *Akhenaten: King of Egypt*, Thames and Hudson Limited, London, England, 1988.

Allen, John, "A Rune with a View: James Frankki scours stone for evidence that proves America's Viking past-or maybe not," *On Wisconsin*, Spring, Madison, Wisconsin, 2012.

Bayley, Harold, *The Lost Language of Symbolism*, Dover Publications, Inc., Mineola, New York, 2006, 1912.

Bernier, Francine, *The Templar's Legacy in Montreal, the New Jerusalem*, Frontier Publishing, The Netherlands, 2001.

Bird, Allison, *Heart of the Dragonfly: The Historical Development of the Cross Necklaces of the Pueblo and Navaho Peoples*, Avanyu Publishing Inc., 1992.

Boorstin, Daniel J., *A Portrait from the Twentieth Century American Civilization*, McGraw-Hill Book Company New York, 1972.

Bowers, Alfred W., *Mandan Social and Ceremonial Organization*, University of Idaho Press, Moscow, Idaho, 1950.

Bray, Warwick, *The Gold of El Dorado*, Times Newspapers Limited, London, 1978.

Brenna, Martin, *The Stones of Time: Calendars, Sundials, and Stone Chambers of Ancient Ireland*, Inner Traditions International, Rochester, Vermont, 1994.

Burgess, Don, "Romans in Tucson? The Story of an Archaeological Hoax," *Journal of the Southwest*, Volume 51, Number 1, Spring 2009.

Burrows, Russell, *The Mystery Cave of Many Faces*, Superior Heartland, Inc., Marquette, MI, 1991.

Castle, Henry A., *History of St. Paul and Vicinity: A Chronicle of Progress and a Narrative Account of the Industries and People of the City and its Tributary Territory, Volume II*, The Lewis Publishing Company, Chicago and New York, 1912.

Catlin, George, *Letters and Notes on the Manners, Customs, and Conditions of North American Indians, Volume I*, Dover Publications, New York, 1973.

Da Silva, Manuel Luciano M.D., *The Portuguese Columbus' Flags!*, da Silva paper, 2011.

De Jong, Dr. Reinoud M. and Jay Wakefield, *How the Sun God Reached America*, MCS, Inc., Kirkland, Washington, 2002.

Downing, Antoinette F., *The Architectural Heritage of Newport Rhode Island: 1640-1915; Second Edition*, Bramhall House, New York 1952/1967.

Ellis, Ralph, *Eden in Egypt: Adam and Eve were Pharaoh Akhenaten and Queen Nefertiti*, Edfu Books, Cheshire England, 2004.

Ellis, Ralph, *King Jesus: from Kam (Egypt) to Camelot*, Edfu Books, Cheshire, England, 2008.

Ellis, Ralph, *Mary Magdalene: Princess of Provence and the House of Orange*, Edfu Books, Cheshire, England, 2011.

Faulkner, Charles H., Edited by, *The Bat Creek Stone: Miscellaneous paper No. 15,* Tennessee Anthropological Association, University of Tennessee, Knoxville, Tennessee, 1992.

Feather, Robert, *The Secret Initiation of Jesus at Qumran*, Bear & Company, Rochester, Vermont, 2005.

Folda, Jaroslav, *Crusader Art in the Holy Land, From the Third Crusade to the Fall of Acre, 1187-1291,* Cambridge University Press, New York, N.Y. 2005.

Gardner, Laurence, *Lost Secrets of the Sacred Ark: Amazing Revelations of the Power of Gold,* Element: An Imprint of Harper Collins Publishers, Hammersmith, London, 2003.

Gordon, Cyrus H., *Before Columbus: Links between the Old World and Ancient America,* Crown Publishers, Inc., New York, 1971.

Gould, Robert Freke, and others, The History of Freemasonry: Its Antiquities, symbols, constitutions, Customs, etc., John C. Yorston & Co., publishers, New York, 1889.

Hall, Manley, *The Riddle of the Rosicrucian's,* The Philosophical Research Society Inc., Los Angeles, California, 1951.

Hall, Manley, *The Secret Destiny of America,* Penguin Group (USA) Inc., New York, N.Y., 1951.

Hall, Manley, *Freemasonry of the Ancient Egyptians*, The Philosophical Research Society Inc., Los Angeles, California, 1965.

Hall, Manley, *The Secret Teachings of All Ages,* Penguin Group Inc. New York, N.Y., 2003.

Hamilton, Ross, *The Mystery of the Serpent Mound: In Search of the Alphabet of the Gods,* Frog, Ltd/North Atlantic Books, Berkeley, California, 2001.

Hammott, Ben, *Lost Tomb of the Knights Templar,* Ben Hammott, London, England, 2008.

Higgins, Frank C., *Hermetic Masonry: The Beginning of Masonry and AUM "The Lost Word,"* Kessinger Publishing Company, Kila, Montana, 1916.

Hodapp, Christopher, *Deciphering the Lost Symbol,* Ulysses Press, Berkeley, California, 2010.

Hoffman, W.J., *The Mied'wiwin or "Grand Medicine Society" of the Ojibwa*, Seventh Annual Report of the Bureau of Ethnology to the Secretary of the Smithsonian Institution: 1885-1886, by J.W. Powell, Director, Washington, D.C., 1891.

Holand, Hjalmar R., *The Kensington Stone, A Study in pre-Columbian History,* Ephraim, WI, 1932.

Jacobovici, Simcha and Charles Pellegrino, *The Jesus Family Tomb: The Discovery, the Investigation, and the Evidence That Could Change History,* Harbor Collins Publishers, New York, N.Y. 2007.

Johnston, Thomas Crawford, ESQ, *Did the Phoenicians Discover America?,* Geographical Society of California, Special Bulletin, 1892.

Limburg, Mark, *The Kensington Rune Stone: More Compelling New Evidence,* Mark Limburg, St. Paul, Minnesota, 2010.

Mahieu, Jacques De, *Les Templiers en Amerique,* Aventure Mysterieuse, Paris, France, 1981.

Mann, William, F., *The Templar Meridians: The Secret Mapping of the New World,* Destiny Books, Rochester, Vermont, 2006.

Mann, William, F., *The Knights Templar in the New World*, Destiny books, Rochester, Vermont, 2004, 1999.

Marsh, Richard O., *White Indians of Darien*, G.P. Putnam's Sons, New York, 1934.

Mertz, Henriette, *The Nephtali: One Lost Tribe*, Henriette Mertz, Chicago, Illinois, 1957.

Mertz, Henriette, *The Wine Dark Sea*, Henriette Mertz, Chicago, Illinois, 1964.

Miller, Crichton E.M., *The Golden Thread of Time, A Voyage of Discovery into the Lost Knowledge of the Ancients*, Pendulum Publishing, Rugby, Warwickshire, United Kingdom, 2001.

Neill, Reverend Edward D., *History of the Mississippi Valley: Explorers and Pioneers of Minnesota*, Minnesota Historical Company, Minneapolis, Minnesota, 1881.

Notovich, Nicolas, *The Unknown Life of Jesus Christ*, R.F. Fenno & Company, New York, N.Y., 1890.

Powell, John Wesley, *Seventh Annual Report of the Bureau of Ethnology to the Secretary of the Smithsonian Institution: 1885-86*, Washington, D.C., 1891

Powell, John Wesley, *Twelfth Annual Report of the Bureau of Ethnology to the Secretary of the Smithsonian Institution: 1890-91*, Washington, D.C., 1894.

Pucha, Francis Paul, *Indian Peace Medals in American History*, University of Oklahoma Press, Norman, Oklahoma, 1971, 1994.

Roux-Perino, Julie, and Anne Brenon, *The Cathars*, MSM, Vic-en-Bigorre Cedex, France, 2006, 2000.

Scherz, James P., and Russell E. Burrows, *Rock Art Pieces from Burrow's Cave in Southern Illinois, Volume 1*, University of Wisconsin/Madison, April 1992.

Secret Societies Illustrated: *Comprising the So-Called Secrets of Freemasonry, Adoptive Masonry, Oddfellowship, Good Templarism, Temple of Honor, United Sons of Industry, Knights of Pythias and the Grange*, Ezra A. Cook; Publisher, Chicago, Illinois, 1909.

Silberer, Herbert, *Hidden Symbolism of Alchemy and the Occult Arts*, Dover Publications, Inc., New York, N.Y., 1971, 1917.

Squier, E.G. and E.H. Davis, *Ancient Monuments of the Mississippi Valley: Comprising the Results of Extensive Original Surveys and Explorations*, Smithsonian Institution Contributions to Knowledge, Volume 1, 1848.

Starbird, Margaret, *The Woman with the Alabaster Jar*, Bear & Company, Rochester, Vermont, 1993.

Stillson, Henry Leonard, and Hughman, William James, *History of the Ancient and Honorable Fraternity of Free and Accepted Masons and Concordant Orders*, The Fraternity Publishing Company, Boston/London, England, 1910.

Tabor, James D., and Jacobovici, Simcha, *The Jesus Discovery; The New Archaeological Find That Reveals the Birth of Christianity*, Simon & Schuster, New York, 2012.

Thomas, Cyrus, *The Cherokees in Pre-Columbian Times*, N.D.C. Hodges, New York, N.Y. 1890.

Weisberger, William R. (Editor), Wallace McLeod and S. Brent Morris, *Freemasonry on Both Sides of the Atlantic: Essays Concerning the Craft in the British Isles, Europe, the United States, and Mexico*, Columbia University Press, New York, 2002.

Winchell, Newton H., *The Aborigines of Minnesota: A Report Based on the Collections of Jacob V. Brower, and the Field Surveys and Notes of Alfred J. Hill and Theodore H. Lewis*, The Minnesota Historical Society, St. Paul, Minnesota, 1911.

Wolter, Scott F, and Richard Nielsen, *The Kensington Rune Stone: Compelling New Evidence*, Lake Superior Agate Inc., Chanhassen, Minnesota, 2006.

Wolter, Scott, *The Hooked X: Key to the Secret History of North America*, North Star Press of St. Cloud Inc., St. Cloud, Minnesota, 2009.

Woodbridge, Dwight E. and Pardee, John S., *History of Duluth and St. Louis County: Past and Present*, C.F. Cooper & Company, Chicago, Illinois, 1910.

Zuckerman, Arthur J., *A Jewish Princedom in Feudal France: 768-900*, Columbia University Press, New York and London, 1972, 1965.

Index